AFRICAN ETHNOGRAPHIC STUDIES OF THE 20TH CENTURY

Volume 37

A MANUAL OF NUER LAW

A MANUAL OF NUER LAW

Being an Account of Customary Law, its Evolution and Development in the Courts Established by the Sudan Government

P. P. HOWELL

LONDON AND NEW YORK

First published in 1954 by Oxford University Press for the International African Institute.

This edition first published in 2018
by Routledge
2 Park Square, Milton Park, Abingdon, Oxon OX14 4RN

and by Routledge
711 Third Avenue, New York, NY 10017

Routledge is an imprint of the Taylor & Francis Group, an informa business

© 1954 International African Institute

All rights reserved. No part of this book may be reprinted or reproduced or utilised in any form or by any electronic, mechanical, or other means, now known or hereafter invented, including photocopying and recording, or in any information storage or retrieval system, without permission in writing from the publishers.

Trademark notice: Product or corporate names may be trademarks or registered trademarks, and are used only for identification and explanation without intent to infringe.

British Library Cataloguing in Publication Data
A catalogue record for this book is available from the British Library

ISBN: 978-0-8153-8713-8 (Set)
ISBN: 978-0-429-48813-9 (Set) (ebk)
ISBN: 978-1-138-58469-3 (Volume 37) (hbk)
ISBN: 978-0-429-50581-2 (Volume 37) (ebk)

Publisher's Note
The publisher has gone to great lengths to ensure the quality of this reprint but points out that some imperfections in the original copies may be apparent.

Disclaimer
The publisher has made every effort to trace copyright holders and would welcome correspondence from those they have been unable to trace.

LAK NUER AND HIS SONG-BULL

Photo: Dr. J. F. Bloss

A MANUAL OF
NUER LAW

*Being an account of Customary Law,
its Evolution and Development in the
Courts established by the Sudan
Government*

By

P. P. HOWELL

Published for the

INTERNATIONAL AFRICAN INSTITUTE

by the

OXFORD UNIVERSITY PRESS

LONDON   NEW YORK   TORONTO

1954

Oxford University Press, Amen House, London, E.C.4
GLASGOW   NEW YORK   TORONTO   MELBOURNE   WELLINGTON
BOMBAY   CALCUTTA   MADRAS   KARACHI   CAPE TOWN   IBADAN
Geoffrey Cumberlege, Publisher to the University

PRINTED IN GREAT BRITAIN

FOREWORD

I ESTEEM it a privilege to have been asked by Dr. Howell to write a foreword to this book. He is well qualified to be the author of a handbook on Nuer law, for he combines anthropological training with administrative experience, a combination very necessary if the principles of Nuer law, which can only be revealed by anthropological research, are to be presented in the form most useful to Officers of the Administration. He took the Anthropological Tripos at Cambridge shortly before the last war and a D.Phil. in Anthropology at Oxford after it. It is greatly to his credit that he has been able to maintain his anthropological interests in the midst of manifold official duties and even more so that he has found time to engage in research and to publish its results; for, in addition to this book, he has made contributions to our knowledge not only of other departments of Nuer social life but also of the Shilluk, the Dinka, and the Baggara Arabs, his papers on the Shilluk being of special importance. Since he is acquainted with anthropological literature, and the theories and problems contained in it, Dr. Howell is in a position to address himself, as he does in this book, to an anthropological as well as to an administrative audience.

The present volume is a valuable addition to the literature on the Nuer, which is now, for a primitive people, quite considerable. There are, apart from a number of articles in journals, no less than seven books, published or about to be published, on their social life: Mr. Jackson's pioneering account, to which I again pay tribute; Miss Huffman's book, which, though slender, contains much useful information and also some acute comments; Father Crazzolara's detailed study of Nuer religion, of which only a condensed account has yet appeared (in the eighth volume of P. W. Schmidt's *Der Ursprung der Gottesidee*); this book by Dr. Howell; and my own trilogy; and there are also excellent studies of their language by Father Crazzolara and Father Kiggen. It is very seldom that we have so many separate accounts of a primitive people written in different circumstances, at different times, in different places, and by people with largely different backgrounds. We have here something similar to the variety of documentary sources which is so important for the historian in reaching a verdict on facts. But, in other respects, we have here also something different, because the sources are not just contemporaneous documents which unintentionally serve to support or weaken testimony, but are successive studies in which each writer in turn has, it may be presumed, deliberately sought to test the statements and interpretations of those who wrote before him. That so many books and articles should have been written on the Nuer is also surely a tribute

vi   FOREWORD

to the Nuer themselves. Twenty years ago they were not highly regarded; but little by little we have learnt to appreciate their qualities, and I think that it is true to say that all of us have persevered in our efforts to record their way of life very largely because we felt that they are a people whose values are worth handing down to posterity.

Dr. Howell's book will doubtless prove of great assistance to Officers of the Sudan Political Service. It is hardly within my province to speak about it from that point of view, and, in any case, its practical value to the Administration will depend largely on the direction taken by political developments in the Sudan in the near future, and this cannot be altogether foreseen. I can speak only as an anthropologist and of its value to anthropology. It is of anthropological value for a number of reasons.

First, it adds, and on some topics quite considerably, to our knowledge of the Nuer. It is true that much of the book summarizes what has been published earlier, mostly by myself. This could not have been avoided if one of its main purposes, to serve as a handbook on Nuer law for the guidance of Officers of the Political Service, was to be achieved. However, not only is there also much that is new, but what is old is presented from a new angle; and I should add further that most of Dr. Howell's book had already been written before much of what I have since published had appeared in print, so that what might appear to someone unacquainted with the circumstances to be a summary of existing knowledge is in fact largely based on Dr. Howell's own observations and enquiries.

Secondly, it provides a most useful check on previous writings on the Nuer, and particularly on my own books. An anthropologist is too often in the unfortunate position of being the sole authority on a primitive people. The value of his account is thereby much diminished since it requires more faith to accept the evidence of a single witness than of several. Dr. Howell has indeed dealt with me with perhaps undue generosity. Nevertheless, he does not hesitate to state, and without equivocation, where he considers my account to be wrong, insufficient, or in other ways at fault. This is all to my advantage because it may therefore be assumed that where he does not find it necessary to correct or criticize my statements it is for the reason that he has tested and confirmed them.

Thirdly, it enables us to view Nuer society in a wider historical setting. Ethnographic studies of peoples usually have only the slightest historical background, and lack altogether historical foreground. They give the appearance therefore of being photographic. Here the value of Dr. Howell's book lies not merely in its description of changes which have taken place among the Nuer during the last twenty-five years. His observations have a further significance. They provide a kind of experimental situation in which the validity of earlier theoretical conclusions can be tested by the movement of events. If they

FOREWORD

were sound, then, given modern developments, certain changes might logically be expected. Moreover, the fundamental values of a society may sometimes be most clearly seen when it is in process of readjustment to new historical circumstances. One then sees what stands the test, what holds firm, what acts as a rallying-point.

Fourthly, it is a contribution to a subject of some importance about which we are not well informed, namely the development of custom into law through the establishment, in this case by an outside authority, of courts and by what amounts to the beginnings of codification; for, as Dr. Howell has shown, the decisions of the courts established and to some extent controlled by an alien government nevertheless express and remain true to the principles of indigenous custom. Yet there are also some strange developments. It is evident that the courts and legal procedures instituted by the Administration have sometimes accentuated or increased the disputes they were intended to settle. All sorts of unintended results have ensued. For example, a premium is put on adultery, for if a wife commits it with more than one man her lovers pay less, or no, compensation to the husband; and to correct this absurdity the offence tends to become more and more treated as a crime rather than as a tort. To take a second example, penal sanctions are now applied where in Nuer custom no civil, far less criminal, action lies; as when a man has congress with another man's concubine (in the Nuer sense of this word). To take a third, a person accused of the evil eye may today be sentenced by the courts to imprisonment, and his, or more often her, sentence has the effect of purification, something like penance. All this is of the greatest interest and, for me at any rate, sheds light on many puzzling features of Nuer custom.

I should like to conclude with two remarks. The first is that we social anthropologists are a very small body who can make our professional studies only here and there, and that we therefore rely very much indeed on the assistance of administrative officers and missionaries. This, however, requires in the administrator or missionary some training in anthropology; and I think that Dr. Howell's book shows how valuable this is. Not only does it enable the administrator, as is here so clearly shown, to make important contributions to anthropology, but also, by adding to his understanding, it makes him a better servant to those whom he serves. Secondly, I would like, if Dr. Howell will permit me this opportunity, to pay tribute to all those Political Officers, of whom he is one, who have served in Nuerland and have, without exception, and in many different ways, encouraged anthropological research among the Nuer in the hope that it might be of benefit to the people with whom they have so obviously bound up their own lives.

E. E. Evans-Pritchard

Oxford
December 1952

ACKNOWLEDGEMENTS

I AM deeply indebted to Professor E. E. Evans-Pritchard for the interest he has taken in this book and for the assistance and encouragement he has given me in this and other anthropological work carried out in the Sudan during the course of my administrative duties. I am also indebted to the following for information and comments: to Captain H. A. Romilly who served for nearly twenty years among the Nuer, first in Western Nuer District and later in Eastern Nuer District, and to Captain G. S. Renny, his successor; to Mr. B. A. Lewis, at one time District Commissioner of the then Zeraf District and later of Pibor District which then included the Lou Nuer; to Mr. John Winder, my predecessor in Zeraf District and later Governor of the Upper Nile Province; to Mr. J. S. R. Duncan, M.B.E., my successor in Central Nuer District; to Mr. H. G. Wedderburn-Maxwell, Mr. J. E. Kennett, Mr. F. D. McJannet, Captain D. K. Rae, Mr. W. P. G. Thomson, District Commissioners of Western Nuer District; to all those who have in one way or another contributed to the information recorded in this book; to Mr. Buth Diu, Nuer representative in the Sudan Legislative Assembly at the time of writing and to all my countless Nuer informants. I must acknowledge with gratitude the advice and encouragement given me by Professor Meyer Fortes, Professor Max Gluckmann, Dr. John Peristiany and others who were at the time on the staff of the Institute of Social Anthropology at Oxford. My grateful thanks are due to Dr. J. F. Bloss for some of the photographs which appear in this book, and to Mr. A. S. F. Gow for his help in correcting the proofs. Finally I am indebted to the Sudan Government and to the International African Institute, who have so generously contributed towards the costs of publication, and to Professor Daryll Forde and Mrs. B. E. Wyatt, who have undertaken so much of the work involved in publication.

CONTENTS

FOREWORD *by* PROFESSOR E. E. EVANS-PRITCHARD . . v

ACKNOWLEDGEMENTS viii

CHAPTER I. INTRODUCTION

1. INTRODUCTORY 1
Sources, Methods, and Objectives 1
Presentation and Orthography 5
Note on Cattle Terminology 6

2. AN INTRODUCTION TO NUER SOCIETY 7
Origin and History 7
Topography and Ecology 9
Social and Political Structure: 16
The Tribe and Tribal Segments 17
The Meaning of the word *cieng* 20
Custom or Law and the Sanctions for Conformity . . 22
Restitutive Sanctions 25
Traditional Scales of Compensation and the Formula of
Compromise 27
Legal Procedures and Political Authority in the Past . 27
The Appointment of Tribal Authorities Today . . 34
Administrative Policy and the Evolution of Nuer Courts 36
Courts and Tribal Structure 37

CHAPTER II. HOMICIDE AND BODILY INJURIES

Part I. Homicide

1. INTRODUCTION. 39
Nuer Concepts Concerning Homicide 39
Definition of Terms 42

2. BLOOD-FEUDS 44
The Process of Settlement and the Functions of the
Leopard-Skin Chief as Mediator 44
The Leopard-Skin Chief concerned with the Individual 44

CONTENTS

The Leopard-Skin Chief concerned with Hostile Groups; *ji ran* and *ji thunge* 45

Ceremonies, Rites, and Acts of Mediation Performed by the Leopard-Skin Chief in the Settlement of a Feud 45

Terminology of Cattle Paid as Compensation. . . 47

Rates of Compensation 48

Persons who are normally concerned in the Collection and Receipt of Compensation 49

The Distribution of Bloodwealth 49

Degree of Responsibility where Homicide is Committed Jointly 51

3. FORMS OF HOMICIDE AND COMPENSATION RECOGNIZED IN NUER
LAW 52

thung ran 52

thung loic ran 52

thung nyindiet 53

thung gwacka 54

thung yüka 54

biem. 55

4. THE STATUS OF PERSONS IN CONNEXION WITH HOMICIDE. . 55

Persons for whom Compensation was paid at Reduced Rates 55

Dinka in the Category of Slaves 56

Witches, Ghouls, and Anti-social Persons . . . 56

Uninitiated Boys 57

Compensation for the Death of a Woman . . . 57

Legal Responsibility for Act of Homicide committed by a Woman 58

5. PEACE CEREMONIES: COMPOSITION ON A TRIBAL SCALE . . 58

6. CONCLUSIONS 59

Traditional Concepts and Action in the Past. . . 59

Observations on the Effects of Government Policy . . 61

Recent Legislation Concerning Homicide . . . 63

Modern Procedure 66

CONTENTS   xi

Part II. Hurt

1. INTRODUCTION 68

2. INJURIES RECOGNIZED IN NUER LAW 69

3. DEFAMATION OF CHARACTER 70

CHAPTER III. MARRIAGE AND DIVORCE

Part I. Marriage and Marriage Laws

1. INTRODUCTION 71
   The Functions of Bridewealth 71

2. DIFFERENT FORMS OF MARRIAGE 73
   Simple Legal Marriage 73
   'Ghost-Marriage' 74
   Categories of Persons on whose behalf 'Ghost-Marriages'
   are made 75
   'Ghost-Marriage' and Bridewealth 76
   The Levirate 78
   Differences between 'Ghost-Marriage' and the Levirate . 79
   Categories of Persons with whom a Widow lives . . 79
   'Widow-Concubines' 81
   Unmarried Concubines 81

3. NOTE ON THE RULES OF EXOGAMY AND INCEST . . . 82

4. THE SOCIAL AND RITUAL PROCESSES OF MARRIAGE. . . 86
   Courting and Betrothal: 87
   luom nyal: 'Courting the Girl' 88
   thiec nyal: 'Asking for the Girl' . . . 88
   cuei: Betrothal 89
   Marriage: 91
   twoc ghok: 'Invocation of the Cattle' . . . 91
   muot nyal: 'The Shaving of the Bride' . . . 94
   loiny deb: 'Loosing the Rope' 94
   noong nyal: 'The Bringing of the Bride' . . 95
   muot nyal: 'Shaving the Bride'. . . . 95
   Conclusion 96

xii CONTENTS

5. THE DISTRIBUTION OF BRIDEWEALTH 97
    The Ideal 98
    Lou Nuer Version 99
    Zeraf Nuer Versions 100
    Kinship Terminology. 100
    Minimum Claims 106
    Western Nuer Versions 107
    Proportions 109
    Other Payments 110
    Claims for Begetting and Fostering Children outside Legal
        Union 111
    Reverse Payments 113
    Examples of Actual Marriages 114
    Number of Cattle Paid Today 121
    Disputes over Bridewealth Payments and Distribution . 122

6. THE LEGALITY OF MARRIAGE 124
    General Principles 124
    Recent Legislation 126

7. THE LEGITIMACY OF CHILDREN 128
    Establishment of Legitimacy by Legal Marriage . . 128
        In Simple Legal Marriage 129
        In 'Ghost-Marriage' 129
        In Leviratic Union. 130
        In 'Widow-Concubinage'. 130
    The Position of Children born of Unmarried Concubines 131
    The Position of Children born of Adultery . . . 133
    The Position of Children on Dissolution of Marriage . 134
    Legitimization Fees: Recent Legislation . . . 134

8. CONCLUSION 135

Part II. Divorce Laws and the Dissolution of Marriage

1. DISSOLUTION OF MARRIAGE ON DEATH OF THE WIFE . . 137
    ghok tuoke 139
    yang muon 140

CONTENTS   xiii

2. DISSOLUTION OF MARRIAGE WHEN BOTH PARTIES ARE LIVING . 140
  Grounds for Divorce 141
  General Observations.   144
  Impediments to Marriage Discovered Subsequently:
    Incest   146
    Blood-Feuds 147
  Circumstances in which Divorce is Considered Impossible 148

3. RULES CONCERNING THE RETURN OF BRIDEWEALTH CATTLE ON
    DISSOLUTION OF MARRIAGE   149
  Deductions: *ruath miemni* and *yang yaatni*   .   . 149
  Original Cattle or Substitutes   150
  Cattle which are not Returnable 150
  Further Rules in Divorce 151
    A Woman may not be remarried until Previous Marriage
      has been Dissolved   151
    Return of Extra-marital Payments   .   .   . 151
    Divorce of Widows living in Leviratic Union or 'Widow-
      Concubinage'   152

4. SUMMARY   153

        CHAPTER IV. THE VIOLATION OF RIGHTS IN WOMEN

1. ADULTERY   155
  Cattle Returnable if a Child is born of the act of Adultery 156
  Legality of Marriage is a Fundamental Consideration   . 157
  The Main Legal Principles   158
  Application of these Principles depends on Circumstances 159
    Impotence of the Husband   159
    Barrenness of the Wife and Age of the Wife   .   . 160
    Morals of the Wife.   160
  Compensation cannot be Claimed more than twice
    where one Woman is Concerned   .   .   . 161
  Adultery with Widows   161
  Adultery and 'Ghost Marriage'   163
  Adultery with the Wives of Kinsmen 163
  Further Qualifying Circumstances   .   .   . 165
  Liability Ceases with the Death of the Adulterer .   . 166
  Return of Compensation Cattle on Dissolution of Marriage 166
  Recent Legislation   166

xiv CONTENTS

2. SEXUAL INTERCOURSE WITH UNMARRIED WOMEN AND GIRLS . 168

Sexual Intercourse with Unmarried Concubines . . 168

The Seduction of Unmarried Girls: *dhu nyal* . . 169

dhu nyal cieng and *dhu nyal dhor* 170

Elopement and Abduction: *kwil nyal* 170

Sexual Intercourse with an Unmarried Girl resulting in
Pregnancy: *ruet nyal* 171

Compensation (*ruok nyal*) and Legitimization Fees (*ruok gaanke* or *muor*) 173

Summary 174

Recent Legislation 176

3. OTHER WRONGS 176

thung yiika 176

thiang 177

CHAPTER V. PROPERTY RIGHTS

1. OWNERSHIP 178

General Considerations 178

Property other than Livestock and Land . . . 179

Changing Values 180

2. LAND TENURE, GRAZING RIGHTS, AND RIGHTS IN WATER . 181

General Considerations 181

Arable Land 184

Grazing Rights 186

Water Rights 188

Fishing Rights and Hunting Rights 188

Conclusion 189

3. INHERITANCE 190

Inheritance of Cattle 190

Inheritance of Other Property 194

4. TRADE AND LOANS 195

Trade in Cattle 195

Exchanges and Loans 196

Loans Arising from the Institution of *Nak* . . . 197

Exchange of Cattle for Grain 197

Gifts given in Friendship (*math*) 198

CONTENTS xv

5. THE INFRINGEMENT OF RIGHTS IN PROPERTY . . . 198
 Self-help 198
 Theft of Cattle 200
 Theft of Other Material Possessions 201

CHAPTER VI. RELIGIOUS CONCEPTS IN RELATION TO LAW

Nuer Religious Beliefs 204
Religious Sanctions and Legal Processes . . . 206
Religious Functionaries and Magical Experts: . . 211
 kuaar kwac or *kuaar muon:* The Leopard-Skin Chief or
 Land Chief 211
 wut ghok: The Cattle Expert 212
 kuaar thoi: The Water Expert 212
 kuaar juath 213
 kuaar yiika 213
 gwan tang 213
Other Types of Religious Expert 214
Beneficial and Anti-social Activities 217
Witchcraft 218
Actions against Witches Today 219
Oaths 219
 kap tang 220
 math 220

CHAPTER VII. THE NATURE OF NUER LAW

Private Law and Public Law 221
Trends and Changing Conditions: The Transformation
 of Custom into Law 225
Modern Procedure 230
'Balanced Opposition' in the Court System . . . 232
The Introduction of Penal Sanctions 234

APPENDIXES

APPENDIX I. NUERLAND: POPULATIONS AND AREA . . . 239
APPENDIX II. CHIEFS' COURTS ORDINANCE, 1931 . . . 240
GLOSSARY 243
BIBLIOGRAPHY 249

INDEX 253

ILLUSTRATIONS

LAK NUER AND HIS SONG-BULL	*frontispiece*	
LEOPARD-SKIN CHIEF	*facing page*	64
THE LITIGANT		65
THE CHIEF. KIC WUR WINYANG OF THE LAK NUER .		80
THE BRIDE		81
THE BRIDEGROOM		160
MAN OF GOD. RIAG LOINYJOK		161
GATLUAK NGINGI		176
BUTH DIU		177

CHAPTER I

INTRODUCTION

1. INTRODUCTORY

Sources, Methods, and Objectives

THE Nuer are a Nilotic people who live in the savannah and swamps of the Upper Nile Province in the Anglo-Egyptian Sudan. My acquaintance with them began in 1942 when I was appointed Assistant District Commissioner of the then Zeraf District which included three of their tribes. In 1943 a special body known as the Nuer District Commissioners' Meeting, and now called the 'Nuer Chiefs' Council', was set up by the Governor of the Province. The object was to enable administrators and chiefs, chosen from all Nuer Districts to represent their people, to discuss common interests, and ensure some consistency in administrative policy. One of the main subjects for discussion was the growing body of 'customary law' administered in Nuer tribunals established by the Government, and the obvious need for standardization of the general principles, although it was agreed that any form of rigid codification should be avoided. One of the first resolutions passed at this first meeting was that an investigation should be made of the principles of Nuer customary law and a record kept. This Manual of Nuer Law springs from that resolution. I was able to study and record the cases which appeared before the courts throughout my service in the Zeraf District, and later, when the Lou Nuer tribe was incorporated to form what is now called Central Nuer District, to extend my enquiries further afield. Subsequently I had occasional opportunities of visiting other Nuer Districts and, although I was not then dealing with administrative affairs, I was able to check some of the information previously recorded. This Manual is, however, largely based on information from the Lak, Thiang, Gawaar and Lou tribes, and it must be appreciated that I have not been able to cover all the detailed variations of customary law which are to be found in so large an area. It would be a mistake to believe that every Nuer court would give judgement always and exactly according to the law I have described, even though there is great consistency in general principles—a consistency which is fortified by decisions made subsequently at meetings of the Nuer Council.

By 'customary law' I mean the body of 'native law and custom' which is administered in Nuer courts under the Chiefs' Courts

BNL

INTRODUCTION

Ordinance of 1931.[1] Such terms appear frequently in the official records of Colonial Governments and in the Anglo-Egyptian Sudan, but they are something of an anomaly if any strict definition of the word 'law' is applied. I shall turn to this question of definition and the nature of Nuer law later. Here such terms are sufficient to indicate generally those customary rules governing human relationships which, among the Nuer, were in the past subject to sanctions too indeterminate to be called legal, but which are now applied with a consistency and organized force sufficient to justify the use of the word 'law' in a more exact sense.

Nuer courts are an innovation. Though there may have been irregular meetings of elders and ritual functionaries to decide matters of local concern, there was no organized political body which could enforce its decisions, even though other sanctions were sometimes strong enough to ensure conformity. Since public security was the primary aim of Government in the early years of the administration of Nuerland and breaches of security usually arose from disputes over matters which to us may appear comparatively trivial, the establishment of such tribunals was the first and perhaps most important move in the development of the Nuer towards management of their own affairs. It was certainly one which brought about the most profound changes, as will be seen later. In those early years most of the decisions were made by the District Commissioner himself, often with curious subsequent results, even though consultation with Nuer representatives was always an important feature of the procedure.

Now that these courts are rapidly developing in most Nuer areas and there are already the beginnings of a proper separation of the judiciary from the executive, the District Commissioner is called upon less frequently for personal arbitration in matters which should be settled with full reference to traditional rules and established precedents. From the time when I first visited Nuerland it was the agreed policy of the Government to interfere less and less in such matters, for not only was it the ultimate object of such courts to provide an indigenous mechanism whereby civil disputes might be settled amicably, but it was realized that the alien administrator can never achieve sufficient knowledge of the complexities of Nuer law to settle such disputes himself. Even if he succeeds in abandoning the conventions which spring from his own environment, he cannot see such cases from the same viewpoint as the Nuer. His only advantage is impartiality which alone is insufficient to justify interference. Criminal law is a different matter, for the concept of punishment was previously unknown to the Nuer, but even in this they must be made to settle

[1] '7 (i). A Chief's Court shall administer—
(a) the native law and custom prevailing in the area over which the Court exercises its jurisdiction provided that such native law and custom is not contrary to justice, morality or order.' Extract from Chiefs' Courts Ordinance, 1931.

SOURCES, METHODS, AND OBJECTIVES

their own affairs and the success with which their courts now deal with matters of criminal responsibility is a tribute to their growing appreciation of the need for internal security. I mention this with some feeling because in those early days it was a real struggle to resist the endless demands of individual Nuer for assistance over civil claims, a most trying experience which every District Commissioner who has served in the area knows. Nevertheless, at the present stage of development and perhaps for some years to come, the appeal from these courts is to the District Commissioner and the Governor of the Province. This being so, a knowledge of the basic principles of Nuer law is essential. It is necessary not only in connexion with specific cases, but also for the direction of policy in the development of the courts themselves. This need will continue even in the changing circumstances of the Sudan as a country whatever the nature of its constitution, and this book is written to meet it, as well as to record the evolution of a system of law.

It is sometimes argued that a government official, especially one with the executive powers of a District Commissioner in an undeveloped area, is an unsuitable person to carry out an investigation of this sort. His position may discourage sincere and truthful answers to his questions. I am aware of this argument and am prepared to accept the criticisms which may follow. Anyone who knows the close and positively wearing relationship of intimacy which exists between Nuer and their District Commissioners will, however, realize that the latter have many advantages. Having heard the details of a Nuer dispute over rights in cattle, and the same sort of dispute over and over again, he can get a pretty shrewd appreciation of the merits of the case and of the principles of law involved. Moreover, though the Nuer have a proper respect for the authority of their District Commissioner, no one could argue that this in any way curbs their blunt methods of expressing approval of his decisions, or more often disapproval. The relationship between the District Commissioner and the Nuer is peculiar and perhaps unique. He becomes a tribal institution adapted by the Nuer themselves to meet their own needs in rapidly changing conditions. He is addressed by his 'bull-name', greeted as an intimate by men and women of all ages, praised, but often severely criticized, by the chiefs. A Nuer 'bull-name' is a passport to the most intimate circles in any Nuer cattle camp or village. I often felt that it was I who had to struggle to maintain at least a vestige of the culture from which I had come.

In cases where my opinion was sought it is true that both sides would try to mislead me both on the principles of law and on the facts. I was fully aware of this. This approach did not apply to me alone; in nearly all legal disputes it takes a most exhausting process of interrogation amid a battery of lies before the truth is reached, for

INTRODUCTION

such is the technique of litigation in Nuerland. This is a necessary opening and not considered reprehensible in the circumstances; in other ways the Nuer are a surprisingly truthful people. It is thought fair tactics for the defendant in a civil case to throw out a screen of fabrications before giving way to the force of public opinion vested in the court, or, as is often the case, reaching some satisfactory compromise. A man must abandon the struggle only when a sufficient flow of ingenious argument has satisfied his honour. This procedure is not even confined to actions in the courts. The negotiations which take place over the payment of bridewealth, for example, are a battle of wits. The Nuer speak of it as a battle (*kur*) and regard it as one of the most exhausting trials of their lives. The idea of a battle is carried into the courts with vigour and in some respects the Nuer regard litigation as a stimulating pastime. The number of cases instituted without any hope of success is enormous, and even the deterrents applied by the Administration have not achieved any substantial reduction.

The sources of my information are therefore from the courts themselves; a close analysis of several thousands of actual cases. These were recorded when I acted as clerk to the appeal courts, or taken from court records. I had the benefit of Professor Evans-Pritchard's account of the social structure and political institutions of the Nuer[1] and more recently his writings on kinship and marriage.[2] In fact he has mentioned, though not always in detail or in the same context, nearly all the subjects recorded in this Manual and since I have rarely had occasion to disagree with the facts or his interpretation, much may appear merely repetitive. My work in the field, however, was carried out independently and largely among different Nuer tribes. Moreover his observations were made of the Nuer as they were some twenty years ago, and since then there have been many profound changes as the result of administrative action. This is especially true in the sphere of customary law. Further, it has been my object to describe only those aspects of Nuer life which are more or less concerned with disputes heard by Nuer courts, though it is obviously difficult to isolate specific aspects from the general background.

This Manual of Nuer Law is not a code or a text-book in which the precise answer to any legal situation may be found. The fine and now rapidly changing distinction between law, custom, convention, and usage will not allow any such precise description. It is rather a study of basic principles as they are now, exemplified by actual examples, as well as a study of a most complex system of law in the process of development. It is, however, primarily intended for the administrator.

[1] *The Nuer*. Oxford, 1940.

[2] In a series of articles and now in *Kinship and Marriage among the Nuer*. Oxford, 1951.

PRESENTATION AND ORTHOGRAPHY

It is also intended to provide further material for those whose interests lie in a more general and theoretical study of 'primitive law', although I have myself rarely attempted to interpret that material in terms of comparative jurisprudence.

These two objectives are not entirely compatible and involve difficulties of presentation. I must therefore seek indulgence in advance for those passages which may appear abstruse and far removed from the practical problems which face the administrator and for those passages which may appear self-evident or over-simplified to the jurist and the anthropologist. Whether the book will be of value in the administration of Nuerland in the near future or in the self-governing Sudan must be judged by posterity. It is dedicated with affection to the Nuer people themselves in the hope that they may find security and fulfilment in the direction of their own affairs with due regard for their traditions.

Presentation and Orthography

Since it is not easy to isolate one aspect of the social and political affairs of the Nuer from another, the system of classification is arbitrary and not based on any conventional legal form. There are also obvious repetitions when a particular institution or concept is examined in different contexts. I begin with a summary account of the social and political structure of the Nuer for the benefit of those who have not studied previous literature on the subject, and this inevitably leads to generalizations which are not equally valid throughout the whole area. The Nuer are, however, sufficiently homogeneous to make generalizations at least possible. For further information the reader may turn to the publications listed in the Bibliography. Chapter II concerns homicide and bodily injuries which are not at all uncommon in Nuerland even today. Chapter III concerns marriage, the means by which it is achieved, the rights and duties which arise and which are often in dispute before the courts. Part II of the same Chapter concerns the dissolution of marriage, a process which is unfortunately more common nowadays than it was in the past. Chapter IV concerns the violation of rights in women, also a common cause for litigation. In Chapter V I have attempted to outline some of the main features of Nuer concepts of ownership and corporeal property which are at present no real problem, but which may well need a more complex and precise system of law in the future. In Chapter VI I have attempted, very briefly, to describe the part played by religion as a sanction for social conformity, and the functions of the various religious and magical experts, some of which are recognized in the administration of tribal law and custom. In Chapter VII I have attempted to analyse in very simple terms the nature of Nuer customary law as it was in the past, and the way in which it is developing under modern conditions.

6 INTRODUCTION

A general index is included, but for easy reference a detailed list of contents is given at the beginning.

For the sake of consistency I have, with few exceptions, followed the orthography adopted by Professor Evans-Pritchard. The full range of phonetic symbols has not been used, but the Nilotic *ch* or *sh* sound is rendered as *c*—a common convention even in administrative documents—and *gh* stands for the phonetic Ɣ. Other forms of spelling are taken from *A Nuer-English Dictionary*, by Fr. J. Kiggen. After initial explanation, I have often had to employ Nuer terms in later passages without further definition simply because such terms have a complicated meaning for which there is no succinct English translation. To assist the reader a glossary of these terms is included among the appendixes.

Note on Cattle Terminology

Nuer law is principally concerned with rights and claims in cattle, and it will be as well, even at this early stage, to give some description of Nuer cattle terms. Cattle are referred to generally as *ghok*. The *ghok thunge*—the indemnity paid to a dead man's kin by his slayer—simply means the 'cattle of compensation', the *ghok gwande* are the 'father's cattle', i.e. the father's portion of bridewealth. A single cow is *yang*, though *yang* is often used indiscriminately to describe all sizes of female cattle. A heifer is specifically *nac*, a young female animal which has not yet calved, but may be expected to do so in the near future. A smaller female calf is *dou*. An entire bull is *tut*, the stud bull being referred to as *tut wec*, 'the bull of the herd'. An ox is *thak* if it is full-grown, all other bull-calves being *ruath*. Cattle obviously have their relative value according to sex and size. A full-grown ox (*thak*) is often said to be worth a cow-calf (*dou*); a pregnant heifer (*nac me liac*) or a pregnant cow (*yang me liac*) is clearly worth more than a similar animal which is not in calf. A barren cow (*yang me but*) is useless except for meat or sacrifice but is often considered the equivalent of a medium size ox.

Conventional claims or rights (*cuong*) are usually specified: for example, the *yang kwoth gwande*, 'the cow of the father's spirit', is one specific item included in the *ghok gwande*, the bride's father's portion of her bridewealth. This is a single animal. The *yang gwande*, another item in the father's portion, however, is usually a cow and its calf, though when referring to the claim, the calf may not be specifically mentioned. At the same time these terms may be subject to agreement between the two parties concerned and not to a strict legal interpretation. Thus, though he may point out that the *yang gwande* should consist of a cow and calf, a father may well be prepared to accept something less than this.

In giving judgement, a Nuer court will almost always specify the

NUER SOCIETY

size and sex of the animal to be paid by the defendant. This is especially the case when the defendant is unable to pay immediately, for otherwise he will be expected to name and describe the exact animal he proposes to pay.

In most cases the nature of the claim will be clear to the reader from the context. The administrator who is concerned with the practical application of Nuer law will be wise to master these terms at the outset. The terms are also set out for easy reference in the Glossary at the end of this book.

2. AN INTRODUCTION TO NUER SOCIETY

Origin and History

The Nuer call themselves *Naadh*,[1] which simply means 'people', '*kon nei te Naadh*', 'we are the people of the People', an expression which is sufficiently descriptive for their own purposes and reveals their arrogant belief in their own superiority over other human beings. By other tribes they are often spoken of as Nuer, and to be explicit to the ignorant stranger they will sometimes say '*kon Nuere*', 'we are Nuer'. Their origin remains obscure. Nuer themselves merely say that their ancestors descended from the sky down a convenient rope or by means of an exceptionally large *akot* (*Ficus*) tree which still grows in Jagei country in the centre of Western Nuer District, an area from which they all came. Other theories of their origin seem to me no less conjectural and in the absence of more convincing evidence, we may as well leave it at that.[2] Culturally they are very near to the Dinka, and the two languages have close affinities. They are clearly of the same stock, but it remains a mystery why the Nuer should have emerged as a separate people with comparative suddenness about the beginning of the nineteenth century, driven the Dinka out of so much of their country, seized so many of their women and cattle, and absorbed whole sections of Dinka into their own society. Their extraordinary vitality, expressed in a peculiar vivacity of speech, in physical courage and endurance, their arrogance and democratic outlook coupled with a most engaging sense of humour, make them outstanding among the peoples of the Sudan.

They are divided into a number of 'tribes', the tribe being the largest group which in the past had any real and permanent sense of corporate unity. Each tribe is further divided into segments and sub-segments, each occupying a common territory with a common name. Administratively they are now divided into three Districts: Western

[1] Sometimes spelt *Nath*.

[2] See Evans-Pritchard, *The Nuer*, p. 3. Fr. J. P. Crazzolara's two recent books on *The Lwoo* (Missioni Africane, Verona, 1950–51) do not provide much further information on Nuer origins.

NUER SOCIETY

Nuer District, which includes the Bul, Leik,[1] Jikany Cieng,[2] Jagei, Dok (and Aak), and Nuong (and Dur) tribes, with its headquarters at Bentiu on the Bahr el Ghazal; Central Nuer District, which includes the Lak, Thiang, Gaawar[3] and Lou[4] tribes, with its headquarters at Fangak on the Bahr el Zeraf; Eastern Nuer District, which is occupied by the whole of the Jikany Dhor people, divided into the Gaajok, Gaajak and Gaagwang tribes, with headquarters at Nasir on the river Sobat. Generally speaking, the administrative system follows the tribal pattern with centres in each tribal area, and in some cases in each primary segment of a tribe, though nowadays there is a tendency for segments to be combined in the development of Local Government based on territorial rather than traditional considerations.

At the beginning of the nineteenth century all Nuer were living west of the Nile. By the end of that century they had occupied an area stretching from the White Nile in the north, north-east of the river Sobat and north-west of the Bahr el Ghazal, eastwards to the Ethiopian frontier, and southwards along the Pibor river to the borders of Murle country and across to the headwaters of the Bahr el Zeraf.

An historical account of their warlike invasions of Dinka country and their gradual migration and expansion eastwards is not part of this book, but there are certain observations concerning their history which are relevant to a study of their customary law. There appear to have been five main periods in Nuer history: (i) The period before their move eastwards, about which little is known, but when they must have been fewer in numbers and more closely united as a people. What was then a tribe would, in numbers, be approximate to a tribal segment today, and tribal boundaries were less clearly defined. (ii) The period of initial invasion when they moved eastwards in a series of waves which began with cattle raids and ended in permanent occupation. This period is recounted in traditions relatively fresh in the minds of the Nuer and not yet merged into tribal mythology. (iii) The period of numerical expansion by natural processes and by the absorption of huge numbers of Dinka and therefore much of Dinka culture. It should be noted that this period was characterized by the facility with which Dinka elements were incorporated into Nuer society without friction or a trace of symbiosis. It is probable that at this time the Nuer lost much of their former cohesion, particularly as they were almost simultaneously subjected to the disrupting effects of slave raids from the north. (iv) At any rate the third period seems to have been followed almost immediately by a period of disharmony, suspicion,

---

[1] Sometimes spelt Leek.

[2] Variously spelt Jikany, Jekaing, Jekain, etc. The Jikany Cieng—lit. 'homeland Jikany'—are the parent tribe from which the Jikany Dhor—lit. 'outside Jikany'—originally sprang.

[3] More commonly, though incorrectly, spelt Gaweir.

[4] Sometimes spelt Lau.

TOPOGRAPHY AND ECOLOGY

internal strife and political fission. (v) As the pressure from the north increased, a return to a semblance of cohesion was necessary and there emerged the great Nuer leaders or 'Prophets' who arose as symbols of tribal resistance to foreign aggression represented first in the Dervish forces who attempted to establish slaving centres in Nuerland and finally by the forces of the present Government. (vi) In the years which followed, administration was limited to an attempt to hold the Nuer from their attacks on the Dinka, to prevent fighting among themselves, and to the collection of taxes. Naturally enough the Nuer resented this, particularly the collection of tribute in cattle and the prevention of cattle raids, and despite the outstanding efforts of individual administrators such as Struvé, Stigand, and Jackson, the attempt to establish ordered administration was only partially successful. Resistance, raids on neighbouring tribes, and lack of internal security reached a climax in 1928. Captain Fergusson, then District Commissioner of Western Nuer, was assassinated; the Lou Nuer led by Gwek Ngundeng[1] had been showing open defiance for some time previously, and in that year too the Gaawar Nuer led by Dwal Diu[2] descended on the Dinka of Bor District and attacked the Government Post at Duk Faiwil. Reprisals followed and took the form of a series of strenuous military operations which were known as the 'Nuer Settlement'. Whatever the moral verdict, the Nuer learnt their lesson and came to heel. A period of pacification followed, and through the just and sympathetic methods of such men as Captain H. A. Romilly, Captain A. H. Alban, and Mr. H. G. Wedderburn-Maxwell, the feelings of fear and suspicion, which were natural enough in the circumstances, were quickly eradicated. It was these men who laid the foundations of the sound administrative system which was to follow. From an excessively arrogant, unco-operative and suspicious people, the Nuer rapidly became what they are now: still proud, still intensely democratic with a fine spirit of independence, but essentially friendly.

Topography and Ecology

Nuer country, set in the savannah and marshland of the Southern Sudan between latitudes 10° N. and 7° N. and with a seasonal rainfall between 800 and 1,000 mm.,[3] has its special topographical and climatic features which account for the present mode of life of the people. The total area of Nuerland in the Sudan is approximately

---

[1] See P. Coriat, 'Gwek the Witch-doctor and the Pyramid of Dengkur', *S.N.R.*, 1939.

[2] The son of Deng Likea, sometimes called the Prophet Diu, who rallied the Gaawar Nuer against the slavers at the end of the nineteenth century.

[3] Averages are: Malakal, 818 mm.; Fangak, 1136 mm.; Bentiu, 797 mm.; Ler, 902 mm.; Abwong, 744 mm.; Akobo, 925 mm.; Shambe, 819 mm. Fangak is exceptional, possibly owing to the heavy bush and Acacia forest in that region.

NUER SOCIETY

32,000 square miles and, as it has a population of about 350,000, it will be seen that the density of population is low. Some areas are, however, more densely populated than others.

During the rainy season, roughly from May until November but varying from year to year, the people occupy higher ground which is better drained and comparatively free from flood. This higher ground, where they build their permanent villages and cattle-byres and have their cultivations, is limited and widely distributed. In some areas it is concentrated in a series of narrow ridges, usually running parallel to the main channels of the rivers, in others dispersed in a series of isolated outcrops. Such natural features have their effects on the size of communities, on communications and therefore social contacts, and, as a result, on political and social structure, producing local variations of detail which make generalizations difficult.

Surrounding the higher ground are the vast areas of open grass plain with thickets of acacia bush,[1] intersected by a network of grass-choked watercourses and the main rivers whose flood-plains produce different ecological conditions and different associations of grass types. Each of these regions has its function in the seasonal activities, which largely concern animal husbandry, but in which crop production, the collection of natural vegetation, and fishing play an important part. It must be emphasized here that the Nuer economy is still essentially at subsistence level and that there is no specialization or organized trade.

I do not propose to enlarge here on the subject of grass associa-tions and pasture utilization. It is worth noting, however, that apart from soil, temperature, and length of day, one of the most important factors in the determination of grass types is the depth and period of immersion during the rainy season. On the higher ground, where the Nuer build their permanent villages, comparatively flood-free condi-tions produce a mixture of perennial and a few annual grasses which are fully grazed when the cattle are unable to move farther afield. Below this level are the vast 'intermediate' plains, subject to accumula-tions of rainfall and overflow from the drainage channels, where the grasses are predominantly perennials (*Setaria spp.*, *Hyparrhenia rufa*, &c.). These grasses are unpalatable and virtually useless except as bulk when in a dry and mature condition. So long as moisture is retained in the soil, however, they produce a green regrowth which provides valuable pasture, but in most areas the moisture is gone by the end of January, sometimes earlier. At this point, the cattle must be driven on to the riverain marshes, which, subject to deeper and longer inunda-tion from the rivers and watercourses as well as from rain-flood, pro-duce other types of perennial grasses (*Vossia cuspidata*, *Echinochloa pyramidalis*, *Oryza spp.*, &c.). These grasses are of variable value during the dry season, but generally speaking provide green nutritive grazing

---

[1] Mainly *Acacia seyal* Del., *Acacia fistula* Schwfth., *Balanites aegyptiaca* Del., &c.

TOPOGRAPHY AND ECOLOGY

throughout that period. This area is known as the *toic*,[1] and is of value for reasons other than pasture, for the pools and lagoons are full of fish which provide an important item of diet at that time of the year. These conditions determine the seasonal migrations of the Nuer in search of pasture for their cattle, cultivation, and other activities which are part of their economy.

Physical conditions varying from thick bush country, sandy ridges, open grasslands stretching mile after mile with scarcely a tree to break the horizon, to marshland and papyrus swamp, are found in all parts of Nuerland. In the Zeraf Valley, a few miles west of that river, there is a long and almost continuous ridge where the Lak, Thiang, and a few of the Gaawar have their permanent villages. The banks of the Zeraf are high and well defined in its lower reaches, and in some places villages are built close to the river's edge, but to the west the country tails away into swampier ground until it reaches the papyrus swamps of the Bahr el Jebel. A large proportion of Lak country and part of Thiang is covered with acacia bush, land which provides only poor grazing and an abundance of biting flies such as the striped *tabanids* which are the agent through which direct infection of trypanosomiasis is conveyed. For this reason Lak country is considered poor for cattle. The area on the east bank of the Zeraf is occupied by the majority of the Gaawar and is much less densely populated. High ground is more limited and dispersed, and the people have to contend with serious floods in their permanent settlements, but such conditions produce more plentiful grazing. In the east is the Duk Ridge, a series of sandy outcrops running parallel to the river about forty miles inland. This area was densely populated in Dinka times and in the early stages of the Nuer invasion, and it remains a refuge for the Gaawar in times of heavy flood. In the exceptional floods of 1917–18, which the Nuer refer to as *pilual*, the Duk ridge was packed with refugees fleeing from the rising waters.

The country occupied by the Lou Nuer has all the characteristics of Gaawar country, though the better drained land on which they build their villages is more concentrated, and there is no perennial river running through it. A few of the Lou move to the Sobat River during the dry season and many to the country bordering the Pibor River, but the rest remain along the *toics* left on the edges of the khor Fullus and its tributaries. Those who move eastwards have been something of a problem to the Administration in recent years, for there is a tendency to settle permanently in Anuak country and sometimes over the border in Abyssinia. The cause of this movement is presumably increasing population in man and cattle and the desire

---

[1] This word has no more precise meaning than 'marshland' in English, and is often used very loosely to describe any area which provides pasture during the dry months of the year.

for better fishing which the rivers provide. It is also possible, and this is a Nuer contention, that the watercourses which flow through Lou country are becoming clogged with silt and vegetation, with the result that water-points dry out earlier in the year though grazing may be improved.

Eastern Nuer District, which lies north of the Sobat up to the borders of Ethiopia, is flanked in the west by the vast Machar swamps, a region which might provide plentiful grazing. In fact, the people prefer to descend to the upper reaches of the Sobat and Baro rivers, where there is not only adequate pasture for their herds, but also exceptionally good fishing and an opportunity to raise a rich crop of maize on the fertile silt left by the flood water.

This whole area, the Zeraf Valley, Lou, and Jikany Dhor, is often referred to generally as 'Eastern Nuer' in contrast to 'Western Nuer', the region west of the Nile. The latter area is known to the Nuer who live east of it simply as *kwi Kir*, 'over the Nile', but it is known that it is the original homeland of all the Nuer and is sometimes referred to as *cieng Naadh*, 'Nuer homeland', as opposed to *dhor*, 'the outside'. This distinction between eastern and western Nuer is only valid in so far as those east of the Nile are all colonizers, for though there are minor cultural differences between western Nuer and the Zeraf tribes, these do not seem to me to be any greater than are those between the latter and the Lou or the Jikany (Dhor). In speaking of the 'Eastern Nuer' therefore, I refer specifically to those people (i.e. the Jikany Dhor) who live in Eastern Nuer District, an administrative classification, and not to all Nuer east of the Nile.

Western Nuer District is divided geographically and to some extent demographically into two distinct parts. There is first the area lying north of the Bahr el Ghazal and partly west of it, and secondly the region south of that river. The difference in terrain is not very great, but whereas the people who live in the north rely on the Bahr el Ghazal itself or the rivers which flow into it, those in the south rely almost entirely on the pastures provided by the natural and seasonal irrigation of the Bahr el Jebel or by the flood waters of rivers coming in from the south-west. In the southern area are the Nuong and Dur, Dok and Aak' and Jagei. These tribes, whose permanent settlements and cultivations are on a ridge of sandy ground which runs parallel to the Bahr el Jebel, graze their cattle in the dry season along the edges of that river or along inland water systems referred to as the Bilnyang system. This system is partly dependent on spill water from the Nile and partly on water derived from a different catchment area. Hence in years when the Nile provides inadequate grazing or is inaccessible owing to heavy flooding, the Bilnyang system gives an alternative. North of these tribes are the Jikany Cieng whose country lies in the triangle formed by the intersection of the Bahr

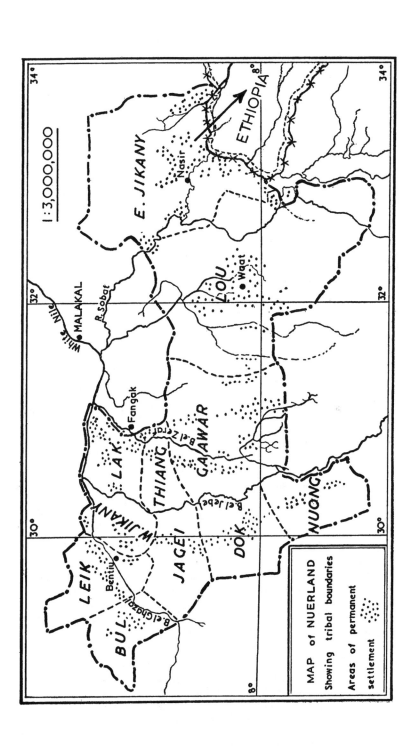

NUER SOCIETY

el Jebel and the Bahr el Ghazal. The Leik and Bul tribes are nearly all on the left bank of the Bahr el Ghazal, although some of them move to grazing grounds across the river during the dry months of the year.

All Nuer are compelled to migrate during the dry season and to set up their cattle-camps near permanent water supplies and where the receding waters of the rivers leave green and succulent grass for their animals. At first their cattle-camps are widely distributed over the 'intermediate' plains, but concentration increases as the season advances until, just before the break of the rains, in late January or February, all cattle are on the *toic*. The distances covered in these seasonal migrations vary considerably. Many of the Lak and Thiang Nuer, for example, move only a few miles from their permanent homes, while many of the Gaawar and Lou move eighty miles or more. These differences, however, have not affected the similarity of movements among the Nuer as a whole. The swing of the seasonal pendulum to and fro is common to all and the difference is one of distance only.

The permanent settlements of the Nuer are not concentrated like those of the Shilluk, Anuak, and some of the Dinka. A Nuer village generally consists of a number of domestic units, each having one or more cattle-byres and a few dwelling-huts, separated by distances varying from a few hundred yards to over a mile. This diffusion of dwelling-sites is partially caused by the nature of the ground, for land which is above the level of the floods is limited in most areas of Nuerland. It is, however, an inherent characteristic of the Nuer to set up his abode sufficiently far from his neighbours to emphasize and retain his individualism, yet sufficiently near to enjoy the privileges and economic advantages which neighbourhood brings. Cultivations are usually opened up in the area immediately surrounding the home-stead, both for convenience and for ease in protecting crops against the ravages of wild animals and straying cattle. Fencing is impossible except in woodland areas, and is in any case a laborious process, but apart from this consideration the Nuer seems to have an intense desire to see his cultivations round his home. When the ground becomes exhausted he will move his home to a new area rather than have his gardens a few hundred yards away from it. During the dry season the settlements are partially or completely abandoned according to whether permanent water is available or not and whether there is sufficient grain to keep the older and less active members of the com-munity. The bulk of the population always moves with the cattle, and by February there are few people left in the villages except where grazing grounds are close enough for daily contact.

The distribution of population in Nuerland is determined by the physical conditions I have described. Communications during the rains are usually difficult, and local communities, large or small, are to

TOPOGRAPHY AND ECOLOGY

a greater or lesser extent isolated at certain times of the year. Such periodic isolation is one of the factors which tend to emphasize the distinction between social groups and strengthen the ties within them, for the people are compelled by territorial proximity to conform to an accepted pattern of behaviour. During the dry season, movements in the pasture areas are comparatively easy, but camps may be far apart and communications therefore tedious. The majority of people from a local community who occupy the same permanent settlement during the rains, tend to join together in the cattle-camps, and their relationship is therefore constant throughout the year. This is not, however, always the case, for people of different descent-groups, normally living together and assisting one another during the season of cultivation, may split up and join different cattle-camps during the summer. The way in which people join together and concentrate during the dry season is usually determined by kinship ties, or ties arising from common residence in the permanent settlements, though it need not be so. For example, the Lak Nuer are sometimes forced to move their cattle into Gaawar grazing areas because their own are insufficient to meet their needs in certain years. They do so by agreement with the Gaawar and graze their cattle there on sufferance. A closer analysis of the relations of Lak with Gaawar will usually show that some form of kinship relationship exists, or at least a relationship through intermarriage between the individual units concerned.

Climatic conditions adverse to the cultivation of millet coupled with widespread cattle disease (rinderpest, contagious bovine pleuropneumonia, trypanosomiasis, &c.) make life extremely precarious. Nuer like to claim that a mixed economy is forced upon them, and that they would scarcely bother to cultivate at all if their cattle were sufficient. This is, I think, largely an ideal. Cattle, though subject to disease, provide a measure of security in an environment where poor drainage and erratic rainfall distribution make crop-production a most risky enterprise and famine a common event. They might well cultivate more energetically if the processes of agriculture were not so laborious and their efforts so often of little avail.

Small quantities of maize are planted in the early rains and the crop matures, if they are lucky, about the end of July, providing temporary relief until the first crop of millet is available. This crop matures a few weeks later, while a second crop is harvested in November or December and sometimes as late as January. During this period the rains may be favourable to both crops and the Nuer are well supplied. In most years, however, one or the other crop fails and in the worst years the early crop is late in starting owing to lack of rain only to be ruined by torrential downpours when it is reaching maturity, while the second crop is often destroyed by floods. In such circumstances the Nuer are short of food, and two unsuccessful years mean famine. The distribution of rainfall is, however, not universally favourable or otherwise to all areas of Nuerland. Heavy rainfall in low-lying regions may prove fatal, while it is suitable for crops planted on better drained, sandier soil. Thus crops are not as a rule universally good or bad throughout Nuerland, nor within one tribal territory. Some families have good crops, others bad, and the position may be reversed in another year.

On a wider scale this leads to trading or a reaffirmation of more remote obligations of kinship; on a limited scale it leads to a re-emphasis of the ties of mutual assistance which are raised both by kinship and by association in a common territory. Economic considerations of this sort are important in the determination and maintenance of social groupings and in the maintenance of peaceful relations. This is a feature of Nuer society which has been at least partially modified by modern administrative methods since grain is often imported and sold in years of shortage.

The other principal factor making for social integration is the need for common defence against opposing groups or, in a much wider sense, defence against foreign aggression. It is obviously another factor which is most readily affected by modern influences and the introduction of an ordered administration. The need for mutual defence is lessened, and doubtless the feeling of opposition to an alien government is less intense now that the Nuer are used to it.

Whatever the factors making for social integration or the reverse, the pattern which extends within and across social groupings is the kinship system, both as a fact and as an ideal. The smaller the social unit the more important these factors are and the greater the need for mutual assistance and co-operation. Later we shall come to examine in greater detail how these factors have altered through normal contacts with other peoples and through the active policy of the Government, and in particular the resulting effect on legal concepts and procedures.

Social and Political Structure

Professor Evans-Pritchard has recorded a full analysis of the political and kinship systems of the Nuer. For the purpose of this work, which aims at the examination of legal processes and procedures in the present and to a lesser extent in the past, it is unnecessary to do more than summarize his observations and conclusions which, with the exception of minor local variations of no great importance in the general picture, are much the same as my own. Where I use examples, I often refer to the Zeraf Valley tribes, Gaawar, Thiang, and Lak, which Professor Evans-Pritchard has not studied. There is therefore some object in this summary, apart from its necessity as an introduction to the subject of law, since it provides further evidence from other parts

THE TRIBE

of Nuerland in support of his views. There is often the danger of over-simplification and generalization in a summary account of this nature and the reader must bear this warning in mind.

Professor Evans-Pritchard has classified the different forms or sizes of local community among the Nuer as follows:

The MONOGAMOUS FAMILY attached to a single hut.

The HOUSEHOLD which occupies a single HOMESTEAD consisting of a cattle-byre and a number of dwelling huts occupied by a POLYGYNOUS family.

The HAMLET, a group of households living in a restricted area, but varying considerably in size and numbers.

The VILLAGE, a group of hamlets and scattered homesteads in a distinct area.

The CAMP, which is essentially a dry season formation, but not necessarily corresponding in the exact number of persons or the same individuals to the hamlet or larger unit from which the majority of its occupants come.

The DISTRICT, 'an aggregate of villages and camps which have easy inter-communication.' This usually corresponds to a small tribal segment.

The TRIBAL SEGMENTS OR SECTIONS of varying sizes.

The PEOPLE (Nuer: *Naadh*).

The 'INTERNATIONAL COMMUNITY', the limits of which are the Nuer's social horizon.

The homestead and the hamlet are essentially domestic units, while larger units are political as well as economic in character. The size and distribution of local communities are largely determined by physical conditions but partly by political considerations—the need for mutual defence, for example—which are variable in time and intensity. Hamlets or villages are usually the smallest political units and are composed of a group of people bound by loyalties which do not spring from kinship association alone but from the need for mutual co-operation in other spheres.

The Tribe and Tribal Segments

Among the Nuer one is faced with the usual problems of defining the segments of a segmentary society. According to Professor Evans-Pritchard the tribe is the largest political unit within the Nuer nation, since it is the largest aggregate of peoples who consider that 'disputes between its members should be settled by arbitration and that it ought to combine against communities of the same kind and against foreigners'. If the Dur (usually classed with the Nuong) and the Aak (often classed with the Dok) are considered to be separate tribes and the eastern Jikany peoples are composed of three separate tribes, the Gaajok, Gaajak and Gaagwang, there are fifteen such tribes in Nuerland, varying in size from approximately 6,700 (Aak) to 67,000 souls (Lou).[1] Each tribe has a dominant clan, round which other clans are clustered. Each has a common name, often derived from that of the original

[1] See Appendix I.

CNL

NUER SOCIETY

ancestor of the dominant clan, from the name of his favourite bull, or having some mythical origin.[1]

The tribe is therefore a unit of society bound by ties resulting from common residence, by the possession of a common territory, by a network of kinship and other social links in relation to the dominant clan from which it takes its name, by the need for mutual defence against external aggression and for co-operation in warfare against other tribes and peoples.

Each tribe is further divided into primary tribal segments, these again into secondary segments, and these into tertiary segments, the lines of cleavage usually but not always following the segmentation of the lineages of the dominant clan. As an example, the primary and secondary segments of the Gaawar tribe are shown in the diagram (Fig. 1).

Within each tribe only a small proportion of the people has the genuine right to claim direct descent from the original ancestor from whom the tribal name is derived. The majority are descended from later immigrants from other parts of Nuerland, or from Dinka accretions absorbed by the fiction of adoption into Nuer society. Genuine descendants are termed *diel*,[2] although this term is rarely used except in a context where the distinction is necessary, for the *diel* do not enjoy any great or noticeable privileges which distinguish them from other lineages which are called *rul*. The distinction exists only within the tribe and within its component segments. Beyond tribal boundaries it no longer has any significance. A Gaawar Nuer, a true descendant of War, is only *diel* within that tribe; he would be *rul* if he lived in Thiang country. Likewise a descendant of the dominant lineage in Thiang would be *rul* in Gaawar. A more common distinction made by the Nuer is between *gaat tutni* (sing. *gat tuot*),[3] the 'sons of bulls', the descendants of the male line dominant in that area, and *gaat nyiet* (sing. *gat nyal*), the 'sons of daughters', i.e. descendants through the female line and by this means attached to the dominant lineage. Others can claim marital relationships and refer to the dominant lineage as *ji cieng thu*, 'in-laws' or more literally, 'people of the in-laws' home', or *gaat nar*, 'mother's brother's sons', so that there is throughout a network of such relationships which provides explanation for political association and occupation of a common territory.

The political significance of the clan system is to be found in its association with the territorial segments of the tribe. The clan is itself

---

[1] For example, the Gaawar call themselves *gaat gan* War 'the sons of the sons of War'. Thiang refers to the bull-name of an ancestor, while *ji kany* (Jikany), the 'people of the gourd', refers to the twin birth of their original ancestor in a gourd together with the ancestor of the Ngok Dinka. Jagei, 'people of Gei or Gea', and so on.

[2] Professor Evans-Pritchard calls the *diel* 'aristocratic lineages'. This is an apt enough description provided it is remembered that there is no class distinction.

[3] A term now used to mean Government 'headman'.

TRIBAL SEGMENTS

segmented, its lineages usually corresponding to the segmentation of the tribe, but this correspondence is not always exact. Thus in Gaawar the Bang, Caam, and Gaatkwa segments are by origin offshoots of the Per lineage, but whereas Per is a segment of the Radh primary segment,

FIGURE I

The Segmentation of the Gaawar Tribe

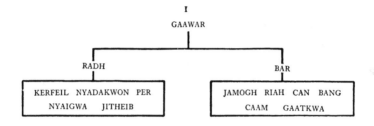

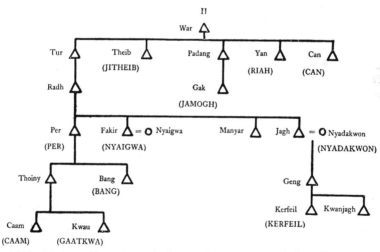

Table I shows the primary and secondary segments of the tribe as they are grouped in political and territorial association. Table II shows the actual genealogies cited by the Gaawar to explain these associations. It will be noted that the segmentation does not entirely correspond with lineal connexions, since Cieng Bang, Cieng Caam, and Cieng Gaatkwa derive from Cieng Per, one of the main secondary segments of Radh.

the former are all segments of the Bar primary segment. There is no conflict of loyalty involved, for kinship allegiance is sufficiently

NUER SOCIETY

remote to be overshadowed by territorial association. If there were
an occasion when the whole of Radh found themselves ranged against
Bar, the Bang, Caam, and Gaatkwa segments would follow Bar rather
than Radh.

The territorial segments of a Nuer tribe have the same characteristics
as the tribe itself, viz. a common sentiment strengthened by tradition
and mythology, exclusive rights in land and common occupation of a
recognized territory, mutual co-operation in certain economic activities
and in warfare both offensive and defensive, and a common name
derived from a central lineage. With these characteristics in common,
and generally speaking the smaller the segment, the greater the reality
and meaning of such characteristics, primary segments are segments of a
tribe, secondary segments are segments of a primary segment, and
tertiary segments are segments of secondary segments. Finally a tertiary segment is divided into a number of villages and villages into
basic domestic units represented in the homesteads which are also
family groups. The smaller the unit, the more nearly it corresponds
with a kinship group.

The Meaning of the word cieng

The word *cieng* is normally used to describe these segments of
society but, like the segments themselves, is a reflection of structural
relativity. Hence it is a term which leads to much confusion among
Europeans unacquainted with the social structure of the Nuer. I can
do no better than quote some remarks of Professor Evans-Pritchard on
this subject because they provide a key to an understanding of Nuer
society and hence to an understanding of modes of behaviour, social
relations, and also of legal concepts, which are the subject of this book.

When a Nuer speaks of his *cieng*, his *dhor*, his *gol*, &c., he is conceptualizing
his feelings of structural distance, identifying himself with a local community,
and, by so doing, cutting himself off from other communities of the same
kind. An examination of the word *cieng* will teach us one of the most fundamental characteristics of Nuer local groups and, indeed, all social groups:
their structural relativity. What does a Nuer mean when he says 'I am a man
of such and such a *cieng*'? *Cieng* means 'home', but its precise significance
varies with the situation in which it is spoken. If one meets an Englishman
in Germany and asks him where his home is, he may reply that it is England.
If one meets the same man in London and asks him the same question, he will
tell one that his home is in Oxfordshire, whereas if one meets him in that
county, he will tell one the name of the town or village in which he lives. If
questioned in his town or village he will mention his particular street, and
if questioned in his street he will indicate his house. So it is with the Nuer.
A Nuer met outside Nuerland says that his home is *cieng* Nath, Nuerland.
He may also refer to his tribal country as his *cieng*, though the more usual
expression for this is *rol*. If one asks him in his tribe what is his *cieng*, he will
name his village or tribal section according to the context. Generally he will
name either his tertiary tribal section or his village, but he may give his primary

MEANING OF *CIENG*

or secondary section. If asked in his village he will mention the name of his hamlet or indicate his homestead or the end of the village in which his homestead is situated. Hence if a man says '*Wa ciengda*', 'I am going home', outside his village he means that he is returning to it; if in his village he means that he is going to his hamlet; if in his hamlet he means that he is going to his homestead. *Cieng* thus means homestead, hamlet, village, and tribal sections of varying dimensions.

The variations in the meaning of the word *cieng* are not due to the inconsistencies of language, but to the relativity of the group-values to which it refers.[1]

Cieng is a word which is used to describe residence, whether common residence implies kinship relationship or not. Thus when a man says he is a member of *cieng* Kerfeil, it does not necessarily mean that he can claim lineal descent from Kerfeil who is the ancestor of the Kerfeil lineage, though he can usually claim some form of affinity with that lineage, which is also the dominant one within that tertiary segment of the Gaawar and from which the name of that segment is derived. The word *cieng* is therefore variable in its application and meaning. In referring to a kinship group without any territorial implications there is another term which is commonly used, *thok dwiel*.[2] It must be remembered that this term is also relative. If asked his *thok dwiel*, his clan or lineage, a Nuer may say, for example, Gaawar, he may say Radh, he may say Kerfeil, or make a further distinction by saying Teng (Kerfeil), or he may refer to the name of some more recent ancestor. Since tribal segments and territorial units are seen by the Nuer in terms of kinship, the word *cieng* is, in many contexts, synonymous with the term *thok dwiel*, but the former is more specifically a term of residence, the latter a term of kinship, and both are relative.

It will be seen, therefore, that the kinship system provides a framework upon which wider political loyalties are extended. Political association is expressed in kinship terms. Thus the Gaawar are *gaat gan* War, the 'sons of the sons of War', and any member of the tribe will speak of himself as such in contrast to other tribes. All Gaawar, however, are not direct descendants of War, and in a context where a distinction is necessary the fact may be stressed. The tribe is usually closely associated with the clan from which it takes its name and which usually has greater numerical representation in that tribe than any other clan, but the clan is not restricted to any one locality and is itself segmented. These segments of the clan or lineages give their names to the component segments of the tribe and so on down the scale until the final unit of society is more nearly a kinship group

[1] Evans-Pritchard, *The Nuer*, pp. 135–6.

[2] Literally 'entrance to the house'. The best translation in English is 'house', in the sense of a lineage—'the House of Bourbon', &c. The Arabic equivalent is *Khashm beit* (خشم بيت) which is often used in Arab society with the same relativity. As in Nuer society, among Arabs social relationships and political associations are expressed in kinship terms.

NUER SOCIETY

occupying exclusively a common territory. Thus the genealogical system runs right through the structure of the tribe and gives it a form which can be visualized by the Nuer in kinship terms. Each individual knows his position in that structure and therefore his relation to other persons in the tribe by reference to the segmentations of the clan which run through it.

I do not propose to digress further on the nature of Nuer society, but must emphasize its structural form and relativity. Further, it is important to note that tribes and segments of tribes exist largely in opposition to each other, a condition which Professor Evans-Pritchard describes as the 'balanced opposition of groups'. Both these conditions, structural relativity and balanced opposition, are of profound importance in a study of customary law, since the sanctions for conformity are relative in strength according to the position in society of the individuals or groups concerned, and 'balanced opposition' is an especially important feature in the institution of the feud and the way in which feuds are composed. I shall therefore refer to these features of Nuer society later.

Custom or Law and the Sanctions for Conformity

The Nuer had no regular institutions for the enforcement of customary law in the past. Social control was not maintained through the systematic application of 'the force of politically organized society',[1] for there is no evidence that anything of such a developed and formalized nature existed. On this strict definition, then, the Nuer had no 'law', but it is clear that in a less exact sense they were not lawless. There were recognized standards for the control of human relationships even though these were maintained by sanctions too indeterminate to be called legal. As will be seen later, a very large and growing body of what should be called 'custom' when we refer to the past is now consistently administered in the tribunals established by the Government and hence is enforceable law in a more precise sense. It is not possible, however, to qualify every statement in reference to the past or the present, so that the term 'law' is used rather loosely in the text which follows.

A Nuer thinks in terms of rights which he calls *cuong* and of wrongs which he calls *duer*. *Duer* in this sense means the failure to recognize a right or the infringement of a right. The Nuer has, by reason of his membership of a kinship group, both rights and obligations. A wrong, *duer*, therefore has two meanings. In the first place it is a wrong when a man actively violates the right of another. It is also a wrong when a man refuses to honour his obligations towards his kinsmen.

Given that there were rules of conduct, expressed in the terms

[1] Roscoe Pound, *An Introduction to the Philosophy of Law.*

cuong, 'right', and *duer*, 'wrong', which controlled the relations of one Nuer with another and of one group with another group, what were the sanctions which made for the observance of those rules? The primary sanction, and one which is most affected by the establishment of public security and ordered administration today, is the sanction of self-help; retaliation if a wrong is committed, or the use of force to claim a right. This applies to individuals, who fear that those they have wronged or those to whom definite obligations have not been fulfilled will take physical action against them, and fear also that, because their action is agreed to be wrong, they will receive no support from their fellows in resisting. Moreover the wronged may receive the assistance of their own kinsmen and neighbours, who will overwhelm any attempt at resistance. This applies to groups of individuals in relation to other groups in the same way, and is expressed in the balanced opposition of tribal segments and kinship groups. A Nuer may owe one of his kinsmen a cow and refuse to pay it. His kinsman will take the cow by stealth or wrest it from him by force, and the success of this action will depend on the extent of the non-intervention of other relatives. In the relationship of individuals there is also the prevailing principle of collective responsibility, so that in fact there is rarely an isolated individual wrong or an isolated right. The strength of the right, or the extent of the wrong, is qualified by the relationship of the parties concerned. Further sanctions are social reprobation, unpopularity, loss of approval and respect of neighbours, and hence loss of the privileges which the individual possesses as a member of a community and which the community possesses as part of a larger social group. Such privileges are both social and political. They are also economic, because so many economic activities must be carried out collectively. For some wrongs there is also a religious sanction, but, as I shall attempt to show later, the religious sanction is often an expression of kinship ideals.

The force of all these sanctions is relative to the position in the social structure of the persons concerned. Clearly social obligations are likely to be more binding on persons not only related by blood but also closely associated in the activities of day to day life. Loss of privilege is a greater loss in such circumstances. Generally speaking, the closer the relationship, expressed in terms of kinship, in association by common residence, and economic co-operation, the greater the need to abide by accepted modes of behaviour. Not only is the need greater and therefore the likelihood of obedience greater too, but also the difficulty of composition, when there is a quarrel, is less, because the sanctions which ensure good relations with other persons within the group in other respects are more intense and therefore more effective. The reaction of indignation is not likely to run to such a pitch of ill-feeling.

NUER SOCIETY

The significance of the 'structural relativity' of Nuer society is therefore most important in a study of customary law, for although the rules and principles which govern the conduct of all Nuer are essentially the same, the extent of their application is relative and largely dependent on the social context. This is best illustrated by use of an example. It is a legal wrong to commit adultery with another man's wife. It is a wrong which, if social relations are to continue between the two parties and the possibility of retaliation on the part of the wronged husband is to be removed, will require the payment of cattle as an indemnity. In the first place, the likelihood of the wrongdoer paying the cattle at all is determined by the relationship of the parties, both in terms of actual kinship and in terms of territorial proximity, in residence and all the sanctions which go with common residence. It will not be paid if there is no pressure on the part of the community in which they live, and there will be pressure in proportion to the extent to which the men's mutual animosity disturbs the tranquillity of that community; generally speaking, the greater the structural distance between them, the less the likelihood of composition. But in another aspect of the law concerning adultery the reverse is found. If we analyse the concepts behind the payment of the indemnity, we find that, of the six cattle required, one has purely ritual significance. It is a cow called *yang kule* ('the cow of the sleeping mat'), the payment of which is demanded as expiation for the spiritual pollution which is caused by adultery, rather than as an indemnity required to appease the indignation of the husband. In disputes over acts of adultery which arise between men who are close kinsmen it is rare that anything more than this one cow will be demanded, for not only is the moral indignation much less, but the group of which they are part is sufficiently well-knit to resist the disturbance caused within it. Not only is the wrong a lesser one because the wronged person has other associations with the wrongdoer which mitigate the offence,[1] but social equilibrium has not been disturbed to a degree which other sanctions making for good relations cannot rectify. Thus we see that the closer the structural relationship of the parties involved, the more likely is the wrong to be rectified, but the smaller is the indemnification required to do so. Conversely, the more remote the relationship the greater the indemnification necessary but the smaller the likelihood that the wrong will be rectified at all. This is a principle which applies to all wrongs which require

---

[1] There is another method of analysis which expresses the same idea. It is that in the payment of indemnification in cattle between two persons closely related the limitation of rights in cattle must be considered. An individual has rights in cattle limited by mutual obligations which apply to him as member of a kinship group. If the wrongdoer is a kinsman of the wronged he has limited rights in the cattle of the wronged, and the closer the relationship, the greater the rights. Hence the recipient of the cattle is also a person upon whom may lie the obligation to assist in the payment. This principle is more clearly illustrated in payment of compensation for homicide, and will be discussed more fully later.

Restitutive Sanctions

indemnification,[1] but is nowadays modified by the fact of enforcement of the law through the agency of Nuer courts.

Restitutive Sanctions

Rules of conduct towards kinsmen and neighbours are upheld by these sanctions. If good relations are to continue, certain breaches of conduct usually require the payment of compensation. Adultery, as we have seen, requires six head of cattle for this purpose; bodily injuries require compensation in proportion to the seriousness of the injury and there are complicated scales laid down in tradition. Homicide requires the transference of forty head of cattle from the kinsmen of the killer to those of the deceased in order to restore the balance between them. Scales of compensation for wrongs can be quoted by the older generation of Nuer with surprising consistency, but this is an indication neither of rigidity of custom nor of constant application. Whether compensation was paid at all and, if paid, whether the scales were strictly followed, depended largely on the relationship of the persons involved. If a dispute arose between groups of people after a wrong had been inflicted on one of them, we have seen that their relationship in the social structure determined the likelihood of settlement. The sanctions for composition operated along lines of social cleavage, being less intense and therefore less effective the greater the structural distance. A man of one tribe could rarely hope to exact compensation for an injury inflicted by someone of another tribe unless there were other links between them which extended beyond the political limits of the tribe. Similarly an individual living within one primary segment would find it difficult to get compensation from an individual living in another primary segment unless there were other ties between them, usually kinship or marital ties, which made composition mutually advantageous. It also depended on the state of the relations obtaining between the two segments, for there was often a feud (*ter*) between them. These observations are less true of members of secondary segments, since the smaller the social sphere the greater the possibility that compensation would be paid, and would be also a matter of extreme expediency. The application of Nuer law was therefore relative to the social structure, and the extent to which it was followed depended on current relations of the social units concerned. It was unlikely that minor disputes involving the payment of compensation to wronged individuals would ever be settled so long as the communities with whom each was associated remained in a state of feud. The situation would be substantially altered if the feud itself was composed by payment of compensation (*thung*) between them. Composition of a feud was

---

[1] Homicide and bodily injury, defamation of character, infringement of rights in property, violation of rights in women, &c.

26   NUER SOCIETY

therefore often followed by the settlement of other and less serious disputes.

In the absence of a legal system for the enforcement of the law, settlement was not easily achieved, and should the situation be such that the disputants were persuaded to come together, there had to be some basis upon which negotiations could be opened. The discussion had to begin somewhere, and an opening was made by reference to traditional scales of compensation which existed largely for that purpose.

There is some evidence that bloodwealth in the form of forty head of cattle was usually paid in full if it was paid at all. In this there was a distinct rigidity which is still maintained in the courts, and it seems that this is not only a result of the enforcement of the law of homicide by the Government. The reason is, perhaps, that the peaceful settlement of a feud required strong sanctions, and negotiations were not usually governed by such considerations as the availability of cattle; a large group of people was involved, and therefore cattle usually were available.

On the other hand compensation for injuries less than death and for other wrongs recognized as demanding indemnification is of a more individual nature, though this does not mean that it is not incumbent on kinsmen to assist in the collection of the cattle. It often happens that a man has not the necessary cattle to pay and, if his kinsmen will not help him, a compromise must be reached. For example, in a dispute over adultery, the wronged husband may eventually agree to accept only three head of cattle. Even though there may be little chance of getting the remainder, his face is saved because six head is the established custom and the rest will be due to him in the form of a debt. 'Saving face' is a primary consideration to the Nuer in the settlement of disputes.

This is true of the past as well as the present, and may be seen in the courts today. In its judgement the court orders that the wrong-doer shall pay the wronged so many cattle known to be in the former's possession. It will further order that the remainder shall be paid at a time when more cattle come into the possession of the wrongdoer; in other words, when some debt, which the defendant is usually called upon to state, is discharged to him; when bridewealth is paid for his sister or daughter or when some other obligation in cattle is fulfilled.[1] All these considerations are thrown into the issue, and a Nuer court is faced not only with the problem of judgement but also with an equally complex problem of execution.

---

[1] The discharge of one debt leads to a claim for another. This is another reason why litigation is increasing. As soon as a man is ordered by the court to pay, he will look around for some excuse to claim cattle from some other party. This sometimes happens immediately after judgement, so that execution often depends on the judgement given in the next case and so on.

LEGAL PROCEDURES IN THE PAST

Traditional Scales of Compensation and the Formula of Compromise

Whatever the sanctions for payment, either in full or in part, of the compensation recognized as traditional, the mere fact that Nuer are able to quote traditional scales of a complicated nature shows that methods of negotiation existed whereby a wrong could be righted and peaceful relations between individuals or groups could be restored. I believe that traditional scales represented a formula through which such negotiations could be opened and were a starting point from which a compromise could be reached. They provided a formula for compromise, but no more. Although, as will be seen later, these scales of compensation have acquired a greater rigidity both in amount and in consistency of application because they are now enforced by the courts, this element of compromise still remains.

Legal Procedures and Political Authority in the Past

It is not the object of this book to describe how incipient legal procedures functioned in the past, if indeed any such procedures existed at all. There is insufficient evidence to justify any generalization, and it is probable that the extent of change in Nuer society, and particularly in the sphere of law caused by the establishment of Nuer tribunals, is already great enough to preclude any possibility of obtaining such evidence. Nuer informants are extremely vague as to how disputes were settled in the past because of the absence of any kind of formalized legal procedure and, above all, the absence of organized legal institutions with powers of coercion. It is sometimes difficult to believe that disputes were settled at all. In fact, they were settled when a combination of circumstances represented in the sanctions already described made it expedient for both parties to come to an agreement.

An act of homicide was instantly followed by a state of feud between the groups concerned. The situation demanded vengeance on the person of the killer or on any of his kinsmen, but, depending on historical circumstance and the conditions in which those groups lived, the need for vengeance could be removed by the payment of compensation. There was no organized political force to compel composition of a feud, but there was a recognized procedure for composition if it was expedient. This procedure, which is described in considerable detail later, centred round the functions of the Leopard-Skin Chief, the *kuaar muon* or *kwac*. This functionary had no political or executive authority to compel the warring parties to come to agreement and no force which he could call to his aid if the opposing parties had no wish to do so. It was, however, expected that he would make

28

NUER SOCIETY

the attempt to intervene. Similarly legal disputes of a less serious nature might be brought before him, but his duties were clearly those of a mediator and not those of a judge. That a dispute was brought to him for mediation at all presupposes that both parties wished for settlement of their differences. On this subject Professor Evans-Pritchard has, I think, rightly stated that 'the five important elements in a settlement of this kind . . . seem to be (1) the desire of the disputants to settle their dispute, (2) the sanctity of the chief's person and his traditional role of mediator, (3) full and free discussion leading to a high measure of agreement between all present, (4) the feeling that a man can give way to the chief and elders without loss of dignity where he would not have given way to his opponent, and (5) recognition by the losing party of the justice of the other side's case'.[1]

That these observations are strictly true is brought out in the procedure followed in the courts today and the characteristic mental attitudes of the disputants which are displayed. The difference is, of course, that there is force behind the decision of the courts, and this means that in the majority of cases recognition by the defendant of the justice of the other party's cause is not so necessary for settlement, and there is also coercion in that a defendant would be compelled to attend when otherwise he might not bother to answer the request of the plaintiff to take the matter before a mediator at all. Nevertheless the elements enumerated above are present in the arguments expressed in the course of a Nuer court sitting, although the concept of neutrality focussed in the person of the Leopard-Skin Chief as arbiter is now inherent in the court itself.

It is possible that Professor Evans-Pritchard underestimates the influence of the Leopard-Skin Chief in bringing disputants together. In the Zeraf Valley tribes at any rate there are indications that some Leopard-Skin Chiefs had considerable powers in this matter, but powers of persuasion based on personality rather than on any established authority inherent in their status. This really means that the Leopard-Skin Chief's actions were dictated by political conditions prevailing within a restricted community. The Leopard-Skin Chief was the focus of political desires and vested in him were the forces of public opinion.

This problem is a controversial one, and the subject of much unpublished criticism of Professor Evans-Pritchard's account of the function and status of the Leopard-Skin Chief. There is, I think, a confusion of thought in these arguments, for Professor Evans-Pritchard is writing in terms of institutions, while his critics write in terms of individual personalities.[2] On the other hand, since there has always been a desire

[1] Evans-Pritchard, op. cit., pp. 164–5.

[2] There is confusion also because Professor Evans-Pritchard's writings are based largely on experiences of the Lou and Eastern Jikany Nuer where there are few Leopard-Skin families, while his critics argue from experience of Gaawar, Lak, and Thiang where the majority of dominant lineages are also Leopard-Skin Chiefs.

on the part of the Administration to find an indigenous foundation on which to graft a system of indirect rule in which authority must be vested in political and legal agents, it may be that their estimate of the powers of the Leopard-Skin Chief is exaggerated. The Leopard-Skin Chief in the early days of administration often acquired political authority because he was chosen to represent the Government. There appears to me to be little or no evidence that Leopard-Skin Chiefs had political authority in the past except in so far as they were the centre of prevailing political cohesion. If a man chose to ignore a ruling given by the chief, he could do so with impunity; but if public opinion was behind the chief's decision, he might lose the privileges which membership of his group gave him. He could always move elsewhere. It is the sanctions which normally operate for the settlement of disputes which are embodied and find expression in the person of the chief, and not a legal sanction derived from his status. Some personalities attempted to further political cohesion within the group, and this was expected of them, but their success depended on the degree of cohesion already existing or the force of sanctions normally making for cohesion. Hence the Leopard-Skin Chief's status and effectiveness are both the expression and the inspiration of collective aims.

Professor Evans-Pritchard writes:

> In taking the view that to regard the leopard-skin chief as a political agent or a judicial authority is to misunderstand the constitution of Nuer society and to be blind to its fundamental principles, we have to account for the part he plays in the settlement of feuds. We have stated that he has no judicial or executive authority. It is not his duty to decide on the merits of a case of homicide. It would never occur to Nuer that a judgement of any kind was required. Likewise ... he has no powerful kinsmen or the backing of a populous community to support him. He is simply a mediator in a specific social situation and his mediation is only successful because community ties are acknowledged by both parties and because they wish to avoid, for the time being at any rate, further hostilities. Only if both parties want the affair settled can the chief intervene successfully. He is the machinery which enables groups to bring about a normal state of affairs when they desire to achieve this end.[1]

In the Zeraf tribes the Leopard-Skin Chief usually had powerful kinsmen, and in the majority of tribal segments Leopard-Skin families were represented in the dominant lineage. In Gaawar, the family of Kerfeil, for example, in Lak in the lineage of Winyang, and in Thiang in the lineage of Toi Thiep, who have always provided leadership in those areas, are Leopard-Skin Chiefs. Moreover, certain personalities often had the backing of a populous community in the sense that political cohesion was sufficient to ensure composition of quarrels and disputes within it. This leads us to the subject of leadership in Nuer society in more general terms.

There is no verb in the Nuer language meaning 'to order', and the

---

[1] Evans-Pritchard, op. cit., pp. 174–5.

NUER SOCIETY

imperative is not used with any sense of authority behind it. To get another man to perform some task on his behalf the Nuer must first draw attention to some special relationship between them, whether it be real or fictitious. It is an appeal to the mutual obligations inherent in kinship and is expressed in kinship terms. *'Gat mar'*, 'O kinsman', is the preface to any request which might otherwise take the form of an order. By this I do not mean that the imperative is never used, but it is used only to persons with whom the speaker has an actual and constant relationship, and usually only when the speaker is a senior kinsman. When telling a foreman wood-cutter, for example, to order his men to cut down certain trees, the District Commissioner, allowed greater licence than others, will use the imperative, but the foreman will pass the order on in more euphemistic terms and include himself in the effort to be made. This is merely an example of the exceptional independence of character of the Nuer and their refusal to admit superiority or domination.

There is, however, a word which implies not so much 'authority', even in a general sense, as 'leadership', or more precisely 'spokesman-ship'. The expression *ruic Naadh*, 'leaders of the people', is frequently used when referring to outstanding personalities of the past. The meaning can only be understood by reference to Nuer history. In the early stages, particularly during the period of invasion and expansion when the Nuer were more closely co-ordinated in tribal groups[1] and united by a common purpose, some form of leadership was not only necessary but more easily achieved. Nuer talk of Buogh Kerfeil, the leader of the Gaawar during their migration across the Bahr el Jebel on to the Zeraf Island and again in their raids to the east into Dinka territory, as *ruic* Ganwaar; Wur Winyang and his father Winyang Kwac were both *ruic* of the Lak Nuer at one time, while in Lou we hear of Bedit Kweinyang, who is associated in Nuer tradition with Latjor of the Jikany and led the people against the Anuak to the east. In Lou, after Bedit's death, Bec Colieth led the majority of the tribe back towards the west into their present habitat, partly because of repeated raids by the Anuak who had the advantage of firearms which they traded from the Abyssinians, and partly because of the ravages of fly on their cattle. The third *ruic* was Nyakong, a Leopard-Skin Chief of Jimem extraction, who at first led the Lou Nuer against the Arab slavers but subsequently, like Nuer Teng in Gaawar, turned traitor.[2] Their position was subsequently acquired by the 'prophet' Ngundeng and his son Gwek.

---

[1] It has already been noted that the Nuer were probably then less numerous and tribal groups much smaller than today.

[2] Bedit Kweinyang was a *kuaar thoi* or water expert. Bec Colieth was a *wut ghok* or cattle expert. Nyakong was a Leopard-Skin Chief—as indeed was Ngundeang, his successor. I am indebted to Mr. B. A. Lewis for this information. See also B. A. Lewis, 'Nuer Spokesmen', *S.N.R.*, 1951.

POLITICAL AUTHORITY

We have seen that the period of invasion from the west, when the Nuer had a high degree of political cohesion, was followed by a period of expansion and absorption of Dinka. In the absence of external opposition a process of segmentation and political fission followed. In Gaawar we find that the descendants of Kerfeil began to lose their influence, particularly during the early period of Arab penetration, and it is at this period too that the division of Gaawar into the Bar and Radh primary segments became particularly marked. The majority of the Radh threw in their lot with Arab slavers and preyed upon their neighbours, and although the line of political cleavage did not follow strictly the distinction between the primary segments of the tribe, the Bar section to the south, joined by certain Radh secondary segments living in that direction and especially those resident on the Zeraf Island, were in permanent opposition to the remainder of the Radh. At this period Nuar Mer, an adopted son (of Dinka origin) of the Kerfeil lineage, is sometimes referred to as *ruic* of the Radh, while in Bar, although there was never sufficient cohesion to allow complete ascendancy, we hear of such leaders as Liaab Liou. Finally, in the event of extreme danger the Bar began to turn to Deng Likea, who certainly had no hereditary claim to leadership but had magical powers and the gift of prophecy much admired by the people. When the Dervishes withdrew he rallied the forces of Bar around him, inflicted a crushing defeat on the treacherous Nuer sections who had assisted them, and killed Nuar Mer. Deng Likea is also referred to as *ruic* Ganwaar. This process can be traced in most Nuer tribes.

For a while the concept of *ruic Naadh* remained vested in the Nuer 'prophets' in opposition to foreign aggression in the form of the present Government, but this has vanished since their defeat and removal, and nowadays if a Nuer is asked who is *ruic Naadh*, he will reply that it is the Government or more likely the District Commissioner.

The term *ruic*, like the word *cieng*, is relative to the social structure. There were also *ruic* whose influence was effective only in segments of a tribe and their significance was greatest at a period when political cohesion on a tribal scale was at its lowest ebb. There was no idea of an institutionalized authority set at the head of a tribe or a tribal segment, though there was perhaps always a tendency for the office to run on hereditary lines within the dominant lineage. Any person might achieve such influence over his fellows by reason of certain qualities which the Nuer consider admirable: generosity in the giving of cattle and in hospitality, which itself indicates a special regard for the obligations of kinship; wisdom and even temper in settling disputes between others; ability to hold the group together, a further expression of the kinship idea; bravery and powers of leadership in war.

These characteristics are also inherent in the conception of the *gat* tuot or *tut wec*, the 'bull of the herd', a position which is acquired within a dominant lineage and extended in relation to other lineages. The expression *gat tuot*, as we have seen, is used in the same sense as *diel* and refers to any member of a dominant lineage, but it has a more restricted meaning and is used nowadays to indicate a 'headman' in the Government system of administrative agents. The *tut wec*, the 'bull of the herd', however, is used generally to refer to the man who is recognized within the segment, whatever its size, as the most important adult male. His position is in the first place derived from his place in the genealogy of the dominant lineage, but it is largely dependent on his personality and prestige. The word *ruic* is sometimes applied to the *tut wec*, but has clearly a much wider significance in political relations and in past history. Finally, it is worth noting that there were never any *ruic* whose influence extended over a unit of society larger than the tribe, which tends to support Professor Evans-Pritchard's contention that the tribe is the largest unit of any permanent political significance.

There is even some evidence that the *ruic Naadh* in much earlier days had greater influence, though the emphasis is placed on their ritual rather than political status. I have heard Nuer say of Buogh Kerfeil that he assumed the stool (*kum* or *kwom*),[1] a fact which suggests some special symbol of office. They also talk of a ceremony in which he was 'lifted up to God' by his fellows, suggesting a ritual investiture. Yet, although Nuer tradition refers to events which happened in the time of old men's grandfathers and, being thus much more recent than Dinka or Shilluk mythology, may have a greater degree of historical accuracy, the story scarcely provides adequate evidence that a form of institutionalized authority was then in existence or that the *ruic Naadh* approximated even remotely to the general conception of an African Chief with political and executive powers.

The essential distinction is that among the Nuer the concept of *ruic* does not imply a crystallized institution in the form of a position in society automatically filled when the present holder dies. In the past, if a hereditary successor did assume the position, this did not mean that his influence would necessarily extend over the sphere affected by the actions of his predecessor. If a *ruic* died his successor gradually established himself by the accumulation of prestige and popularity among the people and gained their acceptance. There is no evidence of a stabilized institution continuing on a permanent level throughout Nuer history. The *ruic* of a tribe only exercised authority, if influence based on powers of persuasion can be called authority, so

---

[1] The Nuer *kum* is an ambatch stick-shield which is also used to sit on. The idea of a stool as a throne is unknown to the Nuer, but may here be derived from the Shilluk. Among the Shilluk the *reth* or king is ceremonially enthroned on the sacred stool (*kwom*) at his installation. See P. P. Howell and W. P. G. Thompson, 'The Death of a Shilluk *Reth* and the Installation of his Successor', *S.N.R.*, 1946.

LEADERSHIP

long as there was a semblance of political unity in the tribe or segment in opposition to other tribes or foreigners. His authority was not at any time equally effective in all segments of a tribe. *Ruic Naadh* is a concept which follows the lines of political cleavage.

It seems, then, that Professor Evans-Pritchard's critics display a confusion of thought when they suggest that there was anything in the nature of a formalized political institution inherent in the status of the Leopard-Skin Chief or indeed in the concept of *ruic Naadh*, but Professor Evans-Pritchard has not made it sufficiently clear that the concept of *ruic Naadh* did exist. Writing of the Nuer political system, he says:

> The Nuer constitution is highly individualistic and libertarian. It is an acephalous state, lacking legislative, judicial, and executive organs. Nevertheless it is far from chaotic. It has a persistent and coherent form which might be called 'ordered anarchy'. The absence of centralized government and bureaucracy in the nation, in the tribe, and in tribal segments—for even in the village authority is not vested in anyone—is less remarkable than the absence of any persons who represent the unity and exclusiveness of these groups.[1]

Yet the Nuer are, and always have been, acutely conscious of the need for unity and are always seeking someone by whom and through whom social disharmony can be averted. Their traditions, which are sufficiently recent to contain at least an element of fact, are full of references to great leaders, as we have seen; and these were persons who achieved at least a semblance of co-ordination and came to symbolize common aspirations. Whereas among some African peoples these aspirations are attached to organized and permanent institutions, among the Nuer they were focussed on personalities. Their principal characteristics are to be seen in Nuer ideals: the desire and the ability to bind the people together; to mediate and to settle internal quarrels and disputes; to negotiate agreements with other tribes and peoples if they are to the advantage of the Nuer; to maintain good relations between neighbours; in fact, to check the process of fission which to the Nuer is highly undesirable. These qualities are stressed in Nuer tradition far more frequently than ability to lead the warriors into battle against the Dinka, and are more important than their sagas of great exploits and daring. The *ruic Naadh* were men who, by outstanding personality and powers of leadership, gained such prestige that they were able to persuade the unruly Nuer to listen to them. They achieved a degree of authority acceptable only so long as the sanctions making for political unity within the group which they swayed were sufficiently strong to maintain it.

The word *ruic* is itself significant. It is derived from the word *ruac* meaning speech or talk. The best translation is therefore 'spokesman'. Nuer also talk of the quality of *ruec*, which really means the

---

[1] Evans-Pritchard in *African Political Systems*, Oxford, 1940, p. 296.

DNL

NUER SOCIETY

ability to speak for the people; in fact, to voice their will. It is in this sense that the word expresses the Nuer idea of leadership, leadership which is derived from powers of persuasion. There is no sense of domination. The concept runs right through the tradition of Nuer leaders in the past who emerged at a time when political unity was required in the face of external aggression or for the furtherance of common enterprise.

The Appointment of Tribal Authorities Today

The concept of *ruic* has been mentioned here, not so much because its existence provides evidence of anything in the nature of formalized legal procedures which operated in the past, but because it is relevant to the appointment of tribal representatives today.

In the early stages of the Administration there was a tendency to use as administrative agents persons who had acquired significance not from their positions in the dominant lineages of the tribes but from their possession of magical or religious attributes. This was at any rate partly due to the fact that at the time of the arrival of the Sudan Government, what leadership existed was vested in the 'prophets' who had usurped the position from men whose status was derived from a traditional and more orthodox background in society.

Minor administrative agents, the representatives of smaller tribal segments, were nearly always chosen from dominant (*diel*) lineages, a fact which finds expression in the use of the term *gat tuot* to denote a 'headman' of a village or a lineage. Clearly, even in the early stages, these minor agents were essentially persons put forward by the people themselves and drawn from sources which would normally provide leaders; they were not nominees chosen regardless of their status in society. A *gat nyal* from a *rul* lineage was usually disqualified from the start. For example, in the Island section of the Radh Gaawar, a man called Gatluak Ngigni was appointed chief of the Per section. I intervened in this appointment rather more emphatically than usual, for there was a shortage of suitable candidates, and Gatluak was a man who had served satisfactorily for many years as a tribal policeman and as personal assistant to the previous chief. There was noticeable opposition from some sections of the community but the majority voted for his appointment. Later he became unpopular and opposition became open. There were clearly other reasons why they wished to get rid of him, but the main reason actually given was that he was a *gat nyal* of recent Western Nuer origin. To be a *gat nyal* does not entirely disqualify a man from gaining authority over his fellows or, nowadays, from holding an official position, but it is certainly a disadvantage, and only a strong and popular character can overcome the handicap.

TRIBAL AUTHORITIES TODAY

In Central Nuer District, at any rate, election of Court Presidents and lesser chiefs[1] has been carried out with the minimum of interference, and the considerations which govern the choice are significant. There is often a tendency to hide the person most closely associated with the aura of the dominant lineage, for the Nuer feel that, in the somewhat precarious position of a chief *vis-à-vis* the Government, that aura may somehow be impaired. This is a religious concept, for the leading man in any lineage is considered to have inherent in him something of the spiritual qualities associated with the ancestral spirits of the kinship group. There is also always a tendency to defer to the supposed wishes of the District Commissioner. This does not necessarily mean that Nuer choose a man known to be popular with the Administration, but rather a man capable of maintaining an even and unirksome balance between the Administration and themselves. In fact, they seek someone who can give the appearance of exceptional zeal while protecting them as far as possible from the more laborious tasks imposed on them by Government. For this reason too there is sometimes a tendency to choose a man of weak character; but on the whole a strong man is chosen because, even if considered tiresome and over-zealous, he will somehow persuade them to perform those tasks, for they know well enough that the performance will in the end be less painful than the punishment imposed for the avoidance of public duties. Since there is often rivalry between opposing segments or lineages, there is finally a tendency to choose from a source which will be neutral in such rivalries, usually from the dominant lineage because this is one of the functions of the dominant lineage in the political structure.

The hierarchy of administrative agents is now largely drawn from dominant lineages, in the case of the tribe from the dominant lineage of that tribe, and so on down the segmentary scale. There are minor differences in the system to be found in the different districts, though the formation of the Nuer Council has tended to standardize Government policy in this respect. In each tribal area, or in some cases in a primary tribal segment, a court is established which is not only a legal institution through which legal disputes are settled and which has recognized forms of legal procedure, but is also an administrative organ through which administrative functions are carried out. In each court there is a president, called by the Nuer *kuaar* 'Book',[2] a number of chiefs representing the larger tribal segments,[3] called in Nuer *kuaar lama*,[4]

---

[1] Technically such chiefs and members are appointed by the Governor of the Province or, in the case of Special (C) Courts, by the Governor with the consent of the Governor-General. Therefore I do not mean anything in the nature of a formal election, but public opinion is consulted.

[2] 'Chief of the book' in reference to the court register held by the president.

[3] Secondary or tertiary tribal segments.

[4] *Lama* refers to the sash given by the Government as a badge of office. From the Arabic *alama*—sash or badge.

36   NUER SOCIETY

and under them a large number of headmen each representing a smaller
community, often a single local lineage. The Nuer court is a judicial,
executive, and administrative body, and there is, at present, only the
beginning of a separation of the judiciary from the executive.[1] It is
with the judicial aspect of its functions we are here concerned.

Administrative Policy and the Evolution of Nuer Courts

Administration of the Nuer up to about 1928 was of an attenuated
form, and in the least accessible areas there was no administration at all.
Action was confined to the attempt to maintain public order, to prevent raids on the Dinka, and to collect taxes in the form of cattle,
efforts which were evaded by the Nuer more often than not, and
occasional meetings for the settlement of disputes. Writing of the
Zeraf Island area in 1924, the then District Commissioner rather
gloomily remarks that he rarely saw more than the distant backs of
Nuer and then only fleetingly. This was not perhaps surprising, for
the Nuer bitterly resented the collection of tribute, which in those
days meant parting with their cattle in return for nothing, or so it
must have seemed to them. I mention this because, in assessing the
effects of contact with European culture and, through the opening of
communications and the maintenance of security, with the peoples of
other tribes and of the northern Sudan, it must be remembered that
external influences are relatively recent.

The military operations against the Nuer which started in 1928
represent a dividing line in recent Nuer history and in the history of
the Administration. Thereafter the Nuer, by then at least partially
subdued and with a wholesome respect for the power of the Government, were approached in a more conciliatory manner. It was a period
of appeasement, and that the objectives of the Government should
be understood by the Nuer at all is largely owing to the efforts of the
District Commissioners already mentioned; and to them is due great
credit. Their contact with the people was essentially personal, and
their approach to the problem the right one, besides being the only
effective means of gaining their confidence.

We are here only concerned with the problems of Nuer law and
the evolution of legal procedures. At this period nearly all legal
disputes were brought to the District Commissioner personally, who
gave judgement with the assistance of the chiefs and saw to it that
these judgements were executed. In the early stages the extent of
litigation was limited, but what statistics are available show the increasing momentum as the years proceed. At the same time the authority
and effectiveness of the tribunals established by the Government

---

[1] Local Government among the Nuer is in its infancy, and only provisional Rural
District Councils exist at the time of writing.

showed little sign of improvement. The decision continued to lie with the District Commissioner, and there was a tendency to avoid any legal procedure in order to approach him direct; for this was the surest and speediest way to get justice, whether it was justice according to the principles of Nuer law or not.

This tendency was formally recognized as retrogressive in 1942, and administrative policy was changed accordingly. Thereafter the policy has been for the District Commissioner to divorce himself as far as possible from any real participation in the administration of tribal law. Further, there is now a more formalized system of appeal courts in which the judgement of a local court, based on a tribal section, can be tested in an appeal court consisting of members from other localities less likely to be biased by local considerations. In these the District Commissioner still acts as clerk to the court, for the Nuer still demand at least the presence of the District Commissioner, who remains a symbol of impartiality and whose presence may be a guarantee for prompt execution.

Courts and Tribal Structure

Although the general policy of the Sudan Government is to build up a system of courts based on territorial groupings rather than on kinship and tribal affiliation, Nuer courts in fact still closely correspond to the traditional divisions of tribal structure. Despite minor modifications, the court system throughout Nuerland is still largely tribal in basis.

Similarly, the court members are representatives of tribal segments. The *kuaar lama* represent primary or secondary segments according to the circumstances. The Awoi court, for example, has six *kuaar lama*, each representing one of the six secondary segments of the Bar primary segment of Gaawar. The Jagei (area) court has one chief for each of the four primary segments of the Jagei tribe. A section chief, a *kuaar lama*, represents a secondary segment, and under him are a number of headmen, *gaat tutni*, who represent tertiary segments or lineages, of which there are a great number.

The way in which these courts operate, the legal procedures followed, and the effect that the very existence of such courts has had on Nuer society in general is discussed more fully in later chapters. It is now necessary to examine the principles of the law administered in those courts. The legality of social institutions and relationships is maintained by the system of cattle exchange between one individual and another or between one group and another. In marital relationships, for example, the transfer of bridewealth cattle is the material symbol of the transfer of rights which in their turn create reciprocal rights. The transfer of cattle is the means by which equilibrium is maintained.

It is also the means by which any disturbance of equilibrium is set right. For this reason most legal disputes concern claims for cattle as indemnities for recognized wrongs—homicide, bodily injuries, defamation of character, adultery, and seduction. Otherwise they concern claims for cattle as part of a system of rights accorded to the individual as a member of a kinship group or acquired by marriage. It is these wrongs and indemnities, these rights and claims, which we must now examine in detail.

CHAPTER II

HOMICIDE AND BODILY INJURIES

PART I HOMICIDE

1. INTRODUCTION

Nuer Concepts Concerning Homicide

SPEAR-FIGHTS between rival factions are not uncommon, and the blood-feud is still a reality among the Nuer despite severe deterrents applied by the Administration. Casualties are sometimes heavy, and most Nuer bear the marks of some armed affray, but fatalities are fortunately comparatively rare. Battles range from the minor clashes of a few individuals within a small community to fights between local lineages and tertiary segments in which perhaps thirty or forty warriors are drawn up on either side. Often the attitude of hostility spreads to much larger groups of people even though actual fighting is limited to a few. On the whole, hostilities on a tribal scale or even between primary segments of a tribe are uncommon. The feeling of antagonism and the call for vengeance may extend through or beyond such larger groups, but it is not usual nowadays for them to combine against each other in full force. I do not wish to exaggerate the incidence of fighting among the Nuer, but it is sometimes believed that although the 'balanced opposition' of tribes or smaller segments is a feature of Nuer society, feuds are merely a conventional expression of that opposition. This is only partially true, and it would be a mistake to believe that the Nuer do not frequently use in earnest the spears and clubs which they keep always at their sides.

Fighting is sometimes described as the national pastime of the Nuer, but it is not so much a pastime as a necessary means of protecting individual and collective rights in the absence of established authority by which wrongs may be righted. This absence is now remedied by the introduction of Nuer courts with powers of coercion, though these have not yet reached a high enough standard of efficiency to eliminate all breaches of the peace. Self-help and retaliation are still common enough in Nuerland. There is still little restraint put on the actions of the young and hot-headed by a body of public opinion consciously opposed to bloodshed as a moral wrong. Nuer will admit that homicide is wrong (*duer*) and that fighting is undesirable, but this is because they realize that these lead to a most uncomfortable state of insecurity. Nuer are always acutely conscious of the need for social cohesion,

There is, however, very little expression of an unfavourable reaction to the taking of life in the abstract, and homicide is not considered a crime against society. On the other hand what we should call 'cold-blooded murder', which is extremely rare, offends Nuer ideas of morality because the victim has had no chance to defend himself. It is the Nuer code of honour which has been contravened. People are profoundly shocked in these circumstances, a feeling which extends well beyond those who by reason of their relationship to the deceased are expected to take a vindictive attitude towards the killer and his kinsmen.

Homicide and blood-feuds arising out of homicide must be considered in relation to the social context. Such feuds are characteristic of the relations prevailing between the political divisions of a tribe. Specifically it is the tie of kinship which demands common action in vengeance against the killer of a kinsman, but the obligation often extends beyond the immediate lineage of the slain to much larger communities, tertiary or even larger tribal groups. Thus the spread of a state of feud follows generally, but not always exactly, the lines of social cleavage, and gives emphasis to the segmentation of the tribe. Generally speaking, a feud between two closely related groups will be settled without great difficulty because common habitation and common economic pursuits, strengthened by the tradition of blood relationship, demand peaceful composition as a matter of expediency. The sustained feud is usually one which has spread to larger units of society and becomes a permanent expression of opposition between them. Hostilities are not continuous, but even comparatively trivial provocation may be sufficient to start further fighting.

In the past there was no conception of individual punishment inflicted on the person of the killer. There was no organized authority to inflict it. We have seen that the Leopard-Skin Chief, who had certain very definite functions to perform in connexion with homicide, had no political power but was essentially an arbitrator called in by hostile groups when a settlement of their differences was desirable. All wrongs were civil or private wrongs as between individuals or groups of individuals and, except in rare cases where collective action was taken against certain anti-social persons, witches and the like, there was no public law. The settlement of a feud arising from homicide, whether the act was committed by stealth, in fair fight, or by accident, required only the restoration of equilibrium between the groups involved. Settlement was in no sense an individual affair. It was not necessary to take revenge on the person of the killer himself; any one of his kinsmen would do instead.

If there was any sense of retributive justice, it was held by an isolated group of persons, the group to which the deceased belonged as opposed to the group of which the killer was a member. The action which

CONCEPTS OF HOMICIDE

followed, whether it was revenge by the former or offers of compensation by the latter, was intended to satisfy the people who had suffered the injury. To kill a person of the other group restored the balance by reducing their numbers proportionately, but it was a negative way of dealing with a situation which required more positive action if a permanent feud was to be avoided. The principle of a life for a life rarely led to permanent peace even if honour was satisfied for the moment. The likelihood of positive settlement by payment of compensation and the performance of the necessary ritual depended largely on the degree of social integration and interdependence of the groups involved. Both were usually segments of an even larger group. Political and historical factors also played their part. Two tertiary tribal segments, for example, previously hostile might have to settle their differences because of the threat of violence from another and less closely related segment of the tribe.

These observations apply to the past, for homicide is now a criminal offence and strong action is taken to prevent the continuation of a feud. The crime is punished, but the feud is settled on traditional lines even though composition is compulsory. The payment of compensation in cattle is still made as a positive and effective way of restoring the balance and allowing social and economic contacts to continue. It involves the fundamental principle that a deceased person must be 'married a wife' so that her children, begotten by some kinsman on his behalf,[1] will bear his name, belong to his branch of the lineage, and may concern themselves with his interests in posterity. *Thung*, the indemnity for homicide, is primarily intended for this purpose. For this reason compensation should theoretically be in proportion to current rates of bridewealth, although, as we shall see later, the proportion is not exact as there are other claims to be met. Part of the cattle at any rate will be used to marry a 'ghost-wife' to the deceased, and although the physical father will be some other member of his lineage, the children will legally belong to his line. The group as a whole also loses in the deceased an economic asset both in ensuring the subsistence of his immediate family and in the collective economic interests of his associates. Therefore other close kinsmen must receive some share of the compensation to meet this loss, to satisfy their indignation and their desire for revenge, and because, were the position reversed, they might be called upon to subscribe towards the payment of compensation to some other group.

Theoretically the question of intention does not enter into the assessment of compensation because the principal object of the payment is to restore the balance which has been disturbed, but Nuer do in fact take it into consideration. It has already been mentioned that in all Nuer disputes scales of compensation are treated more as a basis upon

---

[1] For this institution—'ghost-marriage'—see Chapter III, pp. 74 et seq.

42 HOMICIDE

which a compromise can be reached than an exact rule, and in the case of unintentional killing the indignation of the dead man's kin will be less than in cases of intentional homicide and a compromise more likely. Nowadays it is accepted that accidental killing demands only half the compensation required for intentional killing.

I must stress once more that these observations apply largely to the past. Homicide is now a criminal offence, and is invariably punished. Moreover, the Government insists on the prompt and peaceful composition of feuds arising out of homicide. The method of compensation, however, is no different from what it always was, and is usually assessed in a separate transaction after the trial for homicide is over. It is therefore necessary to describe in some detail the traditional procedures, ceremonies, and ritual involved before turning to modern procedure in the courts, where homicide is treated as a crime.

Definition of Terms

Before turning to the processes by which settlement of a feud is reached, it is necessary to define some of the Nuer terms which will be used. The verb 'to kill' in Nuer is *nak*, and the expression '*ce ran nak*', 'he has killed a man', is used generally for all forms of killing. Nuer further distinguish between killing which occurs in fair fight, whether in battle or single combat (all covered by the term *nak*), and killing by stealth or ambush, which is called *biem*. To them the latter form of killing is particularly reprehensible, although the circumstances are mitigated if it is done in revenge for a previous killing. The word *kur* is used to describe fighting in raids and battles, as opposed to the word *duac*, which is used exclusively to describe single combat or duels. The word *ter* means literally 'a state of feud'.

The two parties concerned in a feud are referred to as *ji ran*, which means 'the people of the man' (i.e. the deceased). These are the people who will seek vengeance on the *ji thunge*, 'the people of the compensation', who are the kinsmen of the killer and will be called upon to pay *thung* or compensation. The killer is usually referred to in the singular as *gwan thunge*, and in cases of homicide where more than one is responsible, the man to strike the first blow against the deceased is called the *ran me koic e-je*, and the second, the *ran me gam e-je*, a distinction which is important in assessing the liability to pay compensation. These expressions are used extensively in describing the processes of settlement, the circumstances of the incident, and the state of opposition between the two parties. The emotional attitude of the *ji ran* is characterized by intense indignation and a reluctance to accept compensation. Custom demands that they express in a conventional manner a sentiment of vindictiveness. Convention also demands that the *ji thunge*, the killer's kin, shall approach the *ji ran*

DEFINITION OF TERMS

in a spirit of conciliation coloured by a genuine fear that vengeance may be exacted. These sentiments are always to the fore if settlement is sincerely desired.

Compensation in Nuer is called *thung*. *Thung* is usually qualified according to the circumstances of the killing, and the number of cattle demanded is graded accordingly. These qualifications are described more fully later, but briefly they are *thung ran*, which is full compensation in cattle for the death of a man killed in a fight whatever the weapon used, and *thung nyindiet*, which means compensation demanded for a man who dies as a result of an injury inflicted a considerable time before. There is another and less usual term (restricted, I think, to Lou and Gaawar Nuer), *thung loic*, which refers to the compensation demanded when the killer has not confessed to his crime until long after the death of his victim. *Thung gwacka* refers to unintentional or accidental killing; *thung yiika* to compensation demanded for a woman who dies in childbirth when the father of the child is not her legal husband.

The special Nuer functionary who is called upon to act as arbitrator in the settlement of a blood-feud is, as we have seen, the *kuaar muon* or 'Land Chief'. His badge of office is the Leopard-Skin (*kwac*), and for this reason he is more usually referred to as *kuaar kwac*, a term which is universally translated as 'Leopard-Skin Chief' and is nowadays used extensively both in works on the Nuer and in Government documents. His powers, however, are derived from his association with the land, and extend to mankind because it is upon the products of the land that mankind exists.

In the settlement of feuds, these 'Chiefs' are called in to remove spiritual difficulties by ritual performances and to act as intermediaries between the warring parties. The Leopard-Skin Chief, by reason of his special association with the land, can curse people, and traditionally he may use these powers to intervene. He can, for instance, interpose himself between the contestants in an actual fight and draw a line on the earth between them which theoretically no man would dare to pass. This action, however, is merely a symbolic expression of general opinion which condemns the continuation of a feud, and if both parties were really determined to come to blows, it is unlikely that it would be sufficient to deter them, although hostilities might be postponed until a time when the Leopard-Skin Chief was not on the scene. I know of only one recent instance when this duty was performed. A few of the more hot-headed warriors did cross the line and were condemned by public opinion afterwards, principally because by doing so they showed an excessive determination to join battle with the other party in a situation where the majority wanted peaceful settlement. In fact, the final result of the Leopard-Skin Chief's action was to provoke a much more serious conflict than would

44 BLOOD-FEUDS

otherwise have been the case, because the side opposed to the youths who had rashly crossed the line were so incensed that they found a way of renewing the fight next day in another part of the area, well removed from the place in which the line had been drawn, and in greater force than before.

In most cases, however, the Leopard-Skin Chief only exerts his influence when he knows that the contestants wish him to do so. He will use threats to break down the opposition and expression of hatred demanded by convention rather than intervene on his own initiative when there exists a real determination to fight. Essentially, so far as the law is concerned, the Leopard-Skin Chief is the mediator who conducts the opposed groups peacefully through the elaborate processes of settlement, who acts as assessor where cattle are concerned, and who deals with the problems of taboo and spiritual observance which arise. He is the appointed and traditional 'Third Party', theoretically impartial, whose duty it is to smooth the path of the negotiations for both sides in a situation which is potentially dangerous. In some parts of Nuerland a special functionary, the *kuaar thoan*,[1] exists to mediate in disputes between two opposing Leopard-Skin families. In Eastern Nuer areas this function must be performed by a commoner or *dwek*.

2. BLOOD–FEUDS

The Process of Settlement and the Functions of the Leopard-Skin Chief as Mediator

The Leopard-Skin Chief concerned with the Individual

Apart from his duties in the settlement of feuds, the Leopard-Skin Chief is concerned with the spiritual welfare of a killer as an individual. The Leopard-Skin Chief's home is sanctuary and the group who seek vengeance may not enter, though they may lie in wait outside. As a mark of the sanctity and neutrality inherent in the office of Leopard-Skin Chief it is traditional that no spears may be carried into his presence or brought into his home.

A man who has killed another may not eat or drink until his blood has been let by a Leopard-Skin Chief; *ce riem-de kam rar* ('his blood has been taken out'). This ceremony is known as *birr*, and is performed by the Leopard-Skin Chief himself or one of his relatives. A fish-spear is taken and the arm of the killer scratched therewith until blood flows. The killer may not shave his head, and his home and cattle-byre are closed. His family may seek refuge with the Leopard-Skin Chief or may rely on the safety of numbers and group themselves round other relatives.

At this ceremony a bull-calf, known as *ruath birre*, is sacrificed by

---

[1] *Thoan*, serval cat (*Felis serval*).

LEOPARD-SKIN CHIEF

the Leopard-Skin Chief. The killer himself is no longer concerned individually and has nothing further to do until the negotiations for settlement are finally concluded except to collect the cattle of compensation of which he will pay a substantial proportion.

After compensation has been paid, a ceremony called *piec mac* is performed by the Leopard-Skin Chief and his assistants at the cattle-byre of the killer. During the period of his seclusion his home has been closed and neglected and weeds allowed to grow. An idiomatic expression in Nuer is *luak-de cerike luak gwan thunge*, which means 'his cattle-byre is unclean like a killer's cattle-byre' and is used in a derogatory manner towards anyone considered dirty or untidy. The byre must therefore be ceremonially purified and swept and fire rekindled (*piec mac*).[1] The Leopard-Skin Chief and his assistants clean the frontage and open the byre and his wife builds the fire-screen (*buor*), the symbol of the Nuer homestead, and kindles fire with fire-sticks. A sacrifice is then made.

The Leopard-Skin Chief concerned with Hostile Groups; ji ran and ji thunge

As soon as a man is killed a state of feud (*ter*) begins between the *ji ran* and *ji thunge*. They must scrupulously observe certain taboos and avoid spiritual contamination, which manifests itself in physical disease known as *nueer*.[2] They may neither eat nor drink together and they may not intermarry (and this rule may continue for many generations after settlement).[3] The Leopard-Skin Chief is able, by the performance of certain rites, to neutralize the effect of spiritual contamination, and he may be called upon to do so when an involuntary breach of taboo has occurred, or in rare cases he may be asked to remove the taboo altogether after compensation has been paid and the case finally settled. This ceremony is known as *math*, and is rarely performed unless the two groups are very closely related.

Ceremonies, Rites, and Acts of Mediation Performed by the Leopard-Skin Chief in the Settlement of a Feud

The Leopard-Skin Chief is first approached by the *ji thunge*, who ask him to call upon the *ji ran* to find out whether they are willing to accept compensation. He then approaches the *ji ran* on behalf of the *ji thunge* and appeals to them to settle the matter peacefully. They are expected by convention to show considerable opposition even though really anxious

[1] *Piec mac* is a normal expression used to denote the kindling of fire with fire-sticks, but in almost all Nilotic languages it has also a ritual meaning associated with the idea of purification.

[2] *Nueer* usually takes the form of painful but not necessarily fatal diarrhoea. The word *nueer* is not confined to cases of illness caused by a breach of taboo associated with a state of feud; other breaches of traditional observance may lead to *nueer*.

[3] 'There is blood between them'—*teke riem kamdien*—refers to the taint of a past feud between kinship groups which may be a bar to intermarriage. See example, p. 147.

46 BLOOD-FEUDS

to come to an agreement, and the Leopard-Skin Chief may resort to threats and curses to override their pretended refusal. After persuading the *ji ran* to consider settlement by compensation, he returns to the *ji thunge* to assess and inspect the cattle they propose to provide.

After the cattle have been collected and seen by the Leopard-Skin Chief, the *ji thunge* gather together and proceed with the cattle to an appointed spot. The *ji ran* collect nearby and send a representative forward to inspect the cattle. Here again there must be a show of opposition; the *ji ran* are not expected to accept too readily, and the Leopard-Skin Chief may again resort to threats. There may even be a mock battle, the Leopard-Skin Chief being chased out with sticks and spears by the *ji ran*. He will eventually cut the matter short by advancing and spearing the first bull-calf which is called *ruath kethe*. If the *ji ran* are too overbearing with the Leopard-Skin Chief, he may turn and run away, in which case the *ji ran*, fearing a curse, are expected to use honeyed terms to get him to come back. All this behaviour is probably pretended only; a symbolic expression of the feelings of the *ji ran*. It is unlikely that negotiations would get thus far if they really meant to refuse. The *ruath kethe* is then skinned and torn to pieces by the *ji ran* and carried away to be eaten.

Shortly after this the Leopard-Skin Chief sacrifices an entire bull called the *tut ghok*—'the bull of the herd'—a purification ceremony required to allow the *ji ran* to drink of the milk of the compensation cattle without incurring spiritual contamination. The milk of these cattle is particularly dangerous to the relatives of the dead man and will not be drunk until all possibility of contamination has been removed by the Leopard-Skin Chief. At a later period, if the parties are agreeable, *ghok pale loic*[1] may be handed over as a sign that the feud is really ended, but it is most unlikely that this ever occurred in the past unless the two groups were so closely related as to make life intolerable without final settlement. Two cows in calf are handed over, one being given to the father or brother of the dead man, the other to his mother, thus appeasing both his kinship group and his maternal relatives. This ceremony is known as *cuil*. Apparently the initiative should come from the *ji ran* rather than the *ji thunge*, and they intimate to the latter through the medium of the Leopard-Skin Chief that they are willing to make final settlement. The final ceremony required to settle the feud for all time is known as *math*.[2] The

---

[1] 'Cattle of appeasement'. *Pale loic* can be best translated as 'to ease the heart'. The custom appears to be more common in Western Nuer than elsewhere.

[2] The word *math* means 'friendship' in the most intimate sense. It is used by Nuer to describe the institution of close friendship which is common. A Nuer will talk of *math-da*, 'my friend', meaning a person with whom he has an altogether special relationship—a voluntary association with another man outside the normal ties of kinship. The ceremony therefore expresses the idea of reintegration on the most intimate plane, and after its performance even the latent hostility which persists after settlement of a blood-feud in normal cases should disappear.

CATTLE PAID AS COMPENSATION

Leopard-Skin Chief then performs certain ritual acts to remove all fear of future contamination between the two groups and to remove the taboo on eating together. A bull called *yang tul coka* is sacrificed and ceremonially divided between the *ji ran* and the *ji thunge*, who partake together of its meat. This ceremony was even more rarely performed than the *cuil*, though instances of its occurrence in the past are quoted, but in all cases the parties were closely related in the lineage system and occupied adjacent territory.

Terminology of Cattle Paid as Compensation

A list of cattle paid in compensation, sacrificed by the Leopard-Skin Chief, or paid to him as fees, is as follows:

ruath birre: 'the bull-calf of blood-letting', the bull-calf sacrificed at the ceremony of letting the killer's blood.

yang kweini or yang jal: 'the cow of the journey', paid by the *ji thunge* to the Leopard-Skin Chief early in the proceedings as a reward for his services in going backwards and forwards between the two parties.

yang jyup: 'the cow of the axe', a cow given to the *buthni* relatives of the *ji ran* by the *gwan buthni* of the *ji thunge*. *Buthni* relatives are representatives of a collateral branch of the lineage (*thok dwiel*), so that this transaction extends the processes of appeasement and compensation beyond the more immediate kinsmen of the killer and the killed to their lineages as a whole. The solidarity of the patrilineal descent group is thus emphasized, and the way in which all persons within it are involved is publicly acknowledged. Traditionally the *yang jyup* should be the first cow to be handed over.

ruath kethe: 'the bull-calf of the gall-bladder', a bull-calf speared by the Leopard-Skin Chief at the actual ceremony of handing over the compensation cattle. It is subsequently eaten by the *ji ran* as a sign that they have accepted the compensation.

tut ghok: 'the bull of the herd', a bull sacrificed by the Leopard-Skin Chief and partaken of by the *ji ran*—a sacrifice to ensure that they will not be contaminated by drinking the milk of the cows included in the compensation.

ruath riem and *yang kwac:*	'the bull-calf of the blood' and 'the cow of the Leopard-Skin'. These cattle are chosen from among the indemnity by the Leopard-Skin Chief and retained by him as fees, though the *ruath riem* is usually given to his personal assistant.
ghok pale loic:	'the cattle of the easing of the heart'. These consist of the *yang tuoke*, 'the cow of the cooking-pot' (*tok*), and a cow-calf referred to as *yang cak*, 'the cow of the milk', which are given to the dead man's mother as a token of her services in cooking for him and suckling him. The terms also bring out incidentally the idea that the ban on eating and drinking together has now been removed.
yang tul coka:	'the cow of the broken bone'. This is usually a bull or a barren cow sacrificed at either the *cuil* or *math* ceremony, divided, and partaken of by the *ji ran* and *ji thunge* together. This sacrifice is held to remove all fear of spiritual contamination in the future.

Rates of Compensation

Traditionally among most Nuer tribes, the number of cattle demanded as compensation for homicide was 40. A few tribes state that 50 were demanded for death caused by an injury from a fighting-spear (*mut*) and 40 for death caused by a wound from a fish-spear (*bith*) or a stick (*ked*) or by some other means. The use of a fighting-spear implies full intent and possibly a degree of premeditation since a fighting-spear has no other use. Moreover, to the Nuer, the probable consequence of a thrust with a spear is death, whereas use of the stick usually results in an injury which is not fatal. I do not know why a fish-spear is considered in the same category as a stick. It is, of course, essentially an economic tool rather than a weapon, but fish-spears are normally carried and used in war. It must be assumed that the use of a fighting-spear was considered a greater wrong and that a higher rate of compensation was demanded simply because the reaction of indignation was more intense. The rates of compensation were at one time reduced in some Nuer Districts to 20 head of cattle instead of 40 or 50, and there is now no distinction made according to the weapon used. As we shall see later, the indemnity is now standardized at 50 head of cattle, of which 10 go to the Government as a fine.

DISTRIBUTION OF BLOODWEALTH

Persons who are normally concerned in the Collection and Receipt of Compensation

We have seen that compensation payments for homicide are linked to bridewealth payments because the ultimate purpose is to provide the dead man with a wife so that children may be raised to his name. In the collection of the compensation cattle it will probably be those persons who normally contribute to bridewealth who will provide assistance. In marriage, when assembling all the cattle for bride-wealth, a man will have a number of recognized claims both by inheritance and on the marriages of female relatives. He may take several years to assemble them even if a part of the bridewealth comes to him not in fulfilment of definite rights but from the spontaneous generosity of his kinsmen. Compensation for homicide, however, will have to be collected without delay, and other than the general obligation of all kinsmen, including as in marriage maternal kinsmen, there is no definite pattern. Moreover it seems that the obligation to assist a killer in the payment of *thung* is cast wider and includes kinsmen who would not normally assist him to marry. By this is meant kinsmen of collateral lineages who have no title to a portion of the bridewealth of the killer's female relatives, but sometimes receive small gifts as a token of their relationship to the bride.[1]

The Distribution of Bloodwealth

The distribution among the *ji ran*, the people of the dead man, is also in many respects similar to the distribution of bridewealth among the relatives of a bride for, apart from those cattle set aside for sacrifice and those paid as fees to the Leopard-Skin Chief, certain categories of kinsmen of the dead man will demand a share. The remainder will go to the man whose duty it is to marry a wife to the deceased. There is in fact a conventional pattern of distribution which is still followed in Western Nuer District.

Leik Nuer (total compensation = 40 head of cattle)

Initial Payments:

ruath riem and *yang kwac* : To Leopard-Skin Chief and assistants.

ruath muon : To the man who buried the deceased.

yang jyup : To *gwan buthni* of the dead man's kin.

thak or *ruath kethe* and *tut ghok* : Sacrificed.

Total: 6 head of cattle.

---

[1] I.e. beyond the limits of the *kethar*: the reader will understand these statements more clearly after reading Chapter III, Section 5, 'Distribution of Bridewealth'.

ENL

HOMICIDE

To the Deceased's Kinsmen:

kwi gwan (father's side):
    gwan (father), a cow and cow-calf.
    gwanlen (paternal uncle), a cow-calf.

kwi man (or *nar*) (mother's side):
    man (mother), a cow and cow-calf (as with bridewealth these go to her own sons).
    nar (maternal uncle), a cow-calf.
                   Total: 6 head of cattle.

To the dead man's heir (usually his son or brother):
    The remainder to marry him a wife.
                     Total: 28 head of cattle.

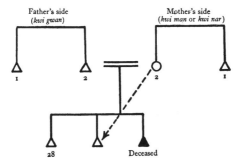

Thus a small portion at least will go to the deceased's paternal and maternal kin, though those set aside in the name of the mother (*man*) will be inherited by her sons and will remain with the paternal lineage.

The Bul Nuer give a more elaborate system of distribution:

Bul Nuer (total compensation = 40 head of cattle)

Initial Payments:
As among the Leik (above) . . . . . Total: 6 head of cattle.

To the Deceased's Kinsmen:

kwi gwan (father's side):
    gwan (father), a cow and cow-calf.
    gwanlen mande (paternal uncle: father's uterine brother), a cow.
    gwanlen gwande (paternal uncle: father's brother by different mother), a cow-calf.
    wac (paternal aunt), a cow-calf.

kwi man (or *nar*) (mother's side):
    man (mother), a cow and a cow-calf.
    nar mande (maternal uncle: mother's uterine brother), a cow.
    nar gwande (maternal uncle: mother's brother by different mother), a cow-calf.
    manlen (maternal aunt), a cow-calf.
                   Total: 10 head of cattle.

To the deceased's heir:
    The remainder to marry him a wife.
                   Total: 24 head of cattle.

It will be noted that in all four lineages are involved, those of the father and mother of the dead man and those of his paternal and maternal aunts' husbands, since cattle given to them will be taken by their sons.

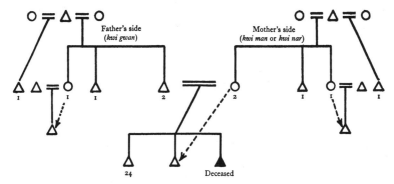

These examples are from Western Nuer where compensation for homicide has always been maintained at 40 head of cattle.[1] Among the Zeraf Nuer, after compensation had been reduced to 20 head, this distribution was not followed. Apart from initial payments, all the remainder went to the dead man's heir to marry him a wife. Since only 14 were left, it was usual to wait until the cattle had increased to the number required for normal bridewealth (not less than 18 to 20). Now that compensation has been increased once more to 40 head of cattle, the Zeraf tribes may well return to the old system of distribution.

Degree of Responsibility where Homicide is Committed Jointly

In assessing the payment of compensation for a man killed by more than one assailant, Nuer do not take into consideration the severity of the wounds inflicted on his body, nor do they attempt to attach the cause of death to any particular wound. Once the fact of homicide is established, all persons involved are considered responsible, but it is the man who strikes the first blow, the *ran me koic e-je*, who is considered to have a much greater degree of responsibility than those who follow him. This applies however superficial the wound he inflicts on the body of the deceased. Most cases of this sort occur in battle, and usually those who fight side by side are kinsmen. The *ran me koic e-je* is therefore in many cases closely related to those who assisted him in the act of homicide, including the *ran me gam e-je* ('second spearer'). The collection of cattle for compensation is not therefore an unusually complicated matter, and is subject to agreement within the

[1] It is worth noting that some Western Nuer tribes say that the Leopard-Skin Chief is entitled to 4 head of cattle in all for his services: two bulls, a cow and a cow-calf. Aak Nuer say that these beasts should be given over and above the total of 40, although this is not a normal Nuer custom (as it is among some Dinka tribes).

52   HOMICIDE

kinship group. In some cases, however, the *ran me koic e-je* is not closely related to those who acted with him, and the collection of compensation becomes more complicated. It seems that, according to usual custom, the kinsmen of the *ran me koic e-je* are expected to pay the bulk of the compensation, although there are no definite rules on this subject. Some Nuer suggest that the 'first spearer' should pay all the compensation.

These rules have caused some confusion in the courts and the matter was standardized in 1945 at a meeting of the Nuer Council. It was then laid down that the *ran me koic e-je* should pay three-quarters of the compensation and the *ran me gam e-je* one quarter, and, if there were more than one *ran me gam e-je*, this quarter should be divided equally between them.

3. FORMS OF HOMICIDE AND COMPENSATION RECOGNIZED IN NUER LAW

The various forms of *thung* or bloodwealth recognized in Nuer Law and graded according to the seriousness of the wrong perpetrated against the dead man's kin have already been defined. It is now necessary to examine these in greater detail.

Thung ran

Thung ran, which is the general term used to describe compensation for homicide, is also used more specifically in circumstances in which a man has been killed intentionally. In the past this was subject, as we have seen, to certain qualifications. The rate of compensation depended on the weapon used, a distinction which perhaps reflected the degree of intent with which the act was carried out.

Thung loic ran

A blood-feud means that a spiritual barrier is raised between the two groups concerned, and that a breach of certain observances and taboos current between them while a state of feud exists leads to contamination which is physically manifested in disease (*nueer*). It is therefore incumbent upon a man to confess when he has killed another. Failure to do so would be a serious breach of moral duty. Moreover, he must do so in order that both groups may not involuntarily contaminate themselves and so that they may scrupulously observe the rules of behaviour necessary in these circumstances. In the event of a man subsequently confessing to homicide or the fact of his guilt being established later, the *ji ran* demand a higher scale in compensation referred to as *thung loic ran*. Nuer feelings are outraged by behaviour of this sort,

THUNG NYINDIET

53

and it takes more to appease the feelings of the *ji ran*: indignation runs high because of the risks which are involved. Moreover they will naturally attribute certain deaths and illness in their family, which have occurred between the killing and the confession, to this cause.

The concept of *loic ran* remains in the category of private law. It is merely that extra compensation is required to restore a balance which has been more acutely disturbed, and to make good the ritual danger which has been added to the original wrong. It should be noted that the concept is extremely vague and is not known to all tribes. It is problematical whether *thung loic ran* was ever paid at all.

Thung nyindiet

The word *nyindiet* is not easy to translate, and I am indebted to Mr. Buth Diu, lately Nuer representative in the Sudan Legislative Assembly, for the following remarks:

> This is a most difficult word, which the Nuer themselves cannot explain. It is not really *nyindiet*, though the majority pronounce it that way, but *nin diet*. The first part of the word *nin* therefore could mean 'days', 'previous', 'old', or 'sleep'. In fact the expression *nin diet* is not only used in the context you have described, but of something which happened in the past implying a previous quarrel. Thus *teke nin diet kam dien ne walke* means 'there was a grudge between them in the old days'. The second part of the expression *diet* is not easily understandable. *Dit* has three meanings: 'bird', 'song', 'deed'. It is presumably the latter meaning which applies here, and the expression *nin diet* then means simply 'deed of the past'.

Thung nyindiet is demanded when a man dies as a result of an old wound. If a man dies a year or so after a fight in which he has sustained a wound full compensation is demanded. This is regarded as a normal killing and not *nyindiet*. If, however, he should die after a period of years, *thung nyindiet* only is called for. The period of time which must pass before *thung ran* changes to *thung nyindiet* is not clearly stated and is often in dispute. Moreover compensation may be sought for a man who dies so long after the infliction of the wound that to attribute death to it is absurd. Cases are continually arising in which men who die at the ripe old age of seventy or more are considered to have been killed by someone who struck them perhaps forty years previously.

As will be seen later, *thung nyindiet* has now been universally abolished, but it is worth noting that disputes arising over *nyindiet* are themselves probably the creation of the Government. The mere fact that *nyindiet* was previously recognized in the courts, and that Government action was taken when judgements were not executed, may account for the fact that what was formerly a very tentative concept, and in all probability never paid, has become a legal reality.

HOMICIDE

Thung gwacka

Compensation for accidental killing is usually paid on a reduced scale. Theoretically this should not be so, for, in the general balance of opposed groups, a life is a life, whatever the circumstances of death. Yet it is natural that when the act is unintentional, the feelings of those who would normally demand redress will not be so intensely inflamed, and they will be prepared to accept less. Here again the relationship of the parties is relevant, and the Nuer make a clear distinction in the terminology of their law. They speak of *gwac mara*, the accidental killing of a kinsman, as a minor wrong which will demand only tokens and ritual expiation. *Gwac gwoka*, the accidental killing of a person who is not related to the killer, is different, and an indemnity in cattle will be demanded, though usually on a much reduced scale. The dividing line between *gwac mara* and *gwac gwoka* is obviously difficult to determine, especially as the fiction of kinship is carried right through the tribal structure as an integrating principle and an explanation of political association. Nowadays the distinction is not valid, though it is doubtful whether compensation would be demanded for the accidental death of a brother or even a father's brother's son, but it is recognized that the full indemnity for homicide need not be paid. Usually half the standard indemnity is considered correct, but circumstances are important, and a Nuer court, though its members would be quite unable to express this as a general principle of law, takes into consideration what we should call negligence and the degree of criminal responsibility. There are certain extreme cases where the principal is held to be liable in theory, even though no compensation is necessary. For example, if a man who is thatching another's house falls and is killed or seriously injured, the owner must pay *thung diit*,[1] a purely symbolic payment in bundles of grass and ropes accompanied by appropriate ritual.

Thung yiika

According to Nuer Law, if a man seduces an unmarried girl and as a result she dies in childbirth, he is held responsible for her death. Her relatives will demand compensation known as *thung yiika*. This concept follows the general principle governing homicide, that the kinsmen, or in the case of a married woman, her husband, are entitled to compensation for the wrong. They should already have demanded compensation for seduction or adultery, which is known as *ruok*,[2] and for this reason it seems probable that the act is considered to be homicide, and not merely a breach of behaviour regarding women. The use of the word *thung* rather than *ruok* indicates that this is so. *Thung yiika* is, however, described in more detail under the heading of violation

---

[1] *Diit*, here meaning 'thatcher'.   [2] See under Adultery, pp. 155 et seq.

KILLING BY STEALTH

of rights in women, a subject which is discussed in a later chapter.[1] *Thung yiika* has now been abolished officially and is not recognized by the courts, but even before that, in most parts of Nuerland, as a custom it seems to have been dying out (except perhaps in Western Nuer) and it is probable that it was rarely paid.

Biem

The distinction between killing a person in fair fight and killing a person by stealth or ambush has already been mentioned, and we noted that the latter arouses in the Nuer a reaction of moral indignation, not because a life has been taken, but because it is an offence against Nuer standards of chivalry. It is therefore somewhat surprising that a higher rate of compensation is not required to appease the more intense feelings of outrage displayed by the dead man's kin. The reaction of horror or displeasure against an act of what we should call 'cold-blooded murder' is almost universal, and one might expect that the sentiment would be expressed in the scales of compensation traditional in Nuerland. There is, however, no suggestion of this in Nuer law, though a feud arising from such circumstances might well be harder to settle than one arising from straightforward homicide in battle or single combat. I think that the explanation lies in the fact that the circumstances rarely, if ever, arise except in the form of an ambush against a particular individual in pursuance of a feud.[2] If carried out as an act of vengeance the circumstances are considered to be mitigated. The literal meaning of the word *biem* is, in fact, 'to kill by ambush'.

4. THE STATUS OF PERSONS IN CONNEXION WITH HOMICIDE

Persons for whom Compensation was paid at Reduced Rates

In the past there was also a recognized distinction in the rates of compensation for the taking of human life according to the status of the person killed. There were certain categories of persons for whom compensation was paid on a much lower scale.

---

[1] See Chapter IV, p. 155.

[2] 'Fair fight' is a Nuer maxim. In the years 1943–4 there was a sudden and unusual incidence of cold-blooded murder among the Lak Nuer. In nearly all cases there was no actual motive, and the offenders gave as an explanation that they were directed by certain spirits (*kuth*) in their actions. Nearly all the accused, both in preliminary police investigations, enquiries, and during trial, displayed characteristics of mental instability, but not sufficient to disable them from conducting their defence. In most cases they revealed a curious persecution mania focussed on the person of their victim, though evidence that no persecution existed in fact was overwhelming. It is interesting to note that these murders, with one exception, were restricted to the Kwacbor primary segment of the Lak Nuer, and all took place within a comparatively short space of time. Public opinion in Lak country was genuinely shocked and other tribes expressed strong disapproval. The Lak had an unsavoury reputation for some time to come.

Dinka in the Category of Slaves

Nuer distinguished between what they called *jaang cieng* and *jaang dhor*. *Jaang dhor* (literally, 'outside Dinka') were Dinka who had no connexion with Nuer and did not live among them. Scales of compensation, which varied according to the tribe, probably depended on their past relations with Dinka with whom their boundaries marched. A scale of compensation was recognized, although this does not mean that compensation was often paid. *Jaang cieng* (literally, 'home Dinka') meant those Dinka who had taken up residence with Nuer, associating themselves with some Nuer lineage and ultimately identifying themselves with it. Dinka recently arrived, and living thus in Nuerland, received compensation at a much lower rate—the scale varying from tribe to tribe. Dinka born in Nuer country and adopted, i.e. in the second generation, were usually treated as pure Nuer. In this connexion it must be remembered that adopted Dinka did not necessarily suffer social or political disabilities and often attained positions of great prominence among the Nuer. Deng Likea, a Dinka of Ngok extraction, became the acknowledged leader of Bar Gaawar through his spiritual powers, and his descendants are still the most important people there; Nuar Mer, an adopted son of Mer Teng Kerfeil, whose real name was Nuar Bul and who was of Dinka extraction, attached himself to the powerful Teng Kerfeil section of Radh Gaawar and gained great power through his treacherous alliance with Arab slave raiders. There are other notable examples. Dinka captured in war were not slaves in the usual sense of the word and were soon assimilated into Nuer society; their descendants, after a generation or two, would trace a fictitious descent relationship to a common ancestor through the lineage of the man who adopted them.

Witches, Ghouls, and Anti-social Persons

For killing a person believed to be *peth*—one who possessed the evil eye—Nuer say that compensation was six head of cattle only. For a *rodh*, a ghoul who performed unnatural rites with the bodies and graves of the dead, no compensation was paid at all if, in killing him, only sticks were used and he was not hit on the head.[1] There are also instances in tradition of witches, *gwan wal* (owners of medicines), *let* (werewolves) and the like, being done to death by general consent of the community and no compensation being demanded.

I know of no recorded instance where a Nuer court has had to deal with a situation of this sort, and it is a matter of tradition rather than the present administration of Nuer customary law. This is true also of the distinction between Nuer and Dinka, for no such

---

[1] The subject of witches and other anti-social persons is discussed more fully in Chapter V. See Howell and Lewis, 'Nuer Ghouls: a Form of Witchcraft', *S.N.R.*, 1947.

DEATH OF WOMAN

differentiation is held valid nowadays. Yet the tradition is strong, and quoted consistently by nearly all Nuer tribes.

Uninitiated Boys

Among the Zeraf Nuer no distinction was made between those having manhood status and uninitiated boys. An uninitiated boy (*dhol*) was held fully responsible for his actions and his kinsmen were bound to assist him. Likewise the killing of an uninitiated boy demanded full rates of compensation. Boys who had not reached the status of warrior, however, were not expected to fight in a serious manner, and it was unlikely that an adult would kill a boy except by accident.

In Western Nuer some distinction seems to have been made even in the past. Writing in 1936, Captain H. A. Romilly records:

> Some doubt still exists about blood-money to be paid when 'ungarred' boys are killed.[1] The new decision in 1936 is: 'ungarred' boys killed by accident: 10 head of cattle; 'ungarred' boys killed on purpose: 20 head of cattle.[2]

It is difficult to say whether these fine distinctions are traditional or the result of past settlements in which the Government had a hand. It is, however, safe to say that theoretically full compensation would be demanded but would probably not be paid, as a compromise was more likely.

This matter was raised at the Nuer Chiefs' Council of 1945, but the only decision reached concerned the killing (usually accidental) of uninitiated boys by uninitiated boys (a fairly common occurrence in Nuerland). The indemnity for intentional killing was set at 20 head of cattle (i.e. half the full indemnity); for accidental killing, 10 head of cattle.

Compensation for the Death of a Woman

Nuer do not, of course, kill women in pursuance of a feud, though a feud might follow from the killing of a woman. Compensation is demanded in full; there is no distinction between the sexes. For an unmarried girl compensation should be paid to her family. For a legally married woman it should be paid to her husband. If he has paid only part of the bridewealth for his wife, compensation will still be paid to him, but some of the cattle will be demanded by the woman's family. He will be expected to hand over to them all cattle with the exception of a number directly proportionate to the number paid by him as bridewealth. The principle of compensation carried to its logical conclusion means that a man does not pay compensation

---

[1] 'Ungarred', 'uninitiated', from the Nuer *gar* to cut the forehead at initiation. Full compensation in that area was then 40 head of cattle.

[2] From unpublished administrative records.

58   HOMICIDE

at all if he kills his own wife—a rare occurrence—for he would have
to pay it to himself.[1]

Legal Responsibility for Act of Homicide committed by a Woman

A man is responsible for his wife's actions if she is legally married
to him, even if only part of the bridewealth has gone to her family.
If she kills someone, it is he and not her family who will pay compensation. A woman who is recognized as *keagh* (unmarried concubine)
is in a different category, and a man is not responsible for her actions
even while she is living as his concubine. Not he, but her family, will
be called upon for compensation if she kills someone.[2]

5. PEACE CEREMONIES: COMPOSITION ON A TRIBAL SCALE

The laws of homicide described in the previous sections concern
feuds (*ter*) which take place between the segments of a tribe. Tribal
boundaries were not in the past so clearly defined as to preclude
payment of compensation between sections of one tribe and sections of
another, but a whole tribe would rarely unite to demand compensation
for one of their number killed by a member of another tribe. When two
tribes had been at war for a long time and there had been many casualties
on both sides, both might decide to make peace; according to tradition
there was a specific ceremony by which peaceful relations could be
restored, and this again was performed by a Leopard-Skin Chief. After
preliminary negotiations, usually initiated by some prominent leader
in one tribe, representatives of both parties met at a chosen spot.
A bull, always a hornless bull (*cot*), was sacrificed, and the Leopard-
Skin Chief invoked the spear names and ancestral spirits of both sides,
calling upon them to maintain peace between their peoples and to
avoid disruption by endless warfare. He cried out, 'He who reopens
this quarrel will cause his people to die and scatter like the hairs of
the head of this bull', and then shaved the hairs of its head, scattering
them in the wind.

We are here approaching an obviously difficult distinction between
the feud and warfare on a wider scale. It seems to me unlikely that
the ceremony was often performed in the past, but the details of procedure have been described to me on many occasions. It is not a
ceremony normally performed between segments of a tribe, though
there was one occasion quoted in Gaawar when Liab Liou, the leader

---

[1] I have known instances. In each case no compensation was awarded, though the
culprit was expected to pay a cow or two as an act of appeasement to his wife's family
and as part of the process of ritual expiation. The courts were always reluctant to
impose a sentence of imprisonment. The culprit had already 'punished himself'.

[2] The question of the legality of the marriage is relevant here. See under 'Legality
of Marriage', Chapter III, p. 124.

TRADITIONAL CONCEPTS

(*ruic*) of the Bar primary segment, called upon the whole tribe, the Radh section included, to unite once more. This was after the separation of the two primary segments of the tribe and when there was a marked deterioration in tribal cohesion, but before the tribe was finally split by the raids of Arab slavers and the treacherous alliance of some of the Radh with the intruders.

6. CONCLUSIONS

Traditional Concepts and Action in the Past

We have seen that the laws relating to homicide among the Nuer are directed towards the maintenance of an equilibrium, and that in Nuer society this equilibrium is expressed in the balanced opposition of the segments of a tribe. Theoretically compensation should be the same whatever the circumstances of the killing and whatever the intention of the killer. These principles still largely apply, but in the past the main objective of restitution in the form of payment was achieved only with difficulty because, whatever the sanctions which exerted pressure on the aggrieved people to accept and whatever their actual feelings, convention demanded that they should accept only after a great display of hostility and reluctance. Moreover the degree of reluctance was genuinely affected by the actual circumstances of the incident. Some, but not all, Nuer tribes distinguished between intentional and unintentional homicide in assessing compensation. Compensation for intentional homicide was usually at least double that for accidental killing. The difference in the weapon used was also a qualification among some Nuer tribes, though it seems probable that they merely considered use of the fighting-spear an indication of intention. In contrast, reactions to homicide achieved by means which the Nuer consider unfair and therefore a greater wrong did not find expression in an increased rate of compensation. Unconfessed homicide was regarded by some Nuer tribes as a much more serious offence, and although this is a theoretical concept and without recorded examples, Nuer say that double the full rate of bloodwealth was necessary before settlement could be achieved. In this case, however, it was not so much an assessment of the quality of the homicidal act as a reaction to an offence committed by the killer afterwards, for he had, by concealing the deed, endangered the whole community including both factions. Nuer believe that the killer enters into a condition of ritual impurity which must be neutralized by the operations of the Leopard-Skin Chief if the community is not to share in that condition. An act of homicide therefore creates a state of grave danger. Actual danger springs from a state of feud, for there is always the likelihood of retaliation and further violence. Spiritual danger arises from the contamination of a man who has

HOMICIDE

spilt the blood of a human being, and this may extend to his kin.[1] Between the group thus tainted and the kin of the dead man no social contact is possible until the pollution is removed by elaborate rites performed by the special functionary who exists for that purpose.

In connexion with the general theory of primitive law it is also worth noting that among the Nuer the composition of homicide was achieved by a payment which varied according to the status of the dead person, but this distinction, which is no longer valid, applied only to Dinka slaves of the first generation, and probably only to those captured in war and not fully adopted. Otherwise there was no differentiation according to class because no class distinction ever existed.[2] Moreover the age or sex of the deceased was not taken into consideration, the compensation for a woman or an uninitiated boy being the same as that for an adult male. It is true that low scales of compensation were demanded for the killing of certain categories of anti-social persons, witches and the like, and it might be argued that such persons were set in a lower status in society because of the evil reputation which attached to them, and in this also the germs of a concept of public law may be detected.

Unlike the scale of indemnities for lesser wrongs, compensation for homicide (*thung*) appears to have been maintained at a more constant level, with the provisos already mentioned. It was set as an ideal, though it is now difficult to say how often it was fully paid in the past, just because homicide and violent retaliation were the very first features of Nuer society to receive the attention of the Administration. The consistency with which these scales are quoted, however, seems to me partly due to its dependence on bridewealth, which is also expressed as an ideal. The main objective in the payment of the indemnity is to provide the deceased with a wife—a 'ghost-wife' who will bear children to his name and enable him to be the founder in posterity of a distinct collateral branch of his patrilineal descent group. It is therefore logical that the number of cattle paid as *thung* should be equal to those paid as bridewealth, though nowadays the difference between the latter ideal and the number actually paid is variable and often considerable. The distribution of bloodwealth among the kinsmen of the deceased follows closely the method of distribution of bridewealth, both maternal and paternal kinsmen having definite claims. It would, however, be a mistake to believe that bloodwealth should be exactly equal to bridewealth just because the former is intended

---

[1] There is also an idea that the spirit (*cien*) of the dead man will haunt his slayer and bring about his destruction and disaster to his kinsmen.

[2] E.g., there is not a higher rate of compensation for a specialist functionary like the Leopard-Skin Chief as opposed to the ordinary people (*dwek*). It is worth noting here, however, that Nuer have in recent years often pressed for official recognition of a higher rate for Government chiefs and policemen when killed in the execution of their duty.

GOVERNMENT POLICY

mainly to provide the dead man with a wife. Other claims must be met first. Of the forty head of cattle some go to the kinsmen in the manner already described, others go to the Leopard-Skin Chief and his assistants, still others are sacrificed, so that only between twenty and thirty are left for the 'ghost-marriage'. These are normally kept until they increase sufficiently to reach the mark of current bride-wealth, and may then be supplemented by other cattle to which the dead man would have had a claim were he alive. Nevertheless Nuer feel that the two payments should be equal; a life for a life or a wife for a life, a logical equation which is entirely consistent with the principles of their customary law.

Observations on the Effects of Government Policy

Nuer are able to quote instances where compensation was paid and blood-feuds settled in the past before the advent of the present Government, but this does not mean that every case, or even the majority of cases, was settled. There is no doubt that blood-feuds, especially between tribal segments remotely related in terms of space and kinship, often continued for many generations, and the tradition of such feuds is still a source of political friction and a problem which faces the Administration today. Even when compensation has been paid and the ceremonies of composition performed the feud may break out again with renewed vigour. Generally speaking, the nearer the social relationship of the opposed groups, the greater the likelihood of permanent settlement. This observation applies theoretically, but only in the sense that in the initial stages feuds between less closely related groups were more likely to continue and no action be taken to bring about an agreement. In fact, they do not often continue nowadays because the Government intervenes and acts as a purely artificial and new medium through which hostile groups are brought together. Paradoxically enough, it is nowadays often the case that feuds between closely related groups are the most difficult to deal with. The reason is, I think, that feelings of hostility receive the permanent reminder of almost daily communication, while the primary sanction for composition, the threat of aggressive action by other groups, is much modified by the action of the Government in maintaining the peace.

The concept of punishment of the individual for offences which we, but not the Nuer, regard as criminal is another innovation which has had widespread repercussions. In cases of homicide capital punishment is sometimes inflicted and imprisonment or fine or both are always applied. Further, in cases of major conflict, fines are sometimes exacted on a collective basis, and in any case, even if the fine is inflicted on the individual culprit, it amounts to collective punishment because in Nuer society the principles governing mutual assistance in

HOMICIDE

the collection of bridewealth, bloodwealth or other kinship obligations automatically come into operation. The fear of punishment is therefore a collective deterrent, and this, with the general realization that payment of compensation will invariably be enforced, has undoubtedly reduced the incidence of homicide. It has also to some extent had the effect of strengthening public opinion opposed to the use of violence, and people are likely to go to greater lengths to restrain their fellows. Conversely, the certainty of punishment and of the enforced payment of compensation has lessened the fear of retaliation and has resulted in a corresponding reduction in the force of those sanctions which make for the fulfilment of social obligations.

Although the concept of punishment inflicted by the State is alien to the Nuer, its introduction has not been difficult, and the deterrent effects are appreciated by chiefs and court members. In general terms, however, a European system of criminal justice is not always understood. Fratricide, for example, is considered a great wrong, and is one which is likely to shock Nuer deeply, but it does not demand any restitution or compensation. A man who kills his brother is injuring himself, and although this may demand a readjustment in matters of inheritance, he cannot pay compensation to himself. Moreover his action runs counter to the very basis of Nuer social sentiment and conflicts with their ideas of kinship solidarity. It is an act almost on a par with suicide, which is fraught with spiritual dangers to the surviving kinsmen. Fratricide is the negation of all social principles. The killer will have to undergo a complex process of ritual purification to appease the wrath of the ancestral spirits and to avoid the misfortunes which may follow, but he will not pay compensation to himself or his brothers. Similarly when a man kills his legally married wife he is causing an injury to himself, for he has paid cattle for her which will now never be returned. Again he will have to undergo ritual purification, will have to give a few cattle or other gifts to his relatives-in-law, but unless he has not completed the bridewealth payments, he will not have to pay compensation in the normal sense. In such circumstances the Nuer find the greatest difficulty in understanding why the Government should seek to punish the culprit, and a Nuer court will usually resist an attempt to do so. If the case is taken out of their hands by the formation of a Major Court under the Presidency of a District Commissioner or Judge, there is little comment and they will accept the sentence, but it would be difficult to persuade a Nuer court to pass sentence itself.

Apart from the difficulties of understanding an alien system of justice, there are other factors which have had repercussions on the application of traditional Nuer law and in particular on the scales of compensation demanded for a wrong. It seems probable that with the absorption of Dinka elements and natural increase, human population

RECENT LEGISLATION

is now much greater in relation to cattle than it was in the past. In addition, diseases have taken a heavy toll and the Nuer are unable to replenish their stock by raiding other tribes. As a result, bridewealth has decreased substantially, and Nuer have at one time or another felt that bloodwealth should be decreased in proportion. In most Nuer districts this has found its own level. In three of the then four Nuer districts the indemnity for homicide was reduced to only twenty head of cattle. This did not occur in Western Nuer District, where compensation remained at 40 head of cattle, but whether this was due to purely economic causes is not easy to discover. The Western Nuer have always had a reputation for being rich in cattle as compared to other Nuer tribes, though this is not entirely borne out by recent statistics. These changes have again been altered by recent legislation.

Recent Legislation Concerning Homicide

At the Nuer Council meeting in 1945 it was generally agreed that compensation for homicide should be raised once more in those districts where it had been reduced, and should be standardized at 50 head of cattle, of which 10 should go to the Government as a fine. In the absence of a sufficiently strong body of public opinion opposed to violence and the taking of life it was felt that this action might serve as a greater deterrent among the Nuer. More remotely related persons would be called upon to subscribe and, since payment of compensation is now rigidly enforced, there would be greater efforts by the people to settle their disputes without resort to force. It must be stressed here that this argument, though put forward by the Administration, was fully understood and appreciated by the Nuer chiefs present at the meeting, and the majority voted for the increase in the indemnity. Yet the argument is itself a doubtful one. In Western Nuer District, where compensation was never reduced, fighting and bloodshed were more common and widespread than in other Nuer districts.

The increase of compensation may have widespread repercussions in other spheres. Captain H. A. Romilly, District Commissioner of Eastern Nuer District, writes:

One of the main decisions reached at the Fangak Meeting of 1945 has been to standardize blood-money at 50 head of cattle and to adjust other compensations accordingly. In Eastern Jikany this has had two main results:

(a) First it has put up bride-price, and a marriageable girl has even less say than before in whom she marries. The heads of families and chiefs are responsible for debts being paid off, so the girl is sold off to the highest bidder, regardless of her feelings. This naturally results in more elopements, adultery, and divorces and consequently an increase in litigation.

(b) The second result of the increase in blood-money is the reluctance of the chiefs to break *mar* which is a system by which relations exchange cattle

64 HOMICIDE

on the marriage of their female relatives. Previously, if relationship was distant, the chiefs would agree to no cattle passing and the 'breaking' of *mar*, but since the Fangak meeting chiefs are very reluctant to break *mar* as the more so-called relations there are available to collect blood-money, the better.[1]

In connexion with the first repercussion mentioned by Captain Romilly, it would appear that the object of this legislation has been defeated. Not only is litigation increased in the courts, but the result has been an increase in the very kind of dispute—elopement, adultery, divorce, &c.—which is so often the cause of violence and bloodshed.

The second result noted by Captain Romilly among the Eastern Jikany Nuer is not necessarily a social evil, as he seems to suggest, and indeed was one of the intentions of the action taken in raising the rates of compensation. We have seen that the social structure of the Nuer has been subjected to severe strains, and since social groups in the past were at least partially maintained as co-operative units by the retaliatory sanction and the need for mutual protection, a reduction in the incidence of violence and of blood-feuds has naturally tended to reduce group solidarity. The lessening of the retaliatory sanction has led to an excessive process of fission without the accompanying process of fusion. Unless this process is checked, or at any rate the speed of the process lessened, there is a tendency towards social decay and even chaos before a new form of social organization based on territorial factors and local government can be substituted. Captain Romilly of course refers to the consequent increase in litigation in the already overburdened courts because the retention of the widest range in *mar*, 'kinship', means a larger circle of people involved in relationships which demand mutual assistance and therefore an increased number of claims in a cattle exchange system.

The Nuer courts which have been established by the Government are a form of machinery through which the social system is maintained. As I have explained previously, this has introduced a political authority upholding the customs of a social system, and custom therefore becomes law in a more precise definition of the term. Customary payments of compensation for wrongs (*duer*), normally only likely to be effective because of the fear of condemnation by a restricted community sentiment and a consequent loss of privilege and security, are now enforced as law. Cases are raised in the courts which would never have had the slightest chance of success in the past, and judgements are enforced because a too literal application of the traditional principles is made. A typical example of this is *nyindiet*. It seems likely that in the past *thung nyindiet* was only demanded in cases where the persons concerned were very closely related and then on a much reduced scale,

[1] Unpublished administrative records (Eastern Nuer District), 1946.

Photo: Dr. J. F. Bloss

LEOPARD-SKIN CHIEF

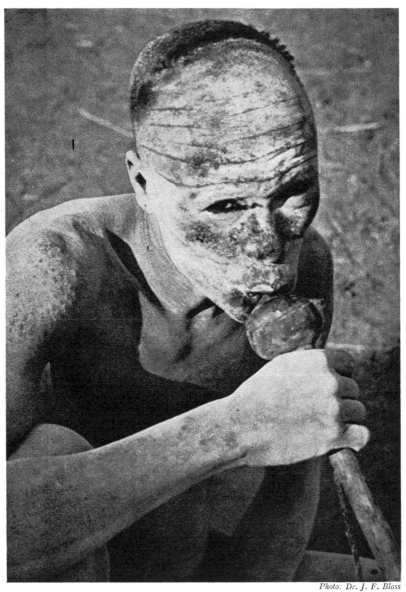

Photo: Dr. J. F. Bloss

THE LITIGANT

RECENT LEGISLATION

probably as a token payment. I have not been able to find evidence of *thung nyindiet* being paid in pre-government times. Yet, until it was abolished in 1945, the demand for *thung nyindiet* was frequent, and although the claims were sometimes carried to extremes of fantasy, they were also frequently enforced. For example, the family of an old headman, Loiny Kur, who must have been over seventy and scarcely able to walk for several years before he died, at once claimed compensation for his death, which, they claimed, was due to a blow on the head. Further investigation revealed that this blow, which caused him considerable discomfort at the time, but no more, was delivered about forty years before his death.

At the meeting of 1945 it was agreed to abolish claims for *thung nyindiet*, but over this a further difficulty arose, because there is no clear distinction between what would be called *thung ran*—compensation for direct killing—and *thung nyindiet*. A man may linger on in a disabled condition as a result of a blow for years before dying. In this case, if compensation for an injury has been paid, the cattle and their offspring will be assessed as part of the claim for bloodwealth, for this is one of the objects of compensation for hurt; but there are some injuries which do not in Nuer custom demand any compensation at all, notably blows on the head. The final ruling given by Chiefs at the 1945 meeting was as follows:

Nyindiet is abolished. Only compensation for a man who dies as a direct result of a wound may be claimed and then full compensation will be paid. The test is this: if a man, as a result of a wound, is confined to his home and is unable to take part in the normal economic activities of the Nuer and finally dies after a period of years, then full compensation will be claimed. If he recovers, then if compensation for an injury is applicable according to Nuer laws it should be paid.[1]

This has subsequently led to much confusion, though the meeting of 1947 recorded that 'a series of test cases with the chiefs of Eastern Nuer straightened out their ideas.' This is an instance in Nuer law in which the circumstances of the case, as deduced from formally recorded evidence, must be the guiding factor and, as medical facilities increase, medical evidence also. In normal homicide cases brought before Nuer courts, the facts are not generally in dispute or concealed by the defendant party.

Recent legislation (in 1947) by the Nuer Chiefs' Council has also abolished the payment of *ghok pale loic*, mainly because in some parts of Nuerland there was an endless demand for such compensation as final payment for cases settled years ago. The idea exists in tradition, but was clearly of very rare application. As we have already seen, *thung yiika* has also been abolished.

[1] Minutes of the Nuer Chiefs' Meeting, Fangak, 1945 (unpublished).

FNL

Modern Procedure

Cases of individual homicide are nowadays often tried by a Major Court[1] convened under the Code of Criminal Procedure of the country. This always applies in cases of murder, since murder is not triable by Chiefs' Courts.[2] The slayer is tried under the Penal Code for murder or, if the act is qualified by one of the five mitigating circumstances laid down, for culpable homicide not amounting to murder.[3] These circumstances can be reasonably adapted to Nuer standards, and the implications are well understood, since murder is *biem*, though even here 'grave and sudden provocation', one of the mitigating circumstances, might still apply in circumstances which the Nuer classify as *biem*. All other forms of homicide are simply *nak*. In the case of a murder for which sentence of death is passed and executed, compensation (*thung*) is naturally not paid, although the kinsmen of the murdered man often demand it. The State has assumed the role of the avenging kinsmen. Where the sentence is commuted to life imprisonment, the indemnity is usually paid.

The more straightforward forms of killing, which take place in collective hostilities, in brawls when the feelings of the participants are roused to extremes of passion, or in sudden unpremeditated quarrels, usually fall within the mitigating circumstances and, as culpable homicide not amounting to murder, may, with the permission of the District Commissioner, be tried by Chiefs' Courts.[4] There are naturally occasions when an act of homicide quickly leads to extensive hostilities and the chiefs appointed by the Government are either unwilling or afraid to intervene and restrain their fellows. In such circumstances the intervention of State police armed with rifles is sometimes necessary. Normally, especially in the more advanced parts of Nuerland— for the effectiveness of Nuer courts is not everywhere the same—the chiefs, their headmen, and tribal police quickly regain control. It is rare that a killer attempts to conceal his guilt, even if in the heat of the battle there are no witnesses, and he will usually give himself up to the nearest authority after performing the necessary purificatory ritual with a Leopard-Skin Chief. Other persons involved are put under arrest, and in most cases a number of cattle are seized, often from both parties and in excess of the number which will later be required as compensation. These are held as surety. A meeting of the court is quickly called, and the relative guilt of the parties is determined. Sentences of imprisonment, sometimes up to the maximum powers granted by law, are imposed on the killer or killers, and

---

[1] Consisting of a Magistrate of the First Class and two lesser Magistrates. Some Nuer chiefs are Magistrates of the Third Class for the purpose of sitting on Major Courts.

[2] Chiefs' Courts Ordinance.

[3] Sudan Penal Code, Section 249.   [4] Chiefs' Courts Ordinance, 1931.

MODERN PROCEDURE

those who participated in or instigated the affair are punished. Fines are often imposed collectively on one or both sides and collected with the minimum of delay. A Leopard-Skin Chief is then appointed by the court to conduct the ceremonies of composition, and these are carried out strictly according to the procedure already described.

It would of course be idle to pretend that all acts of homicide are dealt with so rapidly and efficiently, but in this sphere—in circumstances where public security is most obviously and severely threatened—Nuer courts are surprisingly effective. At any rate, during my time in Central Nuer District there were not many occasions when I had to intervene to restore order, though I was, of course, called in to confirm the judgement of the courts. Indeed, there was one occasion when I interfered too hastily by sending mounted police to round up the culprits and their cattle. As a result I was publicly and most soundly rebuked by the elder statesmen of the area, and was told that such matters should be left to the chiefs themselves. Many feuds were quickly settled during my absence when I was away from the district on leave, sometimes for several months at a time and there was no one to take my place.

PART II HURT

1. INTRODUCTION

NUER demand compensation in cattle for injuries sustained in all forms of affray and individual fighting. Certain definite injuries are recognized in traditional law, and for these there are scales of compensation. There are also notable exceptions. For example, while elaborate scales of compensation in cattle exist for fracture of individual bones of the hand and for different fingers, there is no traditional compensation for a broken skull.[1]

The compensation is intended not only to appease the feelings of the injured party, but also to restore the balance between the conflicting groups. It seems that the fundamental principle involved is that an injury should be met by compensation in direct ratio to its severity, and the severity is assessed by the extent of a man's disability. Disability is judged by the extent to which a man is incapacitated from co-operating in the communal activities of defence and the maintenance of his immediate family and the whole group to which he belongs. It is a collective concern as well as one of individual redress. Fracture of the bones of the hand or the fingers may amount to a very serious injury if the man is unable to hold a spear in defence of his kin or to assist in the cultivation of his fields. In the case of a broken skull, the victim either dies—in which case a feud probably follows or bloodwealth must be paid in full—or he makes a complete recovery.

A second principle inherent in the payment of compensation for personal injury less than death is directly related to the law of homicide. It is that in payment of compensation in cattle the culprit insures himself, in the event of his victim dying at some later date, against the possibility of the deceased's kinsmen attributing death to that wound. This association of ideas has close connexion with the law of *nyindiet*. If cattle have been handed over as compensation for the injury at the time, it is unlikely that a claim for *thung nyindiet* could or would be pressed, for in theory the cattle have increased to a number equivalent to or more than the number normally demanded for *nyindiet*. In this respect it is also significant that most claims for *thung nyindiet* refer

---

[1] Although there is no traditional compensation, a Nuer court will nowadays sometimes award a cow or two to the injured party.

INJURIES RECOGNIZED IN LAW 69

back to wounds inflicted on the head of the deceased, particularly a broken skull.

As in the case of homicide, the existence of traditional scales of compensation for personal injuries does not indicate either a high exactitude of application or the inevitable and prompt settlement of disputes. In the past settlement depended largely on the relationship of the disputants. The principal inducement for payment was fear of retaliation, and in the case of a wound or a blow retaliation was likely to take a more personal and individual form than in the case of homicide. The injured party was on the look-out to avenge himself on the person of the offender. Generally speaking, too, the smaller and more integrated the community to which the disputants belonged, the more likely was it that pressure would be exerted to have the matter settled by payment of cattle and thus remove the danger of further friction within the group. The smaller the group, the greater was this pressure and the greater, too, the opportunity to exact personal revenge on the body of the culprit. Nowadays, injuries are assessed by the court and compensation is awarded with due regard for these traditional scales.

2. INJURIES RECOGNIZED IN NUER LAW

There are many specific injuries recognized in Nuer customary law as demanding compensation in cattle. Most of these injuries are fractures of bones, but it is usually on the subsequent effects of the injury —the stiffening of joints or paralysis causing permanent disablement— that the extent of the compensation is judged. Specific injuries recognized are given in the table (p. 70). Scales of compensation were extremely variable throughout Nuerland, but fairly consistent within one tribe. Elders can usually quote the rates current in the past. As in the case of most indemnities among the Nuer, I think that the rates were essentially idealized and therefore only a basis upon which a suitable compromise could be reached. This principle still operates in Nuer courts today, although there is an increasing tendency to quote past precedents established in case law. An attempt was made in 1945 to stabilize the scales, and the results are also recorded in the table, though it was appreciated that any rigid rule at this stage might be unwise. It is worth noting that theoretically total blindness is tantamount to death among the Nuer, and that loss of both eyes should demand full bloodwealth. At the Nuer Chiefs' meeting where these scales were discussed it was said that a man who loses his sight is 'like one who is dead', and the main object of the indemnity was to provide him with a wife, as in homicide. It was agreed, however, that in modern conditions ten head of cattle should be sufficient.

3. DEFAMATION OF CHARACTER

Defamation of character is a recognized wrong in Nuer law, and is usually associated with false accusation of witchcraft, though sometimes of such offences as adultery. The Nuer expression is *lorjok* (*teke lorjok*). Here the slandered person is likely to suffer a loss of status and privilege and run the risk of destruction at the hands of his fellows. In the case of false accusation of adultery, he runs the risk of retaliation by the husband. Hence, particularly in the latter instance, there is danger of breach of the peace in which opposed kinship groups will be involved, and the offence calls for some form of compensation. Nuer say that cases of this sort were frequent in the past, compensation being made by payment of one cow (*yang lorjok*), and cases are occasionally brought before the courts today.

[1] The distinction depends on the results of the injury—which applies to all injuries, but is here specified.

CHAPTER III

MARRIAGE AND DIVORCE

PART I
MARRIAGE AND MARRIAGE LAWS

1. INTRODUCTION

The Functions of Bridewealth

THE majority of legal disputes which are brought before a Nuer court concern marriage relationships, matters arising out of marriage, claims to a share in bridewealth cattle or a return of bridewealth cattle if the marriage is dissolved. Cattle provide a legal symbol which runs through the whole structure of kinship and marital relationships. A thorough understanding of marriage, the bridewealth system, and rights in cattle raised by kinship is essential to a study of customary law administered in the courts.

The test of legality in all Nuer marriages is found in the transference of bridewealth cattle from the bridegroom and his kinship group on the one hand, to the legal parent or guardian of the bride and his kinship group on the other. The main functions of bridewealth are as follows:

(i) It supplies a material symbol which legalizes the union of man and woman and establishes the legitimacy of the children of the union and their lawful inheritance.

(ii) It gives emphasis and legality to the conventions and patterns of behaviour and the reciprocal obligations which are raised between the kinship groups concerned and must be observed if the union is to be successful.

(iii) It gives stability to the union, particularly in the initial stages when it has not been confirmed and fortified by the birth of children who will subsequently form a link between the lineages concerned.

(iv) To some extent it stands as security for the good behaviour of the wife in her new home and for the observance of her marital duties towards her husband and his kin. It will be in the interests of her kinsmen to encourage her in this matter because her husband can demand his cattle back and dissolve the union. In this they may sustain no loss since the woman can be married again, but it will certainly cause them inconvenience, especially if the bridewealth

MARRIAGE

has been passed on in other marriages. It is also in the interests of the husband to protect and care for his wife, for if harm should befall her through ill-treatment or carelessness on his part, he may lose his wife and find difficulty in getting his cattle back.

(v) It serves as legal indemnity for the loss of the woman's services to her own family and kin, particularly her economic and domestic services, and since, in an exogamous patrilineal society, she cannot bear children to her kinsmen, bridewealth provides them with the means to marry and raise children to their own name. The social equilibrium is thus maintained, the patrilineal identity of the lineage preserved, and its continuity in posterity assured.

(vi) It invokes the interest of ancestral spirits and their blessing, and by doing so fulfils a duty towards them. This is really a religious expression of the principles described in (v) above, but some of the bridewealth cattle are actually set aside and dedicated to the spirits of the lineage.

It is important to remember that cattle are held collectively by the family or kinship group in the sense that their disposal is governed by conventions operative within that group. Kinship relationships govern the limitation of rights in cattle. The collection of bridewealth and its transference are not simple transactions between the prospective husband and the father or legal guardian of the bride. Certain persons standing in special relationships to the bridegroom within the kinship structure, and some of them maternal relatives, are expected to assist him in collecting the required number of cattle. Persons standing in special relationships to the bride are entitled to their shares in the distribution of the cattle when received, and these rights have been raised because they are the persons who co-operated in the collection and giving of bridewealth cattle in previous marriages, particularly the marriage of the bride's mother. This principle runs through the conventional form of reciprocal obligations and rights which are found in the kinship structure.[1]

Bridewealth is not, therefore, a payment in the sense that the bride is purchased from her family, though clearly the cattle are not regarded as merely tokens in the marriage system. They have economic value of extreme importance to the Nuer, since milk and meat products are

---

[1] It should be mentioned at once, though the subject is examined more fully later in connexion with divorce laws, that this does not mean that there is not a measure of individual ownership of cattle. Alienation of cattle is governed by definite rules of inheritance, posthumous rights, and present obligations. A Nuer possesses his cattle as an exclusive right in relation to persons of another kinship group, but the cattle he receives as member of his own kinship group are not his exclusive property; their alienation is not possible without a degree of permission from his kinsmen. This is one of the reasons why Nuer do not on the whole sell their cattle. In contrast, cattle received from other sources, by purchase for example, are his exclusive property even in relation to his kinsmen, though if used for marriage they are, as it were, put into the pool and lose this quality in the future.

FORMS OF MARRIAGE

part of their basic diet. In an article on the subject of bridewealth, Professor Evans-Pritchard says:

> Until very recent years the Nuer had no currency and nothing corresponding to what we mean by 'price' and 'purchase'. The word *kok*, now used to denote the act of purchasing something from an Arab merchant with money, had a religious and sacrificial meaning. It cannot be used to refer to transference of bridewealth. I have heard the word *luil* used in this connection, but only with circumspection or in anger, for it is disrespectful to use it about marriage. It denotes a simple exchange of goods, as when a man who is leaving his neighbourhood exchanges his byre for a bull-calf or when a man exchanges an ox with certain markings for one with his favourite distribution of colours.[1]

The word *kwen* is commonly used to denote marriage, and refers in a general way to the whole procedure of marriage, but more particularly to the distribution of the bridewealth cattle. The word *kwen* is also used to denote the 'counting' or 'division' of money nowadays, but in this connexion it does not have any meaning of payment or purchase. A man will *kwen* or count his own money, *ce yoke kwen*, or he will count a sum of money out, giving each person his portion. He will also use the word in reference to the counting of cattle: to count them as they return from grazing. The use of the word *kwen*, which implies nothing in the nature of purchase, seems to me significant.

2. DIFFERENT FORMS OF MARRIAGE

Among the Nuer there are different forms of domestic union, of which some have a legal basis and some have not.[2] The key to the legality of such unions lies in the transference of cattle in relation to the persons concerned: to whom and by whom. An understanding of the legal principles involved is essential to a study of Nuer Law.

Simple Legal Marriage

The normal legal union which approximates to our own form of marriage consists of the marriage of a man with a girl by the payment of bridewealth and by the completion of the social and ritual processes described later in this chapter. This form of union has been termed by Professor Evans-Pritchard 'Simple Legal Marriage'. The children of such a marriage are usually both legally and biologically the children of the husband, and they trace their descent to his name, since Nuer marriage is patrilineal in basis.[3]

---

[1] Evans-Pritchard, 'Bridewealth among the Nuer', *African Studies*, 1947.

[2] See also Evans-Pritchard, 'Some Aspects of Marriage and the Family among the Nuer', *Zeitschrift für vergleichende Rechtswissenschaft*, 1938. Reprinted in *Rhodes-Livingstone Paper*, No. 11, 1945. The terminology employed in this section is taken from the above article, and I have little to add to his observations.

[3] Nuer call themselves by the name of their father and he by the name of his father, and so on up the line. Dak the son of Gai calls himself Dak Gai; Gai the son of Pan calls himself Gai Pan. To be extremely exact when there is possibility of confusion, Dak will be referred to as Dak Gai Pan.

74   MARRIAGE

'Ghost-Marriage'

It is an accepted rule among the Nuer that if a man dies before he is married or dies without male issue one of his kinsmen, often his brother, must marry to him a wife. This is one of the strongest mutual obligations of kinship.[1] It is considered essential that a man should have an heir who can carry on his name and 'keep it green' in order to further the interests of the lineage in posterity. To die without male issue amounts to oblivion. Female children do not count since their offspring belong to their husbands' lineages, as in any patrilineal society.

This obligation of kinship is nearly always carried out when sufficient cattle are available. Failure to observe the obligation would mean restlessness on the part of the dead man's spirit, who would bring evil (*cien*)[2] upon his kinsmen.

The main characteristics of 'ghost-marriage' are as follows:

(1) It is the dead man, to whose name the wife is married, who is considered the legal father of the children. The ritual processes of marriage are performed in his name, and the bridewealth is paid on his behalf. Therefore, while he is not the physiological father of the children, he is their legal father, and it is from his name that they trace their descent.

(2) The man who marries a wife to the name of his dead kinsman is father in all roles and is in every respect the husband of the woman except in the strictly legal sense.

(3) The physiological father fulfils all the domestic duties of husband and father. In this respect the characteristics are the same as in a normal legal union, and it is only by enquiry that his true legal status can be discovered.

(4) On enquiry, though not in normal circumstances, the wife will be called *ciek jooka*, 'ghost-wife', and the children will be called *gaat jooka*, 'children of a ghost'.

(5) Since the husband is a substitute for his dead kinsman and performs all ritual and domestic obligations on his behalf, the features of a simple legal marriage are found in the structure of this form of union.

(6) The behaviour and obligations of the pro-husband are indistinguishable from those of a man who is both legal and physiological husband and father.

For purpose of definition, the legal father of children will be referred to as *pater* and the physiological father as *genitor*. The difference therefore between a simple legal family and a 'ghost family' is that

---

[1] The Nuer expression is '*ce deman kwen ciek*', lit. 'he his brother married a wife'.
[2] *Cien:* A spirit which haunts or is restless. See also under Homicide, p. 60, n. 1.

'GHOST-MARRIAGE'

the former consists of a man who is both *pater* and *genitor*, a wife, and the children born of that wife, while the latter consists of a 'ghostly husband', who is the *pater* and legal husband, a vicarious husband who is the *genitor*, a wife and the children borne by her.

Since mortality among males is high[1] 'ghost-marriage' is extremely common and, in an analysis of the marital unions of Nuer, will be found nearly, if not quite, as common as simple legal marriage.

Categories of Persons on whose behalf 'Ghost-Marriages' are made

(1) As a general rule, the system is not usually carried back more than one generation. A man would not marry a wife for his grandfather or grand-uncle. It was the duty of his father or uncles to do so.

(2) Kinsmen for whom a wife may be married are: brothers, paternal uncles, maternal uncles, and fathers.[2] The system, except in the case of brothers, is not usually reversible. That is to say, a man would not marry a wife to the name of his son because he would then assume the status of both husband and father-in-law to the wife, which would be incestuous. A man may marry his maternal uncle a wife, but a maternal uncle would not marry his sister's son a wife.

(3) Only kinsmen are expected to marry a wife to the name of a dead man.

(4) In exceptional cases a wife is married to the name of a female relative, but usually only in the case of barren women, who are counted as men and provide a link in the paternal line.

(5) An old woman, especially if she has no paternal relatives living and has the cattle required, will marry a woman to the name of one of them in order to reopen the line. She will invite some unrelated male to act as husband and as *genitor* of the children. In this case the legal husband will be the dead kinsman, whose interests will be guarded by the woman. Sometimes a woman will marry a wife to the name of her dead husband if she has no children and is herself beyond the age of child-bearing. She will do this if she has cattle which are legally the property of her dead husband and there are no heirs in the paternal line to whom they would normally pass.

(6) Sometimes an old man, or one who is impotent, will marry a wife to himself and invite another man to act as *genitor*. This is not

---

[1] The rule applies also to males who die even before they reach marriageable age. An infant is sometimes regarded as a personality in the lineage structure, but not usually before it has cut its second teeth. If it dies before that event, it may be buried without the normal mortuary ceremonies, in which case its name will not continue. After that age it is of more significance in the lineage and 'ghost-wives' are sometimes married to the names of small boys, but usually in a later generation when the boy (whose age on death is no longer remembered) becomes a paternal uncle.

[2] A son will sometimes marry a wife to the name of his father if it is considered that his father had insufficient male issue.

'ghost-marriage', because the legal husband is still living, but the functions of the *pater* and the *genitor* are similar to those found in 'ghost-marriage'.

'Ghost-Marriage' and Bridewealth

Although 'ghost-marriage' is an obligation of kinship, it is obvious that not all men who die without issue are honoured in this fashion. There are too many considerations to make generalization possible, but it seems that the first consideration is the configuration of the lineage. If it is ill-balanced and there are many categories of relatives who simply do not exist, this must be remedied. It is ill-balanced if, for example, a man has no half-brothers or uterine brothers or persons who will be paternal uncles to his children. This links with the second consideration, which is the number of cattle available for bridewealth, for in many cases a man will, on the marriage of a daughter of the house, receive portions which should have gone to some recognized kinsman who is dead or never existed. This will be more easily understood when the principles which govern the distribution of bridewealth have been mastered. The reader should refer to Section 5 of this chapter. For example:

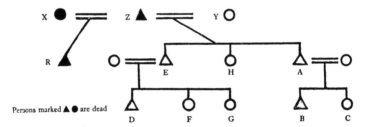

A's father, Z, had two sons E and A by his wife Y. He had one son R by his other wife X. R died without issue. R could have claimed cattle on the marriage of his half-sister H (as *deman kwi gwande*: paternal half-brother), and he might have expected at least some of the cattle which went to his father Z in this marriage (the *ghok gwande*: father's cattle) because it is usual for the major part of this portion of bridewealth to go to the bride's half-brother, i.e. brother by another mother. Again, on the marriages of F, G, and C, he (or his heirs if he had any) might expect the portions called *ghok gwanlen gwande*, 'the cattle of the father's brother by another mother'. Since R is dead and has no heirs, all these cattle must go to A and his brother E or their heirs. They have therefore obtained a number of cattle which would not otherwise have been at their disposal, and one of them, assisted by the other, will marry a wife to Z, their father, so that there will eventually be a collateral lineage descending from him

—the lineage which would have sprung from R had he lived. The configuration will then become:

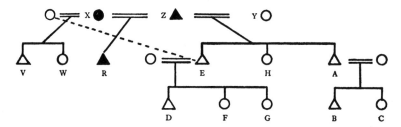

In the initial stages the relations of E (who has married a 'ghost-wife' to his father Z) with V and W will be indistinguishable from his relations with his own children, even though V and W are technically his father's children (*gaat gwan*), and therefore theoretically of his own generation. In normal circumstances he will refer to them as his own children, but their rights in the bridewealth of future marriages will be determined by their legal status in the lineage. The disparity in age will disappear in the next generation. A much more likely alternative, since it will avoid any confusion in status, is for E to marry a wife to R. In these circumstances children born of the 'ghost-marriage' will be legally R's, and hence brother's sons to E and A, and father's brother's sons to their children (*gaat gwanlen*), and therefore no confusion of status or generations will arise. It is also more usual to marry a wife to the brother (rather than the father), because the father already has heirs and ultimately the configuration of the lineage descending from him will be the same. In this case the immediate configuration will be:

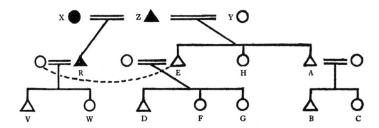

It is very unusual for a man to marry a wife in the name of his grandfather or a kinsman of his grandfather's generation because, unless there are many gaps in the lineage, descendants will be too far removed in the lineage structure for there to be a proper reciprocal interchange of bridewealth claims in subsequent generations; e.g. C marries X to his grandfather A. D, son of C, is too far removed from E (his father's father's father's son) for there to be any interchange.

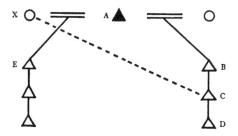

The reader will realize that many possible configurations may result. As a general rule the object is to create two balanced branches of a lineage descending from the sons of one father: sons of one mother or of different mothers, but with a common father. (As an actual example, see the marriage of Deng Rea to Nyalam Dhor, p. 120.)

The Levirate

Bridewealth cattle are not collected by the individual efforts of one man; certain categories of kinsmen co-operate and assist him to get married. Moreover many cattle are held in trust by the family, particularly those inherited by brothers. It is not the legal husband alone who benefits from the domestic and economic services of his wife, and though the children link themselves directly to his name, they are part of the lineage to which he belongs, and his brothers are equally anxious that his offspring shall swell the numbers of their patrilineal group. Therefore, if a man dies, his widow is expected to continue bearing children to his name. Theoretically also she is expected to remain in the vicinity of his near kinsmen and to assist them in normal domestic and economic activities. For both these reasons it is desirable that she should live with one of his brothers or, in certain circumstances, with other categories of kinsmen. The union of a widow with her husband's kinsman does not constitute a remarriage or a 'ghost-marriage': the marriage is already in existence, and legally she is still the wife of the dead man. Any children she may bear after his death are legally his. It merely means that a kinsman, or another man, acts as *genitor* and foster-father of her children.

The levirate is a legal union, and in certain circumstances a man may demand the divorce of his dead kinsman's wife. As will be seen later, this is rarely allowed, and nowadays when the husband is dead a court would only grant a dissolution of the marriage in very exceptional circumstances. Moreover, if an outsider has sexual relations with a widow, her dead husband's kin have a right to demand

LEVIRATE

79

compensation for adultery unless some previous agreement has been reached between them. The legal husband of the woman and the legal father of her children is still the man who has died. The children will be linked in the lineage of his family to his name, and the legality of the marriage is guarded by his heirs. In his name, his heir or heirs will continue to represent his interests, and indeed those interests are their own as members of his kinship group. This point is all-important in the assessment of rights in a widow in legal disputes which appear before Nuer courts. If, as sometimes happens, the bridewealth cattle are returned to the wife's family in the event of her husband's death, no further rights in that woman are retained by the dead man's heirs; but in this case the legal marriage has been dissolved, and the situation is not really different from normal cases of divorce.

Differences between 'Ghost-Marriage' and the Levirate

(i) A 'ghost-marriage' means that the vicarious husband as legal representative of the dead man actually *marries* the wife in the sense that he collects and hands over the bridewealth cattle for her and performs the marriage ceremonies with her on behalf of the dead man. In the levirate, the kinsman merely enters as a substitute into a marriage which is already in existence.

(ii) Generally speaking, in the case of the levirate, since the marriage was not actually initiated and negotiated by the pro-husband, he has less control over the widow than he would over a 'ghost-wife'.

(iii) The levirate differs from 'ghost-marriage' in that the legal husband (*pater*) and his widow once lived together as man and wife.

(iv) Although the leviratic family, like the 'ghost-family', consists of the dead husband (*pater*), the pro-husband (*genitor*) and the children born of the woman, the children, or at least some of them, may have been begotten by the dead man. Therefore in a 'ghost-marriage' the dead man is the *pater* but never the *genitor* of the children; in a leviratic union the dead man is always the *pater* and he may have been the *genitor* of all or some of the children. The distinction is emphasized in Nuer terminology: a child begotten by the dead man is known as *ret*, an orphan. A 'ghost-child' is known as *gat jooka*.

The levirate is established by the previous payment of bridewealth cattle. Therefore, unless the bridewealth is returned for some definite misbehaviour on the part of the widow, the simple legal marriage continues after the death of the husband and children born either before or after his death are legally his.

Categories of Persons with whom a Widow lives

The most usual and correct form of leviratic union implies the cohabitation of a woman with her dead husband's brother, and in

MARRIAGE

rarer cases with a half-brother or more distant kinsman. Sometimes a widow lives with her husband's son (by another wife), but this is usually only in the case of an old man who dies leaving a young widow. Normally, if a man dies young, his children will be too young to inherit his widow. If a man dies old, his wives will usually be old too and will live with their own offspring, not as wife, but as 'mother of the household'. In very rare cases a widow is taken by her husband's sister's son.

According to customary law a widow is expected to live with one of her late husband's brothers. Among the Nuer brothers must marry in strict order of seniority, and the cattle held by them as a family are used in that order. Therefore if a married man dies leaving an unmarried brother, the latter will expect to take over his widow. Legally, he is entitled to do so, and if she refuses he can call for a dissolution of the marriage and return of the bridewealth cattle. The application of this law varies according to circumstances, and also according to the conventions held by different Nuer tribes, but it is rarely employed. If the widow is determined to live with someone else, and particularly if she declares her determination from the beginning, that is at the mourning ceremony of her husband, she is usually allowed to have her way. Moreover, if she has borne two or more children, she is considered to have fulfilled her procreative obligations, and it is less likely that there will be any objection to her taking a stranger as her lover. A widow, according to the circumstances, may elect:

(i) to live with her late husband's brother or kinsman;
(ii) to take a lover who is not a relative from her late husband's village community. In this case her husband's group is not deprived of her assistance in communal economic activities, and they are able to watch over the upbringing and education of her children.
(iii) to return to her own family and live among them, taking a lover or lovers from some stranger lineage.
(iv) to go off to some other vicinity and there live with a lover. If she did so without the agreement of her late husband's family, a divorce could be demanded, unless she had sufficient children to make it unlikely that it would be in the interests of her husband's kinsmen to demand it.

In all the circumstances described above, her children, wheresoever born and by whomsoever begotten, are legally the children of her late husband. This is the hard and fast rule. Only the circumstances set forth in (i) above can be described as the levirate. The other forms of union differ both from 'ghost-marriage' and the levirate. Such unions have been termed 'widow-concubinage' by Professor Evans-Pritchard.

Photo: Dr. J. F. Bloss

THE CHIEF. KIC WUR WINYANG OF THE LAK NUER

THE BRIDE

CONCUBINES

'Widow-Concubines'

The main points are as follows:

(i) The man who performs the duties of husband to the widow is in no sense the legal father of her children, nor is he heir to the legal husband.

(ii) He cannot compel her to live with him or claim compensation if she commits adultery. The compensation for adultery would concern her late husband as represented by his living brothers or legal heirs.

(iii) He cannot divorce her or demand back her bridewealth for there is no legal marriage between him and the widow, only between the widow and her late husband.

(iv) He is not even the legal representative of the dead man and therefore, unlike the levirate or 'ghost-marriage', the characteristics of the simple legal family are not contained in the structure of this union.

The man's position is therefore, in theory, a precarious one. In fact, most of these unions are arranged with the agreement of the dead man's legal representatives and thereby receive social recognition not only from the world at large, but also from the dead man's family.[1] If no such agreement exists the control over the children and the widow may be a source of legal dispute. Such disputes are not uncommon.

Unmarried Concubines

All these forms of domestic and procreative union have one principal common factor: the children of the woman, whether she be wife, 'ghost-wife', widow or widow-concubine, belong to the man on whose behalf the bridewealth cattle were transferred to her family, and they trace their descent through his name to his more remote ancestors. There are, however, forms of union which are in no sense legal because no cattle have been paid as bridewealth for the woman. Children born of such unions will be attached in name to their mother's lineage unless their father chooses to legalize their status and attach them to his lineage by payment of a special fee, or unless the mother is legally married later to some other man who assumes the status of legal father to the children.

The status of women among Nilotic peoples is high. In the question of marriage they usually have a fairly free choice, though there are undoubtedly many occasions when father or brothers will use persistent persuasion or even force to compel a girl to marry a man she

---

[1] A widow living in this form of union with a man is known as *ciek me lak* and her children as *gaat cana*.

GNL

82 MARRIAGE

dislikes simply because they are avaricious for the many cattle he possesses or wish to link themselves to some important family. More often control is exercised in the form of a prohibition rather than positive compulsion. In other words, although they will not use force to compel her to marry a man she detests, they will not allow her to marry the man she loves if he has not sufficient cattle to provide the bridewealth. Whether or not they will take this attitude depends on a variety of circumstances. Some Nuer girls are headstrong and of independent spirit and will not allow their wills to be thwarted by the conventions of the bridewealth system. They therefore live as they please with lovers of their own choice and without either the sanction of bridewealth or the ritual processes of marriage which go with it.[1] A woman of this sort is known in Nuer as *ciek me keagh*. The circumstances in which a woman becomes a *ciek me keagh* are many. Any woman who lives with a man without payment of bridewealth (either on his own behalf or on behalf of the man who is considered her legal husband) is called *keagh*, but she may not be of the restless independent spirit which characterizes most of these women. She may be a young girl who has borne a child to a man who refuses to marry her, though this is rare, or a woman who simply cannot stand life with the husband of her family's choice and has therefore run away and provoked a divorce.

Women who are *keagh* are not regarded as immoral in our sense of the word in these circumstances, but their families are naturally often exasperated by their behaviour and disappointed that no bridewealth cattle have been paid for them. Their social position as unmarried concubines is not generally so high as that of married women, but no distinction is made in the every-day behaviour of their neighbours towards them. The basic difference between widow-concubines and unmarried concubines is that in the former case bridewealth has been paid, even though it has not been paid by the man with whom they live and by whom they produce children. In the latter case bridewealth has not been paid at all or has been returned in divorce.

3. NOTE ON THE RULES OF EXOGAMY AND INCEST

An account of Nuer marriage laws would not be complete without mention of the laws of exogamy. It must be stated at once, however, that breaches of the rules of exogamy and incestuous extra-marital intercourse are not generally the subject of dispute or of litigation in the courts. Both parties are equally guilty, there is no question of compensation, and the spiritual contamination which is considered to follow incest (*rual*) and which is manifested in physical disorders

---

[1] For this reason Nuer do not go to extreme lengths of compulsion for, if the girl runs away, they will lose the chance of getting any cattle at all.

EXOGAMY

(*nueer*), sometimes resulting in death, falls equally on both parties and even upon their relatives. There are therefore strong social and ritual sanctions. For the purposes of this Manual I shall do no more than summarize the laws of exogamy, and refer the reader to published literature on the subject.

Nuer clans and lineages are exogamous. The patrilineal descendants of a common ancestor may not intermarry. The laws of exogamy extend farther than this and include persons who are closely related by marriage; persons related by blood but not legal kinship; and, finally, persons standing in a particular social relationship to each other. The prohibited degrees of relationship and other circumstances may be summarized as follows:

(i) A man may not marry or have sexual intercourse with a clans-woman, and therefore with a woman of his lineage. The limits of clan exogamy are not, however, so rigid as to be unalterable. If the ancestral link is remote (beyond ten generations or so) the prohibition may be ignored or effectively removed by appropriate sacrifice and prescribed ritual.

(ii) A man may not marry or have sexual intercourse with a woman who is a clanswoman of his mother. This prohibition is not, however, carried back beyond six or seven generations.

(iii) As we have seen, a Nuer may be the legal son of one man and the physiological son of another. The prohibited degrees recorded above would apply to the Nuer through his legal father, but the relationship of the *genitor* to his natural child has a degree of social recognition, and it is also not permissible to marry a close kinswoman of the *genitor*. The extent of this prohibition is not as wide as that created by legal kinship.

(iv) Adoption, especially of Dinka children, is a common occurrence[1] among the Nuer, and the links created between father and adopted child receive social recognition and ultimately legal recognition amounting to true kinship.[2] A man would not be allowed to marry or have sexual intercourse with a kinswoman of his adopted father, though in the initial stages this prohibition would be less extensive. In the next generation it would probably be identical, for a man who is fully adopted into a Nuer lineage assumes all the characteristics of that lineage, and in the future his origin may be forgotten. Similarly, an adopted girl would not marry into the lineage of her adoption, and would be bound by the same prohibitions. The reason here is clearer. Members of the lineage of her adoption would be the recipients of her bridewealth cattle and could not also be her relatives-in-law.

[1] Obviously more common in the past.
[2] See also under Homicide, Chapter II, p. 56. The distinction between *jaang dhor* and *jaang cieng* is relevant.

84   MARRIAGE

(v) A man may not marry again into his wife's lineage. Nuer say that a man may not have intercourse with two closely related women at the same period of time. The link is really through the children; a man may not marry his wife's sister because she will also be the maternal aunt of his children and entitled to a portion of the bridewealth of his daughters. A confusion of status of this kind must be avoided.

(vi) A man may not marry the daughter of an age-mate. Common initiation brings about an association similar to kinship. This is symbolized in the giving of the 'cow of the age-mate' (*yang ric* or *ruath ric*).[1] To marry the daughter of any age-mate is to bring him into the category of father-in-law; the avoidance due to the latter is incompatible with the conventional familiarity which exists between age-mates.

Professor Evans-Pritchard summarizes these rules in an article on the subject.[2] He says:

> The exogamous rules ... can be generalized by saying, as the Nuer do, that a man may not marry a woman who is *mar*, kin, to him. In defining exogamy kinship is traced farther in some directions than in others and is of different kinds: the clan kinship of the *mut*, the common spear; the kinship of *buth*, of collateral lineage and of adoption; uterine kinship; kinship through the *genitor*; the kinship of cognation, *mar* in the usual sense of the word; kinship which the birth of a child creates between husband and wife; the kinship acknowledged by acceptance of bridewealth; the kinship by analogy of the *ric*, the age-set, and the *twac*, the leopard-skin.[3]

We shall see that the greatest care is taken during the social processes of marriage to avoid any possible breach of these rules,[4] and it is unlikely that a bar to marriage would be discovered subsequently, at any rate one which involves a prohibition sufficiently strong to be unavoidable. Unless the relationship is singularly remote, however, the union would be dissolved without further delay and the appropriate ritual of appeasement and decontamination performed. This is usually performed by a Leopard-Skin Chief, who neutralizes the effects of the breach of taboo. A cow is sacrificed to the ancestral spirits, and the whole carcase divided into halves,[5] one half being consumed by the relatives of the man, the other half by the relatives of the woman. The presence of the Leopard-Skin Chief and the fact that a cow (possibly only a barren one) is sacrificed would indicate that the breach is a serious one and likely to bring great misfortune to the people concerned. As Professor Evans-Pritchard points out, the value of the sacrifice is

---

[1] See p. 110.

[2] *Social Structure: Studies presented to A. R. Radcliffe-Brown*, Oxford, 1949.

[3] Evans-Pritchard points out that 'a leopard-skin chief may not marry into the family of another leopard-skin chief, even though they are unrelated'. This contention may be true of Lou and eastern Nuer, where Leopard-Skin families are few, but I doubt whether it is applied in the western parts of Nuerland, where they are more common.

[4] See pp. 87, 91, 92.   [5] *Yang me bak ke rual*, 'the cow of dividing for incest'.

EXOGAMY

usually an indication of the seriousness of the breach. For less serious offences of this sort, a smaller animal would be sacrificed, a bull-calf or a ram, and the ritual performed by the kinsmen of the parties concerned would be less elaborate. In some cases it is sufficient to cut in two a wild fruit known in Nuer as *kwol*. I think that the Leopard-Skin Chief is called in more usually when a legal union between persons within the prohibited degrees has taken place, and not in cases of extra-marital intercourse which will not continue. These ceremonies may also be performed before the union takes place, but clearly only in borderline cases where the relationship of the parties is so remote as to be almost fictitious. Similarly, as already mentioned, it would be performed if the impediment were discovered subsequent to legal marriage, but again the union would be unlikely to continue unless the relationship was exceptionally remote, especially, as is so often the case, if disasters (infant mortality or sickness in the family and other misfortunes) have occurred and have been attributed to this cause after searching investigation. As a ground for divorce, should both parties demand it, a breach of the exogamy rules would be indisputable, and I think that a Nuer court would nowadays grant a divorce without much argument.[1] This is, however, a matter of conjecture only, as I have only known one case of divorce brought before the courts for this reason, and then there were circumstances unconnected with exogamy which would have made the dissolution of marriage inevitable. Such matters are strictly limited to the families, or at most to the lineages, of the parties concerned, and are not usually brought to light in a public manner.

We have so far been principally concerned with the laws of exogamy and the prohibition of legal union between persons who fall within the forbidden degrees. We have seen also that these laws are relative to the position in the social and kinship structure of the persons concerned, and if their relationship is sufficiently distant, the prohibition may be permanently cancelled by the performance of sacrifice and ritual. In any case the consequences (*nueer*) may be thus avoided, even if the ritual is not sufficiently effective to ensure a safe continuance of the union. These rules also apply to extra-marital and illicit sexual intercourse, though not necessarily with the same force, and the consequences of infringement may be less serious. There is also an obvious difference between a casual act of sexual intercourse which is not repeated, and intercourse which results in the pregnancy of the woman. The birth of a child in such circumstances is a permanent reminder of the offence, and because the child is a link between the mother and the physiological father the situation is more dangerous. There is a confusion of legal and social status which at all costs must be avoided. Among the Nuer such difficulties can

---

[1] See also under Dissolution of Marriage, p. 146.

86   MARRIAGE

still be overcome by suitable sacrifice, but the implications are clearly more serious.[1]

Incestuous intercourse may sometimes be relevant to disputes which arise in the courts. Examples of this will be seen later.[2] I do not propose to digress further on the subject of exogamy and incest, because the laws of exogamy are not in themselves a subject for dispute. There is now adequate published literature on the subject,[3] of which I have no criticisms to make and little except detailed information to add.

4. THE SOCIAL AND RITUAL PROCESSES OF MARRIAGE

The transfer of cattle as bridewealth does not in itself constitute marriage, although it is certainly the most significant aspect of marriage from the legal point of view. Nuer marriage is a protracted affair involving many negotiations and ceremonial meetings. Those social and ritual processes which are described here apply to the simplest form of legal marriage and the simplest situation therein possible. The same principles are involved in 'ghost-marriage', that is marriage by a living person on behalf of a dead relative, but in leviratic marriage and in what Professor Evans-Pritchard has classed as 'widow-concubinage' there is naturally no repetition of the ceremonies which were carried out by the widow's husband in his lifetime and naturally, too, no further payment of bridewealth. In other forms of union, which are not legal unions, no ceremonies similar to those of true marriage are possible.

The description which follows is applicable to a normal Nuer youth[4] who wishes to marry a normal Nuer girl and has sufficient cattle to do so, and in such cases, unless the union is prearranged by the parents, the youth has probably met his future bride at the dances

---

[1] Among some African tribes children born in incest would be destroyed. It is reported of the eastern Dinka that children born in such circumstances are sold to the Murle. There is, however, no published evidence to substantiate this statement. The idea of infanticide, except perhaps in the case of deformities, is, so far as I know, alien to Nuer ideas.

[2] See p. 164.

[3] Evans-Pritchard, *The Nuer*, Oxford, 1940, pp. 6, 17, 192, 202, 225–8, 235, 257; in *Social Structure: Essays presented to A. R. Radcliffe-Brown*, Oxford, 1949. Further information will be found in various articles by the same author: 'Nuer bridewealth', *Africa*, XVI, 4, 1946; 'Nuer Marriage Ceremonies', ibid., XVIII, 1, 1948; 'Some aspects of Marriage and the family among the Nuer', *Rhodes-Livingstone Paper*, No. 11, 1945; and more recently in *Kinship and Marriage among the Nuer*, Oxford, 1951.

[4] Certain categories of persons who are considered abnormal, by reason of circumstances in their birth, have extra ritual to perform. Thus twins have to undergo special ceremonies; see Evans-Pritchard, 'Customs relating to Twins among the Nilotic Nuer', *Uganda Journal*, Vol. III, 3, 1935. Also a person whose father has been struck by lightning and killed.

PROCESSES OF MARRIAGE

held by young people and has danced and 'flirted' with her for some time.[1]

Only the most important ritual and negotiations are recorded. Moreover it must be remembered that the form and order of ceremonial among primitive peoples usually vary considerably on each occasion, and no marriage ceremony is word for word, act for act, an exact repetition of another. Further, there may be local variations of custom.[2] It does not follow that all the ceremonies described below are necessarily performed in all Nuer marriages, nor that they are always performed with the same degree of ceremonial and publicity. Older men, especially men with many cattle, who already have other wives would think it unseemly to court a girl with the same intensity as would a younger Nuer, and they would not be expected to go through all the preliminaries.

Courting and Betrothal

When a Nuer youth has been accepted by a girl she will hasten to inform her family, provided she knows that her lover has sufficient cattle to legalize the union. It may be that her legal representatives in the family—that is, her more important male kinsmen—will ban the marriage from the start for some reason or other. Relations with the prospective bridegroom's family may already be strained, and they may have no desire to associate with it; there may even be blood between them (*teke riem kamdien*), or the memory of a blood feud. They may know at once that a marriage is precluded by the rules of exogamy. In such circumstances the girl will be discreetly told to avoid her lover in future. If, however, there is no objection she will be encouraged to continue and will receive their permission, though this is not made public. The first ceremony may then take place. This does not concern the older members of either family, and is confined to the prospective bride and bridegroom and their friends and coevals. It is in fact no more than a formal recognition among the younger people that the couple are courting, and it does not involve any legal negotiation. It is known in Nuer as *luom nyal.*

[1] Dances provide the best opportunity for flirtation and courting. In the normal pursuits of daily life the Nuer does not have much contact with girls except those who are related to him, and these he cannot marry. Dances, particularly big dances held in the rainy season, are usually attended by considerable numbers of people from different and unrelated lineages. These dances often lead to quarrels and violence and even bloodshed. Spirits are high, and for this reason tribal authorities (in the Zeraf tribes), representing the Government, sometimes attempt to ban dancing. This has not received the support of the Government, but it is worth noting that a ban on dancing would give the Nuer youth less chance to meet and flirt with a wide choice of girls which is undoubtedly a factor making for stability in marriage.

[2] My description of the ceremonial sometimes differs from the accounts given by Professor Evans-Pritchard. Where there is any great difference I have recorded it in a footnote, but it should be noted that his observations were made in Lou and Eastern Jikany, while mine are drawn from experiences among the Zeraf tribes and later among Western Nuer.

88   MARRIAGE

Luom nyal: 'Courting the Girl'

The meeting is held at the home of some person who is related neither to the girl nor to the young man, often the home of the latter's best friend (*math*). A few friends of both parties are present, and among them is the prospective bridegroom's official spokesman, who is known as the *gwan twac* and performs the duties of a 'Best Man'. The girl also has a personal friend, a girl who is known as *ngi nyal*, and who takes her part in the ceremony, and leads the conversation and the friendly chaff which are characteristic of these occasions.[1] The meeting usually takes place at night, sometimes all night, inside a hut. No elderly people are present, and the time is spent in the exchange of elaborate compliments which sometimes go on for half an hour or more without break.[2] The verb *lum* in Nuer, from which *luom* is derived, is used to describe any form of courting, even casual flirtation at dances, but its use here implies a degree of formality not previously recognized, the recognition of the engagement being restricted to the young people who take part in dances together, and not including the adult members of the communities concerned.

Thiec nyal: 'Asking for the Girl'

After the *luom nyal*, which is not a serious engagement and more often than not comes to nothing, a meeting takes place known as *thiec nyal*, 'asking for the girl'. This again may lead to nothing, but it is a more formal affair than any preceding it, and for the first time the girl's parents or guardian are approached by the prospective bridegroom and possibly by some of his senior kinsmen. It amounts to an opening of negotiations between the two families, but is not binding. If the members of the girl's family are satisfied by this time that the young man is in earnest and has cattle in support of his suit—for they have probably made discreet enquiries long before this—they will ask that the first tokens of formal betrothal be paid. They hope to receive at least four head of cattle (though they may be satisfied with less) known as the *yang gwan nyal*, a cow and calf which are intended to supply the girl's father with milk, *thak deman nyal*, a bull or bull-calf for the bride's brother,[3] and a *yang kwoth*, a cow which will be dedicated to

---

[1] *Gwan twac* and *ngi nyal* might be translated as 'Best Man' and 'Bridesmaid' respectively, but although the part they play in this and subsequent ceremonies is similar to our conception of the functions of the Best Man and Bridesmaid, I prefer to use Nuer terms hereafter.

[2] Complimentary speeches of this sort, often full of subtle and suggestive phrases with a good deal of badinage, are spoken in a language which is almost poetic in form and not easy to understand.

[3] The *thak deman nyal*, by bringing in the interest of the brother who expects to benefit most by his sister's marriage, is in the nature of a personal guarantee, and is important. The prospective bridegroom expects this brother to further his cause with the girl's family and to keep other lovers away from her. These cattle, which are really the father's portion, are sometimes included in the bridewealth payments, sometimes not; i.e. a man will sometimes have to pay a further four as *ghok*

BETROTHAL

89

the spirits of their lineage. The distribution of these cattle is significant. In the first place the girl's father or, if he is dead, her eldest brother or paternal uncle, must receive a guarantee in material form that the prospective bridegroom is in earnest. The ancestral spirits must be called in to bless and assure the future union, and the *yang kwoth* is dedicated to them. Finally, the bride's eldest brother, often a coeval of the bridegroom, must be placated, for it is he who expects to benefit most by her marriage, which will bring in bridewealth which he him-self will use for his own marriage. If the girl's family are in agreement, a day is then fixed for the formal betrothal, in the form of a meeting when the cattle of engagement will be paid over. This is known as *cuei*, and the Nuer will say *ce cuei-de cuei*, 'he has engaged himself'.

Cuei: Betrothal

The *cuei* is part of the betrothal negotiations, and amounts to a more public acknowledgement by the bridegroom's family in paying, and by the bride's family in accepting, the cattle which are considered necessary for that purpose. The cattle are driven straight to the homestead of the girl's father, and there remain shut in the cattle-byre while the meeting takes place. The prospective bridegroom and his *gwan twac* are expected to observe rigidly the special restrictions on their movements in the bride's home, the signs of respect and other observances which characterize behaviour towards relatives-in-law. They are not allowed to enter any of the houses, and they must cover their nakedness with a special cat-skin known as *twac thoan*. It is for this reason that the principal assistant of the bridegroom is known as *gwan twac*, 'owner of the skin', and a husband, is usually expected to wear it in the presence of his wife's mother.[1] Beer has been brewed beforehand, and is handed round among the senior guests; dancing takes place, and a bull-calf known as *yang kwen* or *yang lum* (the 'cow of marriage' or 'of courting') is sacrificed and eaten.[2]

The adult males of the two families (with the exception of the bridegroom himself) have therefore drunk together and the kinsmen of the bridegroom have partaken of meat provided by the girl's father. The

gwan nyal (see p. 102, n. 1). It is, on the whole, unusual for a man to pay as many as four head of cattle on betrothal, especially if there is likely to be delay in the actual marriage ceremonies. If any of those cattle died while in the possession of the betrothed girl's family, the prospective bridegroom would be expected to replace them.

[1] The *thoan* or serval cat-skin is to the Nuer a mark of respect shown to a wife's relatives by any of her husband's kin, and in a sense is a symbol of marriage.

[2] The word *yang*, cow, is used here in a figurative sense, for the animal should more correctly be referred to as *ruath* (bull-calf). Nuer say that in older and better times a cow would be sacrificed, though doubtless a barren one. *Yang* means cow, and it might be supposed that a cow would be slaughtered. It may refer to a past custom when cattle were more plentiful, but nowadays the use of these terms in connexion with sacrificial animals is often elastic, and *yang*, which is certainly cow, is often used to refer to cattle of either sex.

90   MARRIAGE

bridegroom's kinsmen have accepted hospitality and provided the cattle of betrothal to give legal stability to the pledge. This preliminary betrothal feast does not concern the rest of the local community, though many of them will turn up uninvited because of the beer and meat which are available. The formal gathering really concerns only the kinsmen of the girl and the kinsmen of the bridegroom. As in the case of negotiations for the composition of homicide, Nuer have a concise terminology for both parties. The bride's family are through-out known as the *ji nyal*, while those of the bridegroom are known as *ji wuta*. These terms mean no more than the 'girl's people' and the 'man's people', but they are used expressly in connexion with marriage negotiations,[1] and stress the distinction between the two parties.

Sometimes girls are betrothed at a very early age, and quite often when they are ten to fifteen years old. This does not mean that they are pledged by their families without their knowledge or consent, for they are usually approached first by the man concerned and are proud to accept, for girls thus engaged appear to have an enhanced attraction for other Nuer youths. Two cows are paid, which are known as the *dau cieh*, the 'cow-calf of the ring or bracelet' (*cieh*), and a larger cow-calf called *nac pieth*, the 'heifer of up-bringing' (referring to the fact that her family will have to continue to care for her and provide her with food for a long time to come). These cattle are not included in the bridewealth, and are not usually returned if, after the marriage has gone through, there is a divorce. Early betrothals of this sort are not common and, even if made, often come to nothing. If this is the case, the *dau cieh* and the *nac pieth* will be quietly returned; they are rarely a subject for dispute in the courts because, until they are re-turned, it would not be seemly to start the negotiations for another engagement.

Professor Evans-Pritchard speaks of the betrothal as *larcieng* or *bul luom*.[2] It is clear that this is the same ceremony as that described above, which is sometimes known as *dour* in Lou country, and although his description gives the impression of greater formality and more elaborate ceremonial than I have encountered myself, I do not think that there is any difference in principle. The *cuei* ceremony is usually performed in the rainy season when grain is plentiful, but sometimes takes place in the dry season, in which case it is likely to be less elaborate for there will be little or no beer, and the final wedding ceremonies will have to wait until the people return to the cultivations.

---

[1] It is useful to know these terms for they are sufficiently concise to avoid obvious confusion in cases of litigation over marriage payments.

[2] Evans-Pritchard, 'Nuer Marriage Ceremonies', *Africa*, 1948, and *Kinship and Marriage among the Nuer*, pp. 58–74.

'INVOCATION OF CATTLE' 91

Marriage

Twoc ghok: 'Invocation of the Cattle'

The betrothal ceremonies described above are followed by the first marriage ceremony, the *twoc ghok*, 'invocation of the cattle'. The length of time which is allowed to elapse between them is variable, and depends largely on the agreement reached at the *cuei* ceremony. It is not usually in the interest of either of the parties to delay matters, though this sometimes happens if the bridegroom finds difficulty in collecting sufficient cattle and yet retains the goodwill of the girl's family who wish the union to take place.

The *twoc* is the crucial ceremony of all the processes of marriage and is public in the widest sense, although the actual negotiations over cattle and the more intimate ritual are restricted to the closer kinsmen of the bride and bridegroom. Most of the bride's kinsmen who expect to receive a portion of the bridewealth are actually present, and if they are not they will usually send someone to represent their interests. We see therefore that, as the processes of betrothal and marriage proceed, increasingly large numbers of persons from both kinship groups are concerned. This emphasizes the collective nature of a union and the extent of the social ties and obligations which are involved.

Dancing begins early in the morning and the bridegroom, his father, and the *gwan twac*, as well as the senior legal representative of the bridegroom's lineage, appear dressed in cat-skins (*twac thoan*) as a conventional sign of respect to the bride's mother and her kinsmen and those of her husband. It should be noted that the bridegroom and the bride really have two representatives. At the bridegroom's side is the *gwan twac*, who is his personal aide. At the *twoc* ceremony he is represented also by the *gwan buthni*, an agnatic kinsman of a collateral branch of the lineage, whose activities are not so much personal as concerned with the interests of the bridegroom's lineage as a whole. His duties are both legal and ritual. He is expected to take the lead in the arguments which arise about the bridewealth cattle and to see that the claims of all those connected with the marriage are noted. It is also his duty to invoke the ancestral spirits of the lineage and to seek their blessing, to call out the honorific (*paak*) and spear-names (*mut*) of the clan and state any further distinctions so that all possibility of a breach of the rules of exogamy is avoided. Similarly, the bride has her personal attendant in the *ngi nyal*, who is a girl of her own age, usually from another and unconnected lineage, while the *gwan buthni* of her lineage represents them in ritual and legal procedures. The *gwan twac* and the *ngi nyal* are usually age-mates of the bridegroom and bride respectively, they are unrelated to either, and their duties are essentially personal, while the *gwan buthni*, usually much older men, represent the kinship interests of their respective sides.

MARRIAGE

After preliminary dancing and singing, which go on more or less continuously throughout the day, the people most nearly concerned in the negotiations take up their positions in the cattle-byre. The bride's family seat themselves on the left of the entrance facing the bridegroom's party, and her *gwan buthni* sits in the central hearth (*gorei*) of the byre. On the right side mats are laid (*yih*), and on these sit the bridegroom's party with their *gwan buthni* nearest the door. The bride herself and her *ngi nyal* do not appear during the negotiations. They are usually closeted inside the mother's hut (*dwil* or *ghot*) nearby. When all are seated the *gwan buthni* of the bride breaks up some tobacco and hands it to the father, paternal uncles, and other senior relatives of the bridegroom as a symbol of friendship and hospitality.[1] It is also calculated to ease the tension, for Nuer regard the whole procedure as a nerve-racking ordeal, and like to smoke when they are nervous. He then rises to his feet and calls out the honorific and spear-names of the bride's lineage, and calls upon their ancestors to take note of the proceedings. The *gwan buthni* of the bridegroom's family then rises and scatters tobacco at the entrance of and inside the cattle-byre as an offering to the ancestral spirits of the bride. He then calls upon his own ancestral spirits, which are those of the bridegroom's lineage, to witness the negotiations, and calls out their honorific and spear-names. If the honorific or spear-names of the bridegroom coincide with those called out by the bride's *gwan buthni*, it will be obvious that the rules of exogamy preclude all possibility of the union, but the invocation is largely a formality, because it is unlikely that negotiations for the marriage would be allowed to go so far if there were any possibility of incest.

Negotiations about the cattle then begin. The number of cattle subsequently handed over, as well as those actually transferred during the final marriage ceremonies, will vary considerably, but there are a number of persons standing in certain relationships to the bride who expect to receive their share. They are the *ji cuongni*—the 'people of rights'. In theory, the bridegroom must produce cattle to meet the claims of all these kinsmen of the bride, but in fact negotiations usually deteriorate into a heated argument, not always in keeping with the supposed solemnity of the occasion, and the main object of the bride's party is to get as many good cattle as possible, and of the bridegroom's family to avoid payment. It is, however, noticeable that negotiations of this sort are less clamorous than other Nuer affairs. The *gwan buthni* are expected to speak for the parties they represent, but most of those present will have their say. The colours, sex, and qualities of the cattle are fully discussed, and it is probable that the recipients will have a clear idea of what those qualities are. As soon as negotiations

---

[1] For this service he can demand payment of a bull-calf. It is not, however, always paid, and it is not considered good manners to argue about the matter or press for payment.

MARRIAGE CATTLE

have started the immediate kinsmen of the bride will have set to work to find out as much as they can about these cattle. In the initial stages of the discussion, however, a certain formality is observed; it is opened by the *gwan buthni* of the bride, who will speak the names of those persons in the bride's family who have a claim on the cattle and, as the argument continues in connexion with each animal quoted by the bridegroom's family, will state to which relative they should go. No cattle are handed over on this day, though a cow called *yang gorei*, the 'cow of the hearth', which is part of the bride's father's portion, is sometimes handed over on the spot. This is a convention which is not often followed nowadays.

When the negotiations over the cattle are finished, the parties go outside for the feasting which follows. There is no prohibition on the two families eating together,[1] but the bridegroom himself and his *gwan twac* are not expected to eat of the meat or drink of the beer provided by the bride's people. They are allowed to join in the dancing, and the bride and her *ngi nyal* appear for the first time on the scene and enter the dance. The bride wears a black skin known as *twac cara*, usually the skin of a black calf.

After the dancing is over, those who are not closely related to either party go home, but the legal representatives of the bridegroom and the bride's family and some of their close kinsmen, both male and female, go into a hut specially prepared for them which is known as the *dwil koam* for the occasion. There they sit all night joking and conversing with their hosts until dawn. Another hut, known as the *dwil twacni* or *dwil kwen*, is set aside for the young people of both parties, and the bride and bridegroom, their *gwan twac* and *ngi nyal*, sit there with their friends and coevals singing and exchanging courting badinage all night through. This completes the ceremony known as *twoc*.[2] The marriage is not supposed to have been consummated,

---

[1] An ox is sacrificed and the meat divided between the bride's people and those of the bridegroom in a formal manner. The bulk of the meat is given to the bridegroom's family, and much of it is taken back to their home to share with the old people who have not been able to attend the ceremony.

[2] The account of the *twoc* ceremony given by Professor Evans-Pritchard does not differ in any substantial way from my own, but he mentions certain rites which take place on the same day which I have not myself witnessed but which I have heard Nuer mention when describing the ceremonial. One is the ceremony in which the bridegroom and his followers rush the homestead of the bride and he tries to spear the *buor* or mud hearth of his future mother-in-law, while the bride's brothers and the young men of her group try to stop him and to wrest from him his special wedding stick or *dang*. This and other rites symbolize the potential opposition between the two parties and the resistance of the bride's people to the demands of the bridegroom, and the final removal of their resistance by the payment of cattle. All such rites, although not always performed and often substantially different in one part of Nuerland from those performed in another, are part of the enactment of marriage and are highly symbolic of the conventional attitude which both parties are expected to display. From the legal point of view they are significant in emphasizing these attitudes and explaining the rules and conventions which govern the social relations subsisting between relatives-in-law. They are not, of course, the subject of subsequent litigation.

94 MARRIAGE

but has acquired by this time a degree of legality. Some Nuer say that the marriage is now legal in the sense that, were another man to have intercourse with the bride, full compensation for adultery could be claimed by the bridegroom. Lak and Thiang Nuer at any rate say that the significant act which confirms the status of the bride as a wife and which subsequently will be recognized in law, is the ceremony known as *yier nyal*, which takes place on the evening immediately after the conclusion of the negotiations for the cattle, when the bride, and also her brothers and sisters present, are rubbed with butter by the *gwan buthni* of the bridegroom. The legal status of the bride in relation to the bridegroom and his family at this point in the social and ritual processes of marriage (and it must be remembered that the bridewealth has not necessarily yet been transferred in full to the bride's family) is a controversial subject and one which is sometimes disputed in legal arguments. The subject of the legality of marriage is discussed later.

The *twoc* ceremony, at which negotiations over the cattle are completed and the blessing of the ancestral spirits is publicly invoked, does not usually take place before the girl has not only reached puberty but is ready for marriage. When talking of a girl who has reached marriageable age the Nuer will say that she is ready for the *muot* ('shaving') which is the next ceremony to take place. *Muot* amounts to a public recognition of physical consummation, although this does not necessarily mean that the girl has not had sexual relations with her bridegroom before. In fact, previous to the *muot*, he has no legal right to physical consummation and must visit his wife in secret, though her family will usually allow him to do so. *Muot nyal* therefore follows the *twoc* ceremony almost immediately.

Muot nyal: 'The Shaving of the Bride'

The ceremonies which are known collectively under this heading are of distinct legal significance, as will be seen later, and include three important stages.

Loiny deb: 'Loosing the Rope'

First, the bridegroom with his *gwan twac*, again suitably dressed in cat-skins for the occasion, accompanied by other youths of his own age, goes to the bride's home to ask for her people's official consent to consummation. There they enter a hut specially set aside for them and are joined by the bride, her *ngi nyal*, and other girls of her lineage and neighbourhood. They spend the day and the whole of the night in conversation and singing. There is as usual a good deal of sexual badinage, but no physical consummation. Next morning, the bridegroom approaches his mother-in-law on the subject of the *muot* which is to follow. Before giving her consent she will expect to receive, or

'BRINGING THE BRIDE' 95

at any rate obtain the promise of, special presents, which are known as the *nyin daba*.[1] These include a goat or two, a spear, a fish-spear, a ring and other offerings, and if she has any co-wives who stand in the relationship of mother to the bride they will expect to benefit too. There follows the ritual performance known as *loiny deb*, 'loosing the rope', which symbolizes the bride's release from her father's homestead.[2] The bridegroom and his representatives stand on one side of the cattle-byre, the bride and her friends on the other, while her father casts a cattle rope between them. The bride is then ceremonially dressed in the clothes which distinguish a married woman from unmarried girls: a leather apron or a skirt of plaited cotton.

Noong nyal: 'The Bringing of the Bride'

The same evening, representatives of the bridegroom go to inform the bride's relatives that all is ready for them. The bride is then conducted to the bridegroom's home by a party of her girl friends (who are called *nong*, 'bringers'). On her arrival she sits down on a special mat provided for her outside the bridegroom's house by his *gwan buthni*. A bull is brought out and sacrificed, while the *gwan buthni* again calls out the honorific and spear-names of the lineage and calls upon the ancestral spirits to bless the union, to accept the bride, and to give her male children to uphold the spear-name in posterity and girl children to bring cattle to the kinship group. The bride then lies on the mat and is covered with a skin (*twac cara*). Meanwhile the bridegroom presents his mother-in-law with a goat or sheep in order to release her, temporarily at any rate, from the taboo on eating in his home.[3] The bride is then assisted into the hut and the bridegroom, whip in hand, goes after her. After he has given her a thorough beating inside the hut (*woc dhouri nyal*), the couple spend the night together and the marriage is said to be officially consummated. The beating is said to symbolize the bridegroom's authority over his bride who is now his wife, emphasizing the rights he now has in her.[4]

Muot nyal: 'Shaving the Bride'

The next day the *muot nyal*, the actual 'shaving of the bride', takes place. In the morning the bride is usually taken away to the home of some unrelated person nearby, but is brought back to the bridegroom's home towards evening. Her head is then ceremonially shaved by one of the senior female relatives of the bridegroom, usually his elder sister,

---

[1] *Nyin daba*, 'the things of bearing'. In other words the mother's due for bearing the bride and bringing her up.

[2] *Deb* means a cattle rope, and the phrase signifies her release from her father's herd.

[3] She does not, of course, eat with the bridegroom himself, or with any of the male members of his lineage, for women do not eat in the company of men on any occasion, but she is thereby allowed to partake of the food of the house with the other women.

[4] In the case of opposite twins this performance is inflicted on the bride's twin brother as well.

96   MARRIAGE

a co-wife of his mother, or sometimes the wife of his *gwan buthni*. At any rate the shaving should be performed by a married woman of the bridegroom's family, and signifies the bride's reception into the status of married woman in that family. She is then taken once more to her own home.

After these ceremonies are over the bride rarely takes up residence in her husband's home, but lives for a period in her own home, where her husband has the right to visit her. Often a special hut is set aside for her there. There is no general rule in this matter, but it is regarded by the Nuer as proper that she should remain in her own home until her first child is born and weaned, for until then, although the marriage has a legal basis, it is not considered to be confirmed. Sometimes, however, the husband has no one to assist him in his home and to cook for him, in which case he may receive permission from his wife's people for her to live with him permanently as soon as the *muot* has been performed. When the first child is weaned, the wife's mother can claim the *yang doth gata*, the 'cow of bearing a child', a cow which is considered a fee for assisting the girl to give birth to a child. This is usually followed by a formal change of residence. The *yang doth gata* is the last cow which need be paid by the husband, although his wife's family may beg him to give them other cattle when further children are born and weaned; but he is not bound to do so and claims of this sort, if they ever arise, would not nowadays be upheld in a Nuer court.[1]

Conclusion

This concludes a very condensed account of the ritual and social processes of marriage among the Nuer. It is the payment of bride-wealth which legalizes a union, and the fact that some of the ceremonies are sometimes not performed at all is not necessarily evidence in Nuer courts today that a marriage is not a legal union. The payment of cattle, however, usually follows the ceremonies described. As Professor Evans-Pritchard has pointed out, 'payments of cattle and marriage rites therefore tend to alternate, though there is no fixity about the alternation and no marriage is exactly the same as another in this respect'. In fact, it is unlikely that a ceremony would be allowed to take place unless the appropriate stage in the negotiations over cattle had been reached, so that in seeking to determine the legality of a union, a Nuer court will first ask what ceremonies have been performed. The issue in such cases concerns not so much the number of cattle paid or to whom they were paid, but the liabilities and

---

[1] It may be noted here that among some Nuer tribes the husband may claim a cow from his wife's family, the *yang jokni*, 'cow of the spirits'. I do not think this is normally paid unless the first child dies, and it is then given in the form of a dedication to ancestral spirits to ensure that the next child will live.

BRIDEWEALTH

97

rights of the husband in his wife. It would be relevant, for example, if a woman committed a wrong. If she killed someone, the payment of compensation would be a liability on her husband if she was legally his wife, but if there was insufficient legal determination in the union, the responsibility would rest with her own kinsmen. Similarly if a man lies with a woman who is not his wife, he may be charged with adultery (*dhu ciek*) and compensation will be claimed, but he might with justification plead that she is not a married woman in the legal sense, and therefore the act is not adultery. In the event of his proving that the union is not a legal one, he has no liability to the husband, but this will not entirely absolve him from responsibility, for in certain circumstances her kinsmen may claim damages on the grounds of seduction of an unmarried girl. There are, of course, many circumstances which will be considered by the court, circumstances which are discussed later under the heading of wrongs in relation to women. In such cases the legality or otherwise of the marriage is in issue, and it is sometimes difficult to find out what constitutes legality. In most tribes it seems that the ceremony which is considered to legalize the union is the *muot*, but this, as will be seen later, is not a universal law among the Nuer.

5. THE DISTRIBUTION OF BRIDEWEALTH

When a man wishes to get married his relatives will usually assist him to collect the necessary cattle in addition to those already allotted to him in his father's herd. There are no set rules governing the actual assembly of bridewealth cattle, and in any case the circumstances are too varied to warrant generalization on the subject. Brothers should marry in strict order of age, and the majority of the cattle they use for the purpose will be drawn from their father's herd. The legal father of a family is responsible for the distribution among his sons of those cattle which have come to him as his rights in the bridewealth cattle of his sisters, daughters, and other female relatives. If he is dead, his legal representative will be his brother, usually the senior paternal uncle of his sons, or his eldest son. The assembly of marriage cattle is, however, partly dependent on the rules of distribution applied to previous marriages in the bridegroom's family. In the application of these rules we shall see that there is a tendency to alternate because no family is exactly symmetrical. There is usually more than one claimant to one particular portion and none to another. In the first instance the junior claimant will have to await his turn until the next marriage in the family; in the second, the portion will be inherited by the claimant's heirs. In some cases these will be his own sons, in others, his brother's sons. There are conventions which govern the inheritance of rights in such cattle. The portion allotted to the mother

Hnl

98 BRIDEWEALTH

(the *ghok mande*), for example, should go to her own sons; that allotted to the father (the *ghok gwande*) should go to his sons by another wife; the grandfather's portion (the *wangnen gwande*) should go to his sons by a wife other than the bride's father's mother, i.e. to the paternal half-brothers of the bride and so on. These rules are applied according to the circumstances within the bridegroom's family.[1] Some of the cattle which he transfers to the family of his bride will have been acquired in this manner. Others may have come to him from kinsmen or friends as gifts, others in settlement of debts unconnected with marriage. Nowadays he may have acquired cattle by purchase with cash which he has earned. In the past he might have seized cattle in raids on the Dinka.

The Ideal

While the collection of the bridewealth cattle by an individual for his own marriage depends on a wide variety of circumstances, the distribution of that bridewealth among the family and kinsmen of the bride is governed by rules which can be stated as an ideal. In an article on the subject, Professor Evans-Pritchard says:

> Bridewealth should consist of 40 head of cattle. Among the Eastern Nuer 20 are said to go *kwi gwan,* to the father's side, and 20 *kwi man,* to the mother's side, of the bride. Equal division between the bride's paternal kinsmen (including her father) and her maternal kinsmen (including her mother) is thus the first rule of distribution. Of the 20 beasts which go to the father's side, 10 remain with the father (or his sons) and 10 are divided among his family (his parents, brothers, and sisters); and of the 20 beasts which go to the mother's side, 10 remain with the mother (or her sons) and 10 are divided among her family (her parents and brothers and sisters). The second rule, therefore, is that the cattle are distributed in fixed proportions between three families: the bride's own family, her father's family, and her mother's family.[2]

In this version, the mother's portion is included on the mother's side (*kwi man*), whereas in reality the cattle transferred in her name are inherited by her sons, and therefore go to the father's side (*kwi gwan*). Professor Evans-Pritchard draws attention to this difference between theory and fact. This is a matter of some importance when we come to consider the proportions paid to each side, and will be discussed later. It may be noted in passing that the Zeraf tribes and (as noted by Professor Evans-Pritchard) the Western Nuer tribes often refer to the maternal side as *kwi nare*, lit. 'maternal uncle's side', rather than *kwi man*. This is certainly a more accurate description.

In the course of my own investigations on the subject I never heard forty head of cattle consistently given as the ideal bridewealth, nor the exact proportions quoted. This may be because I never put the question in the right form, or because the Thiang and Lak have for a long time been poorer in cattle than most tribes of the Eastern Nuer.

---

[1] See under Inheritance, Chapter V, Section 3, pp. 190–4.
[2] 'Nuer Bridewealth', *Africa*, XVI, 4, 1946, p. 247.

DISTRIBUTION OF BRIDEWEALTH

I have not often heard a specific number given as the ideal, only a list of recognized relations of the bride to whom certain cattle must be paid. My informants were perhaps talking in terms of a minimum. Certainly forty head of cattle is usually given as the traditional rate of compensation for homicide and, as we have seen, bridewealth and bloodwealth should in theory be equal since the object of the payment of bloodwealth (*thung*) is to provide a wife to the name of the dead man.[1] Marriages are nowadays completed by payment of as little as 17 to 20 head of cattle and sometimes even less, though the average in well-to-do families is usually nearer 30. Professor Evans-Pritchard says that the usual payment is from 20 to 30. This is a reasonably accurate estimate of bridewealth today, but it must be remembered that bridewealth varies not only from tribe to tribe but also within the tribe from year to year. A particularly heavy epidemic may carry off as much as 30 per cent. of the cattle population, and bridewealth must drop accordingly.

Lou Nuer Version

I quote the ideal distribution, based on the payment of forty head of cattle, given by Professor Evans-Pritchard in full, before examining, by way of comparison, versions cited among other Nuer tribes.[2]

	Cattle	Total
KWI GWAN (on the paternal side) Gwan (father)	A cow and its calf, a cow and its calf, an ox, another ox, a cow, and a calf*	8
Gat gwan (father's son) . .	A cow and another cow** . .	2
Gwanlen (indit) kwi mane or kwi dwiel (father's elder brother by the same mother)	A cow and its calf, a calf, and an ox	4
Gwanlen kwi gwane or kwi luak (father's brother by a different mother)	A cow and its calf, and an ox .	3
Gwanlen (intot) kwi mane or kwi dwiel (father's younger brother by the same mother)	A cow, and an ox . . .	2
Wac (father's sister) . . .	A heifer***	1
	Total	20

* The single calf is sometimes called *puang* (*de*), and they say: 'It is like a gift thrown in for nothing.' The single cow is sometimes called *yang luak*, the cow of the byre, and is given to conclude the claims on the paternal side. One of the cows is usually the *yang kwoth*, the cow of the spirit of the father.

** These animals join the herd of the claimant's father, if he is alive, and count as his portion also. The father therefore receives 10 beasts.

*** This animal joins her husband's herd if he is alive.

[1] Nuer say and think that this should be so, but as already stated they are not too careful about the mathematics of the transaction. In point of fact a substantial proportion are distributed among the kinsmen of the deceased, so that much less than forty are left to marry the 'ghost-wife'. See pp. 50, 51.

[2] Evans-Pritchard in 'Nuer Bridewealth', *Africa*, XVI, 4, 1946, and in *Kinship and Marriage among the Nuer*, Oxford, 1951.

BRIDEWEALTH

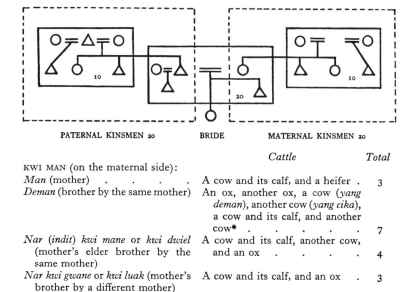

		Cattle	Total
PATERNAL KINSMEN 20	BRIDE	MATERNAL KINSMEN 20	

KWI MAN (on the maternal side):

		Cattle	Total
Man (mother)	A cow and its calf, and a heifer		3
Deman (brother by the same mother)	An ox, another ox, a cow (*yang deman*), another cow (*yang cika*), a cow and its calf, and another cow*		7
Nar (*indit*) *kwi mane* or *kwi dwiel* (mother's elder brother by the same mother)	A cow and its calf, another cow, and an ox		4
Nar kwi gwane or *kwi luak* (mother's brother by a different mother)	A cow and its calf, and an ox		3
Nar (*intot*) *kwi mane* or *kwi dwiel* (mother's younger brother by the same mother)	A cow and its calf		2
Manlen (mother's sister)	A heifer**		1
	Total		20

* The last cow is sometimes a poor beast that has been refused by some kinsman but is taken in charity by the bride's brother to make up the total. The cattle of the brother also count as the cattle of the mother, so that her total portion is 10 beasts. As they all join the father's herd, if he is alive, his actual portion is 20 head of cattle.
** This animal joins her husband's herd if he is alive.

Zeraf Nuer Versions

The principles which underlie the distribution of bridewealth cattle as described by Professor Evans-Pritchard apply to all Nuer tribes, and it would be impossible to improve on his account. There are, however, differences of detail which are worth recording here. My own observations on the Lak and Thiang Nuer of the Zeraf Valley and, to a lesser extent, the Gaawar, were made before the results of Professor Evans-Pritchard's investigations had been published. This work was carried out between 1942 and 1945. Subsequently, in 1949, I had several opportunities of testing out his and my own observations among the Western Nuer tribes.

Kinship Terminology

Before making comparisons, it will be as well to give some account of Nuer kinship terminology, especially as the terminology employed

KINSHIP TERMINOLOGY

by Professor Evans-Pritchard sometimes differs from my own. The difference is one of dialect, and it may be noted that, although all the terms used are understood in all parts of Nuerland, nearly all of them have alternatives which are current in one part or another. There are in fact many ways of saying the same thing. Nuer could, of course, employ the most highly descriptive terminology, just as we could. We could say 'father's brother' or we could say 'paternal uncle'; Nuer could say *deman gwan* or they could say *gwanlen*. To be more descriptive we could say 'father's brother by the same mother' or 'father's full brother'; the Nuer could say *deman gwan kwi mande* or *kwi dwiel*, or they could say *gwanlen gwande* or *kwi luak*.

In normal speech, especially in conversation about or with a particular relative, the finer qualifications are not employed. If the context does not demand any precise distinction, a man will say *gwanlende*, 'his paternal uncle'. The distribution of bridewealth, however, demands such precise distinction. The term used for a particular relative is therefore qualified by the addition of *gwande* or *kwi gwande*, 'on the father's side', or *kwi luak*, 'on the *luak* (cattle-byre) side', and *mande* or *kwi mande*,[1] 'on the mother's side', or *kwi dwiel*, 'on the hut side'. The significance of the 'cattle-byre' side and the 'hut side' is that, since each wife has her own hut (*dwil*) in which she lives with her children, those of the hut (*kwi dwiel*) are uterine brothers and sisters; the cattle-byre (*luak*) is common to the whole family, i.e. the father, his wives and all their children. Hence when a relative is described as *kwi luak* it implies that he is not of the same mother, though by definition he is of the same family group.

Other differences between terminology employed by Professor Evans-Pritchard and myself are:

(*a*) The distinction between elder paternal uncle (*gwanlen indit*) and younger paternal uncle (*gwanlen intot*), etc. *Indit* simply means 'big' and *intot* 'small'.

(*b*) Professor Evans-Pritchard uses *gat gwan*, literally 'father's son', for half-brother of the bride. Another way of describing this relationship is to say *deman kwi luak*, which is more normal in Western Nuer.

The variations are recorded in the diagram on page 102.

Note.—Relationship to the bride is given in the third person, e.g. *Man* (or *Man nyal*), the bride's mother; *Manlen* (or *Manlen nyal*), the bride's maternal aunt.

---

[1] The personal pronoun *da*, *de*, &c., is also difficult. Professor Evans-Pritchard records, for example, the paternal uncle (by the same mother) as *kwi mane*. This is simply because some Nuer tribes (notably Lou) drop the consonant *d* and say *mane* instead of *mande*.

BRIDEWEALTH

NUER KINSHIP TERMS

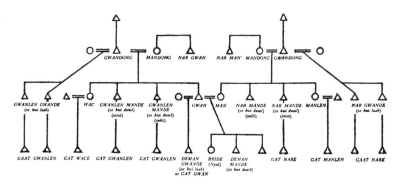

Zeraf Valley Version (Lak and Thiang)

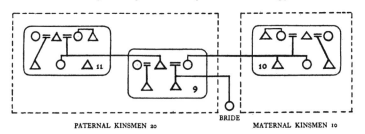

PATERNAL KINSMEN 20   BRIDE   MATERNAL KINSMEN 10

Relationship to bride	Cattle	Total
KWI GWAN (on the paternal side)		
Gwan (father)[1]	*yang gwande*, a cow and its calf. *yang kwoth*, a cow dedicated to his ancestral spirits. *thak gwan nyal*, an ox . . . . (These should go to his sons, often to half-brothers of the bride. The ox is usually considered the right of the eldest half-brother.)	4
Deman (brother by the same mother)	*thak deman*, an ox . . . . . (The bridegroom is usually expected to please his future brother-in-law by finding an ox of the latter's favourite colour.)	1
Deman kwi luak (brother by a different mother)	*thak deman*, an ox . . . . . (This is not always demanded, and is often merely included under the father's portion. See above.)	1

[1] A man will often have paid four head of cattle at his betrothal (*cuei*: see p. 88 n. 3), so the father's portion is sometimes 8 (as in the Eastern Nuer version), but I think that the previous 4 head usually count as the total allotment to the father nowadays. This may account for the disparity.

BRIDEWEALTH DISTRIBUTION

Relationship to bride	*Cattle*	*Total*
Gwanlen mande (father's brother by same mother)	A cow and its calf. An ox. A cow-calf, sometimes called *puong* . . (Nuer refer to this relationship as *gwanlen mande* or, in full, *gwanlen kwi mande*, i.e. the father's uterine brother. The calf called *puong* is sometimes said to be the special right of the youngest uterine brother.)	4
Gwanlen gwande (father's brother by a different mother)	A cow and its calf and (sometimes) an ox . (Nuer refer to this relationship as *gwanlen kwi luak*, but more often *gwanlen gwande*.)	3
Wac (father's sister) .	*yang waca*, a cow . . . . . (This cow goes to the woman's husband and his sons, and is therefore transferred outside the father's lineage.)	1
Gwandong (father's father)	*yang wangnen gwande*, a cow or heifer . (This cow should go to the father's youngest brother and often the youngest half-brother. Among the Zeraf tribes it is usually included whether the father's father is living or not, and even if he died before the bride was born.)	1
Mandong (father's mother)	*yang wangnen mande*, a cow or heifer . . (This cow should go to a younger uterine brother of the bride's father.)	1
Nar gwan (*nyal*) (father's maternal uncle)	Sometimes called *kethar*, a cow-calf . . (This should go to the sons of the father's maternal uncle and hence outside the father's lineage.)	1
Man[1] (mother) . .	*yang man nyal*, a cow and its calf. (This should go to the bride's eldest uterine brother.) *yang kwoth*, a cow . . . . . (Dedicated to the mother's ancestral spirits and usually later inherited by one of her younger sons.)	3
	Total	20

KWI MAN (on the maternal side often referred to as *kwi nare*, maternal uncle's side)

Nar mande (mother's brother by the same mother)	*ghok nare* or *ghok nar mande*, a cow and cow-calf. An ox. A cow-calf (*puong*) . . . . . (The cow-calf called *puong* is said to be the right of the youngest uterine brother of the bride's mother.)	4

[1] The Zeraf tribes include the mother's portion and that of the bride's uterine brother under the paternal side. This is also so in Western Nuer, as Professor Evans-Pritchard observes. This point is discussed later.

BRIDEWEALTH

Relationship to bride	Cattle	Total
Nar gwande (mother's brother by a different mother)	*yang nar kwi luak* or *nar gwande*, a cow and its calf	2
Manlen (mother's sister).	*yang manlen*, a cow-calf . . . . (This goes to her sons and therefore outside the maternal lineage.)	1
Gwandong (mother's father)	*yang wangnen gwande*, a pregnant cow . (This should go to one of his younger sons, e.g. half-brother of the maternal uncle above.)	1
Mandong (mother's mother)	*yang wangnen mande*, a pregnant cow . (This should go to one of her younger sons, e.g. a uterine brother of the maternal uncle above.)	1
Nar man (*nyal*) (mother's maternal uncle)	Sometimes called *kethar*, a cow-calf . . (This goes to his sons and therefore outside the maternal lineage.)[1]	1
	Total	10

Apart from the disparity in numbers of cattle, there are obvious differences in this version from the ideal given by Professor Evans-Pritchard:

(i) Among the Zeraf tribes, the cattle of the grandparents, called *wangnen*, are nearly always included, and usually at least some of them are paid whatever the circumstances. On this subject Professor Evans-Pritchard says:

> It must be added that the four grandparents of the bride are entitled each to a cow in certain circumstances, but they are not mentioned in the distribution given above because it is assumed that by the time their granddaughter is old enough to be married they will be dead. It is a rule that in the event of any claimant being dead his, or her, son inherits the right to cattle.
>
> . . . a grandparent only receives a cow if he, or she, saw the bride before he, or she, died. It is probably for this reason that the cows given to the grandparents or their sons are called *wangnen* (*wang*, eye, *nen*, to see). It is possible, therefore, for there to be four *wangnen* claims, but there are generally one or two at the most.[2]

(ii) Professor Evans-Pritchard's version includes:

> *Gwanlen intot* (father's younger brother by the same mother).
> *Nar intot* (mother's younger brother by the same mother).

---

[1] There is not only a definite division between the bride's paternal relatives on the one hand and her maternal relatives on the other, but also a distinction between the bride's immediate relatives, e.g. her father and his sons (both uterine and half-brothers of the bride) and the more remote relatives on either side who in this context are classed as *ji cuongni*, 'the people who have rights'. The cattle to which they are entitled are known as *ghok cuongni rar*. Those of the bride's father and his sons are referred to as *ghok dieth*, 'the cows of begetting'.

[2] Op. cit. (in *Africa*, 1946), p. 249.

BRIDEWEALTH DISTRIBUTION

Now, it is just these relatives of the bride who inherit in the first instance the *wangnen mande* on the father's side, and in the second, the *wangnen mande* on the mother's side. It may therefore be that they are exactly equivalent, and if, for example, a cow is paid as *wangnen mande* on the father's side, a cow for the *gwanlen intot* is not to be expected. Similarly the *wangnen gwande* (grandfather's cattle on both sides) by right descend to the bride's father's younger half-brother (i.e. *gwanlen kwi luak* or *gwande*) on the one side and to the bride's mother's younger half-brother (i.e. *nar kwi luak* or *nar gwande*) on the other. These relatives are sometimes included, sometimes not. It seems that Nuer often treat these portions as alternatives, and this may explain the fact that not all of them are always included. It must be emphasized here that Nuer find considerable difficulty in quoting the claims of various relatives in a hypothetical marriage. This difficulty does not arise in an actual marriage because all the relatives who claim some portion as a right (*cuong*) are known personalities. Such negotiations over bridewealth are carried out with unusual decorum, and although feelings run high there is generally a spirit of compromise. Talking of these things Nuer sometimes say '*ruoah latke ked de dut*', 'you must put your stick in the grass for your wife's family'. The word *ruoah* is a polite way of speaking about relatives-in-law, and the expression implies that a man must put his anger aside if his wife's family are unreasonable in their demands.

(iii) Professor Evans-Pritchard's version does not include the *kethar* portions which go to the *nar gwan nyal* (the bride's father's maternal uncle) and the *nar man nyal* (the bride's mother's maternal uncle). These portions are nearly always quoted by Zeraf Nuer tribes and, as will be seen later, by Western Nuer. They are often but not always paid. This point is important because these relatives are outside the lineages of both the bride's father and bride's mother, so that when those cattle which go to the bride's paternal and maternal aunts and their sons are included, in all six different lineages are involved in one marriage,[1] as will be seen in the diagram on page 106.

---

[1] Of the *kethar* (or *karthar*) portions, Professor Evans-Pritchard writes:
'A borderline case between bride-cattle properly speaking and such small gifts to distant kinsmen is that of the calf, called *karthar* among the western Nuer, which may be claimed by a collateral kinsman who is a patrilineal descendant of the bride's father's father's father. This payment is sometimes made, as sign that the patrilineal limit of bridewealth claims has been reached and that no demands will be accepted from collateral kinsmen tracing their common descent with the bride from an ancestor yet farther removed' (op. cit. p. 257).
I do not think that the expression *karthar* is used except in the circumstances I have already described, i.e. of a special portion which goes to the maternal uncle of the bride's father on the one side and the maternal uncle of the bride's mother on the other side. Some Nuer tribes, notably the Dok, Nuong and Gaawar, who have a close historical connexion, sometimes say that a cow-calf called *dong* should be paid to the bride's father's father's father and less commonly the mother's father's father's father. I think that this is a claim which is nowadays rarely made, and therefore rarely included in a list of bridewealth claims, though it may have been customary in the past.

LINEAGES INVOLVED IN BRIDEWEALTH DISTRIBUTION
Lou Nuer (as quoted by Professor Evans-Pritchard)

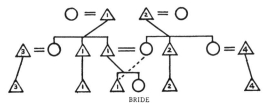

Lineage 1 = Bride's father and agnatic kinsmen.
Lineage 2 = Bride's mother's father and agnatic kinsmen.
Lineage 3 = Bride's paternal aunt's husband and agnatic kinsmen.
Lineage 4 = Bride's maternal aunt's husband and agnatic kinsmen.

Zeraf and Western Nuer Versions

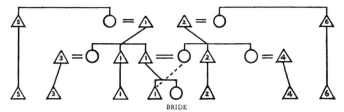

Lineage 1 = Bride's father and agnatic kinsmen.
Lineage 2 = Bride's mother's father and agnatic kinsmen.
Lineage 3 = Bride's paternal aunt's husband and agnatic kinsmen.
Lineage 4 = Bride's maternal aunt's husband and agnatic kinsmen.
Lineage 5 = Bride's father's maternal uncle and agnatic kinsmen.
Lineage 6 = Bride's mother's maternal uncle and agnatic kinsmen.

Minimum Claims

The difference in numbers of cattle is perhaps accounted for by the fact that Professor Evans-Pritchard is quoting an ideal from Lou Nuer, while the Zeraf version given here is not an ideal, but is closer to reality and nearer to what is considered the minimum although not actually the minimum. On this subject, Professor Evans-Pritchard says:

> In any particular marriage there is a minimum definition of rights. Whatever else the bride's family and kindred get they must get certain animals or the marriage cannot take place. Hence these basic claims take precedence and their titles are always the first to be acknowledged. The conventional order is as follows:

1. *wangnen gwane*, the cows of the paternal grandparents . . . 2
   wangnen mane, the cows of the maternal grandparents . . . 2
2. *yang gwane kene doude, ke thakde*, the cow of the father with its calf,
   and his ox 3

BRIDEWEALTH DISTRIBUTION 107

yang mane kene doude, the cow of the mother with its calf . .	2
3. *yang gwanlene kene doude, ke thakde*, the cow of the paternal uncle with its calf and his ox	3
yang nara kene doude, kene thakde, ke puangde, the cow of the maternal uncle with its calf, and his ox, and his *puang* (ox) . . .	4
4. *dou (nac) waca*, the calf (heifer) of the paternal aunt . . .	1
dou (nac) manlene, the calf (heifer) of the maternal aunt . . .	1
5. *yang kwoth gwande*, the cow of the father's spirit	1
yang kwoth mande, the cow of the mother's spirit	1
6. *thak deman*, the ox of the uterine brother	1
thak gat gwan, the cow of the paternal half-brother[1] . . .	1
	22

This, with the exception of the *thak gat gwan* (which in the Zeraf is included in the father's portion) and the *yang nar gwan* and *yang nar man*, approximates very closely to the Zeraf version.[2] It is noticeable, however, that the cattle of the grandparents, the *wangnen*, are included in the minimum, while they are omitted in the ideal. The cattle of the paternal and maternal uncles, the *gwanlen* and the *nar*, are correspondingly reduced in numbers, and since, as we have seen, it is these relations who would inherit the *wangnen* cattle, this is perhaps not surprising.

Western Nuer Versions

In Western Nuer there appears to be considerable variation of detail and, as will be seen later, of proportions, but no difference of principle. The Jikany system approximates very closely to that of Thiang and Lak, with the following variations:

(*a*) Sometimes two cows (*yang kwoth*) are paid in the father's portion instead of one.

(*b*) As in Lou, the *wangnen* cattle are never paid unless the grandparent concerned was alive at the time of the bride's birth. This is, however, balanced by a proportionately higher claim by the bride's paternal and maternal uncles, who are normally considered the heirs to the *wangnen* cattle.

(*c*) The *kethar* cattle—for the father's maternal uncle (*nar gwan nyal*) and the mother's maternal uncle (*nar man nyal*)—are considered essential payments, but it is unusual for a bridegroom to pay more than one. Jikany say that these payments should alternate with the marriages of the daughters of the house: to the *nar gwan nyal* on the first marriage, to the *nar man nyal* on the second, and so on.[3]

---

[1] op. cit., pp. 252–3.

[2] Also the *yang nar gwan* and *yang nar man* are often omitted in actual marriages today—so the minima are virtually the same.

[3] *Nar man nyal*, &c. This is sometimes referred to as *nar mande*, which could also be interpreted as 'maternal uncle'—uterine brother of the bride's mother—and *nar gwande* as 'maternal uncle'—half-brother of the bride's mother. It is really the tone and emphasis which distinguish these relationships.

108   BRIDEWEALTH

(*d*) Every brother of the bride may expect an ox, but only one need be given to the half-brothers.

Among the Bul Nuer, who on the whole are inclined to marry with larger numbers of cattle than most Nuer tribes, there are no essential differences except that there appears to be a more exact definition of claims in the paternal and maternal uncles' portions, and in this their system resembles the Lou Nuer ideal.

Gwanlen mande (father's brothers by the same mother)	eldest, a cow and cow-calf.
	second or middle, a cow-calf and bull.
	youngest is reckoned to get the *wangnen mande*, or if not paid, will get a bull.
Gwanlen gwande (father's brothers by a different mother)	eldest, a cow and cow-calf.
	second, a cow-calf.
	youngest is reckoned to get the *wangnen gwande*, or if not paid, a bull-calf.

This approximates more closely to the system recorded by Professor Evans-Pritchard.

Similar proportions are paid to the maternal uncles of the bride on the mother's side (*kwi nare*) and again the youngest maternal uncles, the bride's mother's youngest uterine and youngest half-brother can claim the *wangnen mande* and *wangnen gwande* respectively. These distinctions, with variation in numbers, apply also to the Leik.

Among the Dok, the system approximates very closely to the Lak and Thiang Nuer systems, but it is worth while noting here that the Dok Nuer were often confused and inconsistent in quoting the ideal, more so perhaps than most Nuer.

I do not think that the variations to be found in the systems quoted reveal any fundamental difference of principle. The key to the problem of distribution lies in the rules of inheritance which are applied during the negotiations or will apply in the future, rather than in the actual relationship to the bride in the name of which cattle are transferred or the portions and number of cattle quoted. Throughout the system there is the principle of alternation and in addition conventional indications, though they are too loosely applied in practice to be more than indications, as to who should receive the cattle.[1] Thus, for example, the cattle classified as those of the bride's mother (*ghok mande*) should go to her sons, i.e. uterine brothers of the bride, while those of the bride's father (*ghok gwande*) should go to his sons by another wife, i.e. half-brothers of the bride. Similarly, a generation higher up the scale, as we have already seen, the paternal grandmother's portion (*wangnen mande*) goes to her own sons (*gwanlen mande* of the bride) and that of the paternal grandfather (*wangnen gwande*) to his sons by another wife, i.e. half-brothers of the bride's father (*gwanlen gwande* of the bride).

[1] This subject is discussed later under 'Inheritance': see Chapter V, Section 3.

BRIDEWEALTH DISTRIBUTION 109

These are conventional rules which essentially apply within each lineage, but do not apply with any exactitude in practice because not all the relatives concerned exist or, if they do, have already received portions on the marriage of another daughter or will do so in the future. The rules are therefore sufficiently elastic to meet almost any situation within a family group yet sufficiently clear to avoid undesirable friction and confusion.

Proportions

In the version current among the Lou Nuer and recorded by Professor Evans-Pritchard, the cattle of the mother (*ghok mane*) and also of her son (*ghok deman*), who is uterine brother of the bride, are included on the maternal side, the *kwi man*. He points out, however, that—

> Among the western Nuer when a man speaks of 'the cattle on the paternal side' and 'the cattle on the maternal side' his description is more in accord with realities because he includes among 'the cattle on the paternal side' those beasts which go to the bride's mother and uterine brother, since the father gets them if he is alive. The western Nuer way of counting bridewealth is therefore less symmetrical than the eastern Nuer way of counting it. This difference is superficial, because in all parts of Nuerland the same relationships are a title to approximately the same number of cattle. The rights of members of the families of the father and mother of the bride are everywhere the same.

It is perhaps significant that in Western Nuer the claims of the maternal relatives are classified under the heading of *kwi nare*, 'the maternal uncle's side', which excludes the mother's portion (the *ghok mande*). In Lou Nuer it appears to be a social fiction that the cattle should be divided equally between the paternal and maternal kin of the bride in the ratio of 20 : 20, for in fact the division is 30 : 10.

On this subject, Professor Evans-Pritchard says:

> I do not guarantee that if one were to ask any Nuer from the eastern part of their territory how bridewealth is distributed in his country he would receive a list identical with the one I have given, for there might be shifts here and there of a cow or an ox, but the balance and proportions would be as I have recorded them.[1]

There are in fact many ways in which these proportions may be regarded. First there is the proportion in theory (when the mother's and uterine brothers' cattle are included on the maternal side) and in fact (when they are not) between the paternal and maternal sides. In the Lou Nuer ideal as recorded by Professor Evans-Pritchard these proportions are 20 : 20 in the first method of assessment and 30 : 10 in the second: ratios of 1 : 1 and 3 : 1 respectively. Among the Lak and Thiang Nuer, and also the Jikany and Dok, they are 16 : 14 and 20 : 10; among the Bul Nuer they are 17 : 17 and

---

[1] Evans-Pritchard, op. cit., p. 249.

BRIDEWEALTH

23 : 11; among the Leik they are 16 : 15 and 22 : 9. Among these last-named people the ratios are therefore approximately 1 : 1 and 2 : 1. These more nearly approximate to the proportions found in the minimum quoted by Professor Evans-Pritchard, and allowing for minor inconsistencies and for the fact that the Nuer do not think of these things in terms of exact figures,[1] the balance and proportions are approximately the same throughout Nuerland.

Secondly, there is the proportion of cattle which go to the immediate family of the bride, the *ghok dieth*, and those which go to the more remote relatives, the *ghok cuongni rar*. In the Lou Nuer ideal version the ratio is 20 : 20 and 8 : 14 in the minimum version. Elsewhere they are: Lak and Thiang, 9 : 21, Jikany and Dok, 10 : 20, Bul, 12 : 22, and Leik, 10 : 21. The ratio throughout is therefore approximately 1 : 2. Analysis of actual marriages (though not necessarily the examples quoted below, where in some instances all payments have not been completed) shows very approximately similar proportions. If, therefore, there has been a reduction in the number of cattle payable as bridewealth, at any rate a reduction from the ideal, it has not been in the portion of the more remote kinsmen but in that of the bride's immediate family. A decrease in the cattle population in relation to human population has not at any rate led to a diminution of the network of claims which marriage involves. Marriage has not become a more individual affair in which only the bridegroom and the bride's father are concerned but has retained its collective nature.

Other Payments

Professor Evans-Pritchard points out that 'any cognatic kinsman up to six or seven generations removed from a common ancestor with the bride may attest his kinship by asking a small gift and it will not be refused'.[2] This is true of all Nuer tribes. There are also certain categories of persons who may claim special gifts which among the Zeraf tribes are known collectively as *thanypiny*:

riu . . . A spear dedicated to the central pole of the bride's father's cattle-byre. This is usually a symbolic offering to the ancestral spirits of the lineage and is often given to the *gwan buthni* of the bride's family.

ruath ric . . A bull-calf or a ram or at least a spear[3] given to an age-mate of the bride's father, often a man who has undergone the ceremonies of initiation with him.

---

[1] A pregnant cow is sometimes assessed at two head of cattle, sometimes one, for example.

[2] Among the Lak, for example, a spear called *dong*, considered the right of the bride's paternal great-grandfather, is usually paid and will be given to one of his male descendants, but in a different line from that of the bride's father.

[3] Sometimes a cow. This is usually a purely reciprocal transaction. *Ric* means 'age-set'.

PAYMENTS CONNECTED WITH CHILDREN   111

wut ghok .   .   A goat or a fish-spear sometimes given to the cattle expert for his services in performing ritual to ensure the fertility of the bride. In some tribes the Leopard-Skin Chief is asked to attend the ceremonies and receives a goat or a spear for his services. These are, however, really only fees for specialist assistance and are in no sense part of the marriage payments, even though the bridegroom will be expected to produce them.

yang mathe   .   A cow for the bride's father's 'best friend' (*math*). This is very often paid.

yang buoth   .   A cow or calf claimed (though not often received) by the bride's father in recognition of his energy in providing for her in times of famine (*buoth*).

yang gorei   .   A cow dedicated to the bride's father's 'hearth'.

There is an infinite variety of such gifts and payments among different Nuer tribes. They are regarded as obligatory on the bridegroom, but such obligations are not necessarily honoured, nor upheld in the courts. They remain a matter of obligatory custom rather than enforceable law.

Claims for Begetting and Fostering Children outside Legal Union

A man who is physiological but not legal father of a female child may claim a cow from her bridewealth when in due course she gets married. The cow is known as *yang leta*, the 'cow of the loins'. This term is not considered polite, and it is more usual to refer to *yang dieth*, the 'cow of birth' or, where the child is born in the more respectable union of 'widow concubinage', *yang laka*, the 'cow of widowhood'. Sometimes it is called *yang twac*, literally, the 'cow of the skin', referring to the serval cat-skin worn in the presence of relatives-in-law and hence politely and euphemistically avoiding emphasis on the illegal nature of the union. *Yang leta* is given to the *genitor* in 'ghost-marriage' and in leviratic union, though it is here often the case that he can claim other portions of his natural daughter's bridewealth by reason of his kinship relationship to her legal but deceased father. This is rarely so in 'widow-concubinage', for here the father is either unrelated to the *pater*, or so remotely related that no legal claim in the kinship system exists. In addition, a man may also claim *yang pithe*, the 'cow of growing', which, however, refers not so much to physical parenthood as to upbringing. It is a definite and quite separate fee payable for the care and attention lavished on a child during its early years. It may be claimed by a man who is neither *pater* nor *genitor* but simply 'foster-father', though the majority of such demands arise in the more stable relationship of 'widow-concubinage'.

BRIDEWEALTH

These fees, which are sometimes taken from the father's (*pater's*) portion of the bridewealth and sometimes demanded from the girl's husband as an extra payment, may even be claimed by an adulterer on the marriage of his natural daughter, for the Nuer recognize physiological ties even if they run counter to legal relationships. There is something of a mystical bond between father and child whatever the circumstances of birth, and Nuer believe that the natural father has power to curse his daughter with perpetual barrenness if his claims are thwarted. For this reason both the girl's kinsmen and those of her husband are usually anxious to placate him. In adultery, when a child is born of the act, the indemnity (*ruok ruet ciek*) is reduced from six head of cattle to one cow. This is the *yang kule*, the 'cow of the sleeping mat', which has a ritual and expiatory purpose only. The principle of reciprocity and of legal claims raised by the transfer of cattle is so strong that even cattle paid specifically as indemnification sometimes lead to a confusion of legal rights in the future. We shall consider this matter more fully later, but it may be noted here that such claims are something quite separate from the *yang leta* which refers precisely to physiological parenthood and *yang pithe* which refers to the fostering of children and the expense of their upbringing. When a child is born to an unmarried, and usually young, girl her seducer would rarely dare to claim such fees. Had no child been born, he might be expected to pay an indemnity of two head of cattle (*ruok dhu nyal*), though in the past he was more likely to meet the violent retaliation of her brothers. If a child is born, the girl's kinsmen may legitimately claim a similar indemnity (*ruok ruet nyal*). Usually they will not press these demands, again to avoid legal confusion in the future, and if this has been the case, the father of a girl-child will scarcely ever have the courage to make claims on her bridewealth at a later date.

Nevertheless, such claims are socially recognized and often upheld in Nuer courts, and hence become legal. They are often paid without question, even in cases of adultery, because after eighteen years or more have passed between birth and marriage, resentment of the initial wrong has long since vanished. In many cases the *genitor* and the *pater* or his heirs are the best of friends. In other cases, however, such claims may be the subject of the most acrimonious disputes and litigation.

These observations apply to female children born out of legal marriage only. A man may expect, obviously enough, no benefits from his natural sons. On the contrary, he may expect certain liabilities, for it is considered that a man should help his sons, even though they have no legal claim upon his cattle. In many cases the *genitor* will be dead by the time his natural son comes of age, and the claims of the latter on the former's heirs are often a source of friction and unpleasantness.

REVERSE PAYMENTS

It is not possible to enumerate here all the various circumstances which establish legal rights to such shares in bridewealth. Without the use of endless examples, generalizations are risky, but the principles described above are usually accepted by a Nuer court and enforced as legal. *Yang leta* is sometimes, but rarely, claimed by the physiological father long before the marriage of his natural daughter; but he thereby forgoes all claim to a larger portion of her bridewealth, especially among those tribes—Western Nuer in particular—where the major portion of the *pater's* share, three cattle in all, is sometimes given as *yang leta* when the *pater* is dead and the *genitor* has had a specially constant and stable relationship with his daughter's kinsmen. This usually happens only in 'ghost-marriage', leviratic union, or 'widow-concubinage', and rarely outside such permanent unions.

Reverse Payments

Among the majority of Dinka tribes west of the Nile payment of bridewealth by the bridegroom to the bride's family is followed by a reciprocal payment by the bride's family to the bridegroom, which is known as *arueth*. The number of cattle varies and may be as much as one-third of the total bridewealth paid. This practice is unknown to the Nuer, though the same concept is to be found in the payment of *thiuk* among the Jagei, Dok and Aak tribes. On final confirmation of the marriage two cows are paid to the bridegroom's family, one from the *kwi gwande* and one from the *kwi mande*. These are reckoned to be the right of the bride's future sons.[1] The payment is accompanied by ritual which symbolizes the removal of the taboo on the two families eating and drinking together and the necessity of wearing a cat-skin in the presence of relatives-in-law. A cow is sometimes paid to the bridegroom on the marriage of his wife's younger sister, but this is not common nor a formal custom as among some Dinka tribes, where as much as five head of cattle (*ariek*) are paid.[2] These payments do not seem to be current elsewhere in Nuerland. I have sometimes heard Nuer say that they used to be paid and on a larger scale in the old days when 'people married with many cattle', but I am inclined to believe that this is not a Nuer custom. The Dok, Jagei, and Aak are in close contact with Dinka tribes, among whom *arueth* is an essential part of the marital system. At the same time, the Bul and, to a lesser extent, the Leik are also in touch with these Dinka, but do not practise the custom or its equivalent, though the idea is known to them.

[1] Some Western Nuer tribes say that a cow—*yang joghni*, 'the cow of the spirits'— should be given to the husband by the wife's father on the birth of the first child.

[2] I have described this in a recent article on 'The Ngork Dinka of Western Kordofan', *S.N.R.*, 1951.

INL

BRIDEWEALTH

Examples of Actual Marriages

When following the principles described above in actual examples of Nuer marriages, it must be remembered that not all the relatives of the bride to whom a portion of the bridewealth should go necessarily exist in fact. In such circumstances, the Nuer would say that the portions should be inherited by their legal heirs. Sometimes a claim is honoured, sometimes not. At the same time it is unlikely that a marriage would be refused, dissolved, or declared illegal if one or more portions included in the 'minimum' of claims were omitted. The procedure is clear. The bride's family will put in their demand for any portion which is considered a definite right; the bridegroom's representatives will name a cow. The bride's representatives will say that this will go as the *yang manlen* or the *yang kwoth mande*, naming a definite portion as the case may be. If in the final assessment the bridegroom has not met or cannot meet all the recognized claims, they will ultimately judge the matter in terms of the over-all number of cattle which he is able to pay. It is usual for representatives of each claim to attend the negotiations in person. Hence there are not only arguments between the bridegroom's representatives and the bride's family, which are on the whole restrained, but arguments between the various members of the bride's family themselves. These discussions are usually more heated.

The examples which follow are not intended as evidence of the principles already described, but rather to show how those principles

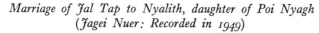

Marriage of Jal Tap to Nyalith, daughter of Poi Nyagh
(Jagei Nuer: Recorded in 1949)

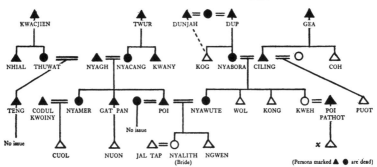

are applied in practice.[1] It will be found that the distribution is made to approximate as far as possible to the ideal. The relationships are

---

[1] It would be difficult to find a marriage in which there was a perfect configuration of both lineages and in which all claims had been met. These examples are chosen at random.

EXAMPLES OF DISTRIBUTION

shown in a chart above the distribution of the bridewealth. Each claim is recorded under the actual relationship term employed (in relation to the bride) and the name of the person who actually received the cow or cattle is given. In many cases the person will be not the actual claimant to a title, but his heir. If the principles are applied, the reasons will be obvious, but where the circumstances are exceptional they are recorded in the text.

BRIDEWEALTH DISTRIBUTION

KWI GWAN
Gwan. A cow-calf ⎫ To NGWEN.
     A bull   ⎬ (as heir to Poi).
Deman. A bull: To NGWEN.
Wac. A heifer: To CUOL.
Gwandong. A cow: To NGWEN ⎫ *Wang-*
Mandong. A cow: To NUON ⎬ *nen.*
Man. A cow and a cow (*yang kwoth*):
                     To NGWEN.

KWI NAR (or MAN)
Nar (*mande*). A heifer: To WOL.
Manlen. A bull: To x.
Wangnen ⎰ *gwandong.* A cow: To PUOT.
        ⎱ *mandong.* A cow: To KONG.

This marriage took place in 1948, only a few months before it was recorded. Full bridewealth has not yet been paid. Jal stated he would complete the payments when he had collected cattle from the marriage of his sister. The *muot* ceremony had been performed, but no *thiuk* cattle had been paid to Jal by Ngwen. In Ngwen's presence, Jal stated he would pay: a cow as *yang kwoth* for the mother's portion, and also a bull-calf; two cows as paternal uncles' portions (*gwanlen*); on the maternal side—a cow as *kethar* (mother's maternal uncle's portion). This in fact would go to Kog, legal, but not physiological son of Dup. It should be noted that other than Ngwen (bride's brother) and Nuon (bride's father's brother's son: *gat gwanlen mande*) there are no living claimants on the paternal side.

Marriage of Tap Mut to Nyamer, daughter of Kwith Leny
(Dok Nuer: Recorded in 1949)

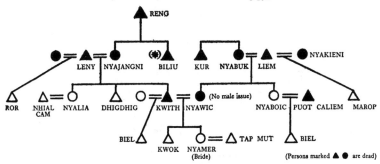

BRIDEWEALTH DISTRIBUTION

KWI GWAN
Gwan. A cow and cow-calf ⎫ To
     A cow (*yang kwoth*) ⎬ BIEL
     A bull   ⎭ KWITH.

KWI NAR (or MAN)
Nar. A heifer and a bull-calf: To KWOK
    (as his mother NYAWIC has no full
    brothers).

BRIDEWEALTH

Deman. A bull: To KWOK KWITH.
Deman kwi luak. A cow:
    To BIEL KWITH.
Gwanlen (mande?). A bull:
    To DHIGDHIG.
Wac. A cow-calf: To NHIAL CAM.
Gwandong. A cow and cow-calf: To ROR ⎫
Mandong. A cow: ⎬ *Wangnen.*
    To DHIGDHIG.   ⎭

Nar gwan (kethar).
  A cow: To JAL LIEP or his son BANGWET (sister's son to BILIU who married a wife in BILIU's name).
Man. A cow and calf: To KWOK.

Manlen. A heifer: To BIEL PUOT.
Wangnen ⎧ *gwandong.* A cow:
          ⎨   To MAROP.
          ⎩ *mandong.* A cow:
                To KWOK.

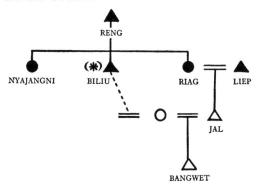

Tap Mut married Nyamer, daughter of Kwith Leny, in 1947. There is as yet no child of this union; Kwith himself predeceased the marriage, and his brother Dhigdhig is senior legal representative. The bridewealth payments are not considered complete, and Tap has promised to pay more when he can do so. The marriage is, however, considered legal and the ceremony of *muot* has been performed.

The following points are significant:

(i) All grandparents' claims (*wangnen*) have been met, although Leny, at least, was not alive when Nyamer was born. It appears that among the Dok Nuer these claims are met, whatever the circumstances.

(ii) Tap stated that he would pay a cow as *yang kwoth* as part of the mother's portion (*ghok mande*) and two cows as paternal uncle's portion (*ghok gwanlen mande*) to Dhigdhig. Dhigdhig stated that no further claims would be made beyond this.

(iii) No *thiuk* cattle (see Reverse Payments) have been paid, but Dhigdhig stated that this would be done when the bridewealth had been completed by (ii) above.

(iv) On the mother's side (*kwi nar*) there are no *nar mande* (mother's brothers by the same mother). Since their portions should go to her father's (Liem's) lineage, it might be expected that they would go to her half-brother Marop. In fact they go to her own son, Kwok. (See also Marriage of Cop Nyang to Nyaliny Rwea, p. 117.)

(v) A man called Jal Liep married a wife to his maternal uncle, Biliu Reng, who had died without issue. Jal's physiological son Bangwet is therefore legal son of Biliu and in fact calls himself Bangwet Biliu. Bangwet is therefore heir to the *yang nar gwan* (father's mother's brother) or *kethar*.

Marriage of Cop Nyang to Nyaliny Rwea (Jikany Nuer: Recorded in 1949)

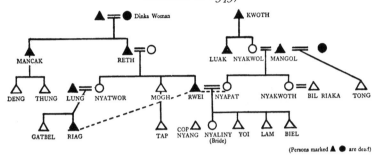

BRIDEWEALTH DISTRIBUTION

KWI GWAN
Gwan.

A cow and cow-calf ⎫
A bull   ⎪ Held in trust
A heifer (*yang kwoth*) ⎪ by NYAPAT
A heifer (*yang kwoth*) ⎬ for her sons,
dedicated to the spirits ⎪ who are
of Reth's father's wife, ⎪ minors.
  a Dinka woman   ⎭

Deman.
Three bulls: To YOI, LAM and BIEL
                                    (minors).

Gwanlen (*gwande*).
A cow and cow-calf: To DENG MANCAK.
A heifer: To THUNG MANCAK.

Gwanlen (*mande*).
A cow and cow-calf: To TAP MOGH.

Wac.
A cow: To GATBEL LUNG.

Man.
A cow and cow-calf ⎫ Held by
and a cow (*yang kwoth*) ⎬ NYAPAT
                                    ⎭ for her sons.

KWI NAR (or MAN)
Nar (*mande*):

A cow and cow-calf ⎫ To NYAPAT,
A cow (*puong*)   ⎬ for her sons
Nar (*gwande*).   ⎭
A cow and cow-calf: To TONG MANGOL.
Manlen.
A cow: To BIL RIAKA'S sons.
Nar man (*kethar*).
A heifer: To the heirs of LUAK KWOTH.

OTHER PAYMENTS

Ghok laka. To LUNG'S son RIAG now
  dead and hence to GATBEL.
    (No cattle yet paid.)
Yang mathe.
A cow: To THUNG MANCAK as RWEI'S
  friend and for bringing up the bride.
Ruath twoc ghok.
A bull-calf: To PAGEM MUT, a distant
  kinsman of RWEI'S.

This marriage took place some six years before recording. There is only one surviving child—a girl aged four. Certain peculiarities about the relationships of the persons concerned are worth noting:

(i) The bride is the legal daughter of Rwei (gen. Rwea), but physiological daughter of Riag Lung. She and her brothers are often referred to as *gaat* Riaka (Riag) but are legally *gaat* Rwea—because Riag married their mother Nyapat to Rwei's name.

(ii) Their physiological father, Riag Lung, was sister's son to their legal father Rwei. Riag died and the children were brought up by his brother Gatbel. Thus the bride has one man as legal father (*pater*), another as physiological father (*genitor*), and yet another as foster-father.

(iii) Rwei had no half-brothers who would normally be entitled to a portion as *gwanlen gwande*. In these circumstances this portion should go to Rwei's uterine brother, Mogh. In fact they go to the sons of Mancak, father's brother to Rwei. This is not usual, but it appears that Mancak made substantial contributions to the bridewealth used by Riag to marry a 'ghost-wife' to Rwei. Hence Mancak (or his heirs) have a special interest in the daughter of this 'ghost-marriage'.

(iv) On the maternal side, Nyapat is the daughter of Mangol, a man of Ruweng Dinka extraction. He had no sons by his first wife Nyakwol, and hence the cattle of the *nar mande* (mother's brothers by same mother) are held in trust by Nyapat and will eventually go to her sons who are now minors. Since Tong is the only living representative of the maternal lineage, one might expect that these cattle would go to him. This would at any rate be correct according to normal usage. Yet the maternal uncle's portions (*nar mande* though not *nar gwande*) are often inherited by his sisters' sons. See a further example of this in the marriage of Tap Mut to Nyamer (p. 116 (iv)).

(v) No *wangnen* cattle were paid on behalf of the grandparents, yet a cow was paid in the name of the bride's father's father's mother (a Dinka woman) described as *yang kwoth jaangni*, literally: 'cow of the Dinka spirits' and included in the father's portion.

(vi) A cow, referred to as *yang kwoth gwande*, was paid in the name of the bride's father's father and included in the father's portion. The explanation given was that both these ancestors were 'restless' and required attention.

(vii) Only one cow was paid as *kethar* (for the bride's mother's maternal uncle). In accordance with Jikany practice a similar dedication should be made on the paternal side (bride's father's paternal uncle) at the next marriage in the family.

Marriage of Kai Gatkwir to Nyaruac, daughter of Kwong Mogh (Dok Nuer: Recorded in 1949)

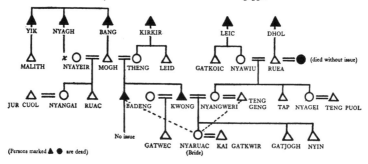

BRIDEWEALTH DISTRIBUTION

KWI GWAN
Gwan. A cow and a bull: To GATJOGH.
Deman. A bull: To GATWEC.

KWI NAR (or MAN)
Nar. A cow and bull: To TAP.
Manlen. A heifer: To TENG PUOL.

EXAMPLES OF DISTRIBUTION

Gwanlen (mande). A bull: To GATJOGH.
Wac. A heifer: To NYANGAI and
  JUR CUOL.

Gwandong. Two bulls:
  To RUAC } *Wang-nen.*
Mandong. A cow: To GATJOGH
Nar gwan. A heifer: To LEID.
Gwan gwan. A heifer (*dong*):
  To NYAGH's heirs *x.*
Gwanlen gwan. A heifer (*dong*):
  To MALITH.

Wangnen { *gwandong.* A cow: To TAP.
  { *mandong.* A cow: To TAP.

OTHER PAYMENTS

Yang laka. A cow: To TENG GENG
  (as *genitor*).

REVERSE PAYMENTS

Yang joghni nyal. A cow: (To KAI
  from GATJOGH) to ensure fertility
  and avoid future calamity after
  NYARUAC's first child died.
Thiuk. A cow: (To KAI through *his*
  mother from GATJOGH).

Kai married Nyaruac about 1933 and has had by her nine children in all, of which six died in infancy. The situation at the time of marriage should be noted. Cattle had died in considerable numbers during the previous years, and bridewealth had been much reduced. Nyaruac's family still say that they would not have accepted so few cattle had this not been so. This marriage is of considerable interest, and several points emerge:

(i) Kwong married Nyangweri as a 'ghost-wife' for his dead brother Badeng. Kwong then died himself and Nyangweri was taken by Teng Geng in leviratic union (Teng being a distant kinsman of Kwong). Teng is physiological father of Nyaruac while her legal father is Badeng. Despite this, she is referred to in ordinary conversation as daughter of Kwong. Kwong (and Badeng) had no uterine brothers, only Ruac, a half-brother.

(ii) In addition to normal payments a cow was paid as *dong*[1] to Kwong and Badeng's father's brother, and similarly a cow referred to as *dong gwanlende*, i.e. father's father's father's brother to the bride. These payments are exceptional elsewhere in Nuerland, but it appears that they are often made in Dok.

(iii) There are no exceptional circumstances on the maternal side except that nearly all cattle went to Tap since he is the only son of Ruea (mother's father).

(iv) One cow was paid to Kai (husband) as *thiuk* and another, as *yang joghni nyal*, on the birth of the first child.

In normal circumstances a cow would have been paid by Kai to his wife's mother on the birth of the first child. This also might be called *yang joghni*, which merely means 'cow of the spirits'. But the child died, and it was held that its father's spirits should be placated.

[1] See p. 110.

Marriage of Deng Rea to Nyalam, daughter of Dhor Thiep
(Thiang Nuer: Recorded in 1944)

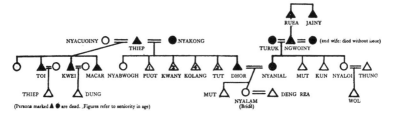

(Persons marked ▲ ● are dead. Figures refer to seniority in age)

BRIDEWEALTH DISTRIBUTION

KWI GWAN

Gwan. A cow and its calf (*yang kwoth*)
A heifer and an ox } To MUT DHOR.
Deman. An ox: To MUT DHOR.
Gwanlen. A cow and calf, an ox:
                    To PUOT THIEP.
and a heifer (*puong*):
                    To KWANY THIEP.
Gwanlen. A cow (pregnant): To KOLANG
          (TUT will get the calf).
(*Mande*) A heifer: To THIEP
                  (heir to MACAR).
Wac. A heifer: To NYABWOGH
                  (to her son).
Gwandong. A cow:
       To THIEP TOI
Mandong. A heifer:
       To KOLANG } *Wangnen.*
Man. A cow and a bull: To MUT DHOR.

KWI NAR (or MAN) *

Nar (mande). A cow and bull-calf
and (*gwande*). A cow and a cow:
                  To KUN NGWOINY.
A bull calf:
                  To MUT NGWOINY.
Manlen. A heifer: To WOL.
Gwandong. A heifer: To MUT
Mandong. A cow and a calf:
               To KUN } *Wangnen.*

OTHER PAYMENTS

Yang dieth. A cow and calf: To TUT THIEP for begetting NYALAM.
Yang pithe. A heifer and an ox: To TUT THIEP for bringing up NYALAM.

      * There are no mother's brothers by a different mother.

The family of Thiep is a powerful one in the Bang primary section of Thiang. They are *kuaar muon*, and Toi Thiep is recorded in early Government reports (1898–1904) as the most powerful personality in this region. His half-brother Puot was for some time Court President, and Thiep Toi is a 'Section Chief'. In all twenty-nine head of cattle were paid, but Deng Rea is expected to give two or three more. The bridewealth is therefore a large one (particularly in 1944 after heavy losses from rinderpest) for the Thiang Nuer, but this might be expected considering the advantages of an alliance with so powerful a family. A claim will be made for Dhor's maternal uncle as *kethar*, and Deng

AMOUNT OF BRIDEWEALTH TODAY 121

admitted this claim in the presence of his relatives-in-law. Certain points should be noted:

(i) Dhor died without issue and his brother Tut married Nyanial as Dhor's 'ghost-wife'. Tut therefore receives the *yang dieth* and *yang pithe* as *genitor* and foster-father of the bride and also a calf as *gwanlen mande*.

(ii) Mut Dhor receives the father's portion as Dhor's heir.

(iii) All *wangnen* cattle have been paid, though Thiep and Nyakong were both dead long before Nyalam was born.

(iv) Thiep Toi receives a cow (*gwanlen mande*) though one would expect this to go to Kolang or Tut. The explanation was that the latter had benefited in excess of their rights on the marriage of Nyabwogh, Thiep's daughter. Thiep and Dung might also be expected to get the *gwanlen gwande* portions, but did not do so for the same reason.

(v) Ngwoiny (on the maternal side) had a second wife, but she died without issue. Hence there are no *nar gwande*, and Mut and Kun receive these cattle as well as the *wangnen gwande* (*gwandong*).[1]

Number of Cattle Paid Today

Professor Evans-Pritchard points out that—

there is good reason to suppose that till thirty to forty years ago cattle were so plentiful in Nuerland that bridewealth was paid at the ideal rate of 40 head. Of recent years the herds have diminished through rinderpest, and the traditional means of recuperation, raids on Dinka stock, has been checked by the presence of the Anglo-Egyptian government. Diminution has been fairly uniform throughout the whole of Nuerland and it would to-day in all parts be impossible for a man to raise as many as 40 head of cattle for marriage. The usual payment is from 20 to 30.[2]

To rinderpest must be added the ravages of trypanosomiasis, a disease which appears to have increased during the last decade owing to mechanical transmission through other biting flies rather than tsetse. We must also bear in mind that the human population may have been less in those days, for although there are no statistical records available to work on, there are indications that the Nuer are increasing. Some tribes are, however, poorer in cattle than others,[3] and bridewealth payments are not everywhere the same. It would probably be unsafe to state an average figure anywhere without an analysis of a very large number of marriages. Some marriages are referred to by the Nuer as *kwen me keagh*. This expression, which is a contradiction in terms, is used very loosely in this context for a literal translation would imply that they are illegal.[4] What is meant is that the number of cattle paid is much less than normal even by present-day standards, but it should be noted that marriages made in these circumstances

[1] Mut stated that as he and Kun had received many cattle which in normal circumstances would have gone to a half-brother, they proposed to marry a 'ghost-wife' to their father Ngwoiny. Mut would do so (see 'Ghost-Marriage and Bridewealth', pp. 76–8).

[2] Evans-Pritchard, op. cit., p. 254.

[3] See Appendix I.

[4] For the various meanings of *keagh*, see pp. 82, 131, 191, n. 1.

BRIDEWEALTH

are often stable. Moreover it is not usual for the wife's family to press for further payments provided the union is confirmed by the birth of children. It is not, therefore, necessarily the number of cattle paid or the fact that sufficient have been paid to meet the minimum claims which makes a marriage stable, but the social relationship of the two families concerned. In examining the legality of a marriage, a Nuer court may ascertain generally the number of cattle transferred, but will not examine each of the many claims. The most telling evidence in this respect is the performance of the marriage ceremonies, for it is assumed that performance indicates the acceptance of the bride's family and this implies that they have been satisfied in the matter of bridewealth cattle.

Disputes over Bridewealth Payments and Distribution

Disputes over bridewealth between the bridegroom and the bride's family do not often arise. Even if the bridegroom does not pay all the cattle required to meet the claims made at the time of marriage, but promises to do so later and then fails, the bride's family can always threaten a divorce which is usually a sanction strong enough to ensure payment. The claims of the *ji cuongni rar* are usually met first, and if any cattle are forgone or postponed, it is by arrangement with the immediate family of the bride. Moreover claims made by the *ji cuongni* will be against the bride's immediate kinsmen, not against her husband, for the distribution of bridewealth among his wife's family is not his direct concern.

The rules of distribution apply within the group of the wife. These are collectively referred to by the husband as *ji twac* ('people of the skin', or relatives-in-law). Further rules govern the distribution between the father's lineage and the mother's lineage and then lineages brought in by other marital relationships. Disputes over these claims are common, and there is an unfortunate tendency to use the courts as a sanction for the fulfilment of kinship obligations. The majority, however, are settled by the elders of the lineages concerned, and the courts often dismiss such cases as *ruac cieng*, 'home talk', which should be settled within the kinship group.

There may be more than one person standing in a special relationship to the bride which carries with it a claim to part of her bridewealth, and if this is so there is always a tendency to alternate. If a man fails to get cattle on the marriage of one of the daughters, he will expect to do so on the marriage of her sister. Disputes sometimes arise, especially over claims that have remained unpaid in the second generation. Such matters are strictly speaking governed by the rules of inheritance, but so far as cattle are concerned, the rules of distribution are part of inheritance. Two examples are quoted below. Both are typical, and it will be noted that the first was dismissed by the

Dispute between family of Cuhcuh and family of Yegh (Gaawar Nuer Case)

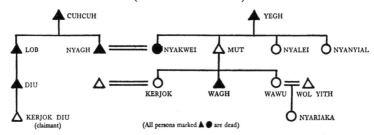

Nyakwei, daughter of Yegh, was married by Nyagh, son of Cuhcuh. Nyakwei died without issue, but there was no dissolution of marriage, Nyagh being content to leave his cattle with Yegh's family. Nyagh, as Nyakwei's husband, would, according to the laws of distribution of bridewealth, be entitled to claim a *yang waca* (cow of the paternal aunt) on the marriage of any of Mut's daughters. In fact the *yang waca* of Kerjok's marriage went to Nyalei and that of Wawu to Nyanyial. Mut promised to give Nyagh the *yang waca* of Wagh's marriage, but it was not paid at the time of her marriage, and she died shortly afterwards. Kerjok Diu as heir to Nyagh (brother's son's son) then claimed *yang waca* on the marriage of Wawu's daughter Nyariaka, on the grounds that it should go to Wagh, whose own *yang waca* should have gone to Nyagh through Nyakwei.

The court was at first puzzled by this case, and said that the *waca* of Nyariaka should go to Wagh's husband. Kerjok Diu then produced evidence that Wagh's marriage had been dissolved as she had died without issue, and pointed out that her sister Kerjok had already received a *yang waca* on the marriage of another of Wawu's daughters. The court was unable to give an exact definition of the law in these circumstances, but dismissed Kerjok Diu's claim on the grounds that it was based on a claim which had not been fulfilled in the time of his grandfather and that his claim had therefore lapsed.

Nyalith Ruac v. Macar Pat (Lak Nuer Case)

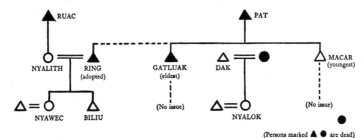

Pat had four sons—Ring (an adopted Dinka), Gatluak (the eldest or *keagh*), Dak (the middle son, or *dar*) and Macar (the youngest or *pegh*).[1] On the

---
[1] For further explanation of these terms of seniority, see p. 191.

marriage of Dak's daughter Nyalok, Macar got a cow (*yang wangnen*) and a cow-calf (*gwanlen*). Ring was by that time dead, but his wife Nyalith received the remainder of the *gwanlen* cattle—the cattle of the paternal uncle—on behalf of her son Biliu, then a minor: a cow, an ox and a bull-calf. On the marriage of Ring's daughter Nyawec, the *ghok gwanlen*—a cow—and the *wangnen*—a cow-calf—were given to Macar again as heir to Gatluak, then dead with no issue. Dak objected to this and, as a protest, seized the cattle held by Nyalith (received on the marriage of Nyalok) for her son. Nyalith then took the matter to court and demanded the transfer of the cattle received by Macar on the marriage of Nyawec, to Dak, so that Dak would give her back her cattle. Court dismissed the case on the grounds that—

> (i) Macar, as heir to Gatluak, has a right to the *wangnen* and *gwanlen* of Nyalok. Dak cannot receive these cattle for the marriage of his *own* daughter.
> (ii) The dispute is strictly between Nyalith and Dak.
> But (iii) it is a purely family matter which they must settle themselves, because Nyalith is living with Dak in leviratic union, he has no male heirs, and all his cattle will anyway go to Biliu to whom Dak is paternal uncle.

6. THE LEGALITY OF MARRIAGE

General Principles

From an analysis of the social and ritual processes of marriage and of the transfer of bridewealth cattle from one group to another, there emerge certain legal principles which are relevant to a study of Nuer law as administered in the courts today:

(i) Apart from the social and ritual processes, the performance of which not only gives stability to marriage but emphasizes the degree of agreement reached at any stage, the key to the legality of a union lies in the transfer of cattle from one kinship group to another on behalf of an individual. The individual thereby obtains rights in his wife which are domestic, economic, and procreative. Even though these are sometimes assumed so far as domestic and economic rights are concerned, they are never assumed in situations where the legal status of the children is concerned unless cattle have been transferred.

(ii) Therefore, in any disputes which concern bridewealth, the return of bridewealth, or rights in the distribution of bridewealth, reference must be made to the individual on whose behalf cattle were transferred. Whether he be alive or dead, he is the nuclear point from which legal discussion must start, and the rights of others are determined by their relationship to him in the kinship structure or the relationship created by marriage. At a later stage, when children are born of the union, all parties concerned become linked through the position of the children in the kinship structure of both sides.

We have seen that, although marriage is still precarious and does not necessarily achieve a high degree of stability until a child is born of the union and the bride takes up her abode permanently with her

LEGALITY OF MARRIAGE

husband, at a certain stage in the proceedings she acquires not only social status as married woman and wife but also legal status. It is at this point that the bridegroom becomes legal husband of the woman.

It is, however, sometimes difficult to determine the exact point at which this occurs. The problem is best examined in reference to wrongs in relation to the woman, and perhaps best exemplified in cases of adultery, for a man cannot claim damages in such a situation unless he is legal husband of the woman concerned. There is in fact considerable variation on this point in Nuerland, and it has become a controversial subject in cases which arise between individuals of different tribes, now brought together through the agency of the courts. Clearly it is ultimately the amount of cattle paid to satisfy the claims of the bride's relatives which determines the legality of a union, but this cannot be expressed as a rigid rule, for an equal number of cattle is not and cannot be transferred in all marriages, and the period over which they are paid is variable. This is particularly true today when there are less cattle in relation to population than before, because to insist on full transfer of bridewealth in one transaction would mean endless delay in collecting bridewealth, and this is not acceptable either to the bridegroom, who is impatient for his bride, or to her family, who wish to use the bridewealth cattle for their own marriages. The legality of marriage therefore finds expression in the degree of agreement reached by the people concerned, this being reflected in each stage of the marriage ceremonies. Some tribes consider that acceptance of the cattle negotiated at the *twoc* ceremony, and particularly at the rite called *yier nyal*, even if they appear totally inadequate when compared to the bridewealth ideal, amounts to legal recognition. Others consider that legality is established at the *muot* ceremony which follows, and certainly it is at this ceremony that the change of status of the bride from a girl (*nyal*) to a married woman (*ciek*) in relation to society as a whole is most clearly symbolized.[1] For the first time she is released from her family (*loiny deb*) and from parental care. For the first time she is introduced publicly into the home of her bridegroom (*noong nyal*) and physical consummation is recognized. Further, she is ceremonially shaved by her bridegroom's female relatives (*muot*), and this not only has ritual significance in connexion with her fertility, but signifies, too, her acceptance as a married woman, her status being determined in relation to other women of the household and through

---

[1] It might be argued that the ceremony performed at the *twoc*, when the bride is dressed in the clothes which signify a married woman, symbolizes a change of status from 'girl' (*nyal*) to 'married woman' (*ciek*). Presumably this is so among those tribes who consider that the *twoc* establishes legal marriage. But it must be remembered that it is not so much her general status, as her status in relation to her husband and his kin which is important from the legal aspect, and this is only brought out at the *muot*. The terms *nyal* and *ciek* do not clarify the problem, because a man will often refer to his affianced bride as *ciek-da* (my wife) at a very early stage in the proceedings, and the woman is often referred to as *nyal* long after the *muot*.

126   LEGALITY OF MARRIAGE

them to all members of their group. These ceremonies are referred to generally as *muot nyal*, and many Nuer tribes consider that this is the point where legal status is established. In these tribes the first question asked at the opening of a legal case will be '*ce nyal mut?*', 'has the girl been shaved?', if the legality of the marriage is in doubt. Nuer assume that if the ceremonies have reached this stage, the girl's family have admitted the legality of the union, whether the cattle paid, in comparison with other marriages, are adequate or not.

As soon as the legality of the marriage is established, the legal husband or, in the case of 'ghost-marriages', his legal representative, who is the man who has married on his behalf, accepts liabilities in the woman's future behaviour. If she kills someone it will be he and his kinsmen who must pay compensation (*thung*), although her own family will undoubtedly assist them in such circumstances; if she injures someone, and this is naturally more frequent than homicide, it will be her husband who has to pay damages. Equally if she is killed or injured, compensation should be paid to her husband, and it will be his legal right to receive it, even if he is usually willing to hand over some of the cattle to her family. These rights are extended to his kinsmen, since his rights are always limited by the position he holds as a member of a kinship group, and in this strictly legal sense the wife must now be regarded as a member of his lineage rather than her own. Cattle have been paid for her; rights in her life have been transferred to those who paid the cattle. This issue is not often in question in disputes which appear before the courts, but, as already mentioned, it is often raised in disputes over adultery. The defendant will plead that the woman is not legally married (*kere kwen ke ghok*—'she is not married with cattle') and that he is only liable to her family. This is usually to his advantage because her family cannot claim damages for adultery; there can be no adultery if the woman is not legally married. They can claim damages for the seduction of an unmarried girl (*ruok dhu nyal*), but the number of cattle demanded is less than in adultery (*ruok ciek*).

Recent Legislation at the Nuer Chiefs' Council Meeting of 1945

The subject of the legality of marriage was discussed by chiefs from all parts of Nuerland in 1945. Opinion was divided, though it was generally agreed that in the past at any rate all ceremonies up to and including the *muot* should be performed before a man could safely claim all legal rights in his wife. The Eastern Nuer tribes, represented by the Jikany Dhoar, maintained that (i) a man has legal rights in his wife as soon as she comes to live with him and has left home with the permission of her family. Other Nuer tribes argued (ii) that it was the *muot* ceremony alone which was important, and that a woman is not legally married until this has been performed. In fact, there is no great difference in these opinions because in a normal marriage a woman's family will rarely allow her to take up residence with her husband until the *muot* has been performed.

Finally in this connexion, I must comment on a statement made by Professor Evans-Pritchard in his most recent book on the Nuer. He says:

> Most broken marriages occur during or shortly after the nuptial ceremonies. One cannot properly speak of divorce at this stage because in Nuer eyes marriage is incomplete till a child has been born. That till the birth of a child the wife is considered to belong to her own kin and not to her husband's kin is shown not only in her continuing to live with her parents but in other ways, most noticeably by the fact that the husband is held responsible for her death should she die in her first childbirth. He then has to pay compensation for homicide (*thung yika*).[1]

The use here of the word 'incomplete' seems to me relative. If a 'complete' marriage is one which is legally indissoluble, then this condition 'is reached only at a much later stage when at least two, and probably three, children have been born. If it is 'complete' when the rights in the woman are legally transferred from her family to her husband, then this occurs much earlier in the proceedings, at some time between the *twoc* and *muot* ceremonies, and usually long before the birth of the first child. Nor does the wife necessarily remain with her family until the first child is born though it is usual for her to return to them to give birth to it, a custom which is common to nearly all Nilotic peoples. At this point and after it any outsider would have to pay *ruok ciek*, compensation for adultery with a married woman, which is payable to her husband, and not *ruok nyal*, compensation for intercourse with an unmarried girl, which is payable to her family.

It therefore seems to me more correct to say that marriage is legally valid after the *muot*, is not dissoluble after the birth of two or often three children, and that the likelihood of divorce diminishes with the birth of each child, but I should not like to say at what point the Nuer consider it 'complete'. Finally it is incorrect to say that a husband will have to pay bloodwealth, *thung yüka*, should his wife die in giving birth to her first child. *Thung yüka* is an indemnity demanded only when the child is the result of an illicit union and is not applicable to the husband within the institution of marriage. I have already explained that a man is not liable to pay bloodwealth should he accidentally or intentionally kill his wife. Such a liability ceases as soon as bridewealth cattle have been transferred and the *muot* ceremony performed. This also applies to *thung yüka*, and the only circumstances in which a woman's family might justifiably demand it from

---

[1] Evans-Pritchard, *Kinship and Marriage among the Nuer*, p. 93.

128 CHILDREN

her husband is before the *muot* and before he has met their claims for bridewealth, in which case strictly speaking the man is not her husband at all.

7. THE LEGITIMACY OF CHILDREN

Establishment of Legitimacy by Legal Marriage

Legal marriage is performed by the transfer of a number of cattle acceptable to the woman's family, and usually also by the performance of ceremonies and ritual observance. Children born of such unions are legally the children of the man who transferred the cattle or on whose behalf the cattle were transferred, and his rights in those children, and the rights which descend to his heirs, are valid and inalienable unless the cattle are returned. No conflict can theoretically arise, for a woman cannot have more than one legal husband at one time. Nor can any one of her children have more than one legal father or *pater*, though sometimes different children of the same mother may have different legal fathers. From the legal aspect, legitimacy brings to male children status and privilege as members of the legal father's lineage and the rights of inheritance from that father. They acquire rights in the cattle of the kinship group—rights which are determined by their position in the kinship structure; rights to cattle inherited and to cattle brought in by the marriages of females of that lineage. Female children provide a means by which cattle will be acquired by the lineage in the future on the normal principles of distribution of bridewealth (*ghok kwi gwande*), and they further stand as a legal link between the lineages of the father and the mother, for the mother's relatives may also claim cattle from their bridewealth (*ghok kwi mande*).

Thus the children of a simple legal marriage will belong to the legal husband by whomsoever begotten (for they may be begotten in adultery—which does not affect the legality of the marriage). In 'ghost-marriage' children are attached to the name of the man on whose behalf the marriage was performed, although in other respects their relationship to their physiological father (*genitor*) is normally the same as that found in simple legal marriage. The *genitor* is usually the principal heir to the *pater* by reason of the fact that he performed the ceremonies on the father's behalf, and also through normal rules of inheritance derived from their relative positions in the kinship structure of their lineage. It is probable that the children will be brought up in their *genitor's* household, and he is therefore also their foster-father. He may die, however, and his position will be assumed by his own heir.

Similarly, in leviratic union or 'widow-concubinage' the status of the children is determined from that of their legal father, although he is dead. Their physiological father will have authority over them and rights in them derived from his relationship to their legal father, although, as we have seen, as *genitor* and foster-father he may acquire certain personal rights to cattle subsequently paid as bridewealth for daughters. These rights in bridewealth cattle, which are not in any case substantial, may be acquired whatever the circumstances, but it is clear that the greater the degree of coincidence in one man as heir to the *pater*, as *genitor*, and as foster-father, the closer the relationship between him and the children and the greater the rights he will hold. If there is a high degree of coincidence there will be no great need for an exact definition of rights.

In these circumstances the legitimacy of children in respect to the acquisition and inheritance of rights is clear. The law is logical and can always be carried to logical conclusions even though there is often a conflict in fact. It is obvious that there is an infinite variety of possible situations depending on the relationships within the kinship structure of the lineage of the persons concerned and the functions performed by persons outside the lineage as *genitor* or foster-father. For the purpose of illustration a number of such situations are recorded.

In Simple Legal Marriage

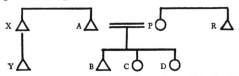

A married P by the transfer of bridewealth to R and his family.

(i) If all the persons recorded above are living, A, who is the legal father of B, C, and D, will be the link through whom their relationship to other members of A's family and lineage is traced, and A will be the point from which the distribution of the bridewealth of C and D will be determined.

(ii) If A is dead, the point of determination will be the same, but X, A's brother or, if dead, his son Y, will represent A, unless by that time B, A's son, has come of age.

(iii) It will probably be X (though it may be another brother or some more distant agnatic kinsman) who brings up A's children and will stand in the relationship of foster-father to B, C, and D, and as he is also A's heir until B grows up, he will perform most of the tasks of *pater*.

In 'Ghost-Marriage'

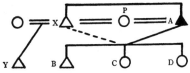

X married P on behalf of his brother A.

(i) Three children, B, C, and D, are born of this union. In this case A is legal father (*pater*) of the children and X is the *genitor*, but since X is also brother of A he will represent him as *pater*, and the distinction is not stressed.

(ii) Hence in all matters concerning kinship obligations and inheritance, particularly in the matter of the bridewealth of C and D, A is the first point of determination in the kinship structure, and X, as his uterine brother and legal heir, comes next. X may expect the *pater's* portion of the bridewealth, a portion which may be inherited by his son Y, though in some cases—depending on their relative ages—B may inherit these as well as claiming the brother's portion.

The position may not be so simple as this. For example:

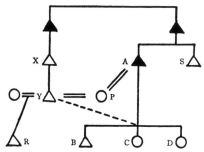

Y, one of A's less closely related kinsmen, marries P on behalf of A with cattle which he has inherited from A. Y is both *genitor* and foster-father of the children B, C, and D, and as heir to A he can claim many of the privileges of *pater*. He would normally claim the *ghok gwande*, the father's portion, on the marriages of C and D, though this will depend partly on the configuration of the lineage, since S or his heirs may have counter claims, but normally they could only claim the *ghok gwanlen*, the paternal uncle's portion.

In Leviratic Union

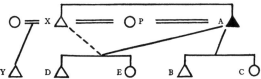

A marries P. She gives birth to B and C of whom A is both *genitor* and *pater*.

A dies and P goes to live with A's brother X, who begets D and E. A remains *pater* of all these children, and they will all call themselves by his name. X is naturally foster-father of B and C and he is *genitor* of D and E. He is also *pater* to all four in the sense that he represents their interests and is legal heir to A, though here the future claims of A's sons will have greater emphasis than in 'ghost-marriage'.

In 'Widow-Concubinage'

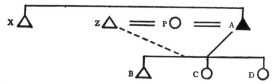

A marries P but dies before any children are born. P goes to live with Z, a relationship which is recognized by X, who is heir to A. Z is the *lum*

CHILDREN OF CONCUBINES

131

or lover of P and has received the formal recognition of her late husband's kinsmen. Three children are born, B, C, and D. All these remain legally the children of A, and their rights are determined from his position in the kinship structure, but X, as heir to A, performs all the duties of *pater*. Z is merely *genitor* and in this case foster-father. On the marriage of C and D, he cannot claim the father's (*gwan*) portion, but he may expect to receive *yang leta*, which in this case may amount to two or three head of cattle since the union is a stable and agreed one. In such cases Z might be the *genitor* only while X brings the children up in his home.

The variety of circumstances in the examples given above is considerable, but all situations are not covered. The legal and sociological relationships of the members of a Nuer family are often a complicated matter. The family preserves the outward appearance of a simple legal union, and in day-to-day affairs the differences are not stressed. Analysis will, however, often reveal a complicated pattern and a variety of legal relationships which are relevant in the distribution of bridewealth and inheritance.

The system may appear complex and sometimes confusing. It is not so to the Nuer themselves and, in a court session, even if the court members are not already aware of the relationships involved, a few introductory remarks and a few pertinent questions will give them a clear picture of the legal aspect of the case before them.

Disputes sometimes arise over inheritance and the obligations of kinsmen in the collection of bridewealth on behalf of others. Clearly in such cases the legality of an individual's position within the framework of the lineage is relevant. Sometimes the *pater* himself, or more often his heirs, refuse to recognize the claims of a legal son who has been brought up in the home of the *genitor*. Sometimes the *genitor* acquires cattle on behalf of his natural son and holds them in trust. At a later date he or his heirs may refuse to hand them over, which amounts to a breach of trust. Such disputes are not frequent, and in the past were usually settled because public opinion will always press for the fulfilment of kinship obligations based on legitimate relationships. The courts are now often called upon to intervene.

The Position of Children born of Unmarried Concubines

Children born out of legal wedlock are illegitimate,[1] and strictly speaking should be linked to the lineage of their mother's father. Sometimes their *genitor* will choose to legalize their position by marrying their mother with cattle, and usually her family will press him to do so, particularly if she is not *keagh*, in the sense of a woman who is unable to remain long with one husband, or has been married before

[1] I am aware that the use of the term 'illegitimate' may be challenged. Children born in wedlock are *legitimately* the offspring of their mother's legal husband; children born of an unmarried woman are *legitimately* linked to their mother's lineage.

CHILDREN

and divorced. There is no moral stigma attached to illegitimate children, though the instability of their position may in later life put upon them psychological strains and cause emotional conflicts. A man who is linked to a lineage through his mother will have to compete with the legitimate members of that lineage, and, since his mother may not have brought bridewealth cattle to the family, he may be poorly treated by them. He will sometimes find it difficult to collect sufficient cattle to marry a wife though this is not by any means always so.

The *genitor* may also legitimize his offspring by payment of *ruok gaanke* (or *ruok muor*). This is a legitimization fee, and in no sense a marriage, for it does not carry with it any rights in the mother of the child, but only in the child itself.[1] It is further a more individual transaction between the *genitor* and the woman's immediate kinsmen, her father or brothers. If the woman is subsequently married to another man by transference of bridewealth, even if the number of cattle accepted by her kinsmen is less than normal, a conflict may arise between the legal father of her first child, who has acquired this position by the payment of *ruok gaanke*, and her legal husband, who has married her with bridewealth. Legal marriage usually implies legal paternity of all the children of the wife, whether born immediately[2] before or after the marriage. Hence, the legal husband will often insist on the return of the *ruok* cattle from the woman's family to the *genitor*; otherwise the first child would in one context be the legal son of the man who paid the *ruok*, in another the legal son of its mother's husband. This is a confusion of legal status and is not proper. Nuer would say that the cattle of the *genitor* of a child, especially in cases of adultery, and those of the legal husband cannot meet in one herd. It is a situation which may not only cause legal difficulties in the future, especially in the matter of inheritance of posthumous rights, but also bring upon those concerned the disapproval of the ancestral spirits. This will lead to sickness and misfortune. Yet the woman may continue to move from one man to another, living with each for a short period and bearing children to some or all of them. If each legitimizes his child or children, it is possible for her to be the mother of several children each of which has a different legal father. Thus, though it is possible for the children of one mother to have different physiological fathers, it is not possible for one child to have more than one legal father. I quote one case by way of illustration taken from court records.

---

[1] A position similar to that of a husband who divorces his wife but allows her family sufficient cattle to legitimize the children (see pp. 134, 139).

[2] I.e. children in arms, but not older children. The point is controversial, and there does not seem to be any set agreement. If the child is weaned before the new marriage takes place it will probably not go to its mother's new husband. If it is born within a month or two before or after the marriage it will almost certainly be accepted as a child of the new husband.

A married B. She gave birth to a son, C, but then deserted her husband and went to live with X. A's marriage to B was then dissolved by order of the court. While living with X, B gave birth to another child, this time a daughter F. B's family strongly objected to X, who had made no attempt to produce bridewealth to legalize the union, and, through the intervention of the court, he was made to leave her. Later he was prevailed upon to pay *ruok gaanke* to retain legal parenthood of his natural daughter F. B returned home, but was later married by T, who agreed to hand over a much reduced bridewealth, all that her family could expect in the circumstances. Her former husband had forgone all claims on C, but, on B's remarriage, T claimed that all the children should be his. X was persuaded to accept return of the cattle he had paid as *ruok gaanke*. The two children, and those born subsequently, were then regarded as T's. This complicated situation was reached in four stages, the final stage being a permanent one and, unless further difficulties arise, it will remain legally valid in the future.

(i)  A married B by payment of bridewealth and is therefore legal father of C.

(ii)  X seduces B, who goes to live with him. A dissolves the union and forgoes all rights in C.

(iii) 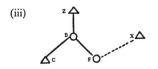 F is born and would normally belong legally to her mother's lineage, i.e. through Z, but X pays *ruok gaanke* and becomes her legal father. X then leaves B.

(iv) 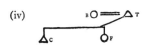 B returns home and is eventually married to T (who in this case paid only seven head of cattle for her). X's *ruok* cattle are returned to him and T claims legal parenthood of F. T also claims that he is legal father of C.

In this particular instance the mother's position is constant, for the legitimacy of the children is not traced through her except in stage (iii) in respect of F but not of C. The position of the *pater* has changed throughout. In future, when C and F have reached maturity, their position will be determined by the final picture shown in stage (iv). C will call himself son of T, though he might—as is often the case—revolt and link himself to his physiological father A. T's lineage will have undisputed claim to the father's portion of F's bridewealth, the *ghok kwi gwande*, while B's family will claim the *ghok kwi mande*, a claim which cannot be altered whatever the circumstances.

The Position of Children born of Adultery

By definition adultery cannot happen unless the woman concerned is legally married, in which case all her children, whoever the *genitor*, belong to her legal husband. He is always *pater* so long as the union remains legally valid. An adulterer cannot under any circumstances

134 CHILDREN

legitimize his child by the payment of *ruok gaanke* while the marriage stands. A child cannot have two legal fathers at one time. It is for this reason that when an adulterer has been prevailed upon, or compelled by a court, to pay full compensation to the woman's legal husband—*ruok ciek* (not more, but sometimes less, than six head of cattle)—if a child is born and attributed to the act of adultery, all those cattle must be returned except *yang kule*,[1] which is not part of the indemnity but has special ritual significance. Unless this is done there may be confusion over the true legal father of the child: a confusion of *ruok ciek*, which is paid as compensation to the husband, and *ruok gaanke*, which should be paid to the woman's family to legitimize the child. In fact, there is not necessarily any confusion, because the compensation (*ruok ciek*) goes to the legal husband as damages, while *ruok gaanke* as a legitimization fee *should* go to the woman's family. A confusion may arise in the future, however, especially if there is a divorce, and usually a wronged husband will return the cattle without argument. This rule applies in all tribes west of the Nile, among the Zeraf tribes, and in Lou, but is not followed in Eastern Jikany.[2] We shall consider this matter again in connexion with divorce and adultery.

The Position of Children on Dissolution of Marriage

As will be seen later, if a legal union is dissolved the husband may retain legal parenthood of any children born prior to dissolution by leaving sufficient cattle as legitimization fees with his wife's family.[3]

Legitimization Fees: Recent Legislation

Fees payable for this purpose have varied considerably from one Nuer tribe to another. At the Chiefs' meeting of 1945, they were standardized as follows:

> for a male child 5 head of cattle
> for a female child 6 head of cattle.

Chiefs said that the fee payable for a girl should be higher than that for a boy because in the case of a girl the mother's family could expect to benefit materially on her marriage.

If a man declares his intention of legitimizing the child at once, he will not be expected to pay more than the five or six head of cattle, as the case may be. If, however, he disowns the child or declares that he will have nothing to do with it, he will have to pay a higher

---

[1] See also under Adultery (p. 156).
[2] See recent legislation on this subject, pp. 166–8.
[3] See under Dissolution of Marriage, p. 149.

STATUS OF *PATER*

rate—up to ten head of cattle—if he wishes to legitimize it later. Chiefs said that he had a right to do so even if the girl's family objected, provided the woman had not been legally married to someone else in the meantime.

If a man pays legitimization fees and the child subsequently dies at an early age, all his cattle must be returned to him except a bull-calf and a cow-calf: in other words, the normal compensation for seduction of the girl, *ruok nyal*,[1] when no child is born as a result.[2]

8. CONCLUSION

The complexities of Nuer marriage and other forms of procreative union may appear chaotic. At first sight the relations of the sexes may even seem to be indiscriminate in the extreme. This is not so, and to the Nuer themselves there is rarely any confusion at all. The terminology which describes special relationships, special circumstances in marriage and descent, besides the normal terminology of kinship, is sufficient to place any man in his correct status both within his patrilineal descent group and in Nuer society as a whole. This status is determined from the status of the *pater*, and the basis of all marital relations lies in the relatively stable position of the *pater*. It is true that the *pater* is sometimes changed, but not without the passage of cattle from one group to another, an event which stamps the change indelibly in the minds of the people concerned. This legal principle runs through the whole structure of Nuer society because it is the basis of the lineage organization upon which other and larger units of society are built. A Nuer finds his position in the lineage through his legal father or *pater* and from no one else, and, as a member of his father's lineage, can ultimately be placed in correct relationship to the members of other lineages within his tribal segment and through them to the tribe. He is a member of a patrilineal descent group (*thok dwiel*), and that group has a recognized position in the community, which is composed of similar lineages. He has through his *pater* a position in the lineage which provides the means for social, economic and political security.

There is adequate literature on this subject, and it is not the purpose of this book to enter into the details of the structure of Nuer society. It must be emphasized again, however, that a full understanding of Nuer law, both the customary law operated by sanctions prevailing in the past and the law now operated by the courts when those sanctions tend to fail, is impossible without a full understanding of the political and social organization of the Nuer. Law is after all only a feature of that organization as well as a means through which the

---

[1] See under Violation of Rights in Women, Chapter IV, Section 2.
[2] Extracts from minutes of Nuer Chiefs' Council, 1945.

CHILDREN

organization can be maintained, and in so far as Nuer courts operate today they are in fact a means by which it is maintained.

The multiple factors and circumstances which have bearing on a dispute over cattle cannot be summarized, but if the principles are understood it is easy enough to see the issues. Cattle provide the key to status within the kinship group and between two kinship groups when marital relationship is established. The payment of bridewealth cattle determines the legality of the union, and if this is not done, the legitimacy of the children can be made valid by the payment of fees in cattle. Disputes often arise over such matters, but it is rarely the legal aspect which is denied; it is rather that certain persons refuse to honour their legal obligations, and the court then enforces the law. As we shall see in the next part of this chapter, other cases arise over the return of bridewealth cattle in divorce and the dissolution of marriage, over the non-fulfilment of the obligations of kinship in the distribution of cattle, and from claims on the bridewealth of daughters, both by the mother's and the father's kinsmen. Disputes also arise over wrongs committed, violations of rights established in legal marriage, and the legitimization of children. Whether, in the settlement of the dispute before the court, the legal principles can be accurately and rigidly applied, depends on the circumstances. The law is not sufficiently exact to cover all situations.

PART II
DIVORCE LAWS AND THE DISSOLUTION OF MARRIAGE

WE have seen that marriage is achieved by the performance of social and ritual ceremonies and the transfer of cattle to the kinsmen of the bride. It is now necessary to examine the reverse process by which a union is dissolved. This involves no public ceremonies or ritual, but only the return of bridewealth cattle, with various deductions in respect of rights received and, in the case of children, rights retained by the husband. A distinction must be made between active divorce in which both parties are living at the time of the proceedings, and dissolution of marriage which sometimes follows the death of the wife, though not the death of the husband. There is no distinction in terminology; both situations are *dak kwen*, 'the breaking of marriage', and the same general principles apply, but the details vary.

1. DISSOLUTION OF MARRIAGE ON DEATH OF THE WIFE

The death of his wife is usually considered to give the husband some right to claim the return of his cattle, although he will not always exercise that right. It will depend on a variety of circumstances. If the union has lasted a long time and the husband is on good terms with his wife's family, he may not wish to sever his connexion with them, though he will usually demand return of the bridewealth cattle if she has borne him no children at all. Her family will not necessarily dispute the case, and often wish to assist him. There is after all a human element in Nuer marriages which a coldly analytical approach tends to ignore. The birth of one or two children will alter the situation substantially. The father will in any case usually leave sufficient cattle to retain legal parenthood over them. The number of cattle varied in the past from tribe to tribe and, in some tribes, according to the sex of the children, but for two children a man will have to leave at least ten head of cattle (legitimization fees have now been standardized at five head for a boy and six for a girl),[1] and, after deduction of these, in some marriages there will not be many cattle left to return. Nowadays many Nuer get married with as little as twelve or fifteen head of cattle, and if some of them have died in the possession of the wife's family they will not be returnable. In other marriages a larger number of cattle may have been transferred, and

[1] See under Legitimacy of Children, pp. 128–35.

138 DISSOLUTION OF MARRIAGE

their progeny may be considerable. There is no hard and fast rule, nor any convention which governs the attitude taken by the husband. At the same time his rights in such circumstances are usually clear, and nowadays a Nuer court will tend to uphold those rights even though they will nearly always attempt to find a compromise.

In fact disputes over the return of cattle when the wife has died are rare because relations between a husband and his wife's kinsmen are not strained, as they must necessarily be in a case of divorce where both husband and wife are living. No generalization is safe on this subject beyond saying that when the wife dies without issue the husband is likely to demand and receive without undue argument all his cattle; that if one child is born the wife's family will retain sufficient only to legitimize that child; and if two children are born the husband may be content to leave all his bridewealth cattle with the wife's family or may demand the remainder after deduction of legitimization fees. A Nuer court will sometimes allow the latter, sometimes not. If more than two children have been born the return of bridewealth is regarded as impossible. It is then considered that the wife has performed her obligations in this respect in full. It must be remembered that the birth of children is also an indication of the time factor and, generally speaking, the longer a union has lasted the less likely is it to be broken. I quote here four actual cases, taken from a large number of similar ones, which indicate both the principles and the tendency to follow them:

(a) Majok Depyang v. Cah Macoat (Dok Nuer Case)

Liah Macoat (brother of Cah) married Majok's daughter. The woman died leaving one male child. Liah then began to claim return of his cattle but died before negotiations were completed. Cah continued this claim as Liah's heir and further demanded return of all cattle and stated that he did not wish to legitimize the child. Chiefs' court ruled that all cattle should be returned with the exception of five head for the boy (*ruok muor*).

(b) Carok Jyath v. Won Teang (Dok Nuer Case)

Carok married Won's daughter, who died after bearing two children. Court ruled that Carok should receive all cattle paid by him after deductions had been made for the children.

(c) Kwic Thowath v. Ngotkek Deng (Bul Nuer Case)

Kwic married Ngotkek's brother's daughter. After bearing him three children she died, and Kwic demanded return of his cattle after legitimization fees had been deducted. Court ruled that the woman had fulfilled her obligations and that Kwic had no right to any cattle. Court, however, stated that Ngotkek should assist by payment of *ghok tuoke*.[1] This judgement was confirmed on appeal.

(d) Cuol Dak v. Liep Balou (Dok Nuer Case)

Liep married Cuol's daughter who died after bearing him four children. Liep subsequently claimed return of his cattle after deductions for the children

---

[1] *Ghok (yang) tuoke*. The significance of this payment is explained later.

DEATH OF WIFE

had been assessed. Court ruled that no dissolution of marriage was possible, but ordered Cuol to give Liep a cow (*yang tuoke*) 'for his sister's sons'. This judgement was confirmed on appeal.

These cases are not unusual, and similar disputes and judgements may be found in any court case book. They provide illustrations of the principle that on the death of a wife who has borne one, and in some instances, two, children, the husband may expect the return of all his cattle with the exception of sufficient for him to retain legal parenthood of those children. If, however, the wife has borne three or more children she is considered to have fulfilled her obligations, and there is no claim on her family at all, though they may be expected to assist her husband by payment of what the Nuer refer to as *yang tuoke*. This privilege sometimes extends to the husband's heirs, if he too is dead, should a cow or cows be required for milk for the children. The distinction is clear. In the first instance the union is dissolved and no longer exists, even though the children continue legitimate and therefore legally members of their father's lineage with all the privileges which that entails. In the second instance there is no dissolution at all, but the wife's kinsmen are expected to assist her widower, either to get married again or at least to bring up the children.

Ghok tuoke

Yang or *ghok tuoke* means literally 'the cow or cows of the cooking pot', and in this sense refers to the loss of the domestic assistance a husband should receive from his wife. It is also sometimes referred to as *ghok pithe gaat*,[1] or 'the cattle of bringing up the children'. There is therefore contained in the idea the necessity both of compensating a widower for this loss of domestic assets, and of providing him with cattle for the subsistence of the children of the union. The number of cattle which may be claimed varies considerably from tribe to tribe. Among the Lak only one cow at most is paid, while some tribes give as an ideal at least six head of cattle. The Leik, who are comparatively rich in cattle, give eight as the accepted number, and state a definite form of distribution among the dead woman's relatives upon whom the obligation falls. The brother and half-brother of the wife (*deman kwi mande* and *deman kwi gwande*) should each pay a cow; her father's uterine brother (*gwanlen mande*) and father's half-brother (*gwanlen gwande*) should each pay a cow; likewise her father's sister (*wac*) and mother's sister (*manlen*), her mother's brother and half-brother (*nar mande* and *nar gwande*) should each pay a cow.[2]

The payment of *ghok tuoke* is not always honoured, but it is a

[1] Here used in a different context from those claimed outside marriage (see pp. 111–2).

[2] In other words, an equitable distribution among the kinsmen of the wife, both paternal and maternal, who have already received a portion of the bridewealth according to the pattern of distribution.

140   DIVORCE

definite right, and a Nuer court will often enforce it. In this it is expressing public opinion, which feels that a reasonable man will in certain circumstances assist his brother-in-law and his sister's sons. There is, however, an obvious difference of opinion which may be seen in the four different views on the subject expressed by the chiefs at the meeting of 1945 as follows:

That if a woman dies after fulfilling her procreative obligations—

(i) The legal husband has a right to at least one cow, and the *ji cuongni rar* (the more remote relatives who have received a portion of the bridewealth) may be expected to give him an additional cow or two to help him to marry another wife; but this should be a matter of agreement and should not be enforced in the courts.

(ii) As above, but that the *ji cuongni rar* should be compelled to assist him if necessary.

(iii) No more than one cow should be given to the husband.

(iv) *Yang tuoke* plus one cow from the wife's maternal uncle's portion (*nare*) and one from the paternal uncle's portion (*gwanlende*) must be given to the husband.

In fact the payment of *ghok tuoke* is largely a matter of agreement; a compromise in the case of a man whose wife has died without issue, or with too few children to prevent him from claiming the return of all the bridewealth cattle; an obligation if his wife has fulfilled her obligations in this respect, and he cannot hope for any return. In the first instance, being a compromise and a convenient way of avoiding dissolution of the union, more cattle will be paid than in the second instance, where the payment is usually restricted to one, or at most two, cows.

Yang muon

When a wife dies without having fulfilled her procreative obligations at all and no children have been born of the union, the husband is sometimes expected to leave with her family one cow known as *yang muon*, 'the cow of the earth or burial', representing a token payment for the woman's death, if he claims the return of bridewealth. This is largely of ritual significance, but is sometimes given in place of the *ruath miemni* and *yang yaatni*, deductions left by the husband in divorce when both parties are living, which will be described later.

2. DISSOLUTION OF MARRIAGE WHEN BOTH PARTIES ARE LIVING

The simplest method of recording the law and circumstances relevant to divorce is to describe some of the commonest situations which arise as exemplified in actual cases brought before the courts. Before doing so, it is necessary to consider what the Nuer believe to be grounds for divorce.

Grounds for Divorce

Marriage implies a stable relationship between the husband and his kinsmen on the one hand, and the wife and her kinsmen on the other. The relationship is maintained by a complex system of reciprocal obligations, duties, and conventional patterns of behaviour. In connexion with the actual relationship of the couple as individuals there are errors, breaches of good behaviour or of recognized rights which the Nuer will quote as the usual causes of divorce. A man may claim a divorce from his wife for the following reasons:

(i) *Barrenness.* If his wife fails to produce children at all, a divorce will usually be demanded by the husband, and all the cattle will be returned to him. If she bears only one child or two at most (again the exact number of children is controversial) and then fails to produce over a number of years, a divorce may follow and the cattle are returned with the exception of those left to legitimize such children as exist. Barrenness amounts to failure of the woman to fulfil those procreative obligations to which her husband has a legal right. Continued mortality among the wife's children is also a common reason for divorce.

(ii) *Nagging and Grumbling.* A Nuer may institute a divorce against his wife if she is an unpleasant character and wearies him with her continual grumbling, especially if, in a polygynous household, she fails to get on with her co-wives or with her husband's female relatives.

(iii) *Laziness.* A Nuer has domestic and economic rights in his wife, and he may call for a divorce if she is lazy in preparing his food, slack in household duties and in milking the cattle or cultivating the gardens. In this case she fails to fulfil her economic and domestic obligations towards her husband.

(iv) *Adultery.* A man may institute a divorce if he discovers that his wife has committed adultery, but he will rarely do so unless she persists in adultery either with one man or with a number of men.

(v) *Desertion.* If a wife runs away to live with another man, her husband is more likely to seek a divorce and the return of his cattle, although he may ignore the loss of her physical assets if she has borne sufficient children to his name.

These are the reasons given by Nuer if asked to quote the usual causes of divorce when instituted by the husband. In this the attitude of mind is not confined to the individual but extends to the kinship group. Therefore there must usually be a reason which is accepted as a conventional one and will receive the backing of the husband's relatives and be recognized by the community in which he lives. The actual cause of divorce is usually a combination of such reasons; the wife is lazy and also an adulteress; or she is lazy besides bearing no children; or she is all of these things. By far the most important consideration, however, is her function in producing male children to further the name of the husband's lineage, or female children to bring to them cattle in the form of bridewealth—in itself a means of marrying women into the group and therefore producing more children to the name of the lineage. It is her function in furthering the continuity of the kinship group in posterity which concerns her husband's kinsmen most acutely.

The reasons given by the husband as grounds for divorce, or the reasons which make him wish for a divorce, are less cogent than those which must be produced by a wife to convince her family that life with her husband is no longer bearable. Her family have in a sense much more to lose, for they must return the bridewealth cattle, and it often happens that they will not receive so many on her remarriage, especially if she has a reputation for barrenness or for being a shrew. In these circumstances they will resist the demands of the wife for dissolution of marriage as much as they can. The grounds for divorce which will receive the support of a wife's family are as follows:

(i) *Impotence or Sterility of the Husband.* A woman may divorce her husband if she bears no children and it is known that her husband, a man of virile years, is impotent. In such a situation her family will usually acknowledge her plea for a divorce and allow her to marry elsewhere, even though her husband has paid a very satisfactory bridewealth for her. If, however, the husband is an old man of failing physical powers they have probably arranged the marriage out of greed for his cattle or the desire for a useful political alliance, which is an important consideration, and may use force to compel her to stay with her husband. But in most cases of this sort the husband will allow his wife to take a lover and will be glad if she begets children by this means, for the children are legally his own.

(ii) *Stinginess.* Stinginess is sometimes cited as grounds for divorce. The husband may resent his wife's hospitality to her friends and neighbours, and meanness of this sort is considered particularly reprehensible by the Nuer. What is really meant by this, however, is that the husband is stingy in the giving of those small items—food, tobacco, presents of spears and so on—which his wife's people expect. These are not legal rights but obligations inherent in the marital relationship, and they symbolize the respect he should have for all his wife's relatives.

(iii) *Failure to support the Wife.* If the husband fails to fulfil his economic duties towards his wife and children; if he is too lazy to cultivate, too lazy or weak to hunt or fish, or too poor in cattle to provide sufficient milk, her family may seek a divorce. A husband, however, who is poor in cattle may make up for the deficiency by industrious cultivation, hunting, and fishing.

GROUNDS FOR DIVORCE

(iv) *Ill-treatment.* A woman may demand a divorce and receive the support of her family if her husband persistently ill-treats her (*ciang jiegh*) or beats her without reason. Her brother will often seek to protect her from serious maltreatment, and her family are interested in her welfare.

Whether the family of the wife will support her depends on a variety of circumstances and a combination of all matters which are conventionally regarded as grounds for divorce. They may agree with her if her husband not only persistently ill-treats her but also is lax in his duties towards them or does not approach them with the respect (*thek*) which is due to relatives-in-law. If he has paid substantial bridewealth for her, it is, of course, in their interests that the marriage should continue, but this may be outweighed by other considerations. It is their desire too that a daughter of the house should have children, though their feeling in this respect is not so intense as that of the husband's family. Her children, although legally placed in the patrilineal lineage of their father, will be an asset to the maternal line. We have seen that in the marriage a substantial part of the bridewealth goes to the maternal kin, and the matter of the husband's potency is therefore of practical concern to them. Moreover the final consideration which will often compel them to seek a divorce, whatever the difficulties and inconveniences to themselves, is the fear that she will run away to some other part of the country, in which case they may lose not only the cattle of this marriage but the possibility of getting others from her remarriage. In extreme cases she may even commit suicide.[1]

It is the interaction of all these considerations and circumstances which determines the stability of marriage or the reverse. They are in fact features of the relations subsisting between the two groups concerned: first between the husband and his wife, then through them between their families and by extension between the two kinship groups as a whole. As children are born of the union, so stability increases and the likelihood of dissolution by the return of bridewealth gradually disappears until, in the event of three or more children having been born and still living, the possibility of a return of the bridewealth no longer exists, and it is no longer legally possible to claim it. This is recognized in Nuer law now administered in the courts, for, as we have seen, it is reckoned that a man cannot have a right to the return of any portion of his bridewealth if his wife has borne him two or, in the case of some tribes, three children who are still living. In fact, he would rarely seek dissolution, even if his wife had left him or was dead, for the disadvantages of her absence from his home are

---

[1] This is not common, but I have known several cases, and in one instance a woman attempted to hang herself from a tree under which I was sitting in an official capacity. The intention, however, may not have been serious, but merely to draw my attention to her grievances.

144   DIVORCE

offset by the existence of the children as well as the advantages he receives from close and amicable relations with his wife's family.

General Observations

Nuer sometimes say that divorce was rare in the old days, and that when the marriage ceremonies had reached the stage of the *muot*, and even more so if a child had been born, neither side was at all likely to seek one. It is also said that if a woman died before or during the birth of her first child, her husband had no right to claim back his cattle: the responsibility rested with him. It is not now possible to assess the truth of a general statement of this sort, particularly as the informant can rarely quote actual examples, but it is clear that the number of cases of divorce which are brought before the courts is considerable and is increasing.

This is, perhaps, a reflection of the wider process of social disintegration which is taking place in Nuerland. The modification in those sanctions which make for social solidarity is likely to react on the institution of marriage as well as on the integration of the kinship group. Moreover, I suggest that the stability of marriage is deeply affected by the attitude of the parties concerned. If there was less chance of recovering bridewealth cattle or less chance of escape by the wife, they would be more likely to make the effort necessary for a successful marriage. Nuer imply that in the past it was not easy for a husband, having entered into marital relations with the bride's group and confirmed the marriage by the performance of the *muot*, to recover his cattle should he no longer want his wife. It was therefore in his interests to make a greater effort to retain his wife's affections and to fulfil the conventional obligations towards her and her relatives. She might run back to her home and, unless he had the support of a numerically superior community, he might find it difficult to obtain redress. Clearly the situation was affected by many different circumstances, and not least of these was the relative position in the social structure of the kinship groups involved and the distance in space between them. Divorce was not so easy, the husband had to make greater efforts to retain his wife, and probably entered marriage with greater care and consideration than he does today, although the slow process of courtship of girls and the eventual choice of a mate is presumably the same as it has always been, and is in itself a factor making for stability when marriage comes.

The comparative facility with which divorce can be obtained through the agency of the courts today means that the husband need not make so great an effort as in the past, because his cattle are nearly always recoverable. It might, of course, be argued that the wife's family must be more conciliatory towards the husband because divorce is

PROCESSES OF DIVORCE

recognized and is enforceable in the courts, and they have a greater chance of losing their cattle. I do not think that these are really major considerations because the Nuer do not think of marriage entirely in terms of cattle, but rather in terms of the union of which the cattle are merely a material symbol. Moreover, and this must be stated at once, the courts do not regard divorce with favour at all, and every effort is made by the court members to prevent it. There is intense feeling on this subject, and divorce is a symptom of social disintegration of which the Nuer are themselves aware. It is not so much the possibility of legal enforcement as the general recognition that divorce is possible at all, particularly after the *muot* and after children have been born of the union, which is the cause of the increase in the number of divorces. Added to this is the fact that union of peoples required for political security is less necessary than in the past, and therefore intermarriage does not serve the same purpose as it did then.

These features are apparent not only in the increased number of divorces but in the growing body of law concerning marriage and divorce which is administered in Nuer courts today. A complex system of law is only necessary when social relations cannot be controlled or maintained by any other means. Now that the sanctions which governed those relations are modified by external influences there is a greater need for law, and an evolutionary process can be seen, particularly because the courts are backed by legal sanctions entirely unknown in the past.

The following are a few representative cases which illustrate the processes of divorce and the circumstances accepted by the courts as sufficient grounds.

Dang Keng v. Nyag Rih (Aak Nuer Appeal)

Dang married Nyag's sister. There were no children, and Dang demanded a divorce on grounds of his wife's barrenness. This was refused by the court in the first instance but was allowed two years later by the appeal court.

Nuer courts will usually allow divorce on grounds of barrenness, but demand adequate proof. The passage of time (in this case about five years—including two years between the initial dispute and the appeal) is therefore relevant. Judgement against divorce by the court in the first instance and then reversal on appeal is therefore a common occurrence. By instituting proceedings the husband is bringing to the notice of the court and of the public his allegation that his wife is barren. The passage of time between this and the hearing of the appeal is then taken into consideration.

In some cases the birth of one child followed by non-productivity is grounds for divorce.

LNL

Kec Kwoyok v. Weir Lam (Leik Nuer Case)

Kec married Weir's sister. During the five years of their marriage she bore only one child, and Kec demanded a divorce. This was refused by the Leik court, but allowed two years later by the appeal court. In this case all cattle were returned to Kec with the exception of sufficient to retain legitimate parenthood of the child.

Kelwal Tutrol v. Kong Kepkeap (Bul Nuer Case)

Kelwal married Kong's daughter. There were no children of the union, and Kong demanded a divorce for his daughter on the grounds that Kelwal was impotent. Kelwal appealed to the court against this demand, but judgement was given against him.

This case is simple enough, but illustrates clearly that impotence or sterility on the part of the husband is equally a ground for divorce. It also shows that Nuer are interested in the children of their daughters, although they will belong legally to another lineage.

Juac Tut v. Pan Rial (Leik Nuer Case)

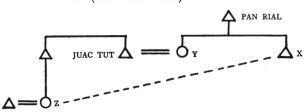

Juac Tut married Pan Rial's daughter Y. X, Y's brother, committed adultery with Z, Juac's brother's daughter. Juac then demanded a divorce from Y on the grounds that the act was virtually incestuous. On the first hearing the court refused the divorce, but on appeal all bridewealth cattle were returned to Juac.

Breaches of this sort of conventional behaviour and normal obligations between relatives-in-law are often compounded by payment of gifts and, in the case of incest, by ritual expiation.

Impediments to Marriage Discovered Subsequently

Two other exceptional circumstances which sometimes result in divorce must be mentioned.

Incest

At any stage of the marriage it may be discovered that the union is incestuous (*rual*), in which case, unless the consanguinity is extremely remote, the marriage must be instantly dissolved. Such an occurrence must be rare[1] among the Nuer, for we have already seen how

---

[1] Within my own personal experience in Nuerland, I have only known of one case in which a marriage had to be dissolved owing to kinship between husband and wife. At the same time such cases are unlikely to appear before the courts or be the subject

IMPEDIMENTS TO MARRIAGE

elaborate precautions against such a contingency are taken at the wedding ceremonies. By previous enquiry and by public invocation of the names and distinctions of the clan at all stages of the process of marriage great care is taken to avoid a breach of the rules of exogamy. There is no great condemnation of extra marital sexual relations with distant clanswomen, and the degree of disapproval and of the severity of the consequences is relative to the position in the kinship structure of the persons concerned. The prohibition of a legal union in such circumstances is more constant, and the discovery of any kinship tie which would normally be an impediment to marriage nearly always necessitates dissolution. There are ritual means by which the contamination may be neutralized, but the risk involved in the continuance of permanent union would be considerable, for the Nuer do not consider that the ritual is infallible.

Blood-Feuds

There are other circumstances which may be a bar to marriage. Nuer will say that there is 'blood between' certain lineages: *teke riem kamdien*, meaning not blood in the sense of kinship, but the spilling of blood and therefore latent hostility derived from a past and unsettled feud. This is not necessarily a serious bar to marriage, and presumably depends on the feelings of the people concerned. Yet if a marriage does take place in such circumstances, and is followed by disasters in the form of sickness and mortality among the children, the existence of a feud between the lineages will often be given as the cause. Yet marital relationships are a means through which blood-feuds can be amicably composed, for unless the indignation is exceedingly intense, the opposed groups will not wish to break with each other if linked by the many ties raised by intermarriage. Dissolution of marriage on these grounds is rare, and I am able to quote only one example:

Kai Bithou v. Lili Gok (*Jagei Nuer Case*)

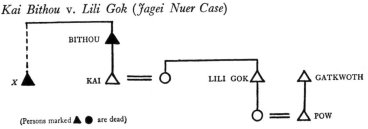

Kai Bithou married Lili Gok's sister. A man called Pow Gatkwoth then married Lili's daughter. Previously Pow's father Gatkwoth had killed a close

of dispute. The spiritual danger involved is sufficient sanction for the immediate dissolution of the union and the return of all the cattle, or, alternatively, for the performance of ritual to break all kinship between the parties (*dak mara*).

148   DIVORCE

kinsman of Kai's (*x*). Kai then claimed dissolution of marriage on the grounds
that there was 'blood between them'. On appeal the court was divided. The
minority were of the opinion that dissolution was essential; the majority ruled
that, since compensation had been paid for the act of homicide and the feud
settled by the Leopard-Skin Chief, no bar to marriage existed. It will be noted
that Lili's family are not involved in the feud, and Kai's contention is that Lili,
by marrying his daughter into a family who are concerned, has brought himself within the range of the impediment. At the same time Gatkwoth was
the actual killer of *x*, not merely an agnatic kinsman of the killer, which
intensifies the feeling of indignation.

In this particular case, it is doubtful whether Kai wanted a divorce merely
because of these circumstances, or whether the 'blood between them' provided a reasonable excuse for a divorce which he desired for other reasons.

For this reason it is safe to conclude that, although the existence of
a feud is considered a serious bar to marriage, the action taken in
such circumstances depends largely on the actual relationship in the
kinship structure (in this case extended to marital relationships) of
husband and wife to the killer and the killed. It also depends on the
actual terms on which the two families are living, for if neither party
wishes for dissolution some means will be found of avoiding it.

Circumstances in which Divorce is Considered Impossible

Nuer consider that the dissolution of marriage, instituted by either
party, is impossible if the wife has fulfilled her procreative obligations.
Generally speaking, though this point is sometimes controversial, two
living children constitute fulfilment in this respect. Three are always
sufficient. This, as we have seen, applies also when the wife dies, and
examples have been given to illustrate the point. Two further examples
are recorded here, there being no difference except that both parties
were living at the time of the dispute.

Riak Teng v. Kuk Diet (Dok Nuer Appeal)

Riak's sister was married to Kuk Diet, twenty-three head of cattle being
paid as bridewealth. Kuk subsequently claimed a divorce on grounds of his
wife's desertion. Original judgement was reversed by the appeal court on
the grounds that two children had been born of the union. Riak was ordered
to arrange the return of his sister to her husband.

Puot Teng v. Biliu Banypiny (Lak Nuer Case)

Puot married Biliu's sister. She bore him three children, and then deserted
him for a man called Jany Mabor. Puot raised the case before the Lak
(Kwacbot) court but the court ruled that no divorce was possible.

These are simple cases. A Nuer court will always attempt to bring
about a reconciliation, but if this fails, which is often the case, the
woman continues to live with her lover, her children and any born subsequently remaining those of her legal husband. There are, however,
borderline cases which sometimes cause perplexity. In particular, the

RETURN OF BRIDEWEALTH

question whether children who have died in infancy should count is a controversial one. Among most Nuer tribes it is generally accepted that those which die in early infancy should not be so counted. From the legal point of view a small child is not considered a being at all, and if it dies before cutting its second teeth no mortuary ceremonies will be performed. Nor will a 'ghost-wife' be married to its name, though there are many exceptions to this rule, especially when there are few adult males to represent the lineage. The test ultimately lies in whether mortuary ceremonies have been performed or not, and the situation is not uncommon owing to the high rate of infant mortality among the Nuer. Opinion, however, is often divided, as is illustrated in the example of Ghuth Bangoany v. Riak Buth recorded below.

3. RULES CONCERNING THE RETURN OF BRIDEWEALTH CATTLE ON DISSOLUTION OF MARRIAGE

Deductions: *ruath miemni* and *yang yaatni*

I have explained that when a marriage is dissolved on the death of a wife who has not fulfilled her procreative obligations, all cattle must be returned to the husband with the exception of sufficient for him to retain legal parenthood of any children (*ruok gaanke* or *ruok muor*), and sometimes a cow referred to as the *yang muon*, 'the cow of the earth' or 'mourning'. When both parties are living, similar deductions are made for children, though naturally there is no claim for *yang muon*. There are, however, other deductions which are deemed necessary. These are known as the *ruath miemni* and the *yang yaatni*. *Ruath miemni* means literally the 'bull-calf of the hairs', and refers to the shaving of the wife's hair at the *muot* ceremony, while *yang yaatni*, 'the cow of the skirts', refers to her ritual dressing in the married woman's skirt (*yat*), and hence her change of status from girl to married woman. These deductions are therefore considered just recompense for the wife's loss of maidenhood. They will not usually be demanded by her family if the husband is willing to leave cattle with them to legitimize any children born of the union. I do not think that *ruath miemni* and *yang yaatni* are often paid when the wife dies. They are essentially payments demanded in divorce when both parties are living, and some Nuer say that they should not be made if it is the wife who is at fault. There are, however, obvious exceptions which the following example shows, and the law on these points is not everywhere consistent.

Ghuth Bangoany v. Riak Buth (Lou Nuer Case)

Ghuth married Nyabieli for 15 head of cattle paid to the kinsmen and heirs of her father Lathuor. She had two sons who died in infancy. Nyabieli

150 DIVORCE

then died, and Ghuth claimed dissolution of marriage and return of the bride-wealth. Court ruled that no dissolution was possible because Nyabieli had fulfilled her procreative obligations by bearing two sons for whom mortuary ceremonies had been performed. Ghuth, however, was granted *yang tuoke*. On appeal Ghuth was granted return of all his cattle save two (*yang mande* and *yang gwande*), these being counted as *ruath miemni* and *yang yaatni*. Both judgements, though entirely different, are logical. The original court ruled that the children though dead should count as living, and that no dissolution was possible. Ghuth could therefore only claim *yang tuoke*. The appeal court ruled that the children could not be so counted, and that therefore Ghuth was entitled to return of his bridewealth cattle. This was tantamount to saying that Nyabieli had borne no children at all. Hence, though Ghuth was entitled to his bridewealth, Nyabieli's kinsmen were entitled to *yang yaatni* and *ruath miemni*.

Original Cattle or Substitutes

Theoretically the original bridewealth cattle must be returned, and with them their offspring, even if born after they have been passed on by the wife's family as bridewealth in their own marriages or further still. This rule is presumably a survival of the days when divorce was comparatively rare, at any rate in instances where all ceremonies had been performed and children born of the union. In the early stages of marriage the cattle will not have moved far afield because there will have been little time for them to do so and their progeny will not be numerous. The complications of collecting thirty or forty head of cattle plus all their offspring born over a number of years will be realized. It is now generally accepted that unless the original cattle are actually in the possession of the wife's family, no return is possible, and that substitutes may be provided. This in itself often leads to dispute because endless arguments arise as to the relative merits of the cattle produced as substitutes as compared to the original cattle. This is, of course, a feature of most disputes which appear before a Nuer court.

Cattle which are not Returnable

Bridewealth cattle are not returnable to the husband on divorce or dissolution of marriage if—

(a) *While in the possession of the wife's family*, they have died of disease or have been killed by wild animals or lost by reason of some other misadventure. The wife's family is not held responsible for providing substitutes, although the husband is not expected to replace such casualties while the marriage continues. Animals passed on in other marriage transactions, or sold or slaughtered for meat, must be replaced by substitutes.

(b) *While in the possession of the wife's family*, they have been paid as compensation for homicide or in payment of fines imposed by the courts. This does not apply to compensation for other offences

RE-MARRIAGE

nor to the normal settlement of debts. This is an interesting point of law because it shows that the enforced payment of compensation (*thung*) and the imposition of punishment in the form of fines are regarded as acts of God rather than the individual responsibility of the offender. It is of course assumed that the bridewealth cattle were used for one of those purposes unwittingly and without previous knowledge that owing to divorce their return would be demanded. The first rule (*a*) appears to be traditional, the second (*b*) is probably a recent development though there are no records of legislation or of intervention by the Administration.

Further Rules in Divorce

A Woman may not be remarried until Previous Marriage has been Dissolved

It is a fundamental rule that a remarriage cannot take place until the previous marriage has been dissolved and all the necessary cattle returned to the husband. Nor may bridewealth cattle from a remarriage be used to pay back cattle owed on a previous one where the same woman is concerned. This sometimes occurs, but is rare because there is a religious sanction as well as a social one involved. Nuer say that the cattle should not mix and that if they did disasters would follow.

Wiea Nyah v. Nyadoiny Yol (Bul Nuer Appeal)

Wiea married Nyadoiny's daughter X, who bore him one son. Wiea then demanded a divorce on grounds of desertion. Nyadoiny is a widow, and her late husband had no close kinsmen. She had already used some of the bridewealth cattle in payment of previous debts incurred by her late husband, and was unable to return all the bridewealth. Seven cattle remained outstanding. Dayim Turuk then began negotiations for marriage with X and paid several head of cattle. Wiea immediately claimed these through the courts. Appeal court ordered return of all cattle to Dayim and return of X and child to Wiea. The union between Wiea and X was still considered legal, while Dayim's cattle had been received illegally.

Return of Extra-marital Payments

Payments made as gifts or as compensation for minor offences against prescribed marital relationships are not normally claimable by either party on divorce. Such payments are considered outside the general bridewealth transactions.[1]

This and other points are illustrated in the following cases:

Gac Cuol v. Mathot Cung (Nuong Nuer Case)

Gac Cuol married Mathot's sister. He then divorced her on grounds of her infertility. All cattle were returned to Gac with the exception of one cow-calf,

---

[1] As will be seen later, offences by an outsider against the husband's physical rights in his wife are treated differently (see p. 166).

152 DIVORCE

which Mathot alleged had been killed by a lion while in his possession. Gac disputed this, and further claimed a cow from Mathot on the grounds that he had previously given Mathot two mosquito nets (value: 150 piastres). Court ruled that:

(i) Cow-calf had been killed by a wild animal while in Mathot's possession. He was therefore not responsible.

(ii) The mosquito nets were a gift outside the transaction of marriage, and were not reclaimable in any form.

Riak Deng v. Gatbuok Nyak (Nuong Nuer Case)

Gatbuok married Riak's sister. In the first year of marriage Gatbuok was profoundly shocked because his wife urinated in his cattle-byre.[1] This nearly led to divorce, but the affair was patched up by Riak paying Gatbuok 40 piastres as compensation to 'ease his heart' (pale loic). With this money and some of his own, Gatbuok bought a cow which subsequently produced five calves. After five years the marriage was dissolved at Gatbuok's request. Riak then claimed the cow and five calves, which in his opinion were his legal right. Court ruled that Gatbuok had the right to retain only the original cow, while Riak should have the offspring. This ruling was given after considerable argument, and was an obvious compromise. The judgement was reversed on appeal on the grounds that the 40 piastres was paid as compensation for a definite offence committed by the woman, was not part of bridewealth, and was therefore not returnable in any form.

Gatkeg Luop v. Tutdel Turuk (Jikany Nuer Appeal)

Tutdel was court policeman under Chief Gatkeg Luop. Tutdel subsequently married Gatkeg's daughter, but divorced her. All cattle were returned to Tutdel, but Gatkeg claimed one cow previously given to Tutdel. Court ruled that the cow had been given to Tutdel as a gift in return for his official and personal services and was not affected by the marital relationship of the two. Gatkeg had no claim on the cow. This was confirmed on appeal.

Divorce of Widows living in Leviratic Union or 'Widow-Concubinage' (see pp. 78, 81)

Generally speaking, the death of the husband precludes the possibility of dissolution of marriage. A Nuer court will not allow proceedings for a divorce to go through unless the husband is present to state his claims. This applies even when no children have been born of the union previous to the husband's decease or subsequently in leviratic union or 'widow-concubinage'.

Can Lony v. Kolang Cal (Leik Nuer Appeal)

Can's paternal uncle married Kolang's sister. The uncle then died, and Can took the woman to live with him. Can then claimed a divorce on grounds of the woman's barrenness. Appeal court upheld previous judgement that no dissolution was possible even though the woman had borne no children at all.

Riek Kwar v. Latjor Kwon (Dok Nuer Appeal)

Gatmac Kwar married Latjor's sister. Gatmac died, and Riek took over the woman in leviratic union. She then deserted him for another man. The

---

[1] A breach of good manners and a particularly reprehensible offence because it was done in the cattle-byre (luak), which is the exclusive stronghold of the male sex.

DISPUTES ARISING FROM DIVORCE 153

woman had one child. Riek then demanded dissolution of the union but this was refused both in the original court and on appeal.

I think that Nuer feel that a widow should have a wide choice as to whom she takes as her lover after her husband's death and that, provided the rights of the deceased husband, including the legal status of the children, are recognized, there should be no interference. Dissolution on grounds of barrenness is, however, sometimes accepted, especially if the marriage had not lasted long before the husband's death. The age of the widow is therefore relevant, and it must be remembered that a young and attractive woman is likely to be guarded more closely by her late husband's kinsmen than an older woman. In the first instance physical rights over her are in issue, in the second only domestic and economic rights, and the emphasis is on her ability to produce children to her late husband's name.

In 'ghost-marriage' the position is different. The vicarious husband is regarded as the principal, and if the reasons were sound and acceptable, a Nuer court would undoubtedly allow dissolution. 'Ghost-marriages' are in fact treated in exactly the same way as simple legal marriages.

4. SUMMARY

Based on these principles the law of divorce is rarely disputed, and cases which appear before the courts usually concern specific claims for cattle which have not been honoured. For example, a divorce takes place, and all cattle are returned save two. The wife's people ask for time to find them, and the debt hangs over for a number of years, possibly until the next generation. A dispute may then arise as to whether the cattle were actually paid or not or whether their theoretical increase in the interim should be taken into consideration. Though there are points which are sometimes disputed, Nuer divorce laws, unlike so much of the customary law administered in their courts, can be conveniently summarized:

Dissolution of Marriage owing to Death of Wife

(i) A △ marries B ◯. B dies before bearing any children to A. A has a right to demand the return of all his cattle paid as bridewealth. Among some tribes he might be expected to leave one cow as *yang muon* (the 'cow of burial') with her family, but this is a ritual payment rather than a specific deduction.

(ii) A △ marries B ◯. B dies leaving one child alive. A is entitled to the return of all his cattle, but will usually leave sufficient to retain legal parenthood of the child (*ruok muor* or *ruok gaanke*).

(iii) A △ marries B ◯. B dies leaving two children. In some tribes B will be said to have fulfilled her procreative obligations, and a dissolution of marriage therefore is unwarranted. In other areas A might expect the return of all his cattle less deductions for the two children.

154   DIVORCE

(iv) A △ marries B ○. B dies leaving three children. In all tribes B is said to have fulfilled her procreative obligations to A and no divorce will be allowed.[1]

(v) In the circumstances described in (iii) and (iv) above, A might expect assistance from his relatives-in-law in the form of *yang* or *ghok tuoke* varying from one cow to eight head of cattle, provided that there has been no dissolution.

Divorce when both Parties are living

(i) A △ marries B ○. A institutes a divorce on grounds of B's misbehaviour, and before any children are born. A can expect the return of all his cattle.

(ii) A △ marries B ○. A demands a divorce for no accepted reason. No children have been born of the union. A can expect the return of all his cattle with the exception of two—*ruath miemni* and *yang yaatni*.[2]

(iii) If children have been born of the union and are living at the time of the proceedings, A will almost invariably leave sufficient cattle to retain legal parenthood. He will not, however, be expected to pay *ruath miemni* and *yang yaatni* in addition to these fees.

(iv) If two children are born of the union, or in some tribes three, a divorce is not considered possible, and will certainly not be allowed in the courts unless the circumstances are exceptional—e.g. if the wife deserts her husband and refuses to return, but even then he will usually waive his domestic and physical rights in her provided she continues to bear children who remain legally his.

These rulings contain the general principles, but it must be emphasized that there are often cases where exceptions are accepted as valid. One does not know how far these rules were followed in the past, or how much they are the product of more recent case law. There are still anomalies and points which are confused, and the law of divorce has not yet developed to its logical conclusion. The general concepts which are behind such claims as *yang muon, ghok tuoke, ruath miemni, yang yaatni* and *ruok gaanke* are known to most Nuer. The precise interpretation in different circumstances varies from region to region, and recent discussions at the Nuer Chiefs' Council have not yet achieved complete standardization.

---

[1] Commenting on this statement, Captain G. S. Renny says of Eastern Nuer: 'I think that even in the case of three children all cattle would be returned to the husband less legitimization fees. Strictly speaking the divorce should go through and the legitimization of the children be carried out as a separate transaction.'

[2] As we have seen, some Nuer tribes say that these payments should be made by the husband whatever the circumstances. See also Evans-Pritchard, *Kinship and Marriage among the Nuer*, p. 91.

CHAPTER IV

THE VIOLATION OF RIGHTS IN WOMEN

1. ADULTERY

NUER courts come into operation only when a recognized wrong is committed, when the validity of some claim is in dispute, or when a man is unable to obtain his rights in cattle from a kinsman, relative-in-law, or debtor. The courts do not operate unless one of the parties resorts to them for one of these reasons, except in cases which are now in the nature of criminal offences: homicide, affray, assault, for example. The law is only clear when the law is broken, and it is in the analysis of disputes brought before the courts that the principles of Nuer law most clearly emerge. Disputes over marriage, that is, over the transfer and distribution of bridewealth or more probably over the return of bridewealth cattle in the event of divorce, do not usually appear before the courts unless a combination of circumstances makes a friendly settlement impossible; and it is symptomatic of the process of social disintegration now taking place in Nuerland that obligations in this connexion are increasingly ignored. In the past a man could only obtain redress if the sanctions for recognized rules of conduct operated with sufficient effect on the wrongdoer or if he had the physical strength, with the support of public opinion, to obtain his rights by force. Adultery, which is in no sense a criminal offence according to Nuer concepts, is now a common cause of legal dispute. There is reason to believe that adultery was less frequent in the past simply because the fear of physical retaliation was greater, and in a sense because acts which are now called adultery were not then treated as adultery at all.

We have seen that the Nuer do not attach great importance to physical paternity. It is legal paternity which is the primary object of marriage, but this does not mean that the relations of the sexes are indiscriminate and uncontrolled, or that a man will not resent encroachment on his exclusive rights to his wife's body. Every Nuer aims at attaching as many children to his name, and through himself to his paternal lineage, as possible. An old man will sometimes allow or even invite a stranger to have intercourse with his wife so that he may have children to further his name and interests in posterity. Whoever may be the physiological father of the children, his legal paternity is in no way impaired. As will be seen later, a man who is impotent may do likewise, though he is not likely to advertise the fact, for impotence is the object of scorn and ridicule among the Nuer.

156 ADULTERY

Despite this general attitude to physical paternity, and despite the fact that birth out of wedlock is in no sense ignominious, a Nuer who is in full possession of his physical powers will bitterly resent an intrusion, and adultery is reckoned a serious infringement of a husband's rights. A husband will take violent steps to prevent it, and it is commonly recognized that a man caught in adultery runs a risk of serious injury or even death at the hands of the woman's husband. There are not, however, nowadays many instances of physical violence or injury arising from adultery (as among some Sudan tribes), and the injured husband will usually resort to the courts.

Adultery is a wrong which demands indemnification in the form of cattle, and this is nearly always enforced by the courts unless circumstances are considered to mitigate the offence. The compensation for adultery[1] (*ruok ciek*) is six head of cattle, and this is common to all Nuer tribes. Of these, five are considered to be direct compensation for the injury caused to the husband, and the sixth, *yang kule*, 'the cow of the sleeping-skin', has a ritual significance. It is considered dangerous for a man to sleep with his wife after she has had intercourse with another man. She is in a state of impurity, and a return to conjugal relations will bring misfortune to them both unless expiation is made by the guilty party. The *kul* or sleeping-skin is symbolic of conjugal relations.

Cattle Returnable if a Child is born of the act of Adultery

The majority of Nuer tribes west of the Nile, the Zeraf tribes and Lou (but not Eastern Jikany), consider that if a child is born of an adulterous union, then all cattle paid previously as compensation must be returned by the husband with the exception of *yang kule*. The reason is not far to seek if we consider the logical principles which underline the concept of legal parenthood already described.[2] It is not so much because the adulterer is considered to have done the husband a service in begetting a child on his behalf—although I have often heard Nuer give this as the reason for the return of the cattle—but because the five head of cattle paid as compensation (*ruok ciek*) have the flavour of legitimization fees (*ruok gaanke*). Unless they are returned there may be confusion of legal concepts. Subsequently, and especially if the marriage was dissolved, the adulterer might claim the child as his legal right.[3]

---

[1] *Dhu*, lit. 'fornication with'. *dhu ciek* therefore means adultery, while if a child is born of the act, it will be called *ruet ciek*. *Ruok ciek*, or more precisely *ruok dhu ciek* or *ruok ruet ciek*, means compensation for adultery.

[2] See Legitimacy of Children, pp. 128–35.

[3] Nuer say that the cattle and the child must not be in the same place together—'they may not meet'. Moreover, the aggrieved husband will always get rid of these cattle as soon as possible even if a child is not born. In the interim between acceptance and their ultimate disposal he will keep them with a friend and well apart from his

CHILDREN BORN OF ADULTERY

Deng Kac v. Nyuon Makwac (Gaawar Nuer Case, 1943)

Nyuon Makwac committed adultery with the wife of Deng Kac. Before the court he admitted his guilt and was ordered to pay six head of cattle. Some eighteen months later, when pressed for execution of the judgement, since he had only paid three cattle, he appealed because Deng's wife had in the interim borne a child, and stated that on these grounds he not only refused to pay the remaining cattle but demanded the return of two head leaving only *yang kule*, for this was the law. Evidence was produced, principally on the admission of the woman, that Nyuon was physiological father of the child. Deng Kac was therefore ordered to return two head of cattle to Nyuon, leaving only one cow as *yang kule*.

This is a simple and typical case, which illustrates the rule that only *yang kule* is due if a child is born as a result of the act of adultery.

Not Pet v. Gac Nyol (Thiang Nuer Case, 1944)

Gac Nyol committed adultery with the wife of Not Pet. Not instituted a legal case against Gac before the Thiang court. The accusation was admitted and Gac ordered to pay six head of cattle as *ruok ciek*. Subsequently the woman gave birth to a child, and Gac appealed for the return of five of the cattle on the grounds that the child was his. Court examined the evidence and ruled that the child was born too long after the act of adultery for Gac to be physiological father. Appeal dismissed.

This raises a point which is of some difficulty to the Nuer. What constitutes proof of physical paternity? There may of course be evidence that the husband was away at the time, and it is in the interests of the adulterer, at this point in the proceedings, to admit access to the woman because he is seeking the return of the cattle. The time element is also of importance and possibly presents a difficulty, but the Nuer are nowadays better able to assess time than they were in the past. Reference can be made to court sittings, inter-tribal meetings, tribute collection, as well as to the seasons. In most cases the evidence of the woman is given weighty consideration.

Legality of Marriage is a Fundamental Consideration

The legality of marriage is also a primary consideration. We have seen that the legality of marriage is established by the payment of cattle and the performance of ceremonies. A man clearly cannot claim damages for adultery with a woman who is not his legal wife, even if he cohabits with her.

Kwol Biliu v. Cuol Puot (Lak Nuer Case)

Kwol Biliu (a government policeman) claimed damages from Cuol Puot for adultery with his wife. Act of adultery was admitted, but Cuol pleaded

own herd. An emotional tie always exists between a *genitor* and his natural child and, I think, Nuer do not wish to give legal emphasis to this by the transference of cattle. As we have seen, even in adultery this tie is recognized, for the physical father may claim a cow on the marriage of his daughter: the *yang leta* or 'cow of the loins'.

158 ADULTERY

that Kwol was in no sense the husband of the woman. She was *keagh* and merely living as his mistress. Court adjourned the case until further evidence could be got from Western Nuer District, where the woman's family lived (obtained through the District offices concerned). The evidence finally produced showed that Kwol had paid her family three head of cattle and a small sum of money. It was also proved that the woman had been living with another man in Malakal (Province Headquarters) until she took up with Kwol. Court ruled that the woman was *keagh* (unmarried) and dismissed the case.

This kind of dispute is, as a matter of fact, not infrequent, and is the result of the increasing number of unmarried women who move from one man to another or live at Government Posts where they have greater freedom and are attracted by the facilities which urban life provides. The men who cohabit with them are often themselves detribalized in the sense that they seek permanent work and cash. They are usually from poor families, and cannot afford to get married in the normal way. In the first instance, they seek work so that they can buy cattle at the auction sales held periodically by the Government, but soon they become attached to an urban life and find that the expense involved gives them little opportunity to save in any case.

Puot Dwil v. Mut Loinyjok (Central Nuer Appeal)

Puot Dwil claimed damages from Mut Loinyjok for adultery with his wife. Mut agreed, and paid two of the six head of cattle awarded, but subsequently demanded their return on the grounds that Puot had not married the woman. This argument was finally taken before a court, which ruled that the union was not legal. The woman was *keagh* (unmarried) at the time because *kere ghoke twoc*, 'he had not performed the ceremony of *twoc*', the cattle had not been bespoken. Further, and this was regarded as all-important, *ce ciekde kere mut*, 'his wife had not been shaved', referring to the ceremony of *muot*. Court ruled that cattle should be returned to Mut. Puot then appealed, and brought further evidence that not only had the bridewealth cattle been paid (17 in all), but that he had full intention of performing the ceremony of *muot* when the incident occurred. He had not carried out his intention because of the incident. Puot further stated that he would insist on dissolution of marriage unless its legality was accepted. Appeal court accepted the evidence that the ceremony of *twoc ghok* had been performed, and that evidence of preparations for the *muot* on his part was also evidence of his intention. Court ordered Mut to pay a total of six head of cattle, i.e. full compensation for adultery.

The Main Legal Principles

The main legal principles concerning adultery can therefore be summarized as follows:

(i) An act of adultery is a wrong against the legal husband of the woman, and requires the payment of compensation in the form of six head of cattle, of which five are intended to appease the wrath of the husband for an infringement of his rights in his wife, and the sixth, called *yang kule*, is to compensate him for the risk of impurity

COMPENSATION TO HUSBAND

and its consequences which he runs in resuming sexual relations with his wife. *Yang kule* is both indemnification and spiritual expiation.

(ii) If a child is born of the act of adultery, the five head of cattle must be returned to the adulterer to avoid any possibility of confusion over the legal paternity of that child, but *yang kule* must always remain with the husband.[1]

Application of these Principles depends on Circumstances

Adultery is therefore an offence because it amounts to an infringement of the legal husband's physical rights in his wife, and also a wrong against the ritual status of the husband which may be impaired by his wife's impurity. This is the law, although its application will depend on a variety of circumstances: the physical condition of the husband and of the wife; the morals of the wife and the age of the wife; the position in the social structure of the parties concerned.

Impotence of the Husband

The physical potency of the husband is sometimes questioned by the defendant, and if the point is proved, the court will rarely enforce the payment of compensation or even of *yang kule*. A man's physical rights in his wife will not be guarded or upheld by the law if he cannot take advantage of them, nor is he likely to suffer any ritual impurity if he is unable to have sexual relations with his wife.[2] On the other hand, it may be argued that the legal husband has acquired rights in his wife by the transfer of cattle to her kin, and if he is unable to enjoy those rights personally, at least he is entitled to dispose of them as he pleases. This at any rate would carry the theory of rights acquired by the transfer of cattle to its logical conclusion, but the Nuer do not look at it in quite this way. We have seen that impotence is recognized as a ground for divorce on the part of the woman, and a man who is impotent has failed in his duties as a husband. In these circumstances he should be pleased that his wife has borne him a child, whoever the father may be. To the Nuer, if he is not pleased, he ought to be.

In cases of this sort a court will sometimes enforce the payment of *yang kule*, though by no means always, but will certainly never allow a claim for the rest of the accepted number of cattle. The concept reflects not so much a definite law as a circumstance which any court

[1] That this rule has been altered by recent legislation will be clear later.

[2] There is, I think, a conscious distinction here. If the husband is impotent and unable to have intercourse with his wife, then there is no risk of the impurity which the *yang kule* is intended to neutralize. If he is able to enjoy sexual intercourse with her, but is sterile and unable to beget children, then the adulterer will still be protected against liability for full compensation (*ruok ciek*), but is liable to pay *yang kule*. The husband, though sterile, still runs the risk of contamination.

160   ADULTERY

will consider in assessing the wrong and the amount of compensation
to be paid. It is a plea which is frequently raised by defendants to
a charge of adultery and is, of course, not easy to prove. Evidence is
based not so much on the statement of the wife as on general reputation
(and it must be remembered that in the intimate life the Nuer lead
there is not much which can be concealed), and also on the existence
or otherwise of other children and the evidence of co-wives if there
are any.

Barrenness of the Wife and Age of the Wife

It is sometimes held that adultery with a woman who is known to
be barren is not an offence, though this view is certainly not universally
held. Adultery with a woman who has borne several children and is
elderly is also considered a minor offence and rarely requires compensation, especially if she has adult children. At most *yang kule* will be
demanded in these circumstances.[1]

Morals of the Wife

The temperament and morals of the wife are also factors which
a Nuer court will consider. If the husband, usually a man who has
been absent from home for a long time, brings charges of adultery
against two or more men and the charge is proven, the court will
order that each shall pay part of the compensation.[2] There is a
limit to this. Nuer consider that a woman who has had sexual relations with more than three men is a *ciek me jok*, a 'loose woman', and
that the men concerned cannot be held responsible. For this reason
the defendant or defendants in a case of adultery will often attempt
to prove that the woman has committed adultery with a fourth man.
In this case a court will not enforce the payment of compensation,
or of *yang kule*, though, if a child is born of one of them, it may
compel him to pay *yang kule*. In such circumstances, the husband
will often institute a divorce against his wife, and if there is any dispute between himself and his wife's relatives, a court will usually
take his side.

Jal Bath v. Gai Nyal (Thiang: Central Nuer Appeal)

Jal Bath claimed compensation (*ruok ciek*) from Gai Nyal on grounds of
adultery with his legal wife Nyandeang. A child had been born in consequence
of the act of adultery, or so Jal alleged. This was admitted by Gai. (It was in
his interests to do so.) Jal claimed *yang kule* only, but Gai refused to pay.
The matter was taken to court and Gai ordered to pay. Some months later,

[1] This was recorded at the Nuer Chiefs' Council Meeting of 1945: 'When a man
commits adultery with a woman who has adult sons or daughters, he is only liable to
pay *yang kule* and not full compensation.'

[2] E.g. if two men, each will pay three head of cattle, if three men, each will pay
two head of cattle.

Photo: *Dr. J. F. Bloss*

THE BRIDEGROOM

MAN OF GOD. RIAG LOINYJOK (*see p. 215*)

Gai appealed on the grounds that he had evidence that Nyandeang had committed adultery with three other men, Koh Col, Ngwom Diu, Top Bath, and had done so during the same period as with Gai, and in the absence of Jal. Appeal court accepted this evidence as true. Jal then stated that he did not deny the allegations of Gai, though he had not heard of them before, but the evidence was not relevant to the case. He had claimed *yang kule* only, not full compensation. He admitted Gai was father of the child, and so did Gai. Court upheld previous judgement and ruled that Jal should keep the *yang kule*.

Questioned on the legal issues involved, the court held that if a man has sexual intercourse with a woman who is the legal wife of another, he is liable to pay six head of cattle which include *yang kule*. If she bears a child attributed to the act of the adulterer, five head must be returned, *yang kule* remains. The fact that the woman is proved to have committed adultery with other men, if more than three men are involved, absolves all of them from paying compensation whether a child is born or not, but if one of them is proved to be the father of the child, he must still pay *yang kule*.[1]

Compensation cannot be Claimed more than twice where one Woman is Concerned

It is also generally held that a man cannot claim compensation for adultery with his wife (the same wife) on more than two occasions. After the fulfilment of two claims of this sort, in which he may have received no less than twelve head of cattle, his wife acquires the reputation of being 'loose'. He will certainly not succeed in a claim instigated out of court, and it is extremely unlikely that a Nuer court would uphold his claim. Moreover he may well be suspected of exploiting his wife's physical charms to his own advantage.

Adultery with Widows

When a woman whose husband is dead has sexual relations with a man without the express permission of her husband's legal heirs, damages for adultery may be claimed, but the right is not often exercised. It depends on a variety of circumstances, particularly the age of the woman, for, if she is young and attractive, one of her husband's kinsmen will wish her to live with him. As we have seen, the main object in the minds of the dead husband's kinsmen is that the woman shall bear children to his name, and they are usually prepared to give her a wide choice, provided she does not go to live too far away from them. They will often object if she goes to live with a man whom they have not accepted as her lover (*lum*), and they will also object

[1] See recent legislation on this subject, p. 167. The idea is a Nuer one, but the exactitude is the result of legislation prompted by the Administration.

Mɴʟ

ADULTERY

if the act of adultery, for it amounts to this in such circumstances, is casual with no permanent basis of cohabitation. In 'widow-concubinage' a stable relationship between the widow's mate and the kinsmen of her husband is naturally desirable. They will expect him to treat them as kinsmen, and between them will arise a relationship which is patterned on kinship. The rights of the husband in his wife are inherited and upheld by his heirs, and they are entitled to compensation for an infringement of those rights.

Tec Nyagh v. Kwoiny Ruok

Jegh married Nyabwogh. Jegh died shortly afterwards without issue. Nyabwogh was a young woman, and Tec, as one of Jegh's heirs, wished her to live with him so that he might benefit from her presence in the home, not only as a mate but in carrying out domestic duties. He had no wife himself. Nyabwogh ran off with Kwoiny Ruok, who was living in another part of the country. Tec made some effort to persuade her to return to him, but she refused. He then went to court and judgement was given that Kwoiny, who was deemed responsible for enticing Nyabwogh away, should pay one cow as *yang kule*. His act was considered to be adultery. Court ordered immediate return of Nyabwogh to Tec.[1]

A case of this sort is not common, and I have no record of a court ordering the payment of compensation in full, only of *yang kule*, although theoretically the deceased's heirs have the right to claim it. In this case Nyabwogh had borne a child to Kwoiny Ruok, who, as physiological father, would in any case only be liable to pay *yang kule*.

From these and other cases of the same nature, it is clear that the death of a husband does not theoretically imply a reduction in his legal rights over his wife and her children whoever their physiological father may be, and that these rights are guarded by his heirs. It is also clear that the husband's domestic, economic, and physical rights are not diminished in theory, but whether his heirs will lay strict claim to them depends on a variety of circumstances. If the wife is young, his heirs will be reluctant to let her go, though they do not usually insist on her staying. In any case she is likely to have a wide choice from among his kinsmen. They will also wish to benefit from her domestic and economic activities and, of course, always prefer that she should stay within their community. Even if she goes to a man outside the community, they wish her relations with him to be stable and permanent and, if accepted, he will be drawn to some extent into the field of kinship and become one of them. 'Widow-concubinage' does not imply complete sexual freedom of an indiscriminate kind. At any time the dead

[1] This was not the end of the case. It was subsequently discovered that Nyabwogh had gone off to live with another man, an arrangement made by her brother, who had also illegally accepted three head of cattle, although she was already legally married to Jegh and there had been no return of bridewealth. Finally, the marriage was dissolved, her brother was punished for what is considered a serious wrong, and Kwoiny received his cow back again.

ADULTERY AND 'GHOST-MARRIAGE'   163

husband's heirs may draw attention to their rights in the woman and, if she has relations with a man who is objectionable to them, they may treat the case as one of normal adultery and claim damages. Such cases are nowadays usually taken to court, and the line adopted by its members will again depend on circumstances. They will, however, admit the validity of the claim even though they are not always prepared to enforce it.

Bang Wic v. Lia Ran (Dok Nuer Case)

Lia Ran committed adultery with the wife of Bang's deceased brother. The case was brought before the Dok court, which judged that no compensation was necessary, 'as the woman is a widow'. This judgement was, however, revised by the appeal court, and Lia ordered to pay to Bang one cow as *yang kule*.

Adultery and 'Ghost-Marriage'

The same theoretical law applies to 'ghost-marriages', but the attitude is different. A 'ghost-wife' is actually married by a man's heir *after* his death, and the vicarious husband in this case performs all the ceremonial of marriage as well as operating the transfer of bride-wealth. Except that legal paternity is vested in the person of the deceased, which fact is of greater significance when the children of the union come of age, the union does not differ from a straightforward simple legal marriage. Moreover the vicarious husband, in his capacity of legal heir to the deceased, stands in the same relationship to the woman and the children as her 'ghost-husband'. The only real difference is that the children will link their names in the lineage structure to the latter, and this is a matter of greater importance in posterity than the present. For this reason, the emotional attitude of the vicarious husband to the wife, their relationship, and their life together are indistinguishable from those found in simple legal marriage, and considering the high proportion of 'ghost-marriages' this is not surprising. The woman is usually his own choice, he has courted her, won her, married her, and his relationship is therefore much more intense and personal than his relationship with his brother's widow. Hence, though a man may overlook an act of adultery with his brother's widow, or the widow of any man to whom he is legal heir, he will certainly not do so in the case of his brother's 'ghost-wife'. The reaction to adultery in 'ghost-marriages' is identical with that found in simple legal marriages, and it is doubtful if a Nuer court would regard the theoretical distinction as relevant to the issue.

Adultery with the Wives of Kinsmen

The full rate of compensation is usually demanded unless the husband and the adulterer are on exceptionally good terms in other

164   ADULTERY

respects, or their relationship in the kinship structure is sufficiently close
to modify feelings of moral indignation on the part of the husband.
Although the wives of kinsmen are brought within the sphere of kinship by the process of marriage, and to have relations with the wife
of a kinsman is in a sense tantamount to a breach of the rules of exogamy, this is modified by the feeling that a wife, acquired by the
transfer of cattle in which other kinsmen have limited rights, is theoretically the wife of all of them. Yet it is not considered correct that
two kinsmen should have sexual relations with the same woman at
the same period. There is no real conflict in these two concepts, but
the attitude behind the payment of *yang kule* includes an idea that
sexual relations with the legal wife of another man create an impurity,
and that there is greater impurity if two men of the same kinship
group have sexual relations with the same woman. It is felt that the
wife of a kinsman is in some degree also a kinswoman, especially as
a potential mother of kinsmen in the next generation. The act is
therefore tantamount to incest (*rual*).

These ideas appear in the arguments put forward in the course of
litigation in the courts today. The court will attempt to persuade the
wronged husband to accept less than five head of cattle, though they
will normally enforce payment of the sixth, the *yang kule*. Talking to
the husband they will say of the adulterer: 'Is not this man your
kinsman? Is it not a man's duty to assist his kinsman?' The implications are that adultery is an offence which brings greater spiritual
dangers when the husband and the adulterer are kinsmen, but just
because they are kinsmen it is an offence which must be wiped out by
expiation in the form of sacrifice and prayer. One does not pay compensation to kinsmen because they are the persons who assist in the
collection of compensation for offences against others. The intensity
with which these ideas operate is relative and depends on the relationship of the principals.

Kin Nyah v. Pagwir Wicdier (Bul: Western Nuer Appeal)

Pagwir committed adultery with Kin's wife. Court awarded reduced compensation of 3 cattle to Kin on the grounds that Kin and Pagwir are kinsmen
(common great-grandfather). Pagwir refused to pay, and was then ordered by
the court to pay full compensation of 6 cattle as punishment. The court
was exasperated by Pagwir's defiance of its orders. The use of the word
punishment is perhaps incorrect here because the additional cattle went to
the plaintiff, but the motive was punishment for flagrant disobedience.

Nin Puor v. Dhoar Muol and Po Gwet (Lou: Central Nuer Appeal)

Dhoar committed adultery with Nyalok, wife of Nin's paternal uncle Uth.
Uth was living at the time, but died before the case was brought to court.
Subsequently Po Gwet also committed adultery with Nyalok. The chrono-
logical sequence is here important, though it was not realized by the court in
the initial stages of the dispute.

Dhoar and Po were absent when these allegations were made against them by Nin, but since there seemed to be no doubt about Po's guilt his father Gwet Thic (himself a chief) was prevailed upon to pay compensation as *ruok ciek*, and had already handed over 3 head of cattle when Po and Dhoar returned. In the meantime Nyalok had confessed that she had also committed adultery with Dhoar, an act which was held to be incest (*rual*), and also that Uth had

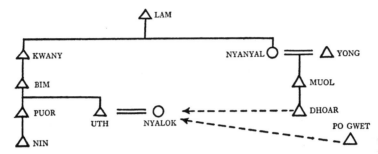

died as a result—he 'had died of incest', *ce lieu ke rual*. This complicated case was naturally the subject of prolonged discussion in the court which finally ruled that:

(i) Po had sexual relations with the woman *after* Uth's death, and even had some encouragement from Uth's family. Court held that he must be treated as the woman's *lum* (i.e. recognized lover in 'widow-concubinage'). Po was therefore in no way liable to pay compensation, and those cattle already handed over to Nin by Po's father Gwet were returned.

(ii) Dhoar committed incest (*rual*) by having sexual relations with Nyalok while her husband Uth was still living, and his act must be accepted as the cause of Uth's death. Dhoar to pay two cattle to Nin as Uth's heir; one cow as *yang kule*, one bull as *yang me bak ke rual*, 'the cow of dividing for incest', to be sacrificed and divided in the manner prescribed by custom in order to avoid further evil effects of the act of incest.

Further Qualifying Circumstances

Nuer sometimes make a distinction between what they call *dhu ciek dhor*, 'adultery with a woman outside (the home)' and *dhu ciek cieng*, 'adultery with a woman in the home'. The distinction is not really a valid one from the legal point of view, and the meaning is sometimes contradictory. *Dhu ciek dhor* sometimes implies an act of adultery committed with a woman who is not living with her husband—a less serious offence than *dhu ciek cieng*—but it can also mean adultery with enticement to desert the husband, i.e. that the adulterer has run away with the woman, or attempted to do so. This distinction is not reflected in the scale of compensation; the maximum is always six head of cattle whatever the circumstances, but in the case of *dhu ciek dhor* in the latter sense, the indignation of the wronged husband and his kin will be more intense and they will not be so ready to accept less than six head as a compromise. For this reason the distinction is now

166   ADULTERY

accepted in court as relevant, and a court will nearly always award full compensation in cases of *dhu ciek dhor* when the adulterer has enticed the woman to leave her husband.

Liability Ceases with the Death of the Adulterer

Mayol Lah v. Dayim Make (*Jikany Nuer Appeal*)

Dayim committed adultery with Mayol's wife and paid five head of cattle in compensation. She then committed adultery with Bul Thic. No compensation was paid because Bul died shortly after. Dayim then appealed on the grounds that if Bul had paid no compensation, why should he? Court dismissed this appeal as frivolous.

There is nothing unusual in this case but it shows that liability for compensation for adultery ceases with the death of the adulterer and does not fall on his heirs. Although a man may expect his relatives to assist him in adversity and to help him in the collection of the indemnity cattle, adultery is regarded as largely an individual offence.

Return of Compensation Cattle on Dissolution of Marriage

It is a generally accepted rule among the Nuer that an adulterer may reclaim any cattle paid by him as compensation for his offence should the husband subsequently divorce his wife. This at least is theoretical law, though whether it was followed in the past is problematical. This rule is at any rate upheld in Nuer courts as the following example indicates:

Gwigwi Keah v. Nyot Lacler (*Jikany Nuer Case*)

Nyot committed adultery with Gwigwi's wife. Court awarded six head of cattle as compensation, of which only four were actually paid. The wife then died, and the union was dissolved. Court then ordered return of these cattle to Nyot with the exception of one cow which had been paid as *thung* (blood-wealth)[1] by Gwigwi in the interim.

This rule, as will be seen later, has been altered recently. It is unlikely that any action would be taken in instances where a considerable time had elapsed between the act of adultery and divorce, but the idea is essentially a Nuer one and not an innovation.

Recent Legislation

At the Nuer Chiefs' Council of 1945, the subject of adultery was discussed with considerable interest, more so perhaps than is usual

---

[1] Cattle which die by misadventure in the possession of the wronged husband are not returnable, a rule which is now extended to cattle paid as compensation for homicide. See p. 150.

RECENT LEGISLATION

on such occasions. It was generally felt that adultery was on the increase and was a threat to the stability of marriage as well as to public security. It was held by representatives from Eastern Nuer District that in their own country there was never any question of returning compensation cattle to the adulterer should a child be born of his act. Chiefs of the Zeraf and Western Nuer tribes were prevailed upon to accept this view, and it became universal law among the Nuer that six head should be paid whether a child was born or not. My own view is that Zeraf and Western Nuer practice is more in accord with Nuer concepts. These tribes admitted that steps should be taken to stop adultery, but said that the way to do so was to introduce penal sanctions as a deterrent rather than alter a principle which to them is fundamental and thus run the risk of confusion over the status and legitimacy of children. This became even more apparent at the meeting of 1949.

At this later meeting, the law that compensation cattle should be returned to the adulterer if the marriage is dissolved, was attacked on moral grounds by one of the British representatives of the Administration present. It was held that an adulterer should not be allowed to benefit in such circumstances, and that there was often collusion between the adulterer and the wife's family in obtaining a divorce so that both might benefit. This argument is clearly fallacious, for whatever the adulterer may gain thereby, the woman's family gain nothing; they will have all the trouble of returning the bridewealth cattle to the husband and will not necessarily receive more from the adulterer even if he chooses to marry the woman. At the discussion which followed it was those tribes who had previously upheld the rule that a husband is entitled only to one cow (*yang kule*) if a child is born of the act of adultery, who most steadfastly opposed the proposal that the husband should retain the compensation cattle in the event of a divorce. They opposed even more strongly the proposal that the cattle should be handed to the wife's family. This latter proposal is at least logical, for the husband in relinquishing his rights over his wife should waive any benefits gained thereby in favour of her family.[1] Yet by accepting these cattle the wife's family would be admitting the adulterer's claim to legal parenthood of the child, and if the former husband had also left cattle with them as legitimization fees there

---

[1] It may be argued that the act of adultery was an offence against the husband alone. This at least would be consistent when we consider what I have termed 'extra marital payments' in connexion with divorce (see p. 151). But the Nuer do not look at the matter in this way, especially if a child has been born. Cattle were only claimable in the first instance because the husband held legal rights in his wife. In dissolving the union and thereby waiving those rights he must forgo any benefits accrued in the past. Nuer themselves explain the matter in terms of rights (*cuong*). The husband had a right (*ce teke cuong*), but now it is the wife's family who have the right. Yet they cannot receive it because of the legal confusion it may cause. Hence the cattle must be returned to the adulterer.

168 INTERCOURSE WITH UNMARRIED WOMEN

would be a clash of interests and a subsequent confusion of status. The embarrassing results are clear enough when we consider the complications which would arise over the claims to bridewealth if the child were a girl, or the claims on the bridewealth of others if the child were a boy. Nuer law is designed to avoid such confusion. The only way out of the dilemma was, as usual, to throw responsibility on the Administration and to decide that, in the event of a divorce, cattle paid as compensation for adultery should go to the Government. The perplexing implications of this decision will be discussed in a later chapter, but it will be seen that adultery is now a civil offence in the first instance and a criminal offence, enforceable under the Chiefs' Courts Ordinance, in the second.

Further legislation at these meetings is recorded here, though the general principles have already been stated:

Chiefs agreed that:

(i) A man who repeatedly commits adultery with the same woman is not liable to pay compensation (*ruok*) more than twice, but shall be liable to punishment by imprisonment or fine.

(ii) Where two or more men commit adultery with the same woman, the following rules are to apply in future:

If 2 men do so, then each shall pay 3 head of cattle=6.
If 3 men do so, then each shall pay 2 head of cattle=6.
If 4 men do so, then no compensation may be demanded by the woman's husband.

(iii) A man can only claim compensation for adultery for the same wife twice; e.g. B commits adultery with A's wife and pays 6 head of cattle (*ruok*). Shortly afterwards C does the same, and he pays 6 head of cattle too. Should anyone else do so, no further compensation is payable, but the third adulterer renders himself liable to a fine or imprisonment.[1]

These rules are not so much an innovation or an alteration as an articulation of existing practice. It is difficult to say whether they are based on exact tradition or whether they represent an evolution of case law based on past precedents. It is probable that each has an element of traditional practice as a basis, but it is unlikely that any were applied in the past with the rigidity implied, even in disputes which reached the final stage of settlement. It is interesting to note too that nowadays when civil liability ceases, penal sanctions may still be applied.

2. SEXUAL INTERCOURSE WITH UNMARRIED WOMEN AND GIRLS

Sexual Intercourse with Unmarried Concubines

Nuer talk of *dhu ciek*, meaning simply sexual intercourse with any woman, but it usually implies that the woman is legally married

[1] Extracts from Minutes of the Nuer Chiefs' Council Meeting, 1945 (unpublished).

SEDUCTION OF UNMARRIED GIRLS 169

whether the marriage is a simple legal union, 'ghost-marriage', leviratic union, or 'widow-concubinage'. Hence the term *dhu ciek* usually implies a violation of marriage rights and closely approximates to the European concept of adultery. We have already seen that, if the wrongdoer can prove that his mistress is not legally married to the man who claims to be her husband, no action for adultery lies. The woman in such circumstances is *ciek me keagh*; she is *ciek*, having the status of a married woman, but she is *keagh*, unmarried. This does not necessarily imply any feeling of disrespect, for the expression is sometimes used of a woman who has not yet completed the full processes of legal marriage with her husband, or sometimes of a woman who has been married and divorced and awaits remarriage of a respectable nature. *Keagh*, however, has a wide range of meaning and, used contemptuously, implies that the woman is wanton and self-willed and that, if she is not legally married, she ought to be. In all these circumstances it is her family who have rights in her, and legally it is for them to claim damages for any infringement of those rights. They rarely do so and, if they did, would be unlikely to receive the support of a Nuer court.

Such women often cohabit with men on a reasonably stable basis, and the union sometimes has the appearance of legality. This is particularly so in detribalized communities to which women of this temperament tend to go, and there are sometimes disputes which appear before the courts. It is noticeable that, although a Nuer court will never award compensation to the man who claims to be husband (*cou*) of the woman, nor, indeed, to her family, they will often punish the offender. Penal sanctions are being applied to offences which must have been comparatively rare in the past and for which there is no traditional remedy.

The Seduction of Unmarried Girls: dhu nyal

The seduction of a young girl (*nyal*) is considered a wrong. Nuer will say it is a great wrong, a *duer medit*, but what they imply is that a girl who gains the reputation of offering herself indiscriminately to any young man will not be approached with genuine offers of marriage. She will be a *nyal me jok*, a 'bitch'.[1] Such girls, once they have gained

[1] This expression is as disrespectful and rude as it would be in our own language, and is not used openly. I recall a girl of this sort in Thiang country who appeared regularly at dances in company with girls obviously much younger than herself. She appeared to me to be attractive, and I asked some youths of my acquaintance whether they did not think so. They replied that she was extremely attractive, a statement which was followed by a good deal of chaffing and laughter on the part of their fellows. Subsequently I was told by one of my followers that she was considered *jok*, and although older men were much attracted to her, none of them wished to marry her, and the young men left her alone because to have relations with her was regarded as slightly ridiculous and they feared the scorn of other girls. The girl eventually took up with an Arab merchant. See example, *Cany Tut* v. *Dar Jal* (p. 172).

170 INTERCOURSE WITH UNMARRIED WOMEN

an unsavoury reputation, may have to wait for a long time for marriage and are also *jut* (which is merely an unmarried girl beyond the age at which girls are usually expected to marry), and when a serious suitor does come along, he will do so because her family are likely to ask less cattle for her than is usual. She is likely to marry a poor man if she marries at all.

Illicit sexual intercourse with an unmarried girl is therefore a wrong in itself, but it is the effects that public knowledge of her wantonness will have on her reputation which are regarded as important. Technically a girl (*nyal*) is supposed to be a virgin, but by the time she reaches the stage of marriage this is unlikely to be a fact. Her family do not necessarily object on any moral principles. Their attitude is a reflection of their real desire to see her properly married so that they may acquire cattle for their own marriages, and they do not tolerate any attention from an outsider which is likely to compromise her chances of making a suitable match with a man who has cattle. A young man with no cattle who pays marked attention to a girl will be warned off by her brothers. But unless her chances are lessened by a reputation for promiscuity in the choice and number of her lovers her family are unlikely to take action, and a complaint on their part will rarely be recognized in a Nuer court. Nuer say, however, that *dhu nyal* is an offence which may require the payment of compensation (*ruok nyal*), and by this they mean that if a complaint is made by a girl's family, and there is proof that they have suffered an injury or potential loss, compensation should be paid to them.

Dhu nyal cieng and Dhu nyal dhor

Nuer also make the distinction between what they call *dhu nyal dhor*, 'fornication with an unmarried girl outside (or in the bush)' and *dhu nyal cieng*, 'fornication with an unmarried girl in the home'. The terms are not very clear, since *dhu nyal cieng* is often used to describe cases of elopement—i.e. when the girl has been taken from her home. The former offence, *dhu nyal dhor*, is considered much less serious, and refers largely to casual encounters at dances held by the young people.

Elopement and Abduction: kwil nyal

It is considered a much more serious offence if a man entices an unmarried girl away from her family and persuades her to live with him. Whether a child is born of the union or not, a Nuer court will take action against the wrongdoer and compel him to marry the girl or pay compensation which will not be returned even if the girl is subsequently married to another man. To seduce a girl, persuade her to take up residence away from her home, so that she appears to be

PREGNANCY OF UNMARRIED GIRL 171

a married woman, without the transfer of cattle, is *kwil nyal*, 'theft of a girl'. The girl will sometimes assume the costume of a married woman (a leather apron or skirt) and, in examining the circumstances of the case, a court will usually ask whether this has happened or not. It is evidence against the wrongdoer, and implies a greater wrong.

Riek Nuon v. Nger Cut (Leik: Western Nuer Appeal)

Nger seduced Riek's daughter. The girl did not become pregnant, but Riek claimed that Nger's attentions were undesirable, and had compromised his daughter's chances of marriage. In considering the case, the court first examined Nger's circumstances, and stated that he should marry the girl. On finding that he had very few cattle and no prospects of more, the court ordered him to pay two head of cattle as *ruok nyal* to Riek. In the course of the discussions it appeared that Nger had several times been warned to keep away from the girl, not only by her family, but by the local headman (*gatuot*), and finally by the chief. For this reason Nger was sentenced to one year's imprisonment, and the sentence was upheld on appeal.

Liep Balou v. Biel Dang (Dok Nuer Case)

Biel eloped with Liep's sister. He was subsequently arrested by the chief's police and brought before the court. It was found that Biel had no cattle at all and no prospects of obtaining any. The girl was not pregnant, and the court noted that this was a single incident. Elopement is, however, a serious offence, and Biel was sentenced to six months' imprisonment, though no compensation was awarded.

It is doubtful whether the present compensation, which most Nuer tribes say should be a cow-calf and a bull-calf, though some say three head of cattle, has any basis in tradition. It is more probably based on past precedents from the courts and, as we have seen, is not often awarded unless there has been a flagrant attempt to avoid the ritual of marriage and the transfer of bridewealth or the girl was betrothed to some other man at the time.

Sexual Intercourse with an Unmarried Girl resulting in Pregnancy: ruet nyal

It is another matter if the girl gives birth to a child. It is clear that in the past violent action might be taken against a girl's lover by her brothers, who would seek to compel him to marry her. They would seize cattle from his home and, depending again on their relationship in the social structure, and the relative strength of the sanctions for social integration between the communities to which they belonged, the seizure would be accepted and regarded as a preliminary move towards marriage. Resistance might lead to an open battle between them and even to a feud. Hence, within a limited community or tribal segment, there were strong sanctions derived from fear of retaliation which made for amicable settlement of a case of this sort. It was

172 INTERCOURSE WITH UNMARRIED WOMEN

also possible to legitimize a child born in these circumstances by the payment of fees (*ruok gaanke* or *ruok muor*).[1]

Cany Tut v. Dar Jal and Kwol Panyal (Lak Nuer Case)

Dar Jal seduced the sister of Cany Tut. She gave birth to a child and, since Dar refused to marry her or to legitimize the child, Cany took the case to court. The court ordered Dar to pay a cow-calf and a bull-calf as *ruok nyal*. Dar was dissatisfied with this judgement and brought the matter to court again on the grounds that another man, Kwol Panyal, was the father of the child. Judgement was reversed and the cattle were returned to Dar. Cany then demanded *ruok nyal* from Kwol Panyal. The latter countered by proving that the girl was wanton, *nyal me jok*. Court accepted this and refused to enforce payment of *ruok nyal*. This judgement was subsequently confirmed on appeal.

Nguot Reth v. Mut Roa (Gaawar Appeal)

Mut Roa seduced Nyadeb Reth, an unmarried girl (about nineteen years of age). She conceived and bore a child to him, and the dispute which followed was referred to the court. Mut had insufficient cattle to marry the girl, and was ordered to pay compensation *ruok (ruet) nyal* consisting of a cow-calf and a bull-calf. The girl was subsequently married to another man, but Mut's cattle were not returned to him. Mut then appealed, not on the grounds that his cattle should be returned to him, but that he had actually paid a full-grown cow in place of the cow-calf ordered by the court. He stated that the traditional scale of compensation in such circumstances was as the court directed, a cow-*calf* and a bull-calf. Court ruled that this was now irrelevant, because had he paid a cow-calf it would by that time be a large cow: it would have grown in the interval.

It is an even more serious offence for a man to return to a girl after he has been made to pay compensation for seducing her. If she has borne one child, her chances of marrying well are not generally lessened. Indeed some Nuer say that her chances are enhanced, for it is thereby proved that she is fertile, and this is a serious consideration to a man contemplating marriage. To return again to the same girl, and particularly to get her with child for the second time, may cause grave loss to her family. A man will be unlikely to look at her as a possible wife if this has happened, and if she gets married at all it will probably be to a man who is poor in cattle and unable to afford a full bridewealth. An offence of this sort is nowadays almost always punished, not only by forcing the guilty party to pay compensation, but by fine or imprisonment as well. Again penal sanctions, previously unknown to the Nuer, are now commonly applied.

Top Bath v. Manyang Tut (Thiang: Central Nuer Appeal)

Manyang Tut got Nyaluk, unmarried daughter of Top Bath, with child. Manyang refused to marry her, and had insufficient cattle to do so anyway. The court ordered payment of two head of cattle as *ruok nyal*. This was paid. Subsequently Nyaluk ran off to Manyang again and lived with him for a short time, though no child was conceived on this occasion. Court ordered the

---

[1] See 'Legitimacy of Children', p. 132.

COMPENSATION

immediate return of Nyaluk to her family, though no further *ruok nyal* was demanded. Manyang was sentenced to five months' imprisonment.

In this case the court punished the wrongdoer because not only had he committed a serious offence, but he had openly defied the original order of the court.

Compensation (ruok nyal) and Legitimization Fees (ruok gaanke or muor)

Legitimization fees for children have already been discussed in a separate section.[1] It is worth mentioning here that a man who gets an unmarried girl (*nyal*) with child is not expected to pay both compensation (*ruok nyal*) and legitimization fees (*ruok gaanke* or *muor*) as well. The two payments are in a sense interchangeable. A man who has paid compensation may increase the payment if it is subsequently discovered that the girl is with child, thereby changing it to a recognized fee to legitimize that child. On the other hand, if there is any likelihood of the girl getting married fairly soon after the event, her family may waive their claim to *ruok nyal*, for then the child will go with its mother to her future husband. In some instances even if legitimization fees have been paid they will be returned on the girl's marriage.

Can Cakwen v. Tutkwac Diu (Thiang: Central Nuer Appeal)

Tutkwac Diu seduced the sister of Can Cakwen, and she gave birth to a child. Tutkwac paid no compensation (*ruok nyal*) for this, and the girl was subsequently married by Buth Jal. Some time later Tutkwac asked to be allowed to pay *ruok gaanke* to legitimize the child to his own name. A dispute arose, and the matter was taken to court. Court ruled that Tutkwac had no right to the child, as the girl's marriage to Buth Jal was by then legally valid. She had performed the ceremony of *muot*, and the child had in fact been born after the marriage.

A man who has paid legitimization fees for his child is not usually able to reclaim them should the child die, as he would be able to do in other circumstances. The legitimization fees become compensation in retrospect.

Lam Twiel v. Jeh Col (Jikany: Western Nuer Appeal)

Jeh seduced Lam's sister and she gave birth to a male child. Jeh was ordered by the court to pay four head of cattle as legitimization fees (*ruok gaanke*), since he refused to marry the girl. This was in 1944.[2] The child died two years later, and Jeh appealed to the court for return of his cattle. The court ruled that the cattle should not be returned. Jeh had refused to marry the girl though he had cattle with which to do so. The four head of cattle must therefore be considered compensation *ruok (ruet) nyal*.

---

[1] See pp. 128–35.
[2] Before the Nuer Chiefs' Council Meeting of 1954, when legitimization fees were standardized (see pp. 134–5).

174 INTERCOURSE WITH UNMARRIED WOMEN

Summary

From the circumstances and examples described above, it appears that—

(i) The mere act of sexual intercourse with an unmarried girl (*dhu nyal*) is considered a wrong and one which may demand the payment of compensation. This attitude is conditioned, not by any idea that sexual intercourse before marriage is morally reprehensible, but by the fact that a girl who is known to be free with her favours and to have had many lovers is often considered an undesirable wife. Her chances of making a good marriage may be compromised. It will be the girl's family and kinsmen who will suffer in consequence.

(ii) Compensation is called *ruok nyal*, and varies throughout Nuerland from two to three head of cattle. The majority of tribes reckon *ruok nyal* to be two head: a cow-calf and a bull-calf. This is rigid and unalterable in the sense that there can be no increase over that figure for a single offence.

(iii) Nuer distinguish between what they call *dhu nyal dhor*, 'seduction of a girl in the bush', and *dhu nyal cieng*, 'seduction of a girl in the home'. The former offence has a degree of social recognition and is not usually regarded as a serious matter; the latter is considered a more flagrant violation of the rights which a girl's family have in her. This distinction is, however, somewhat academic and is certainly not reflected in the actual number of cattle demanded as compensation.

(iv) *Dhu nyal cieng* is sometimes used to describe an act of elopement. This is a much more serious offence, especially if the girl assumes the appearance of a married woman by wearing a skirt and openly living with the culprit. He has stolen the girl, *'ce nyal kwal'*, and the offence will be referred to as *kwil nyal*.

(v) These distinctions, though they do not alter the amount of compensation, are relevant to the action which the girl's family will take. Although the culprit is liable to pay compensation, it is unlikely that the girl's kinsmen will pursue the matter unless he persists in his attentions or actually runs away with the girl. If he does persist their attitude will depend on a variety of circumstances. If he is known to have cattle, they will begin by trying to persuade him to legalize the union by payment of bridewealth. If he is undesirable they will warn him to keep away and, if he ignores the warning, may resort to violence by seizing cattle from his kinsmen. His kinsmen may take steps to recover them by aggressive action, they may ask for them to be returned on the understanding that they will pay the recognized compensation, or they may allow them to remain with the girl's family, thereby indicating that they are willing to open negotiations for legal marriage.

(vi) Nowadays, in most parts of Nuerland and largely depending on

PENAL SANCTIONS

175

the prestige and effectiveness of the local authorities, the girl's family will usually resort to the court. To begin with the man will be publicly admonished by the headman or chief; if he ignores this he will be brought before the court. The court will usually try to bring about a legal union between the pair, but if this is unacceptable to either party or impossible because the culprit has insufficient cattle, it will enforce the payment of *ruok nyal*.

(vii) Penal sanctions now enter into the matter, not only in ensuring that action one way or another will be taken to satisfy the girl's kinsmen, but in the infliction of punishment on the wrongdoer if his act is regarded as a particularly serious wrong. It is noticeable, however, that punishment is usually inflicted only in cases where the wrongdoer has disobeyed the orders of the local authority, usually the headman, or sometimes the orders of the court. The punishment is therefore usually, though not always, applied because the culprit has committed an offence against the authorities, not because his initial offence was punishable in law.

(viii) The birth of a child as a result of illicit intercourse with an unmarried girl in any of the circumstances described above does not alter the law or the amount of compensation payable to compound the offence. But the girl's family are likely to display greater indignation and to force the issue with greater determination. A simple act of sexual intercourse with an unmarried girl is often ignored. If a child is born as a result, whatever the circumstances, the offence will certainly not be ignored.

(ix) This offence is known as *ruet nyal*—impregnation of an unmarried girl. It may be compounded at the same rates as *dhu nyal*. There arise, however, obvious complications over the legitimate parenthood of the child. The culprit may simply pay compensation (*ruok nyal*) and forgo any future claims on his child. The child then belongs to its mother's lineage or, more usually, to the man who subsequently marries her with full bridewealth, especially if she is married fairly soon after the event. The culprit may pay a legitimization fee (*ruok gaanke*).

(x) If he pays *ruok gaanke*, he will not be expected to pay also *ruok nyal*; but should the child die, the cattle will not be returned to him. What he has paid as a legitimization fee becomes compensation in retrospect for the act of sexual intercourse with the girl. As we have seen, a man must announce his intention of legitimizing the child at once. He cannot do so at a later date, at any rate without paying much higher rates.

I rather doubt whether the scales of compensation quoted by Nuer as being traditional, though obviously again a formula for compromise, had any exact application in the past. They seem to me to be the product of more recent decisions in the courts and of case law.

176 INTERCOURSE WITH UNMARRIED WOMEN

Recent Legislation

Rulings given by the chiefs at the meeting of 1945 were as follows:

(*a*) When a man seduces an unmarried girl he must pay compensation (*ruok dhu nyal*) of a cow-calf and a bull-calf to her guardian. If he elopes with her or persuades her to leave home he is liable to pay two cow-calves. This applies only in cases where the girl does not bear a child. This is *ruok dhu nyal*.

(*b*) If the girl bears a child, her seducer is not liable to pay compensation, i.e. *ruok ruet nyal*.

(*c*) In the circumstances given in (*b*) above, the seducer has the option of marrying the girl in the normal way or of legitimizing the child by payment of fees (*ruok gaanke*). If he declares that the child is not his or that he will have nothing to do with it, he can only legitimize it at a later period by payment of from six to ten head of cattle according to the age and sex of the child.

(*d*) Any man who seduces a girl and, after payment of compensation or legitimization fees, returns to her again, renders himself liable to imprisonment.[1]

There appears to be considerable variation of opinion on this subject throughout Nuerland, and it is surprising that this agreement took the form it did. Some chiefs said that if a girl bore a child her chances of getting married to someone else were not reduced. The birth of a child proved her fertility, which was an important consideration to a prospective husband. It may also be noted that these rules give legal recognition to the distinction between mere seduction and seduction which amounts to abduction. A man will now pay a cow-calf and a bull-calf for the former offence and two cow-calves for the latter. Though the latter was regarded as a more serious offence in the past, the distinction was not, as we have seen, reflected in the compensation claimed.

3. OTHER WRONGS

Thung yiika

Thung yiika has already been mentioned under the heading of homicide. *Thung* is the normal word used for bloodwealth and *yiik* refers to the married woman's mat, and hence is a symbol of marriage and childbirth. The expression therefore refers to the indemnity which a woman's family may demand if she dies in childbirth. Nuer opinion on the subject is vague, and the law has now been abolished. Prior to its abolition in 1947 it was generally accepted in Nuer courts that—

(i) The indemnity was never claimed from the husband of a legally married woman. It could not be claimed by a woman's husband from an adulterer should his wife die as a result of the latter's wrong.

(ii) It was demanded for unmarried girls who died in childbirth. The definition of 'unmarried' in this context is not entirely clear. The indemnity might be demanded from a man whose betrothed wife died in childbirth before the final bridewealth payments

[1] Extract from Minutes of Nuer Chiefs' Council Meeting, 1945 (unpublished.)

GATLUAK NGINGI (see p. 34)

BUTH DIU

INTERCOURSE WITH PREGNANT WOMAN   177

had been made or before the *muot*; a woman in such circumstances is *keagh*, still unmarried.[1]

(iii) A man was only liable to pay *thung yiika* in certain circumstances, for example, if the girl died in childbirth before the child was delivered or before she rid herself of the afterbirth.

Up to 1947 there were occasional claims for *thung yiika* through the courts, but this does not necessarily indicate that it was applied either consistently or often in the past. It is worth noting, however, that the special expert known in Nuer as the *kuaar yiika* was concerned with the assessment of compensation in such cases, acted as arbitrator, and performed the necessary ritual. He was concerned generally with the fertility of women, and had a traditional and orthodox position in Nuer society like other experts of that category.

Thung yiika was at one time standardized at six head of cattle. Among the Gaawar, Thiang, and Lak tribes it had previously been set at eight head of cattle (five cows and three bulls), and at six head among the Dok and Jagei of Western Nuer District. I have, however, heard the Eastern Jikany say that it was previously thirty head, and the Bul and Leik sometimes say that it should be twenty. I doubt that such large numbers of cattle were ever paid. *Thung yiika* was abolished at the Nuer Council of 1947, and is therefore no longer law.

Thiang

Sexual intercourse with a woman who is pregnant or is suckling a child is a serious breach of taboo, and will result in harm to the woman or her child. A husband who commits this offence is scorned; his family, as well as that of his wife, will insist on the performance of ritual expiation and sacrifice. If the man who does so is not the legal husband of the woman and his act results in her death, he will be held liable and will have to compensate her husband, though the rate of compensation is not fixed. I have no records of a case of this sort, though I have heard of instances where a man has been prevailed upon to pay. Disputes do not usually arise, for, apart from the fact that the offence is rarely committed, ritual sanctions are usually sufficient to secure payment. The wrongdoer will fear the consequences to himself, although it is considered that the woman runs a graver risk. I recall one case among the Rut Dinka who have the same custom.[2] A man called Thon de Kur had intercourse with a woman who was suckling a child. The child died subsequently, a dispute arose, and he was made to pay a cow as compensation (Dinka: *puk de thiang*).

[1] See under 'Legality of Marriage', pp. 124–8. Nuer simply say *nyal me kaa kwen mi caa liu ba thung yiika col*, '(if) a girl who is not married dies (in childbirth) *thung yiika* will be called'.

[2] The idea is common to all Nilotes, including the Shilluk, and is everywhere known by the same name.

NNL

CHAPTER V

PROPERTY RIGHTS

1. OWNERSHIP

General Considerations

EVEN though radical changes are now taking place with the introduction of a cash economy, the concept of 'ownership' among the Nuer is still largely expressed in terms of kinship. The principles of group solidarity which apply in marriage relations, homicide, and the balanced opposition of social groups extend also to property relations. Nuer speak of ownership in definite terms of speech. They will say *dun-da*, 'my thing', or *nyin-ke*, 'his things', but further analysis shows that these expressions of individual ownership are qualified by kinship relations. A man may well speak of a cow as *his* cow (*yang-da*), but in most instances his ownership of or right to that cow is qualified by his membership of a kinship group. The cow has come to him through one of the many intricate channels in the kinship structure and will not be his for long. Either it will be paid to some kinsman in discharging another obligation of kinship or it will be passed on in marriage. When a man leaves cattle to his sons, these do not become their permanent and inalienable property. They have the right to use them for the time being, but sooner or later it will be incumbent upon them to use them to marry a wife, either on behalf of one of their number or on behalf of some dead kinsman, or they may be obliged to assist some living kinsman to marry. It should be emphasized here that it is obligatory upon them to use the cattle for this purpose; obligatory because the cattle are part of a collective, not an individual system of ownership. A Nuer can rarely sell a cow without the express permission of his kinsmen, and this will probably only be granted if the transaction is both expedient and to the common advantage of them all. This is, of course, one of the reasons why sales of cattle in Nuerland are still so small.[1] Therefore, when a man speaks of his cow as *yang da* 'my cow', he means that he has the right to use that cow for the subsistence of himself and his family, to marry a wife, or to discharge some debt, but he only has that right by virtue of his membership of a kinship group. In this sense ownership of cattle is collective. It must be remembered, too, that although most articles of importance in the material culture of the Nuer are reckoned in terms of cattle, the handing over of cattle

[1] See pp. 195–6.

MOVABLE PROPERTY 179

in marriage is not a financial transaction but an operation which maintains the balance of exogamous groups, defines their limits, and emphasizes the legality of their marriages.

There is, as will be seen later, no concept of the ownership of land by an individual. Ownership of the land, both for cultivation and for grazing, or of stretches of water for fishing, is expressed in terms of kinship and follows the lines of social cleavage. Disputes over land are again associated with the balanced opposition of tribal segments, not of individuals.

Property other than Livestock and Land

Apart from cattle and land there are other forms of property, the ownership of which is in some cases more individual in character. These are articles of clothing, ornaments, weapons (except sacred spears), utensils and domestic tools, pottery, houses, and agricultural implements.

It is necessary here to make some distinction according to actual values in the past. That these values have been altered by the introduction of trade goods which may be bought with cash will be seen later. In the past there appear to have been four categories of such property:

(1) Articles made from local materials easily available, the manufacture of which required no technical skill or knowledge. In this category were such things as cattle-ropes (particularly the less ornamented kind), sandals made from cow-hide, spear-shafts and cattle-pegs. Such articles could always be made by any Nuer with the minimum of trouble. They were of little permanent value and were given away freely. Hence the right to ownership rarely, if ever, became the subject of dispute, and there is no tradition of accepted scales of compensation for misappropriation, nor for that matter any likelihood of legal remedy.

(2) Articles made from local materials, the manufacture of which required both skilled technique and knowledge. Here a further distinction may be made according to the sex of the manufacturer, e.g. pots were made by women, bull-collars by men. Moreover, although there were very few hereditary craftsmen in Nuer society, some individuals acquired the reputation of especial skill and were able to barter their wares for things of equal or greater value, and sometimes for goats, sheep or even cattle. Such articles included clubs, shields of hide, ornaments of leather, pottery, spear-shafts of a more ornate kind, decorated gourds, and wooden or bone spear-heads. These were exchanged freely and were given to relatives without much demur if asked for, but Nuer would object strongly to their removal by a stranger.

(3) Articles of local materials manufactured by skilled and sometimes, though rarely, hereditary craftsmen, the value of which was in

180 PROPERTY RIGHTS

the past nearly always expressed in terms of cattle and often on a conventional basis. Such articles were canoes and ivory bangles (though here the basic value of the ivory must be taken into account). These were of considerable value and, as will be seen, there were in the past scales of compensation demanded for their loss or misappropriation.

(4) Imported articles, chiefly of iron, like fish-spears, iron spear-heads, hooks, iron hoes, &c. There were no iron smelters and few blacksmiths among the Nuer in those days. Iron wares were acquired from other tribes in exchange for cattle. These also had a conventional value and, in traditional legal processes, a conventional rate of compensation (*cut*).

We see therefore that there were various categories of chattels or movable property, some of which (those in the first category) had no definite or standard value because they were so easily obtainable; others which had exchange value, but no conventional rate of compensation for loss in excess of the exchange value (those in the second category); still others which had not only high exchange value in terms of cattle but also rates of compensation for loss, usually far in excess of that value (those in the third and fourth categories). The reason for the heavy damages demanded in such circumstances is discussed later. It may be noted here that it was partly due to the economic advantages obtained from the article (hoes or fish-spears for example) and hence the economic disadvantages caused by its loss, for it could not be easily replaced. Although actually held by an individual, the advantages applied to other members of his community, who would therefore assist him to obtain redress. Moreover, since it was initially purchased with cattle, kinsmen who had interests in those cattle would also have interests in the article.

Finally another form of ownership, which must be mentioned in connexion with property relations, is possession of spirits or 'spirit medicines'. Certain kinds of spirits or medicines which have magical properties may be purchased with cattle. Such spirits are spoken of as being 'owned', but in contrast to more corporeal rights, they cannot be stolen because in the transference there must be some spiritual harmony between the two persons concerned, and the appropriate ritual must be performed. The nature of these spirits is discussed in a later chapter.

Changing Values

These observations apply to the past. Clearly concepts of property relations are undergoing swift and radical changes in Nuer society today. The introduction of a money economy in itself is bound to have repercussions on ideas of property and ownership. Most articles can be bought for relatively small sums of money, and money can be

LAND TENURE

obtained by work or the sale of such products as hides and grain; and money can be used, apart from trade goods now in demand, to purchase cattle, although the market for cattle is still very limited.

Legal concepts based on values related to a subsistence economy only and conditioned by relative scarcity are bound to be modified when the economy begins to change, and the availability of certain articles is vastly increased. For example, although Nuer now practise agriculture on a larger scale than before and it is therefore of greater importance, an iron hoe valued at several head of cattle in the scale of traditional compensation, if it is ever stolen at all, now demands nothing more than material restitution. Another hoe can be purchased for a few piastres almost anywhere, and the threat of hardship from its loss is negligible. Hence nowadays the potential value of the hoe is ignored; only the actual trade value is assessed and, as will be seen, the wrong inflicted on the owner by taking it from him is not considered.

2. LAND TENURE, GRAZING RIGHTS, AND RIGHTS IN WATER

General Considerations

Rights in land, grazing, and fishing and drinking pools are held by those who are considered to be the descendants of the original occupiers of the area. This is particularly true of Nuer east of the Nile, for such rights are held by descent from the original colonizers. An understanding of land tenure, therefore, requires an analysis of the lineal structure of Nuer society and of the way in which areas were seized from the Dinka and occupied, mostly towards the end of the last century. The position and function of the nuclear clan or 'aristocrats' in each area who are called *diel*—as opposed to *rul*, i.e. later accretions who attach themselves to the original occupants—has already been explained. Most Nuer clans or tribes have strong traditions of an original division of land. Later accretions only acquire rights of possession by association with the nuclear lineage. This is in fact the basis of the whole system of Nuer society. Many *rul* lineages attempt to attach themselves to a nuclear lineage by real or fictitious relationship, often through intermarriage. The distinction in the latter case is clear, for, as we have seen, those who link themselves to the *diel* through previous marriages are called *gaat nyiet*, the 'sons of daughters', as opposed to *gaat tutni*,[1] 'sons of bulls'. *Diel* are always *gaat tutni* in the area they occupy; *gaat nyiet* are always *rul*, though *rul* are not all necessarily *gaat nyiet*. It seems that the word *rul* is applied with greater emotional intensity to those who have arrived and settled more recently, while those whose ancestors attached themselves earlier in Nuer

[1] See p. 18.

PROPERTY RIGHTS

history to a nuclear clan have acquired so much associated tradition that the attachment is confirmed.

Land tenure here means the holding of, and rights to, the high ridges and sandy outcrops which the Nuer occupy during the wet season, where they build their permanent villages and cattle-byres and clear their cultivations, and the various forms of land used for pastures and fishing in the dry season. That certain communities, consisting of the *diel* and later accretions by association, have a definite right to distinct areas is clearly recognized by all Nuer. The sanction for possession in the past was, however, physical force and power to resist the encroachment of others, while nowadays the *status quo* is maintained by the Government.[1]

Occupation of the land and prescriptive rights to a certain territory are often expressed in mythological terms linked to the history of the nuclear lineage. The original ancestor is said to have divided land among his sons, themselves ancestors of particular collateral lineages, in the same way as he divided his cattle and sometimes his ritual functions among them. But this is merely an idiom which gives emotional emphasis to ownership of land vested in that nuclear lineage, for land, either arable or pasture, is not a form of property which is normally controlled by the laws of inheritance. A man's eldest son will inherit his huts and cattle-byre, while the other sons continue to occupy them so long as they wish to do so, particularly if they are not married; but, as younger sons, they have no specified portions of their father's land, and there is consequently no individual inheritance of land. When they wish to do so, they will build their houses and set up their homes in some area which is unoccupied, for there is usually no shortage.

As I have explained in the introduction, three types of land are utilized by the Nuer, and each is of definite value at certain times of the year. The 'high land', ridges of higher, better-drained ground, provides for the permanent settlements mainly occupied during the rains from approximately May until November, though the period varies according to latitude and local climatic conditions. This area is largely used for the cultivation of millet (their staple crop), of maize and tobacco and the few vegetables which some Nuer grow. Beyond, and usually surrounding the higher ridges, are the 'intermediate' grass plains which are subject to variable flooding from accumulated rainfall which only drains away with difficulty, especially if the ground is already saturated. These 'intermediate' areas are utilized at the end of the rains for pasture so long as sufficient moisture remains in the soil to allow a green regrowth from the perennial grasses after they

[1] Nuer did not confine their aggressive movements to the Dinka. Other Nuer tribes were often attacked and their territory occupied. For example, the Lou Nuer originally occupied the Zeraf Island, but a military alliance between Thiang and Lak drove them out.

OWNERSHIP OF LAND

have been burnt or close cropped. Later they dry out and become unpalatable, and by this time the inland pools are also dry, so that the people must move their herds to the *toic*. The word *toic* in some contexts merely means 'summer grazing', in others more specifically the marshes bordering the main channels of the rivers, their smaller tributaries, and the network of minor drainage channels found everywhere in Nuerland. Here a combination of soil, depth and period of immersion from river-spill and other factors produces grasses which, to a greater or lesser degree, are valuable as pasture throughout the dry months of the year. Beyond this are the permanent papyrus swamps (*sudd*), which scarcely dry out at all and are useless for grazing and (at present) are not used for crop production.

This classification is necessarily arbitrary and relative, for the difference of level is rarely more than a few feet, and there is no clear-cut boundary between the different types of land.[1] Moreover, though 'high land' is nearly always limited,[2] 'intermediate' land may extend no more than a few hundred yards before *toic* is found in the flood-plain of neighbouring watercourses, or it may continue for more than fifty miles. Such varying distances have their effect on the seasonal movements of the people, but—again as a broad generalization—the main feature, the balanced utilization of all three types of land according to the season, is common to all Nuer.

For these reasons ownership of the land necessarily includes all three, and when a Nuer speaks of his *rol*, his country, or sometimes his *dhor*, he envisages a territory which includes 'high land' for cultivations and permanent settlements, 'intermediate' land for pasture in the early months of the dry season, *toic* for summer grazing and fishing. *Rol* Gaawar is a complete territory in this respect; within it each primary segment has its own complete area, *rol* Radh and *rol* Bar, and within these the secondary segments, *rol* (*cieng*) Kerfeil, *rol* (*cieng*) Per and so on.[3] Thus territory and rights in land follow the segmentary system, but this does not mean that an individual or even a small group of people will necessarily confine their movements to the territory of the segment to which by tradition and practice they should belong. Living in one permanent settlement during the rains, they may well choose to herd their cattle in the dry season pastures of a different segment of the tribe, or in some cases to cross the boundaries of another tribe. They will do so, however, only by agreement with the 'owners' of that territory, though such agreements are often implicit rather than defined. It is clearly recognized that ownership of the land lies with the segment of the tribe from which the name of the area derives; in other words, from the dominant lineage. *Rol* (*cieng*) Kerfeil is theoretically the exclusive property of all descendants of

---

[1] See Jonglei Investigation Team. *Progress Report, 1948–9.*
[2] See map on p. 13.   [3] See p. 19.

184 PROPERTY RIGHTS

Kerfeil and those linked with them by permanent association. Within it each collateral branch of the main clan has definite rights to a certain part, usually specified by reference to villages on higher ground, and elsewhere to pools which provide water and fish and to the pastures which surround them. *Rol* (or *dhor*) is relative like the word *cieng*, which has much the same meaning on a smaller scale.[1]

I must emphasize again that land to the Nuer must include all types, for their subsistence economy is maintained by the balanced and seasonal utilization of all three, but it may be as well to examine separately and in more detail the types of land used for crop production and animal husbandry and the rights in water-points and fisheries which go with them.

Arable Land

From the legal point of view the problem of rights in arable land is not a complicated one among the Nuer, and there is virtually no litigation concerning either individual or collective claims. The reasons are not far to seek. During the cultivation season the Nuer occupy the high ground which is free from river floods or swamping by heavy rain. Such high ground is limited when compared to the total area occupied by Nuer tribes, but there is generally more than enough available. An intricate and complex system of rights in land cannot be necessary unless there is scarcity, and this is not usually the case. Nuer like to have their gardens close to their dwellings, so that they can protect them against wild animals and straying cattle. They do not usually fence their fields, particularly in those areas where wood and thorn are not easily available.[2] The Nuer village, moreover, is not built on a concentrated pattern, and each homestead is separated from its neighbours by a considerable distance ranging from about a hundred yards to over a mile. The Nuer ideal is to live in the bosom of his own immediate family as isolated as possible from his neighbours and free from tiresome intrusions. This individualistic outlook is, however, limited by a variety of considerations. In the clearing of land, in the heavier tasks of cultivation, and in harvesting, collective assistance, dependent on the mutual obligations of kinship and neighbourhood and the provision of beer and meat for workers, is necessary. A Nuer would not wish to live so far away from his neighbours that it would be impossible to take advantage of their help. Further, in the past at any rate, the need for defence and concentration against

---

[1] For definition of the word *cieng*, see pp. 20–21.

[2] Fencing is used in some areas, particularly in the heavily forested regions of the Zeraf Valley, but usually only on newly cleared ground. The branches of trees cut are then used to make thorny enclosures, but these do not last for more than a year or two at most and there is rarely an attempt made to renew them. Fencing is employed particularly when new cultivations are cleared and sown before the homestead has been rebuilt close to them.

ARABLE LAND

attack was another factor of importance in shaping the pattern of the Nuer settlement, but certainly did not encroach on their desire to live freely, unhindered by the irritations of daily contact with neighbours. There is even the possibility that the establishment of public security by the present Government has resulted in a tendency to move farther afield, but there is little evidence to show with any certainty that villages and settlements were any different a hundred years ago.[1] Apart from these factors, the pattern was obviously governed by purely topographical and climatic considerations: the contours of the high ground, its extent in relation to the population of the community, and the fertility of the soil.

The Nuer are not aware of the value of crop rotation, and do not use their cattle to fertilize the soil; when the ground is exhausted they simply abandon it and move elsewhere, rebuilding their houses and cattle-byres on a new site. There is therefore no high degree of permanence of tenure, and no rigidity of rights in arable land. A man and his family have the prescriptive right to use the land they have cleared, and to do so to the exclusion of every other man so long as they choose. They also have the right to the products of the land and of their own labours, though this right may be said to be limited by their obligations to assist kinsmen, obligations which may be extended in terms of kinship to neighbours, should the vagaries of climate affect their crops. We have already seen that the maldistribution of rainfall coupled with an impervious and otherwise badly drained soil makes crop production a precarious undertaking. In bad years Nuer must rely on the generosity of their more successful kinsmen and sometimes take refuge with them (for the widespread failure of crops only occasionally happens) and in years of heavy rainfall, those whose land is high and well-drained enjoy an advantage which is lost to them when the rains are light. There is, of course, no means of enforcing the rules of hospitality and kinship obligations in such circumstances, but refusal to assist hungry kinsmen will lead to fission and the conscious breaking of relationship (*dak mara*). There are other sanctions for maintaining such relationships, not the least of which is the probable need at some future date to demand assistance in return. A man who acquires a reputation for meanness quickly loses the privileges which membership of a community provides, and also the privileges of kinship with Nuer living in other parts of the country.

Claims on the hospitality of kinsmen are often carried to extremes

---

[1] During the period of invasion and occupation of Dinka country there were periods when the Nuer lived in cattle-camps of concentrated form, a circle of huts or shelters, and did so for several years at a time. The camps were built on the same pattern as those used in the dry season today, but it is clear that agricultural activity was extremely limited and there was certainly no need for a complex system of rights governing the distribution of arable land.

186 PROPERTY RIGHTS

and well beyond the limits of the reciprocal distribution of bridewealth cattle, but I do not wish to exaggerate the extent or effectiveness of economic reciprocity in the kinship system. In the past as well as the present, grain and other food were bartered for cattle, other animal stock, and other commodities, and there was considerable trade, which increased in volume in years of famine. Nowadays, with the introduction of a money economy, grain is bought with cash either from other Nuer or from Arab merchants, who, sponsored by the Government, often import large quantities to meet local shortages.

A stranger cannot intrude himself into a community or build his house and clear his fields without its acceptance. Not only will objections be raised which might lead to his ejection, but he could not hope to gain full membership of the community and the advantages which follow. This does not, however, usually arise because strangers are nearly always a welcome addition to the community, which thereby gains in strength, and because the newcomer can nearly always claim some previous link arising from kinship, marital ties, or at any rate close friendship (*math*), with one or more members of that community. In any case a form of social relationship will be forged in the passage of time by intermarriage and adoption into the lineage structure of the community. A change of residence, if it is permanent, means also a change of social and political affiliation.

For these reasons, because crop production is not an important feature of their economy, at any rate in many parts of Nuerland, and because, despite the obvious limitations of flood-free land, there is no great shortage, there are no complex laws of land tenure. Disputes are rare, and still more rarely taken before the courts.[1] Thus, though circumstances may change with the development of agricultural enterprise, land tenure is not at present an important or well-defined feature of Nuer customary law.

Grazing Rights

During the rains the cattle are kept in the permanent settlements and quartered in cattle-byres (*luak*), each family unit having its own. The *luak* is the centre of the family group consisting of the head of the family and his wives, who, each with her children, occupy separate huts which are clustered around it. Grazing is used communally by all members of the settlement, and although pastures are limited, especially at the height of the rains, and although there may be periodic shortages when the cattle lose condition, no more precise division of the territory is necessary. Disputes rarely, if ever, arise, and in the herding of cattle the members of one settlement are united by common

---

[1] The only form of dispute commonly brought before the courts concerns 'animal trespass', where straying cattle, sheep, or goats damage the crops of neighbours. Compensation is often awarded in such cases.

GRAZING RIGHTS

interests. In most parts of Nuerland too the nature of the terrain—isolated outcrops of flood-free ground often widely separated—usually precludes the possibility of clashes between different settlements. Likewise when the rains cease the cattle are widely dispersed in small camps over the 'intermediate' plains. There is no shortage and no need for a clear demarcation of boundaries between the units of one community, or between different communities coming from different settlements.

As the dry season advances, when the 'intermediate' grasses become unpalatable and water supplies run short, concentration increases, and the small camps join together in larger ones in the *toic*. Cattle-camps with five or six thousand animals are not uncommon, and often there are many of such camps clustered along the banks of a river or watercourse in one region. More careful regard for rights in these pastures and in the fisheries which go with them may be necessary if disputes are to be avoided. Yet there is usually plenty of grazing, though this varies according to prevailing climatic conditions. In one year the river may be low and the rains light, with the result that the Nuer must penetrate farther into the riverain marshes; in another, a high river level may limit their movements to the fringes. Both circumstances may result in shortages, and something between the two extremes is probably the ideal; but many Nuer tribes have alternative grazing grounds which are utilized in varying proportions according to the year. For example, the Dok and Jagei Nuer can use the marshes of the Bahr el Jebel in a year when that river is low and much of the flood-plain uncovered, or they can move to the pastures of the Bilnyang system, which are produced partly by water spilling from the main river, and partly by water draining from a different catchment area. Some Nuer tribes do not have these advantages; in some areas periodic plagues of biting flies or mosquitoes, whose incidence also obviously varies with different climatic conditions, prevent the full utilization of their summer grazing grounds. Generally speaking, there are rarely acute shortages, and even in the *toic* the boundaries between tribes or tribal segments need not be closely guarded.

In certain circumstances, however, such boundaries become essential, and their infringement may then cause disputes, which often result in violence and bloodshed. Sometimes there is an unusual shortage both of grazing grasses and water-points, and people who have normally tolerated the intrusion of outsiders less favourably provided than themselves, turn upon them and demand their withdrawal. Again, an epidemic of some contagious disease such as rinderpest or contagious bovine pleuro-pneumonia makes quarantine and segregation of the herds essential. Fear of the spread of disease compels the owners to guard their boundaries more closely. To bring contaminated cattle into an area recognized as the exclusive right of other segments, and

188

PROPERTY RIGHTS

where strangers are only allowed on sufferance, is a particularly serious infringement of grazing rights, and one which raises a storm of protest quickly followed by blows. Disputes of this nature do not usually start on a tribal scale; the initial quarrel arises between two adjacent cattle-camps near the boundaries, but feelings of indignation may extend along the lines of segmentation until two large segments or even two tribes are ranged against each other. Rights in grazing are recognized and follow the lines of the segmentary system, but are not a constant source of friction. Violation of these rights in years when it was necessary to guard them almost invariably led to hostilities in the past. Nowadays, though fights are not infrequent and boundary disputes are a common cause of blood-feuds, disputes of this nature are often settled peacefully in the courts.

Water Rights

Rights in watering places cannot be treated except in relation to grazing. In the dry season it is the availability of water which largely determines the extent to which certain pastures within the territory of the tribe or the tribal segment are used. This applies particularly to those Nuer tribes who are unable to reach perennial rivers like the Zeraf, Bahr el Jebel, or Sobat. Disputes over pools, especially in dry years when they dry out early in the year, often arise and may lead to bloodshed. Water rights, however, follow the same principles which govern the division of territory according to the segmentation of tribal structure. Shallow wells are sometimes sunk, and are the property of the individual who digs them, but subject always to his obligation to share with his kinsmen and neighbours.

Fishing Rights and Hunting Rights

Fishing rights go with the divisions of territory in which the fish pools are situated and are guarded with perhaps a greater intensity of feeling than are rights in land. Fishing in the riverain area is essentially a dry season occupation, and there are fishing pools or stretches of shallow rivers and watercourses attached to and situated within grazing areas. Fishing is also a collective activity, and the right of the individual is limited by his membership of the tribal segment to which the pool belongs. Fishing again depends largely on the climatic conditions prevailing. A season of heavy rainfall followed by an abrupt drop in levels in the rivers and their tributaries is usually the ideal. Fish have been able to move far upstream during the rains, but are prevented from returning to the deeper waters of the main channels and are concentrated in depressions and pools shallow enough for the people to spear them. In such circumstances fish are not scarce, and pools

FISHING AND HUNTING

farther afield may be abandoned for the time being. Other people whose opportunities for fishing may not be so great as their neighbours' may utilize the less accessible pools unmolested, but should climatic conditions cause scarcity elsewhere their owners will demand the right to use them to the exclusion of other people.

Hunting rights are also defined by the limits of recognized tribal or segment territory, but since the Nuer are not very active hunters there is no clear definition, and quarrels rarely arise. There are rules governing the division of the flesh of wild animals killed in collective hunting, though they are rarely followed without argument. The division of meat in these circumstances often leads to violent quarrels but is not a subject which reaches the stage of litigation in the courts. Ivory, a very valuable commodity in Nuer eyes, not because of its market value but because it is the ambition of most Nuer to own an ivory bracelet, is subject to more definite rules. The right tusk must always go to the first spearer, the *ran me koic e-je*, the left tusk to the second spearer, the *ran me gam e-je*. Others who take part in the hunt, even if the wounds they have inflicted have been much more deadly than those of the first two spearers, get no more than their share of the meat. Those who get the tusks must divide them among their kinsmen according to principles similar to those which govern the distribution of bridewealth cattle. The central portion must be given to the *gwan buthni* of the lineage, this portion being sufficient to make one large bangle; of the remainder a portion must go *kwi gwan*, to the father's side, and a portion *kwi man* (or *nar*), to the mother's or maternal uncle's side. Dead elephants are sometimes found, the ivory going to the first and second finder in the same manner. The right to tusks and the way in which they are distributed are not matters which come before the courts, and there are strong ritual sanctions for observing the correct rules. There is a mystical link between man—that is, Nuer—and elephants, which means that killing them is not only a hazardous physical undertaking, but is also spiritually dangerous. It is something akin to homicide, and special ritual must be performed, including the letting of blood (*birr*) from the first spearer.[1] Nuer also believe that if they ignored the rules of distribution, the spirit (*cien*) of the dead elephant would haunt them and would bring them misfortunes.

Conclusion

Rights in land are therefore collective and follow the segmentary structure of Nuer society. They are recognized and nowadays will be enforced in the courts, and they embrace all types of land necessary to the subsistence economy of the Nuer, but they are not in constant

[1] As in homicide it is the first spearer who is held responsible for the animal's death.

190 INHERITANCE

emphasis nor is there any demarcation of boundaries. Within each tribe which owns a territory in opposition to other tribes there is a further division according to primary segments and smaller communities. The lower down the scale of segmentation the less clearly defined are these boundaries, because ultimately they correspond to regions occupied by people closely bound by ties of kinship and by the need for close co-operation in the economic sphere. Individuals and small groups of people cross these boundaries, but must do so with the consent, tacit or consciously given, of those with whom the territory is associated, the *diel*, and those who link themselves to them. Thus with the exception of occasional quarrels over the riverain grazing grounds, land is not often in dispute. In the past rival claims to territory were settled with the spear, and there existed no complex laws of land tenure governing human relationships where land was concerned. Land tenure is not a serious problem in Nuerland nor the subject of much litigation in the courts, and is unlikely to become so while there is no shortage.[1]

3. INHERITANCE

Laws of inheritance might more properly be discussed under the heading of marriage, for they are inseparable from the general kinship system and the rules of bridewealth distribution. Matters of inheritance are not a common cause of litigation; they are essentially *ruac cieng*, private affairs which should be settled in the home. Nevertheless, disputes of this kind are sometimes brought before the courts, even by persons as closely related as brothers or half-brothers.

Inheritance of Cattle

Nuer society is essentially patrilineal where the inheritance of property is concerned, and a man's belongings should go to his sons, or failing that to his brothers or brothers' sons. Property or titles to cattle accorded in the name of a woman (for example, the mother's, maternal aunt's, and paternal aunt's portions in bridewealth) should go to her own sons and hence to the lineage of her husband, not that of her father. This rule is normally applied though it may be ignored in certain circumstances upon which no generalization can be made.[2]

The laws concerning inheritance are not distinct, for the owner is normally expected to divide the cattle actually in his possession among his sons or relatives before he dies. The underlying principle, however, for the distribution of cattle among a man's sons is that brothers

---

[1] As there may be when the Equatorial Nile Project is in full operation.

[2] See for example the marriages described on pp. 115–117. In these, since there were no uterine brothers of the bride's mother, their portions went to their maternal nephews, though one might expect them to go to their paternal kinsmen.

must marry in order of seniority—the eldest first. In a simple family consisting of a man, his wife, and sons, the sons are referred to as *keagh, gur keka, dar, joah* and *pegh* respectively. Thus:

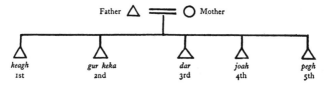

(The 'first', 'the one after the first', 'the middle', 'the (one before the) last', 'the youngest'.)[1]

When a man has more than one wife, the sons of each wife are thus titled separately, each family beginning with *keagh* and ending with *pegh*. The principle of priority in marriage, however, is applied according to age, and does not depend on the status of the wife.

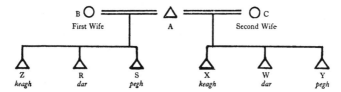

Thus, if X is older than Z, he will marry first. If W is older than Z, he will marry first and so on.

Certain indications of inheritance rights are also given in the distribution of bridewealth, not only between actual claimants standing in a particular relationship to the bride, but also between the persons who should rightfully inherit the title to those claims should the claimant be dead. I do not propose to describe here all the details of these indications because they have already been mentioned in connexion with bridewealth distribution,[2] but certain principles must be emphasized again.

The first of these principles is based on the distinction between the sons of the father (by another mother) and the sons of the mother (in this connexion the mother of the bride). A family group among the Nuer is made up of a number of domestic units each of which consists of a wife and her children. A man who has two wives is in the position of being husband and father to two such units. The children of one unit are uterine brothers and sisters; to each other they are *kwi dwiel*, 'on the side of the house or hut', because each wife must have her own

[1] The terminology is interesting. The word *keagh* is used to describe a woman who is unmarried or has not yet completed the processes of marriage. *Gur keka* (*gur keagh*) means simply 'the follower of the *keagh*'. *Dar* means 'middle', 'in the midst', *joah* or *joagh* means 'last', while *pegh* means 'end or limit'.

[2] See pp. 97–124.

hut (*dwil*). They are half-brothers and half-sisters to the children of another wife of their father; these are *kwi luak* because the *luak* or cattle-byre is common to all, as is their father. The *kwi dwiel—kwi luak* distinction is also brought out in other terms of speech, as we have already seen; those who are *kwi dwiel* are *kwi man* or *mande* ('of the mother'), those who are *kwi luak* are *kwi gwan* or *gwande* ('of the father'). In normal speech these distinctions are not used because the context does not demand a distinction. A man's paternal uncle is referred to as *gwanlen*, whether he is a full or uterine brother of the man's father or a half-brother. A distinction is, however, demanded in matters of bridewealth distribution and inheritance. He is *gwanlen kwi luak* or *gwanlen kwi gwan* and so on. The first principle, therefore, of bridewealth distribution and the inheritance thereof is that there should be an equitable distribution on both sides of a family group described above. We have seen that each of the persons standing in a particular and accurately described relationship to the bride has a title to a portion of the bridewealth according to an ideal. This, however, concerns direct and contemporary claims. It becomes a matter of inheritance when the actual claimant is dead.

If the claimant is a male, the heirs to his title may be any one of his sons, though in bridewealth there is always a tendency to say that his sons by a woman who is not the mother of the bride should inherit in these circumstances. These are in fact half-brothers of the bride, and the system is one of mutual alternation, since the bride's uterine brothers already have a special portion and will expect in return to benefit on the marriage of the half-brothers' uterine sisters. Moreover the paternal grandfather's portion (*wangnen kwi gwan*) should always go to his son born of another wife and not to the son of the bride's paternal grandmother. This rule is applied with considerable exactitude unless no such person exists. If the claimant is a female, then her portion should always go to one of her own sons. For example, the paternal grandmother's portion (*wangnen kwi man*) goes to her own sons (other than the bride's father), i.e. one of the paternal uncles of the bride who are classified as *gwanlen kwi dwiel* or *kwi man*. Similarly, the bride's mother's portion should go to her own sons, i.e. the ʙride's uterine brothers.

These distinctions concern the different domestic units of a family group and of a minimal lineage, and govern the distribution and inheritance of claims on both the paternal and maternal sides. There are also indications within a single domestic unit as to which of the brothers should receive a particular cow. Thus, for example, the paternal grandmother's portion (*wangnen kwi man*) is said to be the right of her younger or youngest son (either the *dar, joah* or *pegh*). Similarly the cow called *puong* of the father's portion should go to his youngest son, i.e. the bride's youngest half-brother.

CATTLE

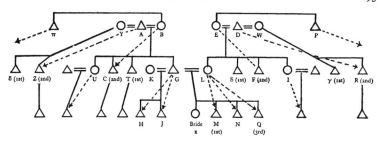

Conventional Indications Bridewealth Portions		Claims on Cattle acquired on Marriage of x From To		
Gwandong	(paternal grandfather)	A	his younger son by Y	=Z
Mandong	(paternal grandmother)	B	her younger son by A	=C
Gwandong	(maternal grandfather)	D	his younger son by W	=R
Mandong	(maternal grandmother)	E	her younger son by D	=F
Gwan	(father)	G	his sons by K	=H and J (the *puong* to J)
Man	(mother)	L	her sons by G	=M, N and Q (the *puong* to Q)

Other portions go to the sons of the actual claimants without distinction.

Gwanlen kwi man	(father's brother by same mother)	=T or C and sons
Gwanlen kwi gwan	(father's brother by different mother)	=Z or δ and sons
Nar kwi man	(mother's brother by same mother)	=S or F and sons
Nar kwi gwan	(mother's brother by different mother)	=R or γ and sons
Wac	(father's sister)	=U to *her* sons
Manlen	(mother's sister)	=I to *her* sons
Nar gwan	(father's maternal uncle)	=π and sons
Nar man	(mother's maternal uncle)	=P and sons

The reader should compare the above diagram with those on pp. 102, 114–23.

There are therefore conventional indications based on distinctions within the family group of the various domestic components and on the seniority of the individual. These are illustrated in the diagram. It must be realized, however, that they are no more than indications because other principles and circumstances intervene. In the first place there is the rule that sons should be granted cattle from the family herd with which to marry in strict order of seniority, as already described. This rule is often incompatible with the conventional indications. In the second place persons to fill exactly the relationships required may not all exist. Finally, while alive, a man will have absolute authority in allotting cattle which are his by right among his own sons, and usually he declares a definite distribution before he dies. Here the indications to inheritance rights are not relevant, but they will be so in connexion with cattle which are acquired after his death, or if he dies suddenly without opportunity to make known his will.

ONL

Cattle which are not necessarily part of the marriage distribution system, for example cattle acquired by a man in compensation for such wrongs as hurt and adultery, are not usually bound by these rules, and a man will allot them to his sons before his death, though he will always bear in mind the order of their marriages.

These rules apply generally to the inheritance of cattle by a man's sons. Sometimes, of course, a man has no sons, and in this case his property goes to his next of kin, his brother, or through his brother to his brother's sons, according to the normal rules of relationship of a patrilineal descent group. It must be remembered also that in inheriting a man's cattle the heir inherits his liabilities and claims—liabilities and claims which are in fact part of the system of obligations inherent in the kinship structure. For this reason, apart from cattle actually in a man's possession which pass in the way described above into the possession of his heirs, the laws of inheritance are extremely complicated. Which liabilities and which claims pass to which of the heirs is a question that is decided, and not necessarily immediately after death, by yet other liabilities and claims already in existence or which come to exist between the heirs. Inheritance is therefore an involved problem which requires a full understanding of the bridewealth system in relation to the obligations of kinship. Except for cattle acquired individually by payment of cash or, in the past, in cattle raids, and to some degree cattle acquired as compensation for wrongs, which are accepted within the kinship group as individually owned, inheritance involves all those rules which govern the collective ownership and distribution of cattle within a lineage.

Inheritance of Other Property

These observations apply mainly to cattle, but also to some extent to sheep and goats. Other corporeal property, including spears, shields, hoes, canoes, ornaments, and nowadays cash, is divided among a man's heirs by common agreement. In the case of cherished objects, particularly spears which have some sacred association, a man will sometimes indicate his heir before he dies, usually his eldest son. This practice is confirmed not only in everyday examples but also in tradition. The original founder of a Nuer clan is often quoted as having decreed that this one of his sons shall perform a particular function in the political and spiritual activities of the clan, and that another son shall receive a particular cow, and so on. Since, however, arguments do not on the whole arise, there is no need for a complicated or exact system of law. Moreover, apart from cattle, or articles which have a recognized value in terms of cattle, Nuer possessions are so easily replaceable that no argument need arise. Disputes over small items of property never appear before the courts.

TRADE

4. TRADE AND LOANS

Trade has never been extensive among the Nuer. There is, of course, a division of labour according to sex, but there are few people who can be accounted specialist craftsmen. Individuals acquire the reputation for making certain specific objects with exceptional skill, but they rarely if ever belong to a family especially associated with such activities. This is an exceptional contrast to specialization in the spiritual sphere, for there are hereditary experts capable of dealing with almost any unusual phenomena: ritual experts, magicians, sooth-sayers and medicine-owners, who demand fees, often in cattle, for their services.

The reason lies, perhaps, in the extraordinary simplicity of Nuer material culture. Most things necessary for their migratory way of life (and this applies to all peoples who move with the seasons) can be made either from wood or grass or from the products of their cattle. Seasonal migration in any case precludes a high degree of virtuosity, for things are liable to breakage and are often an unnecessary encumbrance. Moreover the Nuer, who do not use their animals for transport, must carry everything by hand.

Certain objects were of relatively high value, and were exchanged for cattle or sheep and goats. Nowadays, however, most of these articles—hoes, spears, ornaments and the like—can be obtained for cash, and disputes do not often arise in the courts except over the sale of grain.

Trade in Cattle

Trade in cattle is clearly increasing as a cash economy becomes more important to the Nuer but, as yet, cattle are rarely sold except when the purchase of grain is necessary. A significant paragraph from the Jonglei Investigation Team's *Third Interim Report* (1948) is worth quoting, for the figures given, although taken from all Nilotic inhabitants of the Upper Nile Province, include all the Nuer:

The disposal of surplus livestock is governed by private, family, and tribal circumstances, and is at present tied up with the need to find cash; this is required mainly for the purchase of grain and veterinary vaccines and, to a small extent, for the payment of taxes. There are four channels through which the inhabitants can dispose of their animals:

(a) By sale to the Veterinary Laboratory at Malakal, where they will be used to produce cattle-plague vaccine and serum.

(b) By sale to Malakal butchers for local consumption.

(c) By export to Equatoria Province, in which case most of them will be butchered in Juba.

(d) By export northwards to the markets of Kosti and Omdurman.

In the majority of cases all trade is carried out through merchants as intermediaries. . . . Previously it had often been necessary for the District Commissioner concerned to exercise pressure before the local inhabitants could be induced to sell.

EXCHANGES AND LOANS

*Numbers of Cattle sold in or exported from Malakal in Yearly Totals
from 1935 to 1947 Inclusive*

1935	1936	1937	1938	1939	1940	1941	1942	1943	1944	1945	1946	1947
2,586	2,413	1,590	2,385	2,817	2,116	2,283	3,124	?,204	3,012	5,944	5,380	5,278[1]

When it is remembered that the Nuer alone possess over half a million head of cattle, these sales figures are not impressive, but the increase in sales is significant.

There is still relatively little internal trade in cattle among the Nuer. Cattle are not bought and sold in local markets, and disputes over prices or payment rarely come before the courts. Cattle continue to be exchanged, however, and there are still customary rates of exchange.

Exchanges and Loans

The Nuer word for exchange is *gual*, and is used specifically in connexion with the exchange of cattle. '*Ce thak gual ke dou*', 'he exchanged a bull for a cow-calf.' The expression, which is often loosely applied, refers to a direct exchange. In some cases cattle may be exchanged for sheep. It is generally recognized that a large bull or ox is worth a cow-calf, and a cow-calf is worth anything from 10–20 sheep. Such transactions are frequent.[2] In certain situations of spiritual danger—famine, sickness, or death—or in any situation which demands a sacrifice, a sacrificial animal is necessary, and this may not be immediately available. In such circumstances a man will be forced to make an immediate exchange: a cow-calf for a bull-calf, and so on. More probably he will borrow a bull or in some cases a ram on the understanding that he will pay the owner its recognized equivalent at some later date. This is in the nature of a loan, and involves some measure of interest. A full-grown ox is worth at least a cow-calf if the debt is discharged at some later date, a ram is worth a bull-calf, and so on. In this case the word *ngual* is usually employed. The word *ngual* implies the passage of time before the transaction is complete, and is thus best translated as 'loan'.

In many cases a Nuer will specify beforehand that he will pay the first cow-calf born to such and such a cow. Such loans are a frequent cause of litigation, for a man is often unwilling to repay the loan after his immediate need has been met, or unable to do so.

---

[1] Jonglei Investigation Team, *Third Interim Report*, 1948, p. 20.

[2] Among some Nuer and Dinka tribes there is a considerable trade in this manner with Baggara Arabs from the north. Cow-calves are brought in by the latter and exchanged for large oxen, which are then driven north and sold in the markets. This form of trade is, however, limited, for it seems that Baggara cattle will not survive in the areas south of approximately latitude 9°, and though the Nuer have been tempted to try, the experiment has usually been unsuccessful. In any case, there are no statistics available because the practice is not encouraged by the Government owing to the spread of disease.

INSTITUTION OF 'NAK'

Disputes are easily settled by the courts, though execution of judgement is often slow.

Loans Arising from the Institution of Nak

Slightly different situations arise from the institution known as '*nak*'.[1] It appears probable that *nak*—the common word meaning 'to kill', but in this context meaning 'a slaughter'—was part of the tribal ceremonies concerned with the division of age-sets. Age-mates of the younger age-set would segregate themselves from the rest of the community at the cattle-byre of one of their number and live entirely on the meat of oxen slaughtered for the occasion.

Two or three of the youths would club together to provide an ox and, if their immediate relatives were unable to supply one, they would appropriate one from someone else. In this they were given considerable licence and, should the owner object, they could seize it with impunity. Public opinion would not allow the owner to resist, and certainly he would be unable nowadays to obtain immediate redress in the courts. In return, the youths are bound by convention, with the full force of public opinion behind it, to make return after a specified number of years (usually announced by the *wut ghok*).

The exchange values of cattle provided in this manner are much higher than those recognized in normal exchanges or loans. They are:

1 large bull=2 cow-calves and 1 bull-calf.
1 medium bull=2 cow-calves.
1 bull-calf=1 cow-calf.

The debts were not, of course, discharged with the rigidity which these rates imply, but they are quoted by Nuer as being traditional. Just as a man is expected to hand over his ox without show of reluctance in the first place, so would his debtors be expected to discharge their obligations without argument. Nuer are particularly emphatic on this point, but disputes are, none the less, frequently taken to court.

Nearly all these exchanges are necessary to meet some ritual situation, and are therefore of frequent occurrence. Sacrifice is extremely common, and Nuer consume more meat than is commonly supposed. Recent statistics indicate that a large proportion of the total cattle population is slaughtered.[2]

Exchange of Cattle for Grain

Finally, cattle are sometimes exchanged for grain in times of famine. This has not been so frequent in recent years, because grain, imported

---

[1] I have discussed this institution in more detail in an article, 'The Age-set System and the Institution of 'Nak' among the Nuer', *S.N.R.*, 1948.

[2] See Jonglei Investigation Team, *Progress Report, 1948–9.*

198   THEFT

by Arab merchants, is usually available and bought with cash. Cases
of this kind sometimes appear before the courts. The facts are not
usually denied by the defendant, but execution is often resisted.

Gifts Given in Friendship (math)

Another situation in which cattle are involved, and which is a frequent cause of litigation, is the institution of the 'Best Friend', known
in Nuer as *math*. Two men will often form a bond of friendship by
exchanging cattle either as a one-sided loan or as a direct exchange, each
party taking the other's cow. This can scarcely be described as trade,
but is often the cause of dispute since friends fall out.

Nger Ngwen v. Can Nyoi (Jikany Nuer Case)

Nger and Can were 'best friends' (*math*). Nger gave Can a black cow as
a gift. Can gave Nger a cow when Nger got married. Nger then asked Can
to give him a cow in milk in order to feed his children. Can obliged by giving
him a cow which he had received on the marriage of his daughter. Nger,
however, considered that the cow was a bad one and, after a violent quarrel
with Can, demanded that their 'friendship' should be broken (*dak math*)
publicly and that Can should give back his black cow. The matter was taken
to court, but Nger's claim was thrown out as groundless since Can had
already given him two cows in exchange.

Exchanges of this sort are a corollary to this form of institutionalized
friendship. Disputes of the kind mentioned above are simple enough,
though often heated. It is perhaps surprising that they should
appear before the courts at all, because the issues must be clear to
everyone and there is rarely any doubt.

5. THE INFRINGEMENT OF RIGHTS IN PROPERTY

Self-help

If the seizure of cattle, the property of another man, is defined as
'theft', then theft of cattle is a common offence among the Nuer.
Nuer, however, distinguish clearly between what is considered licensed
seizure, either openly or by stealth, and theft for which the thief can
produce no customary justification. The word *kwal*, which is used
loosely to describe both forms of misappropriation, is employed regularly, but in its more specific meaning it refers to this seizure of what
is considered a man's right. Used in connexion with cattle the word
implies that the culprit, however mistaken he may be, believes that
through kinship ties or in settlement of a debt he has a legal claim
to the cattle. Again, a man may seize for himself cattle which he
regards as his just due in compensation for some injury done to him
by their owner. Thus, for example, a man may seize six head of cattle

SELF-HELP 199

from a man who has seduced his wife because six head of cattle is the accepted scale of compensation for adultery. Having acquired the cattle, he is in a better position to negotiate his terms with their owner. In some cases he may take more than his recognized due, for this will give him an extra lever to get the matter settled, but in most cases he will wish to settle the matter amicably so that he does not run the risk of having them stolen back from him. Some compromise will be reached. In many cases, provided the culprit has reasonable customary grounds for his action, i.e. if he has right (*cuong*) on his side, the owner of the cattle will not bother to resist and will readily agree to negotiate through some mediator, so that the transfer of the cattle may be socially recognized and not lead to blows between them. Moreover the closer the relationship between the man who takes the cattle and the owner, the more likely will it be that the former will have some legal justification for taking them. The expression, *ce yang-da kwal*, so common among Nuer, usually means that someone has seized the speaker's cattle in (according to the speaker) the mistaken opinion that he had a definite right to them.

Frequently the culprit knows that he has only a very thin excuse for taking them, and often removes himself and the cattle to some distance where the owner can get legal satisfaction only with difficulty, for whereas in his own community opinion will be against him, the people with whom he takes refuge are not interested and do not know the full implications of the case. If the injured party agrees that the culprit has a right to the cattle, peaceable negotiations will follow; if he does not, disputes may result between them which may or may not lead to blows. According to Professor Evans-Pritchard, a man will never steal a cow from a fellow tribesman merely because he wants one.

He has, on the other hand, no hesitation in stealing cows from persons belonging to neighbouring tribes and will even go with friends to another tribe in order to steal from them. This theft (*kwal*) is not considered in any way wrong.[1]

This really comes under the heading of cattle-raiding, and depends on the current relations between tribes. If, as frequently happened in the past, tribes were technically at war with each other, then such cattle-raiding was considered a legitimate move in the course of war. Moreover, if a blood-feud existed and homicide cases remained unsettled, the seizure of cattle might have some legal justification behind it. Nuer tribes were not, however, always hostile, and the tribal boundaries did not imply such a rigid line of demarcation as to pre-

---

[1] Evans-Pritchard, *The Nuer*, p. 165. I quote this passage because it refers to conditions some twenty years ago when cattle raids were more common and, since legal remedies through the courts were less effective than they are nowadays, 'self-help' was not unusual.

THEFT

clude social relations and intermarriage. Moreover, a legal mechanism under the control of Leopard-Skin Chiefs existed whereby a state of war could be brought to an end when both sides were heartily sick of the endless danger and insecurity which such major feuds entailed. There are instances quoted in Nuer tribal history when these matters were settled, and though compensation for homicide was usually waived because of the large number of persons for whom compensation would be demanded on both sides, the illicit seizure of cattle was often assessed in the final count.

Therefore the seizure of cattle without legal justification, real or supposed, within a tribal community was extremely rare, and the stealing of cattle from other tribes was really an act of war. Raiding the Dinka, a legitimate Nuer prey, was something different. It was, however, extremely common for Nuer to 'take the law into their own hands' and wrest what they considered their just dues from their debtors without bothering to arrange peaceful negotiations through some mediator or, later, through the medium of established courts. In most cases this action was taken only if the defendant in the case was unwilling to negotiate. These observations apply largely to the past when no courts existed, or when they had not yet developed present standards of efficiency and effectiveness. Nevertheless Nuer still often seize cattle which they consider their just due.

Theft of Cattle

There are certain specific situations which fall within the true definition of theft: when cattle are taken or material possessions misappropriated without any real or supposed reason other than that the thief covets them. It has been mentioned that the word *kwal* applies generally to all situations when the rightful or wrongful seizure of stock or material objects takes place. There is a specific term in the Nuer vocabulary which is applied when stock or personal possessions are taken for no apparent reason other than that the thief wants them. That such a word exists at all and is used to describe these circumstances is evidence of the distinction. This word is *wuan*:[1] a man will say *ce yang-da wuan* or *ce yoka wuan*, 'he has stolen my cow', 'he has stolen my money', and in using this expression he implies that the culprit did so for no accepted reason.

Cases where a man steals cattle from his neighbours merely because he covets them are rare. He would not be able to hide the theft unless

---

[1] Two other words are worth mentioning here. The word *pec* is used to describe situations where superior force is used, e.g. when cattle are raided by a more powerful group from a weaker one and, nowadays, when the Government or local authorities seize cattle by force. The word *mac*, which also means theft or misappropriation, implies deprivation by fraud or cunning, i.e. swindling. *Wuan* also implies stealth or cunning.

COMPENSATION 201

he fled to some other Nuer tribe, and the force of local public opinion would compel him to return them if he wished to continue residence in his own community. Upon occasion a man will steal another man's barren cow or bull and kill and eat it, motivated by greed or hunger. This, which is known as *yang micaa luc* in Nuer, is considered a serious offence, and Nuer say that in the old days compensation of ten head of cattle would be demanded. In the past at any rate restitution in equivalent value was not considered sufficient to appease the feelings of the persons who had suffered the loss. Nuer consciously express the concept of a deterrent when they say that such damages are demanded because otherwise others would do the same. Another offence, which is recognized as such in Nuer law, is to misappropriate someone's cow and try to disguise the fact by altering the ear marks on the animal. Nuer say that the cow would have to be returned or another substituted and a bull-calf paid as compensation to satisfy the wronged owner. The principle of compensation applied in cases where cattle are stolen and secretly eaten by the thief is applied also in the cases of sheep and goats, *del micaa luc*. The traditional scale of compensation for the latter was six head of cattle. Apart from the fact that cases of this sort are nowadays almost unknown, it is doubtful whether more than equivalent restitution would be enforced by the court. It is more likely that the culprit would be sentenced to imprisonment.

Theft of Other Material Possessions

Apart from cattle, there are few material possessions which come within the scope of this term. Nuer are persistent beggars, though they take refusal light-heartedly. They pester friends and relations to give them personal property which has taken their fancy—spears, cloth, beads, tobacco, &c. Sometimes they may take these things without the owner's permission. Depending largely on the relationship of the persons involved, the owner will rarely do more than protest or grumble and demand (later) some equivalent privilege in return. Neither the word *kwal* nor *wuan* would be used in these circumstances. Most articles of personal property are so easily obtainable, being made from raw materials locally available, that a man would scarcely bother to take them, or if he did, their removal would not be missed. Apart, however, from such easily acquired possessions as described above, certain material objects were, in the past, only obtained with difficulty through meagre trade channels, and their misappropriation was considered a cause for litigation or retaliation. It should be noted also that most of these material objects were bought with cattle, and that their removal would cause proportionate discomfort or suffering to the plaintiff because they were one and all

THEFT

important items in the subsistence economy of the people. Their illicit removal by a stranger would again be *wuan*—'theft'.

In analysing some of the customary scales of compensation for misappropriation, it is apparent that in many cases the damages were out of all proportion to the wrong. As in the case of hurt, the compensation was directly proportionate to the suffering of the persons concerned. As has been explained in the introduction, the likelihood of such compensation being paid depended largely on the relationship of the persons involved and the social cohesion of the community in which they dwelt. It is also probable that all these scales of customary compensation date right back to a period of Nuer history when the people lived in more closely-knit groups and before the major processes of expansion began; that is, before they occupied huge tracts of country and absorbed large numbers of Dinka in doing so.

Those material possessions for which compensation (*cut*) was demanded included fish-spears, hoes, and axes—all articles made of iron. The scales of compensation differed considerably from tribe to tribe. The Gaawar, for instance, say that six head of cattle would be demanded for the theft of a fish-spear. Lak Nuer say that one cow was sufficient. The probable reason for this disparity was that compensation was conditioned locally by the relative difficulty of obtaining those articles, and also by the number of cattle paid for them in the first instance. The Gaawar, remotely situated from the trade channels through which iron wares came, could only obtain them from the Anuak to the east or through the Atuot Dinka to the west. In Lak country a cow would purchase a bundle of these things but in Gaawar the cost was much higher.

Again, we find that not only were these articles initially purchased with cattle but all had very considerable value in the subsistence economy of the Nuer. The loss of a fish-spear might cause great hardship because Nuer are often compelled to rely on fish as a major item in their diet, especially when grain is short. Hoes were essential for agricultural processes. Canoes, for which a high rate of compensation was also demanded, were of considerable economic importance not only for fishing, but for swimming cattle across rivers in the course of seasonal migrations. Canoes, however, may have had a trade value nearly equal to the compensation, for suitable timber is rare in Nuerland even today.[1]

It is therefore possible that in these traditional scales of compensation for the loss of certain possessions, there are the germs of deterrent and punitive concepts, but it is more likely that they still fall within the category of private law. There was certainly no organized political

---

[1] Canoes have a high value. Those imported from Anuak, Shilluk or the south and west are worth several head of cattle. Canoes made of doleib palm trunks which are available locally are comparatively cheap and are usually sold for cash.

body capable of enforcing payment. To steal an article of this nature was a private delict and could only be settled by payment of compensation sufficient to appease the owner. Since ownership was in a sense collective, it was necessary to restore the balance between the groups concerned if hostilities were to be avoided. Compensation represented restitution or the equivalent value of the article and in addition recompense for the potential economic loss which might occur.[1] Clearly compensation was not paid rigidly according to conventional rules, but the scales were there to quote—once more as a basis for compromise.

Compensation in excess of the actual trade value of the article stolen is never applied today. For one thing, most of these articles are no longer purchased with cattle but for small sums of money. Moreover they are so easily obtainable from local shops that the owner is scarcely likely to be involved in any real hardship. Ownership of such articles is now a more individual matter, and it is unlikely that two communities will embark on hostilities over such trivial matters as this unless other motives already exist. Even with possessions which still demand a high rate in cattle or substantial sums of money, like canoes, there is never any question of compensation in excess of that value, only restitution or the equivalent.

If the wrong is considered particularly grievous or if there has been a danger of a breach of public security, a Nuer court will usually inflict punishment on the culprit in the form of imprisonment or fine. Thus theft is rapidly becoming a criminal offence, rather than a private delict the seriousness of which was gauged by the potentialities of economic discomfort to the wronged and by the extent of compensation required to restore the balance between opposed groups. No economic discomfort is likely, and if there is any danger of hostilities this is met by penal sanctions. It is gratifying to be able to record that theft of this kind is still comparatively rare in Nuerland, though it is alarming and ominous that it is of more frequent occurrence in communities where detribalization is most apparent.

[1] It is interesting to note that the ordinary fighting-spear (*mut*), though made of iron, was not included in this category.

CHAPTER VI

RELIGIOUS CONCEPTS IN RELATION TO LAW

IN the preceding chapters I have described what may be called the secular aspects of Nuer customary law. The terms of the law described are largely rational, and only at certain points and in certain contexts have religious and magical associations been mentioned. The isolation of rational procedures from the religious background, however, gives an incomplete picture, and some mention must be made of Nuer religion and ritual sanctions in relation to legal concepts. To do so is to embark on a highly complex subject and one which, as an administrator, I had least time and opportunity to investigate. There is also a danger of over-simplification and generalization. The reader must bear this in mind.

Nuer Religious Beliefs

The Nuer are an intensely religious people. As a basis is the concept of *kwoth*, an all-pervading deity associated with the sky but present to a greater or lesser degree in all things, which supplies, directly or indirectly, an explanation for phenomena which cannot be accounted for in terms of everyday life.[1] This applies to material objects, human beings, events, and situations. Thus a particularly vicious snake may be a manifestation of *kwoth*, thunder and lightning are *kwoth*, a magician is possessed by or possesses *kwoth*, an unexplained accident or illness is due to *kwoth*, spirits are *kuthni* (a plural form of the word *kwoth*) and the unpredictable future is *ruac kwoth*, literally 'God-talk' or 'the will of God'. The word *kwoth* also has connexion with the whole range of spiritual forms and concepts: ancestral spirits, household spirits, spirit medicines, talking spirits, sky spirits, earth spirits. The special functions of the ritual experts of the kind already mentioned and their magical powers are derived from and are dependent upon *kwoth*. Nuer themselves find great difficulty in describing their beliefs because *kwoth* is accepted without

---

[1] In a recent article Professor Evans-Pritchard says: 'God is a spirit who is in the sky and also everywhere, he is the creator of the universe, the father and friend of man and the guardian of the social order; and in comparison with him man is an ignorant and puny creature. . . . There is nothing which can properly be called a cult of God, the spirit who is in the sky, and indeed the absence of a cultus is very much in keeping with the whole Nuer metaphysic.' 'A Note on Nuer Prayers', *Man*, Vol. LII, 140, 1952.

NUER RELIGIOUS BELIEFS

query and is an abstract idea which they cannot explain in terms of specific examples; but this does not cause confusion to them because, although all aspects of their religion are an indirect extension of the idea of *kwoth*, there is a special terminology which refers to every kind of manifestation and category.

For example, there are, as will be seen later, *kolangni*, special spiritual forms which come into the possession of and possess individuals or kinship groups, and of these there are many different types of manifestation. They are often the cause of physical illness or misfortune. A particular individual may be subject to epileptic fits or periods of mental instability, and speaking in general terms the Nuer will say *teke kwoth*, 'he *has* or is possessed by *kwoth*'; but they will usually go further and qualify this statement by saying that he is possessed by some particular manifestation of *kwoth* which has a definite name. In some cases the individual will have called upon himself evil effects (though the same spirit may equally bring beneficial effects) in angering the spirit by some action, or more probably by failure to carry out some ritual obligation. There are special functionaries whose duty, in return for fees paid, usually in cattle, is first to diagnose the cause of the trouble and then to suggest a remedy, often assisting in the ritual which follows.

Kwoth is sometimes spoken of in the rôle of creator, but creation is more often explained in mythology by reference to ancestors. Such ancestors are not consciously thought of as manifestations of *kwoth*, although their origin would be explained as *kwoth*.[1] Ancestors are intermediaries between man and God; prayer is offered through them to *kwoth*. There is therefore a close relation between the concept of *kwoth* and religious practices associated with a patrilineal descent group. The word *thek* is used to express the idea of respect to ancestral spirits, and also, by extension, respect for kinship relations. Misfortunes and illness, sometimes referred to as *nueer*, are often believed to be caused by ancestral spirits who are angered on account of a breach of observance—such as neglect of prayers, which should be addressed to them—or by actual relations between living descendants. An offensive action against a kinsman demands not only some compensation in the form of apology or even material indemnification but also prayer and expiation. There is therefore a religious sanction for kinship obligations and observances.[2]

[1] E.g. when asking Nuer to relate their genealogies, one often finds that they get stuck at a particular ancestor—and there is, of course, always an ancestor beyond whom they cannot go. Pressed for an answer they will simply say that this man came from *kwoth*.

[2] *Thek*. A full explanation of the word *thek* is given in an article by Professor Evans-Pritchard in *Man*, Vol. XLIX, 96, 1949. He says: 'We can therefore perhaps best think of *thek* as a term indicating a category of ritual prohibition or taboo, and of *nueer* as a term commonly used both for the infringement and the sanction of this class of taboo.' My own view is that *thek* implies not only negative action in the form of prohibition or avoidance but also positive action in carrying out some observance or duty.

206 RELIGIOUS CONCEPTS

Few disputes derived from religious situations appear before the tribunals established by the Government today except occasional accusations of witchcraft, or violent action against persons believed to be practising witchcraft, and the claims of religious experts for fees from their clients. Before turning to these matters, however, I propose to consider two aspects of Nuer religious belief which are relevant to a study of their customary law. The first aspect is the part which is played by religion as a sanction for the fulfilment of obligations towards kinsmen and to Nuer as a whole, and as a deterrent against breaches of recognized behaviour. The second aspect concerns the part played by religious functionaries in connexion with legal processes. This aspect has been discussed at some length both in the introductory chapter and in the chapter on homicide, but mainly in connexion with the Leopard-Skin Chief. More must be said of other experts who have specific functions to perform.

Religious Sanctions and Legal Processes

Religious sanctions for the operation of accepted rules of conduct have already been mentioned in connexion with homicide and the spilling of blood. We have seen too that in certain offences concerning women there is a sense not only of a secular wrong but also of sin which must be expiated by ritual observance.

It is clear, however, that religious concepts do not provide a deterrent; a man is not deterred from killing another simply because he fears spiritual contamination or the pollution of those with whom he is associated. He might do so were there no definite means by which he can remove the danger, but the means exist. What he and his kinsmen fear is the voluntary, or more probably involuntary, breach of observance which will bring them disaster in the form of natural disease (*nueer*) or of sterility among themselves and their cattle. Religion among the Nuer is therefore not so much a deterrent to homicide as a sanction for carrying out accepted modes of behaviour after the event. It is further a sanction for the immediate confession of homicide, and this is why the Nuer rarely if ever attempt to conceal their guilt. The dangers of concealing an act of homicide are expressed in the concept of *loic*.[1] When a man fails to confess, there is a graver disruption of equilibrium; both his own kin and those of his victim run into the danger of involuntarily breaking the taboos on social contact, and consequently an incident of this sort may demand a higher rate of compensation if peace is to be restored.

There appears to be no formal reaction on the part of the community as a whole to an act of homicide, nor any general expression of reprobation. The killer is not thought of as an evil-doer because of his

[1] See p. 52.

RELIGIOUS SANCTIONS AND HOMICIDE 207

action in spilling the blood of a fellow man. There is no concept of Man as a member of Mankind, only as a member of a kinship group, and reprobation is expressed by them alone. Moreover God is not angered at the death of a human being, for God is not concerned with humans in this general sense of protection and responsibility; but the particular manifestations of God, represented in the kinship group by ancestral spirits and by the spirit of the dead man (*cien*), are indignant and cry out for vengeance.

There are therefore two reactions present: first, the reaction of the kinsmen of the slain, which is a reaction of indignation at personal loss, reduction in their numbers, and the damage to the continuity of their group; and this finds further expression in religious concepts associated with the kinship group. The second reaction is that of the killer's group, who demand that, in their own interests as well as his own, he shall perform those rites of expiation which will neutralize the effects of spiritual contamination emanating from the spirits associated with the dead man's kin. They may also express disapproval of his action, for he has brought upon them not only spiritual dangers but the threat of violence, and more probably the loss of the cattle which they will have to pay to restore the peace and regain their security.

Homicide has not yet become the concern of society as a whole and, except that other persons may find themselves involved in a feud which may spread along traditional lines of political cleavage, those outside the specific groups affected are not interested. The existence of a segmentary system and the absence of organized political authority covering all sections of Nuer society mean that there is no corporate body which will take action against the killer in the interests of society as a whole. The kinship group of the deceased combines against the killer and, by extension, according to the principles of collective responsibility, against the kinsmen of the killer. The latter are then compelled to adopt an attitude of defensive opposition, but within their own group they have also to demand that the killer shall perform those acts which will restore to him his ritual status.

From these observations it will be seen that—

(i) Homicide is considered a wrong, though not against society as a whole. The element of wrongness is relative to the relationship in the social structure of the parties involved. The killing of a stranger, especially of a foreigner, who does not come within the most expanded form of the social structure, is not really wrong (*duer*) at all. It is neither a crime nor a private delict, for there is no political sanction involved and no social relationship which might demand restitution. There is no motive for composition nor any mechanism for achieving it. It is, however, a situation which demands expiation in the form of ritual and sacrifice, which the killer performs with the assistance of the Leopard-Skin Chief. The ghost of the dead stranger,

RELIGIOUS CONCEPTS

no less than that of a fellow tribesman, may haunt the slayer, and the mere act of homicide creates a situation of spiritual danger.[1] This is a religious concept, but it does not provide an effective sanction against homicide because the consequences can be avoided.

(ii) The killing of a fellow tribesman, and to a much lesser extent a fellow Nuer of another tribe who is within the orbit of the killer's social sphere, is a wrong because it is an offence against the stability of society in its most extended form. But it is a private delict and not a crime, and demands only retaliation or restitution. The closer the relationship between the component tribal segments involved, the greater the sanction for restitution. It is also an act which brings spiritual contamination upon the killer and his kin, and expiation and ritual purification are necessary. Moreover the closer the relationship the more dangerous the consequences and the greater the need for purification, because the act of homicide amounts to a more grievous breach of kinship observance.

(iii) Finally in the narrowest definition of blood-relationship, where kinship is a reality and not merely a fictional social form—that is, within the lineage or the extended family group—restitution becomes less and less necessary because the persons who assist in the payment of compensation are also the recipients. To put this in negative form, those who are in duty bound to take vengeance are also those upon whom vengeance should be wreaked. The situation then reached is so near to patricide or fratricide that the idea of vengeance or restitution must disappear. The situation is indeed something akin to suicide, which is the negation of the principle of kinship solidarity, and, as in suicide, the danger is not the threat of retaliation nor the need to pay cattle as compensation to some other group but spiritual damnation from within.[2] Hence the act does not constitute a private delict but is

---

[1] To the Nuer this idea applies to all mankind. The disgruntled spirit (*cien*) of the dead man will haunt his killer and bring him misfortune or even death. The act of spilling blood in itself creates a condition of impurity which afflicts the killer, amounting to an impairment of his ritual status, and therefore requires expiation. Hence the ceremony of *birr*, which includes not only sacrifice but the letting of the slayer's blood. The danger involved in the spilling of human blood is exemplified in the rules concerning the destruction of certain categories of anti-social persons, notably the *rodh* or ghoul, with the consent of the community. No blood must be spilt; the ghoul should be beaten to death with sticks. No such contamination arises from the spilling of animals' blood except that of an elephant. For this the ceremony of letting the blood of the killer must be performed or the ghost (again *cien*) of the animal will haunt him. It is especially interesting to note in this connexion that elephants are closely associated with mankind and are linked in mythology to the genealogies of certain lineages.

[2] This statement is, of course, qualified by the actual relationship of the persons concerned. Between brothers or half-brothers there could be no payment of compensation; between patrilineal cousins some form of compensation might be paid, but conditioned then and subsequently by other mutual obligations in connexion with cattle. The real test probably lies in the obligation to marry a wife to the name of a dead kinsman. If the killer were also the man, or one of the men, who normally might be expected to discharge this duty on behalf of the deceased, then no form of compensation would be necessary.

RELIGIOUS SANCTIONS AND KINSHIP

a sin. No action against the offender is taken, but the spiritual dangers involved are correspondingly greater and more difficult to avoid. Fratricide and patricide and, to a lesser degree the killing of a close agnatic kinsman, is an offence against the objectives of kinship association and therefore a sin against the religious standards which express those objectives. Expiation in the form of prayer and sacrifice is essential; vengeance or restitution is not possible.

These observations apply specifically to homicide. There is no apparent belief that spiritual pollution will result from the infliction of bodily injuries less than death, nor from private delicts such as theft or the destruction of the property of persons who have no kinship or marital relationship with the offender. On the other hand, offences against accepted rules of marriage relationships and behaviour towards women within the lineage have a supernatural sanction, but again it will be seen that this is only a reflection of the idea of kinship. In such cases, however, there is no need for indemnification paid in cattle,[1] which is limited to the relations of opposed groups and the maintenance of the balance between them. In the first place a breach of the rules of exogamy is an offence against the structure of the kinship group, and one which involves the couple and their kinsmen in the gravest danger. Here there is no question of the maintenance of social equilibrium between two groups, only the spiritual safety of the single kinship group within itself and of the individuals of which it is composed, and there is consequently no question of material indemnification. The incestuous couple are themselves liable to the supernatural consequences which may be physically manifested in some form of disease (*nueer*), and their kinsmen may suffer subsequently, particularly from sterility, infant mortality, or a series of disasters which may also apply to their cattle. It is an act which requires expiation in the form of ritual and sacrifice, and the seriousness of the breach is gauged according to the nearness of the relationship of the couple. This dictates the value of the sacrifice and the complexity of the ritual of expiation. In some African tribes incest is treated as a crime, particularly if the offence is repeated, and penal action is taken against the culprits; but among the Nuer the ritual processes required are presumably considered sufficiently efficacious, and no repressive action is taken against the offenders. Theoretically those who consciously repeated the offence would earn the reprobation of their kinsmen, resulting in a loss of privilege which might reach the stage of expulsion, but I can quote no instance of this and have never found a Nuer who could.

There are other breaches of observance which result in similar forms of pollution. It is, for example, an offence to have sexual intercourse

---

[1] For minor infractions gifts—tobacco, food, &c.—may be offered to an offended kinsman.

PNL

with a woman who is pregnant or a nursing mother. If the man who so offends is the woman's own husband, her relatives are likely to express great indignation and, if he is to continue on good terms with them, he will have to take steps to neutralize the consequences by ritual purification and sacrifice; otherwise the woman or her child will die. Moreover the ill-effects may extend to her kin, and in some cases these will demand a cow from the offender, not, I think, as direct compensation for a wrong but as a gift which will probably be dedicated to their ancestral and household spirits who otherwise may bring trouble to them.[1]

If the act is committed by a man who is not the woman's husband, it is certainly considered serious, but it is treated as a normal case of adultery and the compensation (*ruok*) demanded by her husband will not be greater than in normal adultery, although his indignation will be more intense and the likelihood of his taking violent action against the offender greater. For this reason alone such cases are likely to be settled by indemnification more promptly, and in this sense the religious concept is also a sanction for payment; the compensation is conditioned not by the likelihood of the spiritual effects, but by the traditional assessment of the wrong to the husband. Thus in this case religious belief is a sanction for the operation of a recognized process of law but has no effect on the amount of compensation. The idea of pollution is also present in cases of straightforward adultery where, as we have seen, among most Nuer tribes one cow should be paid in order to counteract the pollution involved, the cow called *yang kule* ('the cow of the sleeping mat'), which will allow the husband to resume relations with his wife in safety, and which is something quite different and apart from other cattle paid as compensation for what is regarded as a secular wrong. It is worth noting that if the adulterer is closely related to the cuckold no compensation will be demanded, but the *yang kule* is always paid.

There are also many customs which are not normally the cause of litigation in the courts, nor indeed of much dispute of any kind, but for which a form of compensation is necessary. For example, it causes offence for a man to appear naked before his mother-in-law or any woman who stands in that relationship to him. This applies even if he does so unwittingly, especially in the early stages of marriage. It is an offence which will require some small gift as compensation, and the offender may also be expected to make a token offering, a pinch of tobacco or something of the sort, to the ancestral spirits of his wife's lineage. Observances of this kind and the action taken if they are ignored are upheld by ritual sanctions, as well as by sanctions derived from the purely social relations arising in marriage and kinship.

[1] *Thiang*, see p. 177.

RITUAL EXPERTS

Religious Functionaries and Magical Experts

We have seen that the Leopard-Skin Chief has certain duties to perform in connexion with the composition of blood-feuds and that he may be called upon to arbitrate in disputes of almost any kind. His rôle is purely that of a mediator whose powers, both ritual and secular, are brought into operation only if there is a genuine desire by the hostile parties to reach an agreement. He has no executive powers with political force behind them, although it is expected that he will attempt to intervene in the early stages of a feud, and he sometimes threatens to use his power to curse the disputants if they will not agree. Moreover, in all matters in dispute, the frequency with which he will be approached depends largely on his prestige and personality, and not merely on his hereditary status. Other persons with no hereditary ritual status might easily acquire a reputation for fairness and tact and be employed as arbitrators in minor disputes. Skill in arbitration was considered by the Nuer one of the attributes of leadership (*ruec*), and the *ruic naadh* often extended their influence into the sphere of legal disputes.[1]

There are also other kinds of ritual experts who have specific functions to perform for public welfare: fertility in man and cattle, success in hunting and fishing, in raids and warfare. In this category are the *wut ghok* or cattle expert, the *kuaar thoi*, the water expert, the *kuaar yüka*, who is mainly concerned with the fecundity of women, the *kuaar juath*, who deals with epidemic diseases among humans, the *gwan tang* or *kuaar bith*, who ensures the success of warriors in battle. These experts have regular duties to perform, a fact which distinguishes them from other categories of magical expert; they have an established ritual status in society, and are expected to carry out religious tasks which in some African tribes are less specialized or even embodied in the person of one man.[2]

Professor Evans-Pritchard has mentioned most of these experts in his writings on the Nuer, and has recorded most, but not all, of their duties. They are:

Kuaar kwac or *kuaar muon: The Leopard-Skin Chief or Land Chief*

The functions of this expert in connexion with homicide have been fully described in Chapter II. His is essentially an hereditary office,

---

[1] We are dealing here with the past. The functions of traditional experts are now much modified.

[2] The *reth* of the Shilluk, for example, who is, apart from his political and executive functions, generally responsible for fertility in man, cattle and crops, for success in hunting and fishing. (See Howell and Thomson, op. cit., p. 9; and *Africa*, XXII, 1952.) He is responsible, however, for these matters as affecting the whole tribe. There is also among the Shilluk a number of specialists responsible for local interests, *jal yath, ajwogo*, &c.

but all members of the lineage do not practise. Professor Evans-Pritchard has listed his functions as:

(i) Anything to do with the land—especially the welfare of crops.
(ii) A limited rôle in rain-making and the regulation of the weather.
(iii) The ritual of homicide (see Chapter II).
(iv) The ritual of incest (see Chapter III, Section 3).
(v) The ritual of preventing feuds and protecting warriors on raiding expeditions.
(vi) Arbitration in all kinds of disputes.

Wut ghok: The Cattle Expert

This is also an office the potentiality of which runs in certain families, and it is to that extent hereditary. The functions of the *wut ghok* are purely ritual and, apart from cattle, are concerned with the social processes of the age-grade system.

Other functions may be listed as follows:

(i) To increase the fertility of cattle and milk production and to ensure that cows give birth to cow-calves. To avoid cattle disease.

(ii) To perform the ritual of warfare, and in particular to ensure that many cattle are captured in raids.

(iii) To perform fecundity rites for women and to assist elderly spinsters to secure husbands.

As in the case of the *kuaar muon*, the *wut ghok* is concerned with activities which are both beneficial and widespread. I only know of two cases brought before the court where a *wut ghok* was alleged to have used his powers for personal gain or for revenge upon the cattle of an enemy. One of these cases caused something of a sensation and considerable animosity.

Kuaar thoi: The Water Expert

A hereditary office running in certain lineages, sometimes of reputed extraneous origin (probably Shilluk or Anuak or what the Nuer call Bar). The *kuaar thoi* may be called upon to bless raiding parties and to perform ritual to ensure that they do not drink of water poisoned by the enemy. His principal function, however, is to bless the water, and to see that there is an abundance of fish and that the people are successful in catching them. He also performs ritual against crocodiles, and is indeed particularly associated with crocodiles and often called *kuaar nyang* (crocodile expert). A *kuaar thoi* is often called in to assist when cattle are fording a river. To ensure that crocodiles do not attack them, he takes a pole which he thrusts into the reeds along the bank and places on this an iron ring. He then takes a sheep, ties its legs

RITUAL EXPERTS

and thrusts it into the river alongside the pole, calling upon the crocodiles to desist. This is, in fact, a common practice, since some Nuer are bound to cross rivers or crocodile-infested waterways in the course of the dry season migration.

Kuaar juath

The badge of this office is a cow-skin which he beats with a stick, and by performing this and other forms of ritual the *kuaar juath* stops the spread of disease among humans (notably small-pox). This office is also hereditary.

Kuaar yiika

The badge of this office is the *yiik* or woman's mat. The *kuaar yiika* is called in to arbitrate in cases where a woman dies in childbirth and *thung yiika* is demanded. Some Leopard-Skin families claim that this is their duty and that the *kuaar yiika* is only an assistant who should help in a subordinate capacity.

Gwan tang (sometimes kuaar tang)[1]

The word *tang* means 'spear-shaft'. The *gwan tang* is particularly concerned with the success of raiding parties and the performance of elaborate ritual to avoid spear-wounds to the warriors. Part of the ritual process is to break off the tip of the spear-shaft and cast it in the direction of the enemy. Some of these specialists are known as *gwan bith* (*bith* means fish-spear), but I know of only one family which claims this distinction, and their functions and the ritual they perform appear to be identical with those of the *gwan tang*.

Many of the functions of these various experts appear to overlap. This is true in general terms, but closer analysis will, I think, show that they are not identical. Thus the *kuaar kwac*, the *wut ghok*, the *kuaar thoi* and the *gwan tang* are all concerned with cattle raids and warfare. The *kuaar kwac*, however, is expected to ensure success in a more general and unspecified way, the *wut ghok* has specifically the duty of seeing that the raiders are successful in capturing cattle, the *kuaar thoi* is expected to protect them from poisoned water, and the *gwan tang* to give them success in inflicting spear-wounds on their enemies and in avoiding injuries to themselves. The *kuaar kwac* is also expected to protect them against the ghosts of slain enemies, which is one of his specific duties in cases of homicide. All experts of this kind are known as owners of *twac* (*gwan twac—ji twac*),[2] stressing their right to wear a particular skin as a badge of office, although some of them, notably the *wut ghok*, have none; the rest of the

---

[1] *Kuaar* is best translated as 'expert', though the word 'chief' is more often used; *gwan* (father) here simply means 'owner or possessor of'.

[2] *Twac* is a generic term for skin: *kwac* means leopard-skin, *thoan* serval cat-skin, and so on.

214 RELIGIOUS CONCEPTS

people who have no such distinction are known as *dwek*. There is no suggestion of a caste system or, indeed, any social distinction, but only of the possession of a special ritual status in society which is emphasized by the hereditary nature of their functions and in tribal tradition and mythology.

I do not propose here to discuss in great detail the part played by these experts in legal procedures. We have already seen that the *kuaar kwac* or *kuaar muon* had special functions to perform as a mediator in blood-feuds and in other forms of dispute. The *kuaar yiika*, though his functions were almost purely ritual, was called in when an unmarried woman died in childbirth as a result of illicit sexual intercourse. Yet it would not be true to say that the *wut ghok* intervened in disputes concerning cattle for his functions were entirely ritual. This applies also to other kinds of religious functionary and, as will be seen later, magical experts of other categories. It is, however, true to say that any man of influence would intervene in disputes, both between individuals and between lineages or tribal segments, and since possession of spiritual attributes brings influence of this sort, doubtless such experts played their part in political and legal affairs. Again, it is necessary to stress that these observations, though still partially true, concern principally the past. It will be obvious that whatever political and legal functions were performed by these people in the old days are now much modified by the introduction of modern tribunals with the sanction of government action behind them.

Other Types of Religious Expert

Religious experts of the second category have no analogous traditional status or specialization of social and economic function, although in most cases their position becomes hereditary. These are the *ji kuthni* (sing. *gwan kwoth*), of which there are many kinds. The first are the possessors of 'sky-spirits'—direct and identified manifestations of *kwoth*—some of whom gained considerable political power and widespread fame during the last century. Professor Evans-Pritchard speaks of these as 'Prophets', and suggests that the concept was of Dinka origin. Many of these prophets were themselves of Dinka extraction.

It must be remembered that the great majority of these people gained no widespread prestige and had no political influence at all, their activities being limited to the ordinary ritual divination and diagnosis of the cause of the minor misfortunes which beset the individual. Nowadays they are unlikely to gain any extensive political power, although there are many who have exceptional influence over the Nuer, and it is interesting to note that they are never brought forward as possible representatives of the people to the Government. For example, there is a *gwan kwoth* called Macar Teng, who lives in comparative

SPIRIT POSSESSION

isolation among the few Gaawar who occupy the southern and almost inaccessible part of the Zeraf island, and has considerable influence over Gaawar affairs. Another, Riak Loinyjok, commonly called by his bull name, *tut me bor*, has recently acquired tremendous prestige and, although he lives among the Lak, is known and visited by people from as far away as the Eastern Jikany. His activities have no political aspect, and he concerns himself with the curing of the sick.[1] These are exceptional cases; the vast majority have no such fame.

There are also owners of lesser spirits, and the multitude of persons who operate through 'talking or spirit medicines', which are described very briefly below. 'Prophets' and persons possessed of spirits and magicians of lesser importance are clearly distinguished from the *ji twac*, religious functionaries who have a traditional right to a skin (*twac*) as a badge of office. These distinctions may be summarized as follows:

(i) The *ji twac* have not only hereditary status, but status which is firmly established in tribal tradition. Their ancestors, themselves operating as *kuaar kwac*, *kuaar thoi* and the like, are figures of great repute in Nuer tribal history.[2] Other types of religious expert can acquire their powers suddenly, alleging possession by a spirit after a trance or epileptic fit, or even by purchase from someone else, but although these qualities may thereafter become hereditary, it is never a hereditary status which goes far back into the history of the lineage.

(ii) The *ji twac* have no particular manifestation or spirit linked to themselves as individuals, only ritual association with earth, cattle, water, &c., as the case may be, while the *ji kuthni* are possessed by much more definite manifestations, each of which has a distinguishing name and sometimes even a known personality.

(iii) The *ji twac* have functions to perform in connexion with the people as a whole or with natural phenomena or events which are likely to affect the whole community or the tribe. The *kuaar kwac* is associated with the land and is therefore responsible for control of the weather, the *kuaar thoi* with the abundance of fish in the waters, the *wut ghok* with the welfare of cattle. Owners of spirits are more concerned with individuals, and are approached by individuals to perform ritual tasks for them in return for an agreed fee.[3]

The distinction given above is not, of course, always crystallized. The *kuaar kwac* may, for example, be approached by an individual, who will ask him to bless his land or his wives and ensure

---

[1] Since the political activities of *ji kuthni* have been so severely repressed by the Government, those who now practise are usually at pains to emphasize the purely spiritual nature of their activities.

[2] See pp. 30–31.

[3] This does not mean that the *ji twac* do not also receive fees. There are recognized fees for specific functions: for example, fees paid to the *kuaar kwac* for arbitration in blood-feuds, &c.

216   RELIGIOUS CONCEPTS

fertility. Moreover it is clear that those of the second category who acquire great prestige and influence often seek to misappropriate the functions and insignia of more reputable experts. There is a tendency to assume the leopard-skin. Deng Likea, Prophet of Gaawar, did so, and his son Gaw Bang—for many years President of the Bar Gaawar Court—often conducted the ritual of homicide although he had no traditional right to do so. Riak Loinyjok (mentioned above) wears the leopard-skin, though he would not be accepted as arbiter in blood-feuds. There is clearly a desire by these people to establish themselves in a ritual and traditional, and therefore more orthodox, status in society.

A *gwan kwoth* of repute will also claim that he possesses or is possessed by a large number of different spirits, not a single spirit. Deng Likea, whose principal spirit was called Diu, possessed many others, and he married a wife in the name of each. His sons are usually referred to first by their own names and then by the name of the spirit in whose name the mother of each was married, and not by that of their father, according to normal Nuer custom. Thus Deng Likea's sons were called Macar Diu, Gaw Bang, and so on.

There is a large number of different categories of spirit owners: owners of 'sky-spirits' (*kuth nial*), owners of 'spirits' of the wind (*kuth dange*), owners of 'earth spirits' (*kuth piny*) and 'talking medicines', these last being divided into a large variety of different forms, and finally, possessors of *wal*, medicine, which is usually present in more tangible form.

It is not within the scope of this book to describe at length the multitudinous concepts concerning *goah* and *kolangni*. *Goah* is said to be of Dinka origin, while *kolangni* are essentially Nuer. Under these two main headings are numerous spirits which have special names— *biel, maluth, gulung, mathiang*, &c.,—and special characteristics. The spirits are used to assist in the diagnosis of ills and misfortunes, the possessor acting as a medium and often going into a trance at a seance attended by a considerable number of people. The spirit is said to speak from the mouth of the medium, from a special pot or gourd, from the ground, or sometimes only through dreams.

Wal is a word which has the more literal meaning of medicine, since it is also applied to herbs, purges, and astringents as well as nowadays to medicines supplied by the government medical service. In this connexion it refers to magic roots and sometimes to other objects which have intrinsic magical power and which are operated by the performance of ritual for some specific purpose. There are different forms of *wal* (one called *nyeth*, for example, is believed to be particularly potent and also dangerous), but the Nuer do not consider themselves to be experts in their use, and regard them as being of foreign origin. In fact such roots are usually obtained from other tribes, and a Nuer will sometimes go on a special journey to purchase them.

MEDICINE AND DIVINATION 217

They can be and are used for beneficial purposes, but they are associated more often with the practice of witchcraft, and owners of such medicines are often greatly feared. This fear has perhaps been particularly impressed on the Nuer by the action of the Government in banning the possession of roots or medicines and inflicting severe penalties on their owners, whether they were believed to use them for good magic or for witchcraft. This reaction has not applied so much to the ownership of spirit medicines, presumably because, being for the most part entirely incorporeal, there was no proof of possession, and Government intervention was therefore much more difficult. Spirit medicines, *kolangni* and the like, can none the less be used for anti-social purposes, although they are normally regarded as beneficent and used as such.

A further category of Nuer magic experts is the *tiet*, who have special powers of divination,[1] but their techniques are not usually dependent on a particular spirit manifestation or on possession of a medicine. Their methods are more mundane in character, for they often use cowrie shells or pebbles, which are cast on the ground, and an interpretation is given of the formation in which they fall.

Beneficial and *Anti-social Activities*

We see, therefore, that the functions of all these experts are generally considered to be beneficial; those of the *ji twac* to the people as a whole; those of other experts or possessors of spirits and medicines to their individual clients. Their power can, however, be used for purely anti-social purposes. The *ji twac* have the power to curse by invoking the element or object with which they are particularly associated. We have seen that the Leopard-Skin Chief may call a curse upon those who refuse to listen to his exhortations in connexion with blood-feuds and homicide,[2] but he is not expected to do so for his own benefit or from personal animosity. Similarly the *wut ghok*, who has the power to benefit the people by ensuring the good health and fertility of their cattle, can also curse their cattle. Yet none of these religious functionaries can be regarded

[1] *Tiet:* a common Nilotic word used to cover a very large variety of magical experts.
[2] In connexion with warfare and cattle raids they are expected to work magic against other tribes; to make the infliction of wounds upon them easy; to destroy or weaken their defences. This is not witchcraft so far as the Nuer are concerned, for their action is pro-Nuer and to them in no sense anti-social. The definition of witchcraft is here relative. It will also apply to cases of warfare against other Nuer tribes or even tribal segments. An expert who performs ritual to bring about the downfall of enemies in another tribal section is acting in the interests of his own tribal section. His action is beneficial magic to his own people, black magic to those of the opposing segment, and there is no formalized community to which both belong and which would consciously react against his performance. His action is not witchcraft in the more exact definition of the term. Nefarious practices against an individual or even a kinship group within the community are a different matter, because there is a body of collective opinion which considers such action anti-social and, as we shall see in the next section, is prepared to take collective steps to remove the danger.

as a sorcerer or witch in normal circumstances. Similarly, other categories of magicians and spirit-owners are generally expected to act in the interests of their clients, although in some cases the client may, by paying a fee, gain the assistance of one of them to work witchcraft against his private enemy. Some spirit-owners have an unsavoury reputation in Nuerland. There are, however, persons whose activities are considered entirely anti-social, and who thus fall into the category of witches, whatever the circumstances.

Witchcraft

Apart from *gwan wal* or owners of medicines who have acquired an evil reputation, witches are possessors of the evil eye, called *peth* in Nuer, who are believed to cause harm and even death to those who cross their path in anger, and sometimes without any motive at all other than the inherent evil of their personalities. The *rodh* or ghoul is also a kind of witch who is particularly associated with the performance of hideous rites upon the bodies of the newly dead, thereby gaining some control over the souls of their surviving relatives.[1]

In the common action of the community against witchcraft we find perhaps the only conception among the Nuer which even approaches the notion of criminal or public law. Nuer say that in the past witches of these kinds were often killed with at least the tacit consent of the whole community to which they belonged. There are, however, no authenticated cases on record. The *rodh* might be killed with impunity, provided that blood was not spilt and no injuries to his head were inflicted by his assailants. The *peth* might be killed without grave danger of retaliation and, if composition was demanded, only six head of cattle need be paid to the kinsmen. It is doubtful if anything was paid in such circumstances. Accusations of the evil eye are fairly common today, but I have no details of the possessors being killed in the past.

It is worth adding that among many primitive peoples unnatural offences and bestiality are treated as public delicts and punished by ostracism, exile, or even death. Such offences are conspicuous by their absence among the Nuer. During several years in Nuerland I only heard of one actual instance. This occurred in Gaawar country, where a headman of considerable standing admitted such an offence with a cow. This was regarded as a grave misfortune, though the reaction was one of pity for the culprit rather than indignation. It was held that both he and the cow would die. As an act of expiation he cut off one of his own fingers with a spear and, accompanied by sacrifice, this was considered an effective antidote. In the absence

[1] See Howell and B. A. Lewis, 'Nuer Ghouls, a Form of Witchcraft', *S.N.R.*, 1947.

WITCHCRAFT

of further evidence it is not possible to expand on this subject. Nuer simply say that a man who commits such an offence will surely die. The ritual sanctions must be very effective.

Actions against Witches Today

In all cases of accusations of witchcraft appearing before modern Nuer courts of which I have any record, the accused was submitted to searching examination and evidence of a sort was taken. The facts seemed hard to prove, but by reference to the character of the accused (anything in the nature of incessant ill-temper, shrewishness, and general unpopularity backed by definite instances of misfortune among the accusers), the members of the court usually came to a decision. The matter was not treated lightly, and it is a fact that the large majority of such cases were dismissed as frivolous, and in some instances the plaintiff was punished for false accusation (*lorjok*)[1]. Sentences of imprisonment were sometimes inflicted, in most instances on women who were suffering ill-treatment from their neighbours and would be better out of the way for a while. Imprisonment, an idea entirely alien to the Nuer, somehow acted as a form of expiation or purification, and I have noted that in nearly all cases the woman went back to live unmolested among her neighbours.

Oaths

In connexion with Nuer religious beliefs which have bearing on the study of law and the procedure of courts today, oaths must be mentioned. The ceremony is usually performed by the Leopard-Skin Chief, who is called in for this purpose. There are two common forms of oath, the first called *kweng*, *kwil*, or *kap tang* ('to hold the spear-shaft'), which is used in a variety of circumstances, while *math* (literally, 'to drink') is the form often employed in cases of unconfessed homicide. The taking of an oath is not an individual process carried out by one man alone. In the former ceremony both accuser and accused are expected to take part, and it amounts to something of an ordeal between them; in the latter, where there is no known accused, those suspected and all their kinsmen are expected to participate.

It should be noted that the use of such oaths, especially in court, is not encouraged by the Government. Moreover, although the participants are often willing enough, the onlookers are afraid for them and nearly always persuade them to take some other course. Nuer chiefs and court members frown on the practice for this reason and not only because they know that the procedure is not in keeping with Government policy.

[1] See p. 70.

Kap tang

In this ceremony, although the name *kap tang* refers to the spear of the Leopard-Skin Chief, the most important ritual association is clearly with the earth, and the ceremony amounts to a symbolic and sympathetic enactment of the process of burying the dead. A small hole is dug in the ground by the Leopard-Skin Chief, and this represents the grave; over it are placed sprigs of *Calotropis procera* and *Balanites aegyptiaca*, for these are usually placed over the newly buried dead as a protection against the diggings of hyenas. Over this hole the Leopard-Skin Chief puts his spear, while the disputants squat on either side and place their right hands on the spear-shaft and each swears his innocence or belief in the other's guilt as the case may be. It is believed that the one who is telling a lie will be seized with sickness possibly followed by death unless an antidote is applied. If either party falls ill he will hurry to the Leopard-Skin Chief, who reverses the process and thereby removes the contamination. Sometimes the ritual is less elaborate; the disputants simply pass under the outspread leopard-skin held by the owner.

Math

This is usually, but not always, applied in cases of homicide where the killer has not confessed or is quite unknown. It is performed by the Leopard-Skin Chief, who fills a gourd with milk from one of the cows belonging to the dead man. Those who protest their innocence are then expected to drink of the milk. This act openly defies the taboo on drinking or eating which automatically comes into operation between the hostile parties in a blood-feud. Indeed there could be no graver danger than drinking the milk of the dead man's cow if there is blood between them. Since contamination is extended to all kinsmen of the unknown killer, it is unlikely that anyone would agree to take the oath unless he was absolutely certain of the innocence of all his kin.

CHAPTER VII

THE NATURE OF NUER LAW

Private Law and Public Law

WHEN speaking of Nuer systems of social control in the past we should not be justified in making a distinction between criminal and civil law, though we might, in some instances, be justified in doing so now. Such a distinction is based on the conventions of legal principles inherent in our own culture, and these are not applicable. We can, instead, as recommended by Professor Radcliffe-Brown, distinguish between 'the law of public delicts and the law of private delicts'. He points out that—

in any society a deed is a public delict if its occurrence normally leads to an organized and regular procedure by the whole community or by the constituted representatives of social authority which results in the fixing of responsibility upon some person within the community and the infliction, by the community or by its representatives, of some hurt or punishment upon the responsible person. This procedure, which may be called the penal sanction, is in its basic form a reaction by the community against an action of one of its members which offends some strong and definite moral sentiment and thus produces a condition of social dysphoria. The immediate function of the reaction is to give expression to a collective feeling of moral indignation and so to restore the social euphoria. The ultimate function is to maintain the moral sentiment in question at the requisite degree of strength in the individuals who constitute the community.[1]

It is worth while examining this statement in the light of what has emerged in the preceding chapters. Our first difficulty among the Nuer is, of course, to define a community. Nuer society is segmentary, and therefore a group of persons or a segment of a tribe may have political significance at one moment, and at another moment no significance at all. This difficulty is accentuated by the process of fission and fusion described by Professor Evans-Pritchard.[2] A tertiary segment of a tribe has, in this sense, a more constant political existence, and a localized lineage even more so, than a secondary segment or larger unit until we reach the tribe which is, or was, the limit of political unity. The fact that political co-ordination, especially in matters of law, now extends beyond tribal boundaries, because the Government provides the link, in no way alters this argument, for we are still considering the past. Even with this qualification, however, and with full realization that the sanctions for conformity have a variable social range and that a

[1] *Encyclopaedia of Social Sciences*, New York, 1933.
[2] Evans-Pritchard, *The Nuer*, p. 148.

NATURE OF NUER LAW

community among the Nuer is relative, like the Nuer word *cieng*, which roughly describes a territorial and social unit whatever the size,[1] we can still safely say that there was little or no public law among the Nuer in the past.

The sanction, even for the most serious of offences, homicide, was retaliatory, requiring only an act of vengeance against the killer or any one of his kinsmen, and thereby maintaining the balance and satisfying the indignation of the kinsmen of the deceased. Alternatively restitution might be made, the payment of which fell not individually on the killer but again on all his kinsmen and which, though primarily directed to providing the dead man with a wife, thus to raise children and restore the balance, was in part divided among the dead man's kinsmen. This division, which still applies today, is itself of particular significance for it shows that the cattle paid as 'blood-money' are in no sense merely a punishment or punitive damages inflicted on the group of the killer, but are primarily directed to the restoration of the balance between them and the group of the deceased. This balance is disturbed by the act of homicide, and the two groups or segments of a tribe are at once in a state of feud (*ter*) and will suffer spiritual pollution if the ordinary contacts of daily life continue between them. They are the *ji ran*, the 'people of the (dead) man', and the *ji thunge*, 'the people of the compensation', and between people in this condition social intercourse is not only unsafe, because at any time an act of vengeance may happen, but also spiritually dangerous. There is therefore a disturbance of equilibrium, which finds expression, on the one hand, in the feeling of intense indignation—often, as we have seen, more conventional than actual—of the dead man's kin and, on the other, in the fear on the part of the killer's kinsmen that violent retaliation may follow. Between them there is the fear of mutual contamination.[2] The balance is restored by the performance of ritual, the purpose of which is to remove the danger of this spiritual contamination, and by the complicated processes of payment of 'blood-money', the main object of which is to remove the feeling of indignation of the *ji ran* by giving them compensation in cattle for their loss. That this loss extends to a group larger than the immediate family of the dead man is seen in the fact that a small portion of the compensation is paid to his maternal relatives, the distribution following a pattern which is similar, though much restricted, to the distribution of bridewealth. The majority of the cattle go to provide a 'ghost-wife' for the dead man, thus assuring the continuance of his line in the lineage structure and also the unimpaired continuance of that lineage as a whole. There is nothing in these processes which

---

[1] The Nuer *cieng* has already been discussed; see pp. 21–22.

[2] It may be argued that the fear of contamination and the consequent avoidance are only a psychological expression of the fear of retaliation.

PRIVATE AND PUBLIC LAW

may be described as public law. There is no evidence of a penal sanction applied by anything which resembles 'politically organized society', nor anything which indicates that such procedure is enforced by the will of the community; the community, that is, which extends beyond those segments which are actually at feud. Nor again can the Leopard-Skin Chief, the functionary through whom the ritual and compensatory processes may be successfully carried out, be described as a 'constituted representative of political authority', for there is nothing behind him to enforce a decision other than a vague and not very effective sanction in his power to curse. It is only when both parties are willing to negotiate that his particular functions are effective.

A further point of significance is the fact that the Nuer distinguish between intentional and accidental killing. It might well be argued that, since they make this distinction, there is at least an element of the idea of punitive damages contained in the scales of compensation according to the circumstances of homicide. I do not think this is so for two reasons. In the first place the Nuer often say that there really should not be any distinction at all. In the second place it seems that the variations spring from an original principle of compromise. The indignation of the *ji ran*, the dead man's kindred, is undoubtedly affected by the motives of the killer, and is likely to be less intense if there is no motive at all. In the past a compromise at a lower figure was therefore more probable. Since then there have been many homicide disputes from which precedents have arisen, and many of these were due to the direct influence of administrators at the time. Precedents of this sort have now become standardized by usage and, recently, by formal recognition at the Nuer Chiefs' Council; there is now a complicated body of laws concerning homicide which are consistently applied.

In the past, then, the outcome of blood-feuds depended on the social relations of the groups involved, even though the division over these events might follow the lines of segmentation until a whole tribe was split. There was no all-inclusive community within which an act of homicide could become a public delict, nor any political association outside the parties concerned sufficiently institutionalized to enforce a decision. There was only a traditional procedure by which the affair could be settled if both parties were willing.

Similarly other legal wrongs required the payment of an indemnity to the injured party and, since the individual does not stand alone or acquire rights except as a member of an integrated kinship group, we may say that this action, though less collective in extent than the composition of homicide, was directed to the re-establishment of the balance between the groups concerned. If the maintenance of the balance was not necessary, either because the two individuals were closely related and the disturbance was in consequence less acute, or because the groups concerned were too remotely connected, the likelihood of composition was small. In the first instance the indemnity was not paid, or was paid on a much reduced scale; in the second instance it was not paid at all. Again, analysis of the concepts which concern sexual congress of persons between whom such relations are forbidden shows that such offences are not treated as public delicts. Adultery requires the payment of an indemnity in cattle, and we have noted that some of these cattle are regarded as direct compensation for an infringement of marital rights in the wife, while one in particular is an expiatory payment necessary to remove the pollution which results and to rectify any impairment of the husband's ritual status. There is no evidence of public law here. Even a breach of the laws of exogamy, which, among some African tribes, is followed by a reaction of moral indignation and organized action against the culprits, is not a public delict among the Nuer. Certainly no punitive action is taken against the guilty parties even though all their kindred are subjected to considerable spiritual danger. The sanction here is supernatural, and although the pollution caused by such an act may extend beyond the principals to persons who are related to them, penal sanctions are not applied. Moreover such offences are relative in gravity according to the proximity of relationship between the principals. Even in the most serious breach the contamination (*nueer*) may be removed by the performance of the prescribed ritual, which is considered effective and in which the Nuer have considerable confidence.

We have also considered theft. Here, in the case of material possessions of a certain type, all of which had an exchange value in cattle, the Nuer tell us that damages could be claimed which appear much in excess of the current value. This certainly suggests a concept of punitive damages; but further analysis shows that compensation was directed again to the restoration of equilibrium. The disturbance had been considerable, not only because articles of this nature had a high intrinsic value owing to their scarcity and the difficulty in obtaining them, but also because their loss might cause severe economic hardship to the individual and to his family group, and perhaps to a wider circle of associates in the subsistence economy. It is doubtful, in the absence of any institutionalized body to enforce payment, whether compensation was ever paid on the high scales which the Nuer tell us are traditional but, whatever the circumstances, it is clear that theft was not considered a public delict.

The only form of procedure which might fall within the category of public law was the repressive action taken against witches and ghouls. Although the Nuer themselves say that this action was sometimes taken and, in quoting instances in their history, refer to individuals who have at least an established position in known genealogies,

CUSTOM AND LAW

there is no documented evidence, and we are again approaching a subject which is a matter of conjecture. It may be presumed, however, that violence probably resulting in death was sometimes used against persons who had acquired such an evil reputation that their continued existence in the community became intolerable. Nuer tell us that in the case of ghouls (*rodh*) no indemnity would be demanded by the dead man's kinsmen, and only a much reduced indemnity in the case of possessors of the evil eye (*peth*), and sometimes magicians (usually *tiet*) who were alleged to have used their powers for strictly anti-social purposes. This does not necessarily suggest that anything in the nature of organized or concerted action was taken but that the act of revenge on the person of a witch by an individual, or a few individuals who supported him, was condoned by public opinion to such an extent that the kinsmen of the deceased dared not retaliate, or perhaps themselves condoned the act, considering themselves well rid of a dangerous factor within their own lineage. At any rate a blood-feud was unlikely to follow, and although vague statements of this kind must be substantiated by actual examples[1] before any definite conclusion may be drawn, we might be justified in saying that here at least is the germ of public law.

Trends and Changing Conditions: the Transformation of Custom into Law

We have seen in the introduction and throughout the descriptive passages of this book that among the Nuer there are recognized rules of conduct which find expression in the terms *cuong*, 'right', and *duer*, 'wrong'. These concern the relations of one Nuer with another and, since the individual cannot be considered in isolation, one group with another. The distinction between custom and law has also been mentioned. The term 'law' is sometimes used of all processes of social control, and by this definition any of the obligations, customary actions, and conventions inherent in the social system might be described as law. It is less confusing to adopt the hypothesis that the extent of the law is limited to social control which is maintained by organized legal sanctions and applied by some form of organized political mechanism. By this definition, the Nuer had no law, for, as we have already seen, there was in the past nothing in the nature of politically organized society. There were in a sense courts of arbitration dependent on the person of the Leopard-Skin Chief, but resort to this functionary only occurred if both parties were willing or found it expedient to do so, and there was certainly no means through which a judgement could be enforced even if it was given.

On this subject, Professor Evans-Pritchard has written:

[1] It is perhaps now too late to collect reliable evidence on this subject.

QNL

NATURE OF NUER LAW

> In a strict sense Nuer have no law. There are conventional compensations for damage, adultery, loss of limb, and so forth, but there is no authority with power to adjudicate on such matters or to enforce a verdict.[1]

When this statement is applied to the past, no criticism can be made. So far as it is now possible to discover what happened in those days, we may safely say that arbitration only occurred when it was expedient for both parties to submit to it. We may also conclude that the conventional compensations referred to were in the nature of a formula for compromise. A start in the negotiations had to be made with reference to some scale, especially when the disputants were under the stress of heated emotions, but although such scales have a traditional consistency, there was no constancy or rigidity of application. Finally we may say that there was no mechanism for enforcement should either party refuse to continue negotiations at any stage of the proceedings.

Professor Evans-Pritchard goes on to say:

> The recent introduction of Government courts, before which disputes are now sometimes settled, in no way weakens this impression, because one well knows how among other African peoples cases are brought before courts under Government supervision which would not previously have been settled in a court, or even settled at all, and how for a long time after the institution of such Government tribunals they operate side by side with the old methods of justice.[2]

This was written of the Lou Nuer as they were some twenty years ago, and the rapidity with which Government tribunals have developed since then is considerable. If it is argued that these tribunals are now applying the law beyond the limits of reality in the past, this statement is entirely true. If it is argued that the courts are administering a system of law which has no foundation in tradition at all, the statement is less true, though it is manifest that there are many innovations which are the result of an evolution of case law based on precedents, some of which are the natural development of Nuer ideas, some of which are due to the direct intervention of the Government. Rules of behaviour administered in the courts are none the less law, provided they are administered consistently on recognized principles and are enforced.

We have considered almost all those aspects of Nuer life which are subjects of discussion and dispute in the courts today: homicide and bodily injury; marital relationships, rights, and obligations; divorce and dissolution of marriages; the legitimacy of children; violation of rights in women; the infringement of grazing and fishing rights; theft and the misappropriation of property; witchcraft and other nefarious practices. In the past the sanctions for conformity with rules of conduct and for the composition of wrongs, if a breach of those rules

---

[1] Evans-Pritchard, *The Nuer*, p. 162.   [2] Ibid.

TRANSFORMATION OF CUSTOM INTO LAW 227

occurred, were forceful retaliation or self-help; social reprobation within the community and unpopularity, loss of prestige and privilege, and so on. The force of these sanctions was neither constant nor continuous, but they were certainly effective in some instances. The sanctions were variable and their effect was relative to the position in the social structure and the actual daily proximity of the persons concerned, and depended also on the political relations prevailing between the tribal segments to which they belonged. Nowadays these matters are to a greater or lesser degree brought before the courts and a settlement is enforced. Customary procedure has become law in the more precise definition.

This may be attested by reference to the examples already recorded in detail. It is, for instance, customary, on the death of a wife who has not fulfilled the required procreative obligations, for the bridewealth cattle to be returned to her husband, thus dissolving the union, though the wife's family may usually claim certain deductions. The Nuer regard this procedure as logical and correct, though it is doubtful whether it was followed in the past, especially as the dissolution of marriages appears to have been less frequent or even impossible after some years of marriage had elapsed. If the marriage is not dissolved, either because the husband does not wish it or because the wife has already borne sufficient children to stabilize the union for all time, her family may be expected to assist the widower by payment of certain cattle (*ghok tuoke*), which will be used to feed the children or to enable him to marry again so that 'there may be a mother in the home'. This may be regarded as a matter of custom, for in the past the payment doubtless depended on the terms on which the husband and his dead wife's family continued to live. This is also true today and most situations of this sort call for no dispute. If this custom becomes a subject for litigation and appears before a court, payment may be enforced. The court will begin by saying to the wife's family that it is customary to give *ghok tuoke* in such circumstances and that the husband is in the right: *teke cuong*, 'he has a right'. They are taking as a criterion what a reasonable Nuer may be expected to do in similar circumstances, and will call upon the wife's family to conform to that criterion, but, after persuasion, they will in the final event enforce this decision with the threat of punishment if it is not followed. To quote another example: in marriage, it is customary for the bride's father's age-mate to receive a cow called *yang ric*. The special relationship between the bride's father and his age-mate, and symbolically the intimate association of all age-mates, is thus socially recognized. If questioned the Nuer would undoubtedly say that the age-mate has a right (*cuong*) to this cow. Further, there are three different sets of people involved in this transaction. In the first place the bride's family are concerned with

228   NATURE OF NUER LAW

the bridegroom. The question arises whether or not he will meet
this particular claim. If pressed he will probably do so because
the bride's family might terminate the negotiations, though this is
unlikely to happen over so remote a claim as the cow of the age-mate.
In the second place the bride's father is concerned with his age-mate,
and here there is an element of reciprocal exchange.[1] A cow is not
given to all age-mates of the bride's father, only to one who has a
particularly close connexion with him and has probably undergone with him the ritual processes of initiation which impart a
mystical association analogous to kinship. We see therefore that
the custom is a complicated one involving two separate transactions and subject to different sanctions. If a dispute over this payment reached a Nuer court, payment would in most instances be
enforced. When there are sufficient precedents to constitute a
consistent application of a custom of this sort, we should be justified
in speaking of the claim as a legal and enforceable right.

Again, certain categories of magical experts are entitled to a fee for
their services. Such claims often appear before the courts. The court
will consider the circumstances, estimate whether the alleged benefits
have been received or not, and if necessary order the client to
pay the fee. The transaction is in the nature of a contract which is
now enforceable in law. In the past the sanctions were retaliatory,
though in this particular instance forceful retaliation would be unlikely
since more commonly the magician's supernatural powers, which might
be used against his client, would be feared.

Compensation for wrongs, recognized in tradition, expressed in
traditional scales, and originally a basis for compromise, is now
enforced in the Courts. Adultery, for example, is a recognized wrong
and one which should be rectified by the payment of a suitable indemnity. Whether or not this was paid in the past depended again on the
sanctions prevailing, but nowadays the wrongdoer will in the final
event be compelled to pay. This applies to other legal wrongs, such as
the seduction or impregnation of unmarried girls, and theft or damage
of property.

Among the Nuer there is a vast field of custom and convention
which is now supported by legal sanctions and thus becomes the law.
Moreover this transformation of custom into law is being carried to
extremes among the Nuer, for there is an increasing tendency to treat
all social customs and conventions as enforceable laws.

Throughout this discussion of Nuer customary law we have sometimes been speaking of the present, sometimes of the past. Under
the influence of modern administration systems of social control are

---

[1] The age-mate will receive the cow if the bride's father has received a like privilege
on the marriage of the age-mate's daughter or has the expectation of doing so. See
p. 110 and n. 3.

NUER COURTS

changing very rapidly, so that this distinction in time is clearly essential. We have seen that most social obligations and systems of social control were maintained in the past by sanctions which made conformity essential or at least expedient. Such sanctions were operative upon individuals or groups and their force was variable according to the position in the social structure of the parties concerned. Theoretically at least, the law was the same but its application was relative. For the most part the establishment of Nuer tribunals, with the threat of force behind them, has provided a substitute for other means by which the political balance was maintained.

In the initial stages of administration the policy was to intervene only in those affairs which constituted a breach of the peace: affray, continued blood-feuds, or individual fights. This action was to modify or even remove the retaliatory sanction. The next stage was to intervene in matters which were likely to lead to a breach of the peace, and to see that disputes were peaceably settled. Both actions took the form of direct intervention by the District Commissioner, his decisions being enforced, as far as was then possible, by State police. The next stage was the appointment of tribal agents. This led to the establishment of Nuer courts whose authority was backed in the first instance by the tribal retainers or 'Chiefs' police', some of whom were armed with an outmoded pattern of rifle, but was upheld in the final instance by the District Commissioner. Since then Nuer courts have gradually developed in efficiency, power, and formality of procedure, until in some areas they may be said to compare favourably with similar courts in the more developed parts of the Northern Sudan.

This raises another important point which is relevant to a study of Nuer law. The courts are not equally effective or efficient in all parts of Nuerland. The extent to which past sanctions have already changed, and the rapidity with which they are changing now, are therefore not constant. For example, the difference between such tribes as the Lak and the Nuong is considerable. The Lak of Central Nuer District, whose country is close to the administrative headquarters of the province and the district centre at Fangak, who are easily accessible at all times of the year, and whose permanent settlements are concentrated, have been closely administered for the past twenty years or more. The courts have reached, comparatively speaking, a high level of efficiency, and a man can usually obtain redress for wrongs committed against him. The Nuong, whose country lies in the southern extremity of Western Nuer District, which as a whole has perhaps been less closely administered than Central Nuer District, are not easily accessible at any time of the year. There are no roads leading to their permanent settlements and only one moderately easy approach to their country by river. At most they have received the personal attention of a District Commissioner for a few weeks each year. The courts,

230 NATURE OF NUER LAW

established it is true for many years, can scarcely be described as efficient and, unless other considerations are present or other opportunities arise,[1] a man can only obtain redress with difficulty.

I do not propose to digress further on this particular aspect of the changing political situation in Nuerland, but must draw attention to these facts because generalizations about the law as it is administered to-day are qualified accordingly. We can say, for example, that in Lak country a Nuer will almost certainly obtain compensation for an act of adultery committed with his wife and in that area there can be few adulterers who escape the penalty, but this statement would not be true of Nuong. In Nuong country the courts may be instrumental in bringing a similar dispute to a satisfactory conclusion or they may not. If a dispute is not settled by the intervention of Government-sponsored authorities, then the likelihood of the indemnity being paid to the wronged husband depends largely on sanctions similar to those operative in the past. It is true to say that in those areas where the courts are least effective these sanctions are proportionately stronger, mainly because there is in consequence less public security, and retaliation, the strongest sanction of all, is for this reason much more likely. It would be unsafe to make further generalizations because the likelihood of a dispute being settled, even in these days and even in the most advanced areas, still depends on so many variable and unpredictable circumstances.

Modern Procedure

Where courts are concerned we must distinguish between judgement and execution. It is one thing for a court to give judgement and quite another for the judgement to be carried out. Many cases which appear before the courts and appeal courts are no more than demands for execution of a previous judgement. It must be presumed that, if a dispute reaches this stage of legal procedure, it is unlikely that other sanctions unconnected with the court will be effective in bringing about execution once judgement is given. Yet in many cases the main function of the court is to establish publicly and to the satisfaction of both disputants that one of them is in the right. In the past it may have been fully recognized within a community that a man had a definite right to certain cattle, either in fulfilment of some obligation, in settlement of a debt, or as compensation for an injury. There was, however, no organized body representing public opinion to enforce payment. It is true to say that such a body now exists in the court itself and in the administrative agents with executive powers appointed by the Government; but the action taken by them

[1] Such as personal relationships or close friendship with chiefs or notables who have a degree of authority accorded to them by the Government. Similar comparisons may be made between all the different tribal areas in Nuerland. I was struck by the contrast in this particular instance on a visit to the Nuong Nuer.

MODERN PROCEDURE

in such matters is not always consistent and certainly not equally effective. Moreover there is still everywhere a reluctance to give anything in the nature of a judgement. In many disputes, where the rights of one or other of the disputants are abundantly clear, a rapid and clear-cut decision might be expected. This is rarely forthcoming. Argument swings from one side to another during the course of the proceedings until agreement is reached. When a compromise is not reached to the satisfaction of both complainant and defendant, although the decision is recorded in the court registers, execution is often avoided even though the guilty party is well able to pay the cattle demanded. More often still an appeal is lodged. A dispute frequently passes through all possible stages of litigation; from preliminary negotiations, in which the elders of the community may be consulted, to appearance before the tribal court, to appeal court.[1] Even then there are many instances where attempts are made to bring the same case again and again. This lack of finality is a distinct characteristic of Nuer litigation.

Nevertheless, the general and most obvious effect of administration in the form and application of what we may now call Nuer law is, as already stated, on its relativity. Here we must make a further distinction, because Nuer courts are in fact operating in two different ways. In the first place they are upholding a network of positive obligations inherent in the social system, and in this sense they are becoming more and more the sole mechanism through which the social system is maintained. In the second place they are the means through which definite legal wrongs are righted. A man who does not fulfil a particular duty towards a kinsman may now be brought before the courts in just the same way as one who has infringed a specific right. More and more of what can only be described as custom, convention, or even usage finds its way into the arena of the courts and is applied as law. Evidence of this may be seen in the growing amount of litigation which appears before the courts. The Nuer are pressing, through this means, claims for the fulfilment of obligations which were not in the past normally subjects of dispute at all. There is another reason for this increase in litigation. Paradoxically enough, although there is now greater certainty of obtaining redress through the agency of the courts, the sanctions which in the past made for greater conformity with accepted patterns of behaviour, have themselves been modified by the very existence of the court system, which aims at the maintenance of public security. These sanctions, as we have seen, were principally retaliatory. For example, a man may nowadays commit adultery with another man's wife with the knowledge that he will at least escape death or severe injury at the hands of her husband, even though he knows that detection will almost

[1] Branch and Main Courts. See Appendix II.

certainly mean that he will be called upon to pay compensation and forced to comply. In the past there was no certainty that he would be compelled to pay compensation, but there was always present a real danger of vindictive retaliation, and the latter sanction appears to have been more effective in the past than the former is in the present. For this reason adultery is a more common offence than it was, or so the Nuer say, and here again there is an increase in litigation.

We find, then, that the establishment of the courts, though in one sense preserving the social system from complete breakdown, is in another sense contributing to social maladjustment. Moreover the establishment of courts with powers of coercion behind them tends to stimulate litigation because the courts provide a mechanism through which claims may be pressed which, by reason of the social or spatial distance between the parties concerned, would formerly have had little or no chance of success. In other words, claims in the courts receive the sanction of alien authority which has a wider range than the sanctions which previously made for their fulfilment. The relativity of application is now fast disappearing. We find at one end of the scale increased litigation due to the enforcement of claims which in the past could have had no legal reality. At the other end of the scale we find the modification of sanctions which in the past would have ensured unquestioned fulfilment of reciprocal obligations; a modification which leads to social disintegration of which increased litigation is a symptom. In the first place the Nuer are bringing before the courts actions which previously would have stood no chance of settlement. In the second place the obligations of social existence are more and more maintained only by direct action through the courts. The problem of increasing litigation is a serious one. It is one of the basic problems of administration among the Nuer.

'*Balanced Opposition*' *in the Court System*

In the past each social unit of Nuerland existed largely in opposition to other units. The need for common defence, mutual co-operation, and collective enterprise in economic activities were the principal factors which maintained the identity of territorial groupings, the relation between the territorial and political aspects being expressed in kinship terms. Each tribe, each tribal segment, each local community, was identified with a dominant clan or lineage. These formed the nucleus of groups of people not otherwise related, and links were forged between them on a kinship analogy. Such cohesion, which was not in any case constant, was therefore the result of the inter-action of several factors. Although the Nuer were involved in aggressive warfare with the Dinka during the period of their expansion westwards in the last century, it is clear that tribal segments

'BALANCED OPPOSITION'

were often at feud with each other. Scarcity of food, an annual occurrence among the Nuer, made mutual assistance in the subsistence economy essential, and this in turn created mutual obligations and reciprocal duties which extended beyond the sphere of economics. Isolation during the rains, varying degrees of necessity to migrate during the dry season in search of pasture, and the variable quality of the grazing available affected the quality and cohesion of the community and its relations with other communities.

These factors are much modified today. The need for common defence or aggression is considerably less because of the intervention of the Government. The scarcity of food and the fear of famine is reduced because in the last resort the Government has, at any rate for the past fifteen years, arranged to import grain for sale to the Nuer, should it be necessary. Isolation at any time of the year is less complete since communications have improved. The integration of the territorial groupings of Nuer society is for these reasons much affected. Communities are essentially territorial in basis and integrated by common sentiments which naturally arise. Through them stretch the concept of patrilineal descent and ties arising from marital relationships. Any modification of the sanctions which uphold the balance of this social system leads to a conflict of loyalties and a tendency to revert to kinship ties alone, even though kinship ties are themselves loosened by the growing process of social disintegration. Fission is caused by the modification of those sanctions which make fusion necessary. In the past, as Professor Evans-Pritchard has pointed out, the latter process was a complement of the former. When a group broke away from its homeland or split owing to a feud within itself, unless the members were sufficiently numerous to retain their identity and resist external aggression, they had to find a place in society somewhere or suffer political or economic insecurity.

Nowadays, when security against the opposition of others and the need for economic insurance are no longer so acutely necessary, the process is confined to splitting into smaller units of segmentation. This is a fundamental tendency apparent in Nuer society today, and the political aspect of the process is manifest in the endless demands for further and yet further representation in the courts by headmen (*gaat tutni*) who are the leaders of smaller and smaller segments. Representation in the courts so that personal claims in legal disputes may receive personal backing is the real motive behind this tendency. Yet the factor of 'balanced opposition' is still evident in the procedure of Nuer tribunals. It is more particularly manifest when a joint meeting is held between tribes or secondary segments. The attitude of the chiefs in such circumstances is always 'if you settle these cases, we will settle those'. Thus, to take an example, a court meeting of the Thiang Bang (primary segment) may appear chaotic so long as

234 NATURE OF NUER LAW

disputes are confined to tertiary or lesser segments within it. A man of *cieng* Bedit (a secondary segment) will receive the backing of court members who represent *cieng* Bedit when arguing a case against a man of *cieng* Juagh (another secondary segment), and the decision reached is in the form of a compromise between them. Even though judgement is given, it will depend on the spirit of compromise between those segments whether the chiefs will see to it that the judgement is promptly executed. There is also present a neutral body represented by the chiefs of other segments who, with the segments concerned, make up the sum total of the people over whom the court has jurisdiction. These will tend to act as arbitrators, while those who represent the segments to which the disputants belong are really acting as advocates rather than judges, but it will be the latter upon whom the responsibility of execution will fall. This is how a Nuer court functions, and if there is a joint meeting between the whole of Thiang and another tribe, all representatives of each side, previously at loggerheads with each other over internal affairs, will join together in forwarding the interests of their own people.

The spirit of compromise usually prevails. In disputes which are hotly contested it has been usual to bring in chiefs from other tribal areas to act as neutral arbitrators, and from this appeal courts have been formed, although in the recent past it was the District Commissioner who acted in this capacity. The balanced opposition of groups is therefore still an essential feature of the Nuer court system, and in this sense the courts are a stabilizing factor in the maintenance or re-emphasis of group identity.

The Introduction of Penal Sanctions

Some of the more general effects of the introduction of ordered administration and the establishment of Nuer tribunals have already been mentioned. We must now consider the effects of these influences on the nature of the law itself. We have seen that in the past, with the exception of the most rudimentary form of public and collective action which was sometimes taken against witches and other anti-social persons, there was nothing to suggest the existence of public law among the Nuer. The law, if we are justified in speaking of the law in reference to the past, comprised all those rules of conduct which regulated the behaviour of individuals and of groups, were maintained by indeterminate and relative sanctions, and were directed to the continuance of equilibrium in society. Since society among the Nuer is segmentary, this aspect is particularly obvious in what we have called the 'balanced opposition' of the component segments. Nowadays people who refuse to conform to the accepted pattern of behaviour, whether by the avoidance of duties or by the violation of the

PENAL SANCTIONS

rights of others, may be punished by fine or imprisonment. Moreover certain legal wrongs, which in the past were never more than private delicts and were composed by the payment of compensation aimed at the restoration of this balance, are now becoming criminal offences in a more exact definition.

Under the influence of the Administration over the last twenty years or more the Nuer, as represented by their local authorities, are rapidly becoming conscious of the value of punishment as a deterrent. Court members will sometimes say that they are punishing a man both because his action has been detrimental to society as a whole and has created a disturbance, and also because such disruptive actions must be checked. Public opinion as a whole is not advancing very rapidly in this respect, and it is significant that there is still no social stigma attached to imprisonment. The average Nuer does not understand why imprisonment should be inflicted at all, especially if compensation is also paid to the injured party. This is apparent, but it is perhaps worth while to consider this attitude in connexion with certain offences. We have already noted that the Nuer cannot understand why a man should be punished for killing his wife.[1] The damage done has been done to himself, and though he must make peace with his ancestral spirits, for he has sinned against the whole concept of kinship and the continuity of the lineage, and must pacify his wife's relatives with gifts and acts of atonement, nothing more should be demanded of him. His act, like suicide and fratricide, is the negation of the basic principles which underlie kinship. He has used the cattle of his lineage to marry a wife, he has killed her, lost the cattle, and compromised his position in posterity. His act is reprehensible enough for these reasons, but why should he also receive punishment at the hands of the Government? Similarly, an act of adultery requires an indemnity to be paid to the man whose rights have been infringed. Once paid, what need is there for fine or imprisonment? This is a general attitude, even though punishment is so frequently applied that the Nuer have come to expect it and even demand its application to those who have transgressed against them.

When we come to analyse the position more closely, however, we find that there are few offences which can yet be classified as criminal. Homicide and bodily injury are the main exceptions to this observation. Murder is often punished by death and other forms of homicide are now settled by the payment of fifty head of cattle.[2] Forty of these go to the kinsmen of the deceased in the traditional manner, but ten go to the Government and must be called a fine. In addition, unless there are exceptional circumstances which mitigate the offence, the killer is sentenced by the court to imprisonment for a period varying from one to six years. Though in the early stages of administration

[1] See p. 62.   [2] See pp. 63 et seq.

NATURE OF NUER LAW

this was usually inflicted by the District Commissioner sitting as a magistrate, or by the court on the advice of the District Commissioner, this form of sentence is now imposed almost automatically. Yet although there are clearly some Nuer chiefs who realize the value of imprisonment as a deterrent, the majority would not impose such a sentence without pressure from the administration. Moreover such punishments are often inflicted without due consideration of the circumstances of the case, and it is symptomatic of the general attitude to punishment that court members have a habit of asking for fixed sentences to be laid down for specific offences. It is, indeed, one of the problems of the Administration to explain to the Nuer that, though there may be a maximum penalty for an offence, this need not necessarily be applied. The reason is that, although Nuer chiefs and court members may be aware of the value of punishment, they are still reluctant to inflict it, especially as they are often subjected to recrimination by their fellows after the case is over. A fixed penalty absolves them from this and throws the responsibility on the Government. Nevertheless homicide and hurt must now be classed as criminal offences among the Nuer because they are habitually treated as such, albeit under protest. This observation may be applied also to theft.

In other offences in which punishment is sometimes but not always applied, we find that it is not usually the offence itself which is treated as a criminal action but the offender's action in disobeying the orders of the local authorities or the court. The punishment is inflicted for the defiance of authority by the offender rather than for the offence he had originally committed.

It is also clear that the introduction of penal sanctions has sometimes led to a curious mixture of legal concepts. For example, adultery is, as we have already seen, an offence which is normally compounded by payment of compensation to the wronged husband. Even though offenders are sometimes punished for persistent attention to the wives of others or for flagrant defiance of the orders of their chiefs, adultery remains essentially a private delict. For the reasons already described,[1] if a divorce follows an act of adultery, it is a fundamental principle among the Nuer that the compensation cattle must be returned to the adulterer and should not be retained by the woman's husband, who would otherwise pass them to her family. To do so is to risk a confusion of legal status which Nuer law seeks to avoid. Owing to a recent decision by the Council of Nuer Chiefs, these cattle must now be paid to the Government and thus become a fine. Adultery, initially a private delict, becomes a public delict, and a criminal offence should the husband decide to dissolve the union subsequently. There is therefore growing up a curious admixture of traditional Nuer law, which in basis and principle is essentially private law, and European

[1] See pp. 166–8.

legal concepts. This process of admixture may be seen in other legal matters and is leading to an illogical and confusing evolution. It is no part of this book to predict what will occur in the future, but it is obvious that some sort of order must be applied to a system which may otherwise become chaotic.

We have been considering throughout these chapters a system of law in a segmentary society which is in a state of evolution. In the first place this evolutionary process is rooted in the traditional methods of controlling the acts of individuals and groups, none of which methods was rigid or enforceable. The application of the principles which we have found was not constant in time or place, but was subject to the balanced opposition of the segments of Nuer society. The evolution has also been deeply affected by decisions made in the courts, often by the direct intervention of British officials who had neither knowledge nor understanding of the principles involved. Often, too, these decisions were made in the mistaken idea that this was justice, without realizing that Nuer ideas of justice are often different from our own. Further decisions have been made which spring directly from the penal code of the country and the penal sanction enters as an active force in the administration of the law, but often without order or consistency. An attempt is being made in one direction to introduce a system which recognizes the fundamental principle of individual responsibility, in another to preserve a system which is essentially based on the principles of collective responsibility. These latter principles will continue to be effective so long as Nuer society remains homogeneous and retains its present form. Yet despite these conflicting forces, we cannot say that the customary law now administered in the Nuer courts is based not on Nuer principles but on our own. If this were so the Nuer, who are a headstrong and independent people, would not submit to it.

APPENDIX I

NUERLAND

Populations and Area

Central Nuer District

Tribe	Humans[1]	Cattle[2]	Area in square miles[3]	Courts
Lak . . .	37,000	44,000*	1,500	
Gaawar . .	39,000	48,000*	5,120	11 (B) Regional Courts
Thiang . .	13,000	15,000*	970	1 (C) Main Court
Lou . . .	63,000	126,000*	5,290	

Western Nuer District

Tribe	Humans[1]	Cattle[2]	Area in square miles[3]	Courts
Bul . . .	32,000	50,000	2,320	
Leik . . .	27,000	40,000	2,140	
Jagei . .	14,000	31,000*	1,220	5 (B) Regional Courts
Dok (and Aak) .	21,000	35,000*	1,930	2 (C) Main Courts
Nuong (and Dur)	14,000	16,000	2,490	
W. Jikany . .	18,000	29,000*	1,100	

Eastern Nuer District

Tribe	Humans[1]	Cattle[2]	Area in square miles[3]	Courts
Gaajok . .	45,000	45,000	} 7,190	4 (B) Regional Courts
Gaajak . .	33,000	33,000		11 (A) Branch Courts
Totals . .	356,000	512,000	31,270	

[1] Based on recent tax-payer figures multiplied by 4·5 to nearest 1000 (1952). This multiplier is purely arbitrary and is probably high, but the figures given are consistent.

[2] Figures marked * are statistics taken from veterinary inoculation campaigns and represent a *minimum* figure. It is clear that all cattle were not counted, and possibly up to 20 per cent. should be added. Other figures are merely a rough estimate.

[3] Areas estimated by planimeter, but boundaries are not clearly demarcated or mapped and the areas are necessarily only approximate.

APPENDIX II

CHIEFS' COURTS ORDINANCE 1931

Nuer courts are established under the Chiefs' Courts Ordinance 1931, which applies to the three southern Provinces of the Sudan: the Bahr el Ghazal, Equatoria, and the Upper Nile. The Ordinance has been reprinted in full in *The Laws of the Sudan, Supplement to Volume 4*, pp. 76-81. It should be noted that this Ordinance has been altered by the terms of the Self Government Statute (1953), section 76, i.e.:

'(5) There shall be vested in the Chief Justice all the powers conferred upon the Governor-General . . . by . . . the Chiefs' Courts Ordinance 1931. . . .

(6) There shall further be vested in the Chief Justice all the powers conferred upon Governors by the Chiefs' Courts Ordinance 1931. . . . Provided that:

(*a*) the Chief Justice may delegate all or any of the said powers to the Governor concerned;

(*b*) the Chief Justice may delegate any power, other than the powers of establishing and convening Courts and of appointing Presidents and members of Courts, to the Judge of the Civil High Court of a Province;

(*c*) neither the Chief Justice nor a Judge of the Civil High Court shall exercise any of the said powers except after consultation with the Governor concerned.'

As a result of the various constitutional changes which will take place during the next few years, further modifications of the Ordinance may be expected.

Each court is established by warrant—under the hand of the Chief Justice—which lays down the jurisdiction, constitution, powers, etc., in accordance with the provisions of the Ordinance, but subject to the Regulations which accompany the warrant. A 'Main Court' has jurisdiction over a District or part of a District. For example, the Central Nuer Court has jurisdiction over all tribes in that district including a few small Dinka tribes. In Western Nuer District there are two Main Courts. A Main Court sits only occasionally, five members in addition to the president forming a quorum, of whom at least two must be presidents of Regional Courts or Magistrates under the Criminal Code of Procedure. There are then a series of 'Regional Courts' within each District. The area over which each Regional Court has jurisdiction corresponds to the territory of a tribe, an amalgamation of tribes, or in some cases the primary segments of a tribe, although the name of the Regional Court often derives from that of the place at which the court

CHIEFS' COURTS ORDINANCE 1931

centre is situated. In some districts there are also 'Branch Courts' of more limited jurisdiction and powers.

Under section 7 (1) of the Chiefs' Courts Ordinance 1931:

'A Chief's Court shall administer—

(*a*) the native law and custom prevailing in the area over which the Court exercises its jurisdiction provided that such native law and custom is not contrary to justice, morality or order;

(*b*) the provisions of any ordinance which the Court may be authorised to administer in its warrant or regulations.'

Right of appeal is from the court to the District Commissioner or 'to such Chiefs' Courts as the Governor, with the consent of the Governor-General (now of the Chief Justice) may authorize to hear appeals'. In most cases appeals from Regional Courts go to a Main Court and only in very exceptional cases to the District Commissioner or higher authority.

Apart from the technicalities of the legal procedure, which the Nuer litigant so often ignores, a civil dispute of the kind already described usually follows a standard course. The dispute is first discussed within the local group or kinship circle and some attempt is made by the elders and headmen to settle it. Up to this point the dispute is *ruac cieng*, 'home talk'. Failing a settlement the plaintiff refers the case to a Branch or Regional Court and, if dissatisfied with the judgement, then appeals to the Main Court of the District.

RNL

CENTRAL NUER DISTRICT COURTS

SCHEDULE I. 'B' COURTS (REVISED UP TO 1951)[1]

No. and Name	President	Jurisdiction	Quorum	Powers	Appeal	Remarks[2]
B.1 Wath Kec .	Head of Wath Kec L.G. Area	Wath Kec L.G. Area	President and 3 members	Imprisonment up to 2 years: Fine up to £E.25—15 lashes; 10 strokes cane. Civil suits up to £E.100[3]	To 'C' Court	Lak Nuer: Jenyang Primary Segment
B.2 Fagwir .	Head of Fagwir L.G. Area	Fagwir L.G. Area .	,,	,,	,,	Lak Nuer: Kwacbor Primary Segment
B.3 Mareng .	Head of Mareng L.G. Area	Mareng L.G. Area .	,,	,,	,,	Thiang Nuer
B.4 Jumbiel .	Head of Jumbiel L.G. Area	Jumbiel L.G. Area .	,,	,,	,,	Gaawar Nuer: Those on Zeraf Island
B.5 Ayod (Awoi)	Head of Ayod L.G. Area	Ayod L.G. Area .	,,	,,	,,	Gaawar Nuer: Bar Primary Segment
B.6 Falagh .	Head of Falagh L.G. Area	Falagh L.G. Area .	,,	,,	,,	Gaawar Nuer: Radh Primary Segment
B.8 Thul . .	Head of Thul L.G. Area	Thul L.G. Area .	,,	,,	,,	Lou Nuer: Gun Primary Segment
B.9 Muot Tot . (Fattai)	Head of Muot Tot L.G. Area	Muot Tot L.G. Area	,,	,,	,,	Lou Nuer: Gun Primary Segment
B.10 Ful Burra . (Yuai)	Head of Ful Burra L.G. Area	Ful Burra L.G. Area	,,	,,	,,	Lou Nuer: Gun Primary Segment
B.11 Faddoi .	Head of Faddoi L.G. Area	Faddoi L.G. Area .	,,	,,	,,	Lou Nuer: Mor Primary Segment

[1] Powers increased to three years' imprisonment in cases of homicide or recidivists in affray cases.

[2] Not included in warrant, but inserted to show the way in which the court system follows the segmentary structure of the tribes. Court B.7 includes only Dinka tribes and is omitted here.

[3] The schedule has been brought up to date up to the end of 1951. From time to time there have been alterations as and when Courts have been amalgamated.

GLOSSARY

ariek . . . Dinka term for cattle claimed by a man on the marriage of his wife's younger sister. There is no formal equivalent in Nuer.

arueth. . . Dinka term for cattle given to the bridegroom by the bride's father or guardian: a 'reverse payment' of which the Nuer equivalent is *thiuk*, but only customary among some western Nuer tribes and in a reduced form.

bak (baɣ) . . to split or divide in two, as in *yang me bak ke rual*, 'the cow of dividing for incest'—used in the ritual required to avoid the consequences of incest.

biem . . . to kill by stealth or ambush.

birr (biir) . to scratch the arm of a killer during the ceremony performed by a Leopard-Skin Chief to remove the pollution which follows an act of homicide.

bith . . . fish-spear, usually barbed.

buor . . . mud hearth or fire-screen used for cooking and hence the symbol of the wife or mother in the house.

buthni . . *gwan buthni*, an agnatic kinsman of a collateral branch of the lineage who represents its ritual and legal interests.

cieh . . . bracelet: of significance in marriage.

ciek . . . woman, and by inference a wife or married woman as opposed to *nyal*, girl, or an adult woman who is not married and is, specifically, *ciek me keagh*. *ciek jooka*, a 'ghost-wife'; the wife of a spirit, a woman who is married to the name of a dead man. *ciek me jok*, a 'loose' woman, lit. 'a bitch'. *ciek me lak*, widow living with a man in 'widow-concubinage'.

cien . . . the revengeful spirit of a dead man, usually one who has met a violent end.

cou . . . husband.

cuei . . . betrothal. *'ce cuei de cuei'*, 'he has betrothed himself': a formal step towards marriage.

cuil . . . a ceremony performed in the final stages of composition in blood-feuds.

cuong . . . a right. *'teke cuong'*, 'he is (has) right', as opposed to *duer*, wrong.
ji cuongni (rar), 'the people of rights' (outside), i.e. those relatives of the bride, other than her immediate family, who have rights to definite portions of her bridewealth.

244 GLOSSARY

cut . . . indemnity. A general term for indemnity or compensation. Nuer say that certain wrongs (*duer*) *teke cut*, 'have compensation'.

dak . . . to break, sever, breakage.
dak kwen, divorce.
dak mara, the severing of kinship.

dap (*dab*) . . to give birth.
nyin daba, the 'things of birth'—given to the bride's mother as something apart from her claims on the bridewealth cattle.

dar . . . back or middle. Hence the 'middle' (usually third) son in a family.

deb . . . rope, tethering rope for cattle.
loiny deb, a ceremony symbolizing the bride's release from her father's herd.

dhu . . . to fornicate with; *dhu ciek*, adultery.

diel (*dil*) . . original occupants of a specific area, often referred to in literature as 'aristocrats', as opposed to *rul*, 'newcomers'.

dou . . . cow-calf.

duac (*dwac*) . . to hit; hence duel between two persons.

duer (*dwer*) . . a wrong, mistake, as opposed to *cuong*, right.

dun (pl. *nyin*) : . thing or possession as in *dun-da*, my thing, *nyin-ke*, his things.

dwek (*duek*) . . 'commoners' as opposed to 'experts' (*kuaar*) or the *ji twac*, the 'people of skins' who wear skins as insignia of office.

dwiel (*dwil*) . . house, hut. *thok dwiel*, 'the entrance to the house', i.e. lineage, genealogy. Also *kwi dwiel*, 'the hut side', i.e. mother's side as opposed to *kwi luak*, 'cattle-byre side', i.e. father's side; terms used to distinguish half-brothers in a polygynous household.

gat (pl. *gaat*) . child, son.

gat jooka . . 'son of a ghost' (in 'ghost-marriage').

gat laka . . son of a widow (in 'widow-concubinage').

gat nyal (pl. *gaat nyiet*) 'son of a daughter', 'sons of daughters', i.e. those attached to the lineage through marriage and descent through the female line.

gat tuot (pl. *gaat tutni*) 'son of a bull', 'sons of bulls' i.e. of the paternal line; headman.

ghok (ɣ*ok*) . . cattle.

ghot (ɣ*ot*) . . dwelling hut.

gorei . . . the central hearth of the homestead and therefore a symbol of the family unit.

gual (*gwal*) . . to exchange or barter: direct exchange as opposed to *ngual*, which implies a loan, usually with profit.

GLOSSARY

245

guk (guh) . . 'prophet', owner of a 'sky spirit' (*kwoth nial*): a 'spirit owner', *gwan kwoth* of exceptional powers and prestige.

gurkeka . . the 'one who follows the *keagh*'; hence the second son in a family.

gwan (guan) (pl. ji) lit. father, father of. Hence 'owner of', as in *gwan bith* or *tang*, 'owners of spears', who have special ritual functions.

gwan nyal, the father of the bride.

gwan thunge, one who has to pay *thung*, compensation, and hence a killer.

gwan twac, owner of a skin (badge of office), as opposed to *dwek*, ordinary person or commoner. Also the bridegroom's representative in marriage because he must wear a skin (*twac*), symbol of respect for relatives-in-law.

gwan wal, owner of medicine, magician.

jal . . . journey.

ji . . . people, as in *ji kany* (Jikany tribe), *j(a)gei* (Jagei tribe): a common Nilotic root, *ji, ja, jal*. Also used in some senses as the plural of *gwan*, father, owner, as in—

ji nyal, 'bride's people', as opposed to the *ji wute*, 'bridegroom's people'.

ji ran, 'people of the (dead) man', as opposed to the *ji thunge*, 'people of the compensation', i.e. kinsmen of the killer.

ji twac, 'people of the skin', ritual experts (pl. of *gwan twac*).

jut . . . a girl past the normal age for marriage not yet betrothed.

kap tang . . 'hold the spear-shaft', a form of oath.

kethar (karthar) . kinsmen (of an older generation) standing at the limits of relationship to the bride which carries a legal claim on her bridewealth.

KINSHIP TERMS . The reader should refer to the chart on p. 102. These are given throughout in the third person singular in reference to the bride.

kok . . . a word now used to denote the act of purchase, as in '*ca bel kok ke jilab*', 'I bought grain from the merchant'.

kolang . . a form of spirit of which there are many manifestations.

kuaar . . . expert, chief: thus:

kuaar kwac or *kuaar muon*, Leopard-Skin Chief or Land Chief.

kuaar thoan, lit. 'Serval Cat-Skin Chief', a special kind of Land Chief who arbitrates between two Leopard-Skin lineages.

	kuaar juath, expert in diseases, especially small-pox.
	kuaar nyang, 'crocodile expert'.
	kuaar thoi, 'water or river expert'.
	kuaar yiika, 'chief of the skirts', ritual expert responsible for the fertility of women.
kul . . .	skin, sleeping-skin, and hence a symbol of conjugal rights. *cf. yang kule*, 'the cow of the sleeping-skin'; the cow paid to the wronged husband by an adulterer as expiation and to remove pollution.
kur . . .	battle, fight, war.
kwen (kuen) . .	to count out, assess; hence assessment of the bride-wealth cattle in marriage—therefore the act of marriage, the institution of marriage.
kwi (kui) . .	on the side of. Thus *kwi gwan*, 'bride's father's side' in marriage, as opposed to *kwi man*, 'mother's side', or more often *kwi nar*, 'maternal uncle's side'. See also under *dwiel—kwi dwiel* and *kwi luak*.
kwil (kuil) . .	from the verb *kwal*, to steal. Theft.
kwil nyal . .	abduction.
luak . . .	cattle-byre.
luc . . .	to disguise an animal wrongfully by altering the owner's markings.
luk (luɤ) . .	case, trial. *ce luk de luk*, 'his case has been tried'.
mar . . .	kinship.
math . . .	to drink; hence a ceremony of composition in feuds where the opposing parties partake of food and in particular drink together.
math (maath) .	'Best Friend'; an institutionalized and formal relationship between persons.
muon . . .	earth, land. Hence also mourning, burial.
muot . . .	ceremony of shaving the bride's hair, which has legal as well as ritual significance. From *mut*, to shave. Nuer say '*ce nyal mut?*', 'has the bride been shaved?'
mut . . .	spear.
Naadh (Nath) .	the 'People', i.e. the Nuer.
nac . . .	heifer.
nak . . .	to kill, slaughter.
ngi nyal . .	'bridesmaid'—the bride's special representative who accompanies her through all the ceremonies of marriage.
ngual (ngwal) .	loan or debt; to borrow an animal and repay it with another (better) one.
noong . . .	bring; hence *noong nyal*, the ceremony of 'bringing the bride'.
nueer . . .	a form of spiritual pollution which follows the infringement of certain taboos, notably incest, manifest in physical disease.

GLOSSARY

nyin . . . things (sing. *dun*).

nyindiet . . compensation due for a man who dies from wounds a considerable time after they were inflicted.

pale loic . . lit. 'easing of the heart'; hence *ghok pale loic*, cattle paid to the kinsmen of the deceased in the final stages of settlement of a feud.

pegh (pek) . . limit, boundary; hence youngest son.

piec mac . . to kindle fire—usually a ritual performance.

puong (puang) . portion of the bridewealth usually set aside for the bride's youngest brother or the youngest in the family.

ran me gam e-je . the second to inflict a wound, used in reference to homicide or hunting.

ran me koic e-je . the first to inflict a wound.

ret . . . orphan, one whose legal and physiological father is dead, as opposed to *gat jooka*, 'son of a ghost', one whose legal father is dead, but whose physiological father is alive having married his mother to the name of his legal father. *cf.* also *gat cana*, son of a widow (also *gat laka*).

ric . . . age-set.

riem . . . blood. *ce riem de kam rar*, 'his blood has been let'—during the ritual of *birr* (see under *birr*), and *teke riem kamdien*, 'there is blood between them'—in the sense of a feud, not kinship.

riet . . . a decision, judgement.

ruac . . . talk. *ruac cieng*, lit. 'home talk', i.e. a matter which should be decided in the home rather than in court. *ruac kwoth*, 'the will of God'—hence also, 'an act of God'.

ruath . . . bull-calf.

ruec . . . spokesmanship in the sense of expressing popular ideas or the will of the people.

ruet . . . to get with child. *ciek me ruet*, pregnant woman.

ruic . . . spokesman, leader.

ruok . . . compensation; to indemnify violations of rights in women:
ruok dhu ciek, indemnity for the act of fornication with a married woman.
ruok ruet ciek, indemnity for adultery resulting in pregnancy and birth of a child.
ruok nyal (as above, *dhu* and *ruet*), fornication with an unmarried girl.
ruok gaanke, often *ruok muor*, 'legitimization fees', fees paid by a man outside marriage or in divorce to acquire or retain legal paternity of children.

tem . . . cut, tear.

ter . . . blood-feud.

GLOSSARY

thak (pl. *thaak*)	.	ox, castrated bull.
thanypiny .	.	certain gifts given in addition to bridewealth.
thiang, thiany	.	spiritual pollution caused by sexual intercourse with a woman who is pregnant or nursing a child.
thiuk .	.	cattle given by bride's family to her husband (*cf. arueth*).
thok dwiel .	.	entrance to the house; hence lineage or patrilineal descent group.
thu . .	.	in-law. *man-thu, gwan-thu*, mother-in-law, father-in-law.
thung . .	.	indemnity for homicide. *thung gwacka*, indemnity for accidental killing; *thung yiika*, compensation for an unmarried woman who dies in childbirth.
toic (*toc*)	.	riverain (summer) pasture. Grazing grasses produced by inundation from rivers or watercourses.
tul . .	.	break, as in *tul coke*, to break a bone.
twoc . .	.	invocation of the cattle during the negotiations of marriage—usually at the *larcieng* ceremony; hence the main ceremony of marriage.
yang . .	.	cow.

yang dieth or *dithe*, 'the cow of birth'.

yang doth gata, cow given by a man to his wife's mother on birth of first child.

yang kule, 'the cow of the sleeping mat', given by an adulterer to the wronged husband as expiation.

yang kwoth, lit. 'cow of God', a cow dedicated to the spirits of the lineage.

yang leta, 'the cow of the loins', or *yang laka*, 'the cow of widowhood': portions of a girl's bridewealth claimed by her natural father if she has been born outside marriage or in widowhood or concubinage. Also *yang pithe gaat*, claimed by a man, not the girl's legal father, who has brought her up in his household.

yang tuoke, 'the cow of the cooking pot', cow or cows given to bereaved husband by his dead wife's family.

yang yaatni, 'the cow of the skirts', cow (together with a bull-calf, *ruath miemni*) deducted from the bridewealth in divorce and retained by wife's family as compensation for her loss of maidenhood.

See also under portions of bridewealth, pp. 102 et seq., and bloodwealth, pp. 47 et seq.

yat (pl. *yaatni*)	.	married woman's skirt—hence a symbol of married woman's status.
yiik (*yih*) .	.	a mat, sleeping mat and symbol of conjugal rights and maternity; *cf. thung yiika*.

BIBLIOGRAPHY

Alban, A. H., 'Gwek's Pipe and Pyramid', *S.N.R.*,[1] 1940.

Brun-Rollet, A., *Le Nil Blanc et le Soudan*, Paris, 1855.

Butt, A., *The Nilotes of the Anglo-Egyptian Sudan and Uganda*, Ethnographic Survey of Africa, International African Institute, 1952.

Capri, P., 'I Nuer—una tribù indomita', *Le Missioni del Comboni*, 1938-9.

Coriat, P., 'The Gaweir Nuers', *S.N.R.*, 1923; republished with 'The Nuer of the Upper Nile', by H. C. Jackson.

—— 'Gwek, the Witch-Doctor and the Pyramid of Dengkur', *S.N.R.*, 1939.

Crazzolara, J. P., 'Die Gar-Zeremonie bei den Nuer', *Africa*, 1932.

—— 'Outlines of a Nuer Grammar', *Anthropos*, 1933.

—— 'Pygmies on the Bahr el Ghazal', *S.N.R.*, 1933.

—— 'Die Bedeutung des Rindes bei den Nuer', *Africa*, 1934.

—— 'A Nuer Story: Goor kene Nyaang', *The Messenger*, 1937.

—— *The Lwoo: Part I. Migrations*, Missioni Africane, Verona, 1950.

—— *The Lwoo: Part II. Traditions*, Missioni Africane, Verona, 1951.

Duncan, J. S. R., 'A Dry Season Trek', *Blackwoods*, November 1948.

Evans-Pritchard, E. E., 'The Nuer, Tribe and Clan', *S.N.R.*, 1933-5.

—— 'The Nuer: Age-Sets', *S.N.R.*, 1936.

—— 'Customs and Beliefs Relating to Twins among the Nilotic Nuer', *Uganda Journal*, 1936.

—— 'Daily Life of the Nuer in Dry Season Camps', in *Custom is King: Essays presented to R. R. Marett*, 1936.

—— 'Economic Life of the Nuer', *S.N.R.*, 1937-8.

—— 'Nuer Time-Reckoning', *Africa*, 1939.

—— 'Some Aspects of Marriage and the Family among the Nuer', *Sonderabdruck aus Zeitschrift für vergleichende Rechtswissenschaft*, 1938, and republished in *Rhodes-Livingstone Papers*, No. 11, 1945.

—— *The Nuer*, Oxford, 1940.

—— 'The Nuer of the Southern Sudan', in *African Political Systems* (ed. Fortes and Evans-Pritchard), 1940.

—— 'Nuer Bridewealth', *Africa*, 1946.

—— 'Bridewealth among the Nuer', *African Studies*, 1947.

—— 'A Note on Courtship among the Nuer', *S.N.R.*, 1947.

—— 'Nuer Marriage Ceremonies', *Africa*, 1948.

—— 'A Note on Affinity Relationships among the Nuer', *Man*, 1948.

—— 'Nuer Modes of Address', *Uganda Journal*, 1948.

[1] *S.N.R. Sudan Notes and Records.*

250 BIBLIOGRAPHY

Evans-Pritchard, E. E., 'The Nuer *col wic*', *Man*, 1949.

—— 'Burial and Mortuary Rites of the Nuer', *African Affairs*, 1949.

—— 'Nuer Rules of Exogamy and Incest', in *Social Structure, Essays presented to A. R. Radcliffe-Brown*, 1949.

—— 'Two Nuer Ritual Concepts', *Man*, 1949.

—— 'Nuer Curses and Ghostly Vengeance', *Africa*, 1949.

—— 'Nuer Totemism', *Annali Lateranensi*, 1949.

—— 'The Nuer Family', *S.N.R.*, 1950.

—— 'Kinship and Local Community among the Nuer', in *African Systems of Kinship and Marriage* (ed. Forde and Radcliffe-Brown), 1950.

—— 'Nilotic Studies', *Journal R.A.I.*, Vol. LXXX, 1950.

—— 'Some Features and Forms of Nuer Sacrifices', *Africa*, 1951.

—— *Kinship and Marriage among the Nuer*, Oxford, 1951.

—— 'Some Features of Nuer Religion', *Journal R.A.I.*, Vol. LXXXI, 1951.

—— 'A Note on Nuer Prayers', *Man*, 1952.

The Story of Fergie Bey, 1930 (biography of V. H. Fergusson).

Fergusson, V. H., 'The Nuong Nuer', *S.N.R.*, 1921.

—— 'Nuer Beast Tales', *S.N.R.*, 1924.

Howell, P. P., 'A Note on Elephants and Elephant Hunting among the Nuer, *S.N.R.*, 1945.

—— 'On the Value of Iron among the Nuer', *Man*, 1947.

—— 'The Age-set System and the Institution of "*Nak*" among the Nuer', *S.N.R.*, 1948.

—— 'Some Observations on the Distribution of Bloodwealth among the Nuer', *Man*, 1952.

Howell, P. P., and Lewis, B.A., 'Nuer Ghouls: A Form of Witchcraft', *S.N.R.*, 1947.

Huffman, R., *Nuer Customs and Folklore*, 1931.

—— *English-Nuer Dictionary*, 1931.

Jackson, H. C., 'The Nuer of the Upper Nile Province', *S.N.R.*, 1923. Republished as a monograph.

Kiggen, Fr. J., *Nuer-English Dictionary*, 1948.

Kingdon, F. D., 'The Western Nuer Patrol, 1927-28', *S.N.R.*, 1945.

Kohnen, B., 'Mein erster Besuch bei den Nuer', *Bericht Negerkinder*, 1905.

Lewis, B. A., 'Nuer Spokesmen', *S.N.R.*, 1951.

Mlakic, S., 'Nuer Religion', *The Messenger*, 1943-4.

Petherick, Mr. and Mrs. J., *Travels in Central Africa*, 1869.

Poncet, Jules, 'Le Fleuve Blanc', extrait des *Nouvelles Annales des Voyages*, Paris, 1863-4.

Prina, M., 'Il Segno distintive nazionale dei Nuer', *La Nigrizia*, 1935.

BIBLIOGRAPHY

Redaelli, E., 'Fra i Nuer', *La Nigrizia*, 1926.

Seligman, C. G. and B. Z., *Pagan Tribes of the Nilotic Sudan*, 1932.

Stigand, C. H., 'Warrior Classes of the Nuers', *S.N.R.*, 1918.

Werne, F., *Expedition to Discover the Sources of the White Nile*, 1849.

Westermann, D., 'The Nuer Language', *Mitterlungen des Seminars für Orientalische Sprachen*, Berlin, 1912.

Other References

The Sudan Penal Code.

The Chiefs' Court Ordinance, 1931.

Sudan Intelligence Reports.

Reports of the Jonglei Investigation Team, 1946 to 1953 (Sudan Government).

Agriculture in the Sudan, ed. Tothill, Oxford, 1948.

The Nile Basin (Hurst, Philips, Black and Simaika), published by Ministry of Public Works, Cairo.

INDEX

ABDUCTION OF UNMARRIED GIRLS, 170-1
Accidental killing, compensation for, 43, 54
Adultery as grounds for divorce, 141
children born of, 133-4, 155-8
indemnity for, 24, 156-68, 224
main legal principles regarding, 158-9
of 'ghost-wives', 163
of 'widow-concubines', 81
of widows, 161-2
recent legislation on, 166-8
resulting in woman's death in child-birth, 54-5, 65, 176-7
with several men, 166, 168
with same man more than twice, 161, 168
with wives of kinsmen, 163-5
Arable land, rights to use of, 184-6

BALANCED OPPOSITION OF TRIBAL SEG-MENTS, 22, 232, 234
Barrenness of wives as grounds for divorce, 141
in cases of adultery, 160
Bestiality, 218
Betrothal ceremony (*cuei*), 89-90
biem (killing by stealth), 55, 66
birr (purification of killer), 44-5
Blindness, compensation for inflic-tion, 69
Blood-feuds, 27, 39-44, 223
as impediment to marriage, 147
composition of, by cattle payments, 25, 26, 47-52
by ritual ceremonies, 27-8, 44-7
See also Compensation, Homicide.
Bloodwealth, collection and distribu-tion of, 49-51. *See also* Com-pensation for homicide.
Bodily injuries, compensation for in-fliction, 25, 26, 70
Bridewealth and 'ghost-marriages', 76-9
and leviratic marriages, 78-9
cattle terminology, 104-5
claims by physiological and foster-fathers, 111-12
distribution among relatives, 72, 97-110, 114-21
disputes over, 122-4
functions of, 71-3
minimum claims, 106-7
negotiations, 88-94
other payments, 110-11

Bridewealth—*cont.*
proportions, 109-10
return on death of wife, 137-40, 227
return on dissolution of marriage, 149-51
reverse payments (*thiuk*), 113

CATTLE AS BETROTHAL PAYMENTS, 88-9
as bridewealth. *See* Bridewealth.
as compensation. *See* Compensa-tion.
as gifts between friends, 198
exchanges of, 196
for grain, 197-8
expert (*wut ghok*), 211-14
for widower on wife's death, 139-40, 227
inheritance of, 190-4
loans of, 196-7
raiding, 199-200
seizure of, 23, 171, 198-9
terminology, 6
blood-feuds, 47-8
bridewealth, 102-4
theft of, 200-1
trade in, 195-6
Ceremonies in settlement of blood-feuds, 27, 44-7
intertribal, 58-9
marriage, 91-7
purification, after acts of homicide, 44-5
after breach of incest rules, 84-5
oath-taking, 219-20
Chief, killing of, 60
leopard-skin. *See* Leopard-skin chief.
See also Tribal authorities, Leader-ship of tribe.
Chiefs' courts. *See* Courts.
Children, legal position of adopted, 83
of adulterous union, 133-4, 156-7, 159
of 'ghost-marriages', 74-5, 79, 129-30
of leviratic marriages, 78-9, 130-1
of 'widow-concubines', 81, 130
of simple legal marriage, 73, 128-9
of unmarried concubines, 131-3
on death of mother, 134, 137-8
on divorce, 154
See also Legitimization fees.
cieng, meaning of, 20-1
Compensation for adultery, 24, 25, 133-4, 156-68, 244

INDEX

Compensation for adultery—*cont.*
  liability on death of adulterer, 166
  resulting in birth of child, 133-4,
    156-60
  returnable on dissolution of mar-
    riage, 166
  for bodily injuries, 26, 68-70
  for homicide, 25-6, 41, 47-58
    cattle terminology, 47-8
    collection and distribution, 49-51
    rates, 48
  for seduction of unmarried girls,
    135, 169-70, 174
    resulting in pregnancy, 171-3,
      175-6
  for theft, 201-3
  traditional scales of, 27
Courts and administrative policy, 2,
    36-7, 66
  appeal, 4, 37
  branch, 241
  chiefs', and tribal structure, 37-8,
    232-4
  appointment of members, 35
  evolution of, 26-7, 229
  ordinance of 1931, 2, 66, 241
  major, 62, 66
  modern procedure, 66, 230-2
  regional, 241
Courtship, 87-8
cuei (betrothal), 89-90
cuil (final ceremony of composition in
    blood-feuds), 46
cuong (rights), 6, 22, 199, 225, 227

DEATH AS RESULT OF OLD WOUND, 43,
    53, 64-5
  in childbirth resulting from adul-
    tery, 43, 54-5, 65, 176-7
  of unmarried girls, 43, 54-6, 65,
    176-7
  of wife, 137-9, 140, 176
Desertion of wife as grounds for di-
    vorce, 141
dhu nyal (seduction of unmarried girl),
    135, 169-76
Dinka, 7-9, 14, 31, 33, 181
  adoption of, 56
  reciprocal marriage payments, 113
  religious experts, 214
  slaves, 56, 60
Dissolution of marriage on death of
    wife, 137-40, 153, 227
  on subsequent discovery of impedi-
    ment, 84-5, 146-7
  See also Divorce.
District commissioner, role in courts,
    3, 36, 37, 229, 241
Divorce, grounds for, by husband,
    141-2
  by wife, 142-3

Divorce—*cont.*
  of 'ghost-wives', 153
  of widows, in leviratic union, 152-3
  in 'widow concubinage', 152-3
  return of bridewealth on, 149-51
  return of extra-marital payments on,
    151-2
duer (wrongs), 22-3, 225

ECOLOGY, 12-16
Elopement, 170-1
Exchanges of cattle (*gual* and *ngual*),
    196
  for grain, 197-8
Exogamy, rules of, 82-6
  divorce for breach of, 84-5, 146-7
  offences against, 85-6, 163-5, 209,
    224
Extra-marital payments, return on di-
    vorce, 151-2

FISHING RIGHTS, 188
Friendship (institutionalized—*math*),
    111, 198

ghok tuoke (compensation to husband
    on death of wife), 139-40, 227
'Ghost-marriage', 41, 60, 74-9, 153,
    163
Gifts of cattle to friends, 198
  to bride's kinsmen, 110-11
Grazing rights, 186-8
gwan tang (war expert), 211, 213
  twac (bridegroom's representative),
    89, 91, 93
  buthni (bride's and bridegroom's re-
    presentative), 91-4
  kwoth (prophet), 214-16
  wal (medicine expert, magician),
    216-18

HOMICIDE, DEFINITION OF TERMS, 42-4
  degree of responsibility for, 51-2
  modern legal procedure, 66-7
  Nuer concepts of, 39-42
  punishment for, 61-2
  recent legislation on, 63-6
  See also Blood-feuds, Cattle, Com-
    pensation.
Hunting rights, 188
Hurt, indemnities for, 68-70

ILL-TREATMENT OF WIFE AS GROUNDS
    FOR DIVORCE, 143
Impotence of husband, 159
  as grounds for divorce, 142
Incest. *See* Exogamy.
Inheritance of cattle, 190-4

INDEX

255

Inheritance—*cont.*
  of land, 182
  of other property, 194

JOINT RESPONSIBILITY IN HOMICIDE, 51-2

kap tang (oath-taking ceremony), 220
Kinship terminology, 100-4
kuaar juath (disease expert), 213
  muon (*kwac*). *See* Leopard-skin chief.
  thoi (water expert), 212-13
  yiika (ritual expert), 171, 177, 213, 214
kwen (marriage), 73
kwoth, meaning of, 204-6

LAND TENURE, 181-6
Law and custom, definitions of, 225-30
Leadership of tribe, 28-35
Legality of marriage, general principles of, 124-6
  recent legislation on, 127-8
Legitimacy of children. *See* Children, legal position of.
Legitimization fees (*ruok gaanke*), 81, 132-5, 137, 156, 172-3, 175, 176
Leopard-skin chief as mediator in disputes, 27-9, 40, 43-6, 58, 211, 220, 225
  as political authority, 29-30, 33, 223
  in homicide ritual, 44, 46, 59, 66, 207, 220
  in incest ritual, 84-5
  payments to, 47, 48, 49, 61, 228
Leviratic marriage, 78-9
Loans of cattle, 196-7
loiny deb ('loosing the rope'), 95
luom nyal (courtship), 87

MARRIAGE (*kwen*), 73
  ceremonies, 91-7
  impediments to, 82, 146-7
  legal aspects of, 124-8
math (i) (oath of innocence in homicide ritual), 200
  (ii) (friendship), 198
  (iii) (final ceremony of composition in homicide), 46-7

OATHS AND OATH-TAKING, 219-20
Origins of Nuer, 7-9
Orthography, 6

PATERNITY, ESTABLISHMENT OF, 157
Peace ceremonies, inter-tribal, 58

Penal sanctions, 61-2, 66, 234-7
Population statistics, 239
Pregnancy of unmarried girls, 171-3
  resulting from adultery, 156-7
  sexual intercourse during, 177
Property, ownership of, 178-9
  other than livestock and land, 179-80
  theft of, 201, 224

RECENT LEGISLATION ON ADULTERY, 166-8
  on homicide, 63-5
  on legality of marriage, 126-8
  on legitimization fees, 34-5
  on seduction of unmarried girls, 176
Religious functionaries, 211-18
  payments to, 48, 49, 61, 228
Religious sanctions applied in cases of homicide, 206-7
  applied for offences against kinship rules, 209
  applied for offences against women, 209-10
Remarriage after divorce, 151
Restitutive sanctions, 25
Rights, fishing, 188
  hunting, 188
  in arable land, 184-6
  in grazing land, 186-8
  of inheritance, 182, 190-4
  of ownership, 178-81
ruic naadh (spokesmen and leaders of the people), 30-4, 211
ruok ciek (compensation for adultery), 156. *See also* under Adultery.
  gaanke (*muor*). *See* Legitimization fees.
  nyal (compensation for seduction), 172-6

SANCTIONS, PENAL, 61-2, 66, 175, 234-7
  religious, 206-10
  restitutive, 25-6
  social, 22-5
Seduction of unmarried girls, 125, 169-70
  resulting in pregnancy, 171-3, 175-6
  resulting in death in childbirth, 54-5, 176-7
Seizure of cattle as compensation, 23, 171, 198-9
  in warfare, 199-200
Slander, compensation for, 70
Slaves, killing of, 56
Status (of persons in connexion with homicide), 55-7

THEFT OF CATTLE, 200
  of other property, 201, 224

INDEX

256

thiang (sexual intercourse during pregnancy), 177
thiec nyal ('asking for the girl'), 89
thiuk ('reverse payments' in bridewealth), 113
thung (indemnity for homicide), 25, 41-43
   gwacka (for accidental killing), 43, 54
   loic ran (for intentional killing confessed later), 43, 52
   nyindiet (for killing when death results from wounds inflicted earlier), 43, 52, 65
   ran (intentional killing), 43, 52, 65
   yiika (for death of woman in childbirth), 43, 54-5, 65, 176-7
Topography, 9-12
Tribal authorities in past, 27-34
   today, 34-6
   See also Courts, Chiefs, Leopardskin chief.
Tribal segments, 17-20, 221
   as represented in courts, 37-8, 232-4
twoc ghok ('invocation of the cattle'), 91-4

UNINITIATED BOYS, KILLING BY, 56
   killing of, 56
Unmarried concubines, children of, 131-3
   sexual intercourse with, 168-9
   status of, 81
Unmarried girls, abduction of, 170-1
   compensation for death in childbirth, 43, 54-5, 65, 176-7
   pregnancy of, 171-3, 175-6
   sexual intercourse with, 135, 169-70
Unnatural offences, 218

WATER EXPERT, 211-13
   rights, 188
Widows, adultery of, 161
   leviratic marriage of, 78-9
   legal position of children, 130
   living arrangements for, 79-80
Witchcraft, 218-19
Witches and ghouls, action against, 219, 225
   killing of, 56, 225
Women, killing by, 57
   killing of, 57
wut ghok (cattle expert), 211-14

Printed in Great Britain by
The Camelot Press Ltd., London and Southampton